BINARY ECONOMICS

The New Paradigm

D1499975

Robert Ashford
&
Rodney Shakespeare

University Press of America,® Inc.
Lanham • New York • Oxford

330.1
A 82 b

𝓜 Copyright © 1999 by
University Press of America,® Inc.
4720 Boston Way
Lanham, Maryland 20706

12 Hid's Copse Rd.
Cumnor Hill, Oxford OX2 9JJ

Library of Congress Cataloging-in-Publication Data

Ashford, Robert
Binary economics : the new paradigm / Robert Ashford & Rodney
Shakespeare.
p.   cm.
Includes bibliographical references and index.
1. Distribution (Economic theory) 2. Right of property. 3.
Distributive justice. I. Shakespeare, Rodney. II. Title.
HB523.A84 1999   330.1—dc21   98-51042 CIP

ISBN 0-7618-1320-9 (cloth: alk. ppr.)
ISBN 0-7618-1321-7 (pbk: alk. ppr.)

∞™The paper used in this publication meets the minimum
requirements of American National Standard for Information
Sciences—Permanence of Paper for Printed Library Materials,
ANSI Z39.48—1984

This book is dedicated

to the memory of

Louis Kelso

and to

Patricia Hetter Kelso

whose seminal writings and years of courageous work have
inspired the binary movement

and to

Kathleen Shakespeare

for her staunch support during a long and difficult time

Contents

v

List of Figures

Preface

A paradigm is a basic mental construct which organizes experience and information. Paradigms enable an understanding of the world. With them, people make a rational approach to reality.

Binary economics provides a new way of approaching economic reality. As a new paradigm, binary economics contains a uniquely powerful set of ideas. It provides a new way of enhancing everyone's economic well-being.

Among its many benefits, binary economics offers:–

- an economy of more equal opportunity, fairness and respect for *all* people individually;
- a free market way for all people to achieve increased levels of economic prosperity and autonomy;
- a systemic solution for poverty, by way of a far more inclusive and efficient private property system;
- a practical market alternative to the redistribution of wealth;
- the potential for beneficial political realignment drawing upon those of the left, right and center who are sincerely committed to a better world;
- a strengthened democracy;

- an economic foundation for voluntary control of population levels;
- a lessening of pressures to emigrate;
- a practical means for helping to protect flora, fauna, and the environment; and
- a practical basis for a new honesty, optimism, and generosity of spirit.

A binary economy offers enhanced growth and distributive justice, whether in times of boom and bust, or anything in between. It offers material assistance to poor and middle class people, and even the rich will benefit. It offers help to all nations, rich and poor.

This book is written for both specialists and non-specialists in economic matters. Intended for anyone who believes that economic principles, theories and practices have a major impact on life, it is essential reading for all people who want to exercise their full rights and responsibilities as citizens. It offers indispensable insights for fiduciaries (including trustees, lawyers and pension advisers), business leaders, and churches. It gives new options to advocates for the disadvantaged, and to public servants responsible for economic policy.

With the binary paradigm, people will be better able to identify and secure their essential economic rights and responsibilities in a market economy. With the binary paradigm, individuals, private companies (including insurance companies and banks), financial specialists, and investment bankers will be better able to meet their aspirations and obligations with greater mutual respect, harmony, and efficiency. In the same way, universities, colleges, labor unions, political parties and organizations, and fiduciary and charitable institutions will find themselves better able to achieve their objectives.

In particular, with the binary paradigm, people will be able to co-operate with their governments to make needed reforms to existing capital markets. These reforms, although modest, will establish the market foundation for substantial, sustainable, economic growth, together with distributive justice for all people.

The essential economic rights and responsibilities revealed by the new binary paradigm are those related to capital acquisition. Binary economics holds that universal, individual market participation in capital acquisition is essential to individual prosperity and sustainable growth for the economy as a whole.

The *binary property right* therefore secures for *all* people individually the right competitively to acquire capital and then pay for it using the earnings of the capital acquired. This right makes use of the very same credit, insurance, and financial principles and techniques presently employed by existing owners to acquire capital with the earnings of capital. In practice, binary economics makes simple reforms of the market structure so that those without capital are also enabled to become owners.

With the binary reforms in place, binary economists predict that more and more (and eventually all) people will individually acquire sizeable capital estates with growing capital earnings to enhance their standards of living. Over time, by way of entirely voluntary market transactions, this wealth-broadening process will reduce and ultimately reverse the present tendency which is to concentrate capital ownership in the hands of existing owners. At first, the broadening capital base may grow slowly, but the growth will increase considerably over time; and in the mature binary economy, everybody will own substantial capital estates.

Over time, moreover, the capital earnings potential of the broader market participation in capital acquisition will increasingly link supply with demand. This market linkage will provide the basis for substantial, broadly based *binary growth*. Binary growth is a distribution-based growth that is presently impeded by the prevailing pattern of concentrated capital acquisition. Thus the binary paradigm reveals a potent distributive relationship between capital ownership and economic growth, a growth which is not comprehended by conventional economics and which is suppressed by conventional economic practices and institutions. Consequently, just as the economies of the existing so-called 'free market' economies are much larger and more affluent as compared to socialist economies, so the binary economies of the future will be much larger and more affluent than any existing economy today.

In general, societies will eventually replace an old, widely accepted paradigm with a new paradigm if the new one helps to explain and resolve an important anomaly left unexplained and unresolved by the old one. Today's important anomaly is the presence of widespread unmet needs and wants existing alongside a capacity to produce the very things needed and wanted. In short, the productive capacity exists, but millions of people are unable to buy the potential output. Despite increasing affluence for a small portion of the population, most people live with many unmet needs and wants, struggling just to get along modestly with an ever-present, gnawing sense of economic insecurity. Many others live and die prematurely in economic desperation.

Notwithstanding all the material progress over the last hundred years, the anomaly persists. The laissez-faire and neo-classical approaches have not resolved it. Nor have communism, forms of socialism or Keynesianism. Moreover, the general acceptance of the conventional economic paradigm gives people the sense that nothing much better can be reasonably expected.

Binary economics, however, reveals that something much better can indeed be reasonably expected *if* people are willing to consider a new approach. In particular, binary economics resolves the anomaly by providing sound theory and concrete proposals for greater growth and broader distribution based on true private property, free market principles. Rejecting both state ownership and wealth redistribution, and finding grave problems with the present so-called 'free market' economies that largely restrict capital acquisition to existing owners, the binary paradigm offers a new, more efficient, truly open private property approach based on universal, individual capital ownership. Starting from a more accurate understanding of economic reality, binary economics reveals that much of the present scarcity of basic necessities and simple comforts around the world is an unnatural scarcity that would be efficiently eliminated with open capital markets in which participants are free to capitalize on the potent distributive relationship between broader capital ownership and growth.

Thus, for those concerned with the welfare of humankind, the anomaly left unresolved by the conventional paradigm raises two important questions:–

- How does the scarcity persist despite the capacity to eliminate it?
- What can be done to eliminate it?

Binary economics provides new, satisfying, effective answers.

Acknowledgements

The authors thank Patricia Hetter Kelso and Cynthia
Hendershott Egan (both of the Kelso Institute for the Study of
Economic Systems, San Francisco) for work and encouragement
and the staff of the University Press of America for guidance. A
grateful record is made of the help and commentary on earlier
drafts given by the following:–

Dulcie Balagumyetime, Tony Bays, Tony Gentles, Fabian
Thompsett and Margaret Westcott, in the United Kingdom; and

John Carter, Michèle Courtney, Jerry Gauché, John Jones,
Stephen Kane, Mark Reiners and Michael Sarofeen, in the United
States of America.

Patricia Hetter Kelso has also generously allowed quotation
from *Democracy and Economic Power* (Louis Kelso & Patricia
Hetter Kelso), *Two-Factor Theory* (Louis Kelso & Patricia
Hetter), *The Right To be Productive* (Louis Kelso & Patricia
Hetter Kelso) and *The Capitalist Manifesto* (Louis Kelso &
Mortimer Adler).

The drawings of the vase and faces (Fig. 2 – 2 and Fig. 2 – 3)
were contributed to the cause of binary economics by Michèle
Courtney. The figure on the historical development of economic
theory (Fig. 3 – 2 and Fig. 10 – 2) is taken from K. Cole, J.
Cameron and C. Edwards, *Why Economists Disagree: the
Political Economy of Economics* (1983) and reproduced by kind
permission of Longman Group Limited.

Book I

Introduction

In order to provide the just and affluent world that most people desire, the binary approach begins with a new fundamental way of viewing and explaining reality. That is to say, a new paradigm.

Chapter One generally discusses paradigms and their important influence on human thought, and then describes key features of the new binary paradigm. Chapter Two presents a broad overview of binary economics. It opens by examining the economic and political situation that people and nations face in the wake of the collapse of much explicit state-sponsored socialism, and then explains the significance of the new binary paradigm. At points, Chapter Two is intense reading because it summarizes many of the key points that are discussed more fully in Books II, III and IV.

Book I

Chapter One

Overview of the new binary paradigm

1. On paradigms

A paradigm is the basic mental framework which organizes experience and information. A major paradigm can be so persuasive as to affect, even govern, all the institutions and practices of a society. It may even make individual members of the society believe that there is no other way to think about a particular matter (because *everyone* thinks that way). Simultaneously, of course, people believe they are completely free to think for themselves.

Historically, the way humans view the world has changed from age to age. Even now, it differs from place to place. Consequently, what is thought to be a rational approach to reality in one age or place can come to be modified, even rejected as irrational, in another.

Because a paradigm is the basic mental framework for viewing and explaining the environment – the reality which is the world around us and of which we are a part – it will be understood that, *when the environment undergoes substantial change*, what was once rational may no longer be so. Indeed, in the face of substantial change in the environment, the maintenance of an obsolete rationality – an outdated paradigm – can be unhelpful, dysfunctional, perilous, even completely disastrous. Consequently, it is essential for humans to understand how paradigms govern their thinking. It is likewise essential for humans to recognize when a paradigm becomes outdated or false; to ascertain substantial environmental change; and, above all, to discover the new paradigm which makes possible successful adaptation to that change.

The change from an obsolete paradigm to a new one, however, is never easy. Learning a new way of thinking requires effort. The change rarely occurs without fierce resistance from those clinging to the old paradigm out of self-interest, fear, or failure of imagination. What is sensible and rational in the new paradigm seems nonsensical and irrational to those who cling to the old. Understanding the power of the new paradigm therefore requires suspending belief in the seemingly rational, basic, unquestionable, truths of the old.

2.   The meaning of 'rational'

So what is 'rational'? Obviously, some sort of definition or set of standards against which 'rationality' can be measured must be identified. Because humans are creatures having to survive as best they can in an uncertain and changing environment, 'rational' has to include that which is practical, efficacious, and which gives the most satisfactory means of controlling the environment for the benefit of human, and other, life. In other words, 'rational' must:–
• take account of fact and circumstance;

- rest on reasonable assumptions;
- be coherent (internally consistent); and
- most easily and naturally explain in a comprehensive way what has happened, and predict and influence what will happen.

These are the standards, the scientific standards, by which societies eventually drop an outdated paradigm in favor of a more helpful one.[1] They are also the standards by which binary economics will eventually replace conventional market theory as the proper foundation for a just and affluent market economy.

3. Calls for a new economic paradigm

Significantly, growing numbers of people, both within and beyond the economics profession, have come to recognize that the conventional paradigm for understanding the operation of a modern industrial economy is simply not working.[2] Although

---

[1] A paradigm reveals its quality by the *ease* (the principle of Occam's razor) with which it describes, explains and gives ways of controlling the environment. There can often be two very different ways of describing things or doing things but the better is obviously the one which is simpler, less contorted, less expensive, less likely to have undesirable consequences and more likely to have further beneficial consequences. Eichner in *Can Economics Become a Science? (Challenge*, Nov./Dec., 1986) offers coherence, correspondence, comprehensiveness and parsimony as the four attributes by which alternative paradigms may be judged in terms of scientific rigor. See also T. Kuhn, *The Structure of Scientific Revolution* (2nd edition, 1970).

[2] Political and religious doubt as to the efficacy of the conventional paradigm can be found in many newspaper articles published, for example, in the U.K. in 1993:– (*The Times*), *What is the moral basis of the capitalist system?* (C. Longley); *World has shrunk from optimism to a failure of reason* (Lord Beloff); *Labour lacks the vision we need* (D. Selbourne): (*The Sunday Times*), *Politicians lost in a time*

4   Binary Economics – *the new paradigm*

technology promises the increasing abundance of substantially increased output with much less human effort, there is widespread poverty amidst the economic cycles of boom and bust. Even in boom times, too many people remain poor.

'Trickle-down' theory cannot solve the poverty – for too many people, the 'trickle' is usually only of menial, low-pay jobs, private charity and public welfare. Nor can education and training *in themselves* solve it: they are necessary for prosperity, but far from sufficient. Even when economies seem to experience steady, low-inflationary, job-providing growth, the reality is that most people do not earn enough to sustain their reasonable needs and, instead, are heavily in debt and/or dependent upon some form of earnings redistribution. Inevitably, conventional economic theory is divided, often polarized, on the fundamental strategy for making all individuals properly productive and for achieving sustainable growth. As a result, there is continual discord on issues of just and efficient distribution.

It is therefore not surprising that, repeatedly, voices are now calling for a new benign understanding, beyond left and right, to provide better guidance for the future.[3] Showing creative insight, they are also calling for a new understanding beyond the usual confines of economics.[4] In response to those voices, we offer the

---

warp (A. Kaletsky); *The end of politics* (M. Jacques); *Politics RIP – killed off by boredom and bickering* (A. Burnet).
[3] See, for example, David Marquand, *The life after death of socialism*, (UK, *The Guardian*, June 5, 1991). In *Macro Theory and the Recession of 1991*, Robert E. Hall outlined eight explanations for the 1991 recession based on all accepted schools of thought, and concluded that the available evidence confirmed none of the explanations as satisfactory.
[4] Thus the call for 'a new socio-economics' made by Amitai Etzioni in *Founding a New Socio-Economics* (*Challenge*, Nov.-Dec., 1986). Etzioni says, "Since the economy is nestled within society and rooted in its institutions, economists should join psychologists and sociologists to study human behavior."

new binary paradigm as decisively the best candidate for exploration.

4.   Important aspects of the new binary paradigm

The new paradigm accurately apprehends reality. Among other things, it reveals that in most economic tasks, and in the overall economy, *capital* (not labor) is doing ever more of the work, is creating ever more of the wealth, and is contributing to ever more of the economic growth.[5] Further, it reveals that growth is primarily the result of increasing capital productiveness rather than increasing human productivity. Moreover, it reveals that *capital* is the primary source of affluence, whereas labor rarely produces more than subsistence.

Binary economics therefore answers in a new way the all-important question of who or what physically creates the wealth. In so doing, it provides a new understanding of economic phenomena and opens the way to new, efficacious policy capable of producing much greater growth and distributive justice far beyond the grasp of conventional economic theory. Among its most important aspects are:–

- an entirely different understanding of the relationship between people and things as they work together to produce goods and services;

---

[5] In binary economics, 'capital' means *productive capital* or some form of *wealth-creating asset*. 'Capital' therefore includes land, animals, machines, structures, tools, and intangibles such as patents, trademarks, trade secrets and processes, i.e., those things which physically produce goods and services. As will become apparent, the binary use of 'capital' needs to be distinguished from what is commonly called 'financial capital'. Put simply, it is the distinction between what physically produces wealth and money.

- a new explanation for growth and poverty in an industrial economy;
- a wholly different view of the industrial revolution and all of history to date; and
- a new optimism for the future based on a new strategy for achieving general affluence on private property free market principles.

With the benefit of the new understanding of economic fact and circumstance, people will be able to establish a just, efficient and broadly affluent economy based on democratic, private property and true free market principles. In short, the new paradigm gives a benign and effective understanding of how to go about achieving a richer, freer world for everyone.

5.   Binary productiveness

If the study of economics is to have any substantial relation to the real world, it must first accurately address the question of who or what creates the wealth and who or what creates economic growth. Since the start of the industrial revolution, there has been a massive growth in per-capita productive capacity and per-capita economic output. The massive growth constitutes a massive change in the environment.

But what fundamentally explains the growth? *Who or what is doing the extra work?*

Under the conventional economic paradigm, the explanation is grounded in notions of productivity, primarily human (labor) productivity. Put simply, conventional economics says that humans (and not capital assets such as machines) are mainly or wholly responsible for the growth. In effect, conventional economics views a machine as but an extension of the human hand.

However, in an important new way, binary analysis draws the productivity explanation into serious doubt. Using, in particular, the paradigm-altering concept of *binary productiveness*, binary analysis provides a new and different explanation for the main (but not the only) cause for the growth. Put simply, it says that while humans undoubtedly make contribution to the growth, the capital assets such as machines and technological processes are making an even bigger, ever-increasing, contribution. In percentage terms, most binary economists estimate that the capital assets are now doing at least 75% of overall production (and some binary economists think the figure is 90%). So, from a binary perspective, growth is primarily a function of increasing capital productiveness rather than increasing labor productivity.

Thus binary productiveness provides a new understanding of who or what creates the wealth and, in so doing, also provides a new understanding of other economic phenomena. This new understanding is quite distinct from the conventional rationale, and quite distinct from anything that has ever come before.

6. The binary property right and binary growth

The benefits of the understanding and the efficacy of the policy coming from binary productiveness are then enhanced by the introduction of two additional paradigm-altering concepts:–

- the *binary property right* which is at the heart of the binary private property system and is the right of all people to acquire, on market principles, private and individual ownership of wealth-creating capital assets; and
- *binary growth*, which holds that economies grow steadily larger as private capital acquisition is distributed more broadly among the population on market principles.

The three concepts – *binary productiveness*, the *binary property right* and *binary growth* – interact with and reinforce one another. Thus once binary productiveness has enabled the main cause of economic growth to be identified, it is possible to understand the universal significance of the binary property right for individual prosperity, sustainable economic growth and distributive justice. With the property right firmly established, the principles of binary growth can then be understood both in respect of the individual capital acquisition transactions and in respect of their cumulative growth effect throughout the aggregate binary economy.

The overall result is a revelation, new to economics, which:–

- identifies a key environmental change that has occurred largely in the last two hundred and fifty years;
- identifies an old, false paradigm that fails to comprehend this change but which still governs human thinking; and
- establishes the new, true paradigm that accurately comprehends economic fact and circumstance.

With the benefit of the new comprehension of fact and circumstance, people will be able to establish a just, efficient, and broadly affluent economy based on democratic and free market principles.

Several words of caution, however, are in order. The binary paradigm must be understood first in its own terms as an entire systematic description of economic reality. It cannot be understood by dismembering its integral parts and conceiving of them as they might operate under the influence of left-wing, right-wing, or mixed centrist theories and practices. The great benign potency of binary principles and institutions to promote broader capital ownership on market principles, and the substantial benefits of that broader ownership, cannot be appreciated with an analysis built on conventional theories and practices. Moreover, the benefits of binary growth will be compromised to the extent that binary market principles are not respected.

Book I

Chapter Two

Overview of binary economics

Chapter One briefly discussed the new binary paradigm. Chapter Two now generally introduces binary economics and starts by noticing that, in a world of competing socio-economic systems, so-called 'free market' capitalism appears to be victorious. But binary economics denies the prowess of 'free market' capitalism finding the victory to be merely that of the strongest among a bunch of weak competitors.

1. A victor's prowess denied

The Cold War was the struggle between competing socio-economic systems. With its ending, state communism has collapsed in many countries as has extreme socialism.

Moreover, viewing the remaining socio-economic systems, it would seem that even moderate socialism and forms of social democracy have an uncertain future. Although superficially appealing as a compromise between left and right, they are unable to combine fairness with both freedom and a proper standard of living.[6]   Thus it appears that only 'free market' capitalism (or, more accurately, unfree, unfair and inefficient market capitalism)[7] stands as victor astride the field.

Now it may seem unwise to deny an apparent victor's prowess, but binary economics does just that.   It denies, firstly, the unfree market's claim to make an accurate apprehension of economic reality.   Unfree market thinking, like all conventional economic thinking (which includes all left-wing, centrist and right-wing thinking), is obsolete.   Failing to understand the increasing role of capital in the production of goods and services and in the distribution of real earning power brought about by the industrial revolution, conventional economic thinking is over two hundred years out of date.   It therefore fails to understand the true dynamics of efficiency, growth and distributive justice, and fails to provide effective strategies for achieving them on market principles.

Secondly, binary economics denies the unfree market's claim to be free.   The basic requirement of a free market is that it have no significant barriers to entry.   For competitive efficiency, therefore, a market must be open to anyone willing to play by the market rules (i.e., voluntary participation, free exchange, and respect for private property).   Increasingly, the most potent markets in any economy are those for productive capital and they are *not* open to everyone.   Indeed, living in a closed property system structured on obsolete conventional economic thinking, 90% of people in all economies are unnecessarily excluded from effective participation in the (productive) capital markets.[8]

---

[6]   In practice, social democracies have high taxation, growing government (particularly welfare) expenditure and loss of competitiveness.   They experience a growing need for earnings redistribution as well as a suppressed ability and diminishing willingness to pay for it.

[7]   Throughout this book the term 'unfree, unfair and inefficient market capitalism' is generally shortened to 'unfree market'.

[8]   While controversial in the minds of some, the idea that most people are effectively excluded from productive capital participation is only a

Worse, those people are excluded even though they are willing to play by free market rules. Consequently, they are restricted in their economic participation to the generally less potent markets for labor.[9] In the unfree market, although everyone is *theoretically* free to acquire productive capital, *effective* freedom to acquire it is unnecessarily denied to the many and enjoyed by only a few.[10]

Thirdly, as a consequence of the unnecessary exclusion of most people from effective participation in capital acquisition, binary economics denies the unfree market's claim to be efficient. The inefficiency of the unfree market manifests itself in the chronic problem of ample supply failing to generate adequate

---

more precise expression of the widely accepted adage that it takes money to make money. But the adage is superficial because it focuses on money (which can be used to acquire capital) rather than the productive capital itself. Of the billions of dollars in new productive capital acquired each year, almost all of it is acquired by *existing* capital owners using the earnings of the capital to pay for the acquisition. Ninety per cent or more of the population have little or no participation in this capital acquisition.

[9] That is not to say that millions of middle class people do not have some savings and investments (as in the U.S.A., U.K. and Japan); but, for most individuals, those savings and investments are so small that they can never produce more than a pittance. Nor is the situation ameliorated by pension fund holdings. Pension funds pay out nothing until retirement so they do nothing to help people during their working lives. Moreover, for most people, the amounts in the pensions and retirement schemes are not only small, but do not return their full economic potential to their owners. In contrast, the binary economy offers a much more potent form of economic participation in productive capital acquisition which, over time, promises to enable *all* people to acquire private and individual ownership of wealth-creating assets so that eventually they can earn from those assets at least half of their income.

[10] That the exclusion is unnecessary will become apparent once it is understood that capital markets promote and distribute more bounty when they are effectively open to *all* people on market principles.

demand. At present, and for many years now, although the technical means of production undoubtedly exist, the consumer needs and desires of most people (from the poorest up through the upper middle class) are not being met no matter how hard they work. Something is profoundly wrong when society has the technical capacity to produce but people cannot earn enough to consume adequately even if they work hard.

Because unfree market economies have endemic excess capacity, willing but redundant workers, and unsold products and services, the inefficiency is quite obviously *not* in the ability to produce. Indeed, the unfree market economies are undoubtedly able to produce more than their people can afford to buy. Rather, the inefficiency lies in the failure of the closed private property system to distribute sufficient consumer earning power on market principles to those expected to purchase what is increasingly produced by capital. In truth, most people have needs and are willing to work to satisfy their needs but either they cannot get jobs or, if they can, cannot earn enough in those jobs to purchase what the society is able to produce. At the same time, many of the machines that have replaced them in the production process also lie idle for lack of consumer demand for their (the machines') potential output.

This chronic failure of supply to generate demand is the direct effect of the present closed private property system which excludes most people from capital acquisition. It will continue as long as most people are effectively prevented from competing to acquire the ownership of productive capital on free market principles. Supply *can* efficiently generate optimal demand in an industrial economy, however, *if* all people have competitive rights to participate in capital acquisition on market principles so that the earnings of capital can be increasingly distributed to those expected to purchase its incremental output.

Fourthly, binary economics denies the unfree market's claim to be democratic so long as most people are denied the economic participation necessary for full participation as citizens of the democracy. Democracy presupposes that ultimate power resides individually with the people. Yet, even in the societies commonly considered the most democratic (e.g., the U.S.A., U.K., Japan, Germany, France, Italy and Canada), even with the right to vote, most people feel powerless. This sense of powerlessness reflects the limits on the effectiveness of democratic *political* power when it is not supported by democratic *economic* power.[11]

The powerlessness occurs because the U.S.A., U.K. and other countries may be 'politically democratic' in that they extend the right to vote to almost all adult citizens; but the right to vote is in reality only a tiny power exercized at lengthy intervals.[12]   In contrast, a proper democracy (i.e. a binary democracy) is much more than the right to vote. Proper democracy is premised on all its citizens having an *effective* freedom over, or a large power to control, their everyday lives as long as they do not interfere with the rights of others. A 'large power to control' includes rights to life, liberty, and property. The right to life itself must include the right to support life. Consequently, unless it means no more than the right to be a ward of private charity or public welfare, or unless it is taken to mean no less than a license to steal, this right to life must mean for most people *the right to earn a legitimate income by participating in production.* In practice, this requires sufficient *economic* power to produce enough to acquire not only the basic necessities of life but also (if the life is to be a properly

---

[11] Economic power is the power to produce goods and services. In a private property economy, the power to produce goods and services is exercised either by way of labor or by way of capital ownership. The more broadly capital is acquired the more democratically economic power is dispersed. Thus, compared with the power to vote, economic power (the power to produce goods and services) can be a very large power. It can directly put bread on one table or many, and otherwise support the autonomous lives of a few people or many.

[12]   As a power, the right to vote does not directly produce wealth, although it can redistribute wealth and promote or thwart its creation. Nevertheless, at elections, frequently less than half the electorate bother to vote. Even if a favored political party or candidate wins an election, the feeling of powerlessness usually remains.

democratic life) the material goods and services necessary for the development of individual talent and the shaping of individual destiny.

Many people rightly understand their lack of power over their lives to be directly related to their lack of sufficient economic power. But fewer people realize that sufficient economic power in an industrial economy requires participation in production not only by laboring but also, and increasingly, by being able to acquire productive capital on market principles. This would result in a full and continuing market participation in the economy which is essential for a democratic private property system.[13]

Lastly, building on all the foregoing reasons, binary economics denies the moral authority of the unfree market. Unless all individuals are provided with an effective, *legitimate* means to produce the goods and services necessary for their basic survival, they will be forced to seek either charity or illegitimate means. Without a legitimate means of survival (going beyond menial, low-pay, low-security jobs, private charity and public welfare), the unfree market will fail to elicit people's loyalty, fail to provide them with the productive means to pursue higher callings, and fail to satisfy their yearning for justice.

2. The binary offer

Having denied the apparent victor's prowess, binary economics then offers an alternative fundamentally different from

---

[13]   Thus the unfree democracies unnecessarily deny most people the full and continuing individual economic power which is required for full democratic citizenship. Without taking anything from the wealthy, and with full respect for the property rights of all, the binary economy would democratize not only political power but also economic power by opening the private property system on market principles for benefit of the poor and middle classes as well as the well-capitalized.

both the unfree market and communism. The binary alternative is a new, positive, consentual and concrete approach to private property and free market economics. It is structured to develop a vital, just, democratic and broadly affluent free market economy. It provides the promise of growth, efficiency and distributive justice beyond the understanding of all conventional thinking.

Moreover, these advances would not be achieved through central planning, market intervention, or redistributive strategies. Nor do they depend on the false promise that sufficient benefits from conventional investment will trickle down in the form of increased wages and jobs together with more welfare. Nor do they rely in any way on strategies that assume that technology does (or may) create more jobs than it destroys. To the contrary, binary economics denies the systemic efficacy of all of these conventional strategies.

Instead, the growth, efficiency and justice in a binary economy would be achieved by opening up our private property system so that it becomes possible for all people to acquire capital on market principles. By eliminating what amounts to an effective monopoly on capital acquisition, the binary economy offers to eliminate the unnatural scarcity that now prevails even in the most advanced economies and to replace it with the greater bounty and leisure that was promised, but never universally delivered, by the industrial revolution.

In the binary economy, as capital is increasingly acquired over time by people of the poor and middle classes, that capital will (after returning its acquisition costs) begin to pay a capital income to its new owners thus supplementing their labor income and reducing their welfare dependence.[14] Each year, with growing

---

[14] 'Welfare dependence' includes state pensions as well as direct and indirect receipt of redistributed earnings. All people receive such earnings in some way. Thus a child's 'free' state education results from redistributed earnings, as does subsidized housing and, in the U.K., 'free' health care. Education, housing and health are directly

participation in capital acquisition among people of the poor and middle classes, capital will increasingly distribute to its new owners the earnings necessary to buy what capital increasingly produces. Thus all people will increasingly be able to afford to buy with their capital earnings what is increasingly produced by capital. In open binary capital markets, supply (in the form of increased capital investment) can increasingly be financed by way of voluntary market transactions to provide the capital foundation (in the form of capital dividends) for growing poor and middle class consumer demand.

Therefore, directly through the private property system, the binary economy establishes the market conditions for sustainable growth. In other words, the growth and justice promised by a binary economy rest on a unique distributional premise related to capital in a private property economy:–

The more broadly capital is acquired over time on market principles, and its income fully distributed to its new owners, the larger the economy will grow.

Let us call this premise, which expresses a distributive growth effect of capital, the principle of binary growth. Although beginning slowly and cumulating only with efficient capital investment, the distributive growth effect (which conventional economics either ignores or trivializes) becomes great indeed over time and, within a decade or so, begins to yield a level of growth far beyond any strategy built on conventional economic theory.

Thus readers are presented with a clear choice based on two paradigms for economics:–

either

• the promised binary growth should be dismissed as an illusion or so trifling as not to be worth bothering about (which is the contention of conventional economics);

or

---

perceived benefits but vast sums are also spent on law and order, environmental protection, defense and a host of other areas.

- the promised binary growth should be explored to determine whether it is a great untapped, natural, market source of wealth and distributive justice that is available to us just for the price of a new understanding (which is the contention of binary economics).

However, whatever the size of the binary growth, it is important to understand that it can be achieved on market principles with *no* expropriation of existing assets, *no* redistribution of earnings, and *no* estate or inheritance tax. Nor is there any 'command' in the binary economy other than the democratic command to honor (on voluntary market principles) the capital acquisition rights of *all* individuals. The only involvement of government is to open the legal and market infrastructure to the extent necessary for upholding the rights of all individuals. The market infrastructure largely exists already by way of laws and institutions that facilitate capital acquisition for existing owners. So, with a binary understanding, the infrastructure merely needs to be modified to honor the capital acquisition rights of all people. Once the infrastructure is opened so that all people may participate on market principles, the growth and distributive benefits of binary economics will be achieved entirely as a result of voluntary market transactions between willing buyers and sellers.

Even-handed analysis will show that binary theory is more faithful to free market principles than the theories, critiques and proposals of even the most ardent 'free market' advocates. Moreover, the binary economy is structured to operate in a way more faithful to free market principles than any existing economy. It is a true free market effectively open to everybody instead of a few. In accordance with true free market logic, it eliminates unnecessary market barriers so as to allow the law of supply and demand to work more efficiently for all people individually. It therefore offers a level of efficiency well beyond that which can be achieved in the existing unfree market economies.

At the same time, the binary alternative offers to realize the goal of just and effective economic opportunity for all. This goal has long attracted people of good will and today motivates many people involved in politics and social reform. However, a goal is one thing and achieving it is another. Thus the communist or socialist economies attempted to give just opportunity by socializing the means of production. The attempt failed.

Today, whilst performing more efficiently than communist economies, the unfree market economies also attempt to give just opportunity and they, too, fail. The unfree market attempt usually involves a two-part policy of:–

- investment incentives for existing capital owners (with the object of providing more growth, productivity and jobs); and
- direct jobs and welfare programs for everyone else.

But the jobs and wages which actually result are *never* enough. Consequently, in attempting to supplement the always inadequate wages of the bulk of the people (and to pay for those who do not have jobs), the unfree market economies are forced to redistribute the earnings of capital through the political structure. This breaches free market principle, stultifies the market mechanisms, and does nothing to answer the key question as to why people are insufficiently productive in the first place.

So, not surprisingly, although producing more than the socialist alternatives, the unfree market economies continually exhibit gross discrepancies in wealth; material insecurity; and great swaths of poverty. They lurch unsteadily from boom to bust with endemic, unexplained inflation and, of course, much unemployment that, in the conventional economic analysis, is ignored or assumed to be inevitable. Just like the various forms of moderate socialism and social democracy, the unfree economies experience a growing need for earnings redistribution while, at the same time, they experience an increasingly suppressed ability, and a rapidly diminishing willingness, to pay for it. Binary economists ask whether it is not time to consider a new alternative.

As a new alternative, a binary economy would achieve substantial growth and just opportunity by opening the private property system to *all* people, individually, on true free market principles.[15] As a result, *all* individuals will be able to acquire their own capital by using the earnings of capital. In this way, people have harnessed for them the productive power of capital to pay for its own acquisition and thereafter to earn income indefinitely.[16] Therefore they will *actually become more productive*. Subsequently, they can enjoy their own capital income rather than having to struggle for their livelihood solely by way of their labor or by living on the redistributed income of others.[17] Their efficient participation in capital acquisition will likewise establish the market conditions for sustainable growth. This will happen because the incremental productive capacity of capital is being linked, on market principles by way of an open private property system, with those expected to purchase its output. By extending to all people the competitive means to acquire capital and thereby enjoy a measure of financial independence that springs from private capital ownership, the

---

[15]   In binary terms, true free market principles are those of open participation, voluntary exchange and respect for private property.

[16]   The idea that capital pays for its own acquisition and restoration, while seeming somewhat mystical to people unacquainted with the direct benefits of capital ownership, is deeply understood by the well-capitalized. The strategy of investing in things expected to pay for themselves in a competitive period of time is the fundamental logic of corporate finance and a cardinal principle in the personal investment strategy of any successful investor. The idea that capital then goes on to earn an income indefinitely, or in perpetuity, may likewise seem fanciful to those systematically shut out of the capital acquisition process, but it is in fact a time-tested strategy employed by the rich to get richer.

[17]   In the binary economy, the redistribution of earnings or income is not necessary because all individuals will be able to pay for what they consume. Thus they will pay for the costs of their education and housing while criminals will pay for their prison accommodation. A possible exception is health because illness does not have an even incidence in the population but some form of insurance, state or private, covers the situation.

binary economy also reduces the need for earnings redistribution, taxes, deficit spending, and inflation of the monetary system, while honoring the property rights of all people.

Furthermore, based on widely shared values, binary economics offers an organic conception of society.[18] The conception elicits people's loyalties, upholds their dignity, provides them with the legitimate productive means to pursue higher callings, and satisfies their yearning for justice. The justice is not an absolute equality of income by any means for there will always be differences in income based on ability, hard work, frugality, wise investment and good fortune including birth. Rather, the justice is realized by providing the effective opportunity for all people to earn, by way of their labor *and their capital,* sufficient income to live well.[19] As will become clear, this justice is *not* inimical to economic efficiency (as some unfree market apologists would have us believe). In the binary economy, *the justice creates the efficiency* and vice versa.[20]

Nor is the great promise of a binary economy limited to the largest of the industrial economies whose markets have some measure of competitiveness, although such economies are likely to yield the most immediate results. The same promise extends to *any* society which understands the new binary paradigm and embraces the theory and practice of the steady, just and true free market.

---

[18] There is an "I-aspect" for all healthy individuals but also a "we-aspect". See A. Etzioni, *The Moral Dimension: Towards a New Economics*, (1988).

[19] The meaning of 'live well' has to be judged with reference to what the economy as a whole can produce.

[20] Thus the choices in a binary economy are not limited to the dismal conflicts embraced by conventional economic theory. See Arthur Okken, *Equality and Efficiency: The Big Trade-off* (Brookings, Washington DC, 1975); and Richard Coughlin ed., *Morality, Rationality and Efficiency: New Perspectives in Socio-Economics* (M.E. Sharpe, Inc., 1991).

Moreover, the phrase 'true free market' is not some sort of coded formula designed to give the developed countries an unfair advantage over the lesser developed ones. Binary economics has a unique ability to evolve the best possible economy in *every* country by making all individuals productive and by bringing supply and demand into balance. It is thus highly relevant to the future of, for example, the nations of Eastern Europe, South America, Africa, the republics of the former Soviet Union, all of Asia and the Islamic world.

3.   The new paradigm

At the heart of the binary offer is the new paradigm which accurately apprehends reality.   It answers the all-important question of who or what physically creates the wealth and, in so doing, it provides:–

- *a new understanding* of the relationship between humans and things as they work together to produce goods and services;

- *a new explanation* for industrial growth, poverty and affluence; and

- *a new strategy* for achieving general affluence for all people on free market principles.

In addition, it provides an entirely different view of the industrial revolution (and all of history to date).

The new paradigm, moreover, founds the new democratic system of economics and private property structured to transform politics peacefully and consentually. Ultimately, it will transform human society globally.   The new system extends to all individuals *effective* capital acquisition rights. Operating entirely on market principles, these rights enable any individual to acquire efficient, income-generating capital assets such as land, animals, structures, machines, patents, processes and other legally protected intangibles. The assets pay for themselves out of their earnings.[21]

The result is a true free market economy in which everybody *privately* and *individually* participates in the increasingly potent capital markets. That economy, moreover, is one in which supply (in the form of capital investment) is increasingly linked, through private property rights, (in the form of dividends on broadly based, individually owned capital) with consumer demand. As a result, technology is unleashed more efficiently to meet the productive and consumer needs of all people thereby occasioning massive economic growth.

The new paradigm has three key elements which are the concepts of:–

- *binary productiveness* (which is distinct from conventional productivity);
- the *binary property right*; and
- the principle of *binary growth*.

They will be discussed more fully in later chapters. For the moment, though, it can be noted that they rest upon an underlying premise which seems in no way exceptional or, for that matter, particularly profound, viz.:–

*There are two, and only two, **independent** factors of production – the human and the non-human.*

The premise is discussed in the next section.

---

[21] A cornerstone of wise investment strategy that serves the wealthy so well is to use credit and invest only in things that pay for themselves in a competitive period of time. Binary economics lets poor and middle class people build on the cornerstone as well.

4. 'Binary' means 'composed of two'

a) The two factors of production

Binary economics is unique among schools of economics in that it accurately addresses the question of who or what physically creates wealth. In so doing, it recognizes that not only people do work to produce goods and services but that *non-human things* (like land, machines and patents) *also do work* as well. And that is true even though the non-human things must be tilled, conceived, constructed, operated, exploited, maintained or repaired by humans.

The recognition of the work of non-human things is a critical and fundamental aspect of the binary understanding which can best be illustrated by an example. A man carries a heavy sack on his back for a mile and is exhausted. But with the help of a donkey, *five* sacks can be carried twice as far in half the time, leaving the man with enough energy to go dancing. From the conventional viewpoint, human productivity has increased by a massive 2000%.

However, from the binary viewpoint, the great increase in per-capita output is *not* caused by an increase in human productivity. Rather it is caused by the fact that the non-human factor (the donkey) is doing most, if not all, of the extra work. Indeed, the man is doing *less* work by employing the donkey rather than doing the carrying himself. The *productiveness* of the donkey has both replaced and vastly supplemented the former labor *productiveness*[22] of the man so that the donkey is doing nineteen times as much work.

In binary economics, two points are critical:–

---

[22] Note the distinction between the conventional term 'productivity' and the binary term 'productiveness'. The distinction is crucial to an understanding of the principle of binary growth (the distributional quality of capital), and the overall binary key to achieving sustained growth and distributive justice.

- the human and the non-human factors are *independently* productive (even though they work or co-operate together); and
- the claim on their productive output (the income it yields) is a property right.[23]

Thus, binary economics sees two broad categorical factors of production: –

- *human labor*

and

- *non-human* (capital) *assets* such as the donkey.[24]

'Binary' means 'composed of two' and the reference is to the two factors of production – *human labor* and *non-human capital assets* (which include land, animals, tools, machines, structures, patents, processes, intangibles, and anything else that can be owned and is capable of producing an income).

The division into two categories extends to all non-human things whose productiveness can be used to replace and vastly supplement human labor productiveness. For example, when a truck and driver carry one thousand sacks fifty miles in the same time as it took one person to carry one sack one mile, the truck and driver together have done fifty thousand sack-miles of work.

---

[23] This means that the man (who owns his own labor) takes the income representing his percentage of the work done. Similarly, the owner of the donkey takes the income representing the percentage of work done by the donkey.

[24] Some further examples of non-human capital assets are:– hand tools, machine tools; minerals, raw materials; arable land, grazing land, woodland; seed, agro-chemicals, tractors, farm animals; lorries, trains, cranes, ships, aeroplanes; roads, railways, docks, airports; quarries, mines, oil and gas wells; dams, power stations; foundries, brick-works, cement-works; technological and bio-technological processes; legally protected capital intangibles such as patents; radio and television stations, telephone networks; hotels and offices – anything which is not human, which is owned and which is capable of providing an income.

But the binary economist sees the *truck* doing its work just as the donkey and person do. And recognizing that the truck is doing work, just like the donkey and the person, the binary economist also concludes that the *truck* is doing most, if not all, of the extra work – approximately *fifty thousand* times the work of human hauliers per unit of output. It is to be admitted that truck-driving requires certain skills different from those required for human-hauling and those required for tending donkeys. However, both per unit of output and per hour, as a percentage of the total work done, the truck driver is doing *less* work than the person tending the donkey or hauling the sacks. So, with the advent of the truck, capital productiveness has replaced and vastly supplemented labor productiveness.

Thus, focusing on the extra work done by donkeys, trucks and countless other 'labor saving' examples leads a binary economist to conclude that the extra work done (i.e. the growth) during any period of time:–

- has very little to do with higher labor productivity expended during that period; and

- has almost everything to do with the additional capital productiveness expended during that period.

Those two conclusions are of the greatest significance because they are at odds with a fundamental assumption of conventional economic theory that analyzes all growth, *including growth caused by capital investment,* as ultimately a function of (increased) labor productivity. The productivity assumption was central to the analysis of Adam Smith in his famous *Wealth of Nations* (1776) and is preserved to this day in modified form as the foundation of *all* conventional schools of economics from the far left to the far right.

In contrast, binary economics is founded on the distinct concept of productiveness. Therefore understanding the binary view of growth (based on productiveness) and how it differs from the conventional view of growth (based on productivity) is of fundamental importance in appreciating the great promise of the new binary paradigm to deliver widespread affluence and distributive justice on free market principles. It is a matter to which we shall return later.

The idea that labor and capital are the two primary categorical factors of production is not of itself new. There are schools of conventional economics which also count labor and capital as the two factors. The schools consider not only labor's input, but also focus on such issues as the rate of return on capital, capital-labor substitution, and factor shares of production.

Other schools then count more than two factors. These other schools distinguish, for example, between land, fabricated physical capital (such as structures machines, tools), and intellectual capital (such as patents, trademarks, processes, trade secrets, computer software and other intangibles).[25] Still other schools focus on knowledge and training as a form of so-called 'human capital', even though in market terms it sells as if it were labor. Those schools also separately consider entrepreneurial activity, though it is likewise a form of labor.

But careful analysis will show that *all* of these conventional categorizations of factors of production are ultimately grounded in measures of conventional human productivity[26] rather than binary productiveness.[27] Consequently, *none* of the schools places the critical, unequivocal, and independent emphasis that binary economics places on the effective right of each person to acquire capital on market principles as a necessary condition for individual economic well-being and distributive justice. Likewise, *none* of the schools understands that the acquisition of capital on

---

[25] Adam Smith focused on three factors – land, labor and capital – but saw all wealth and value creation as ultimately a function of labor. See Chapter Three.

[26] K. Cole, J. Cameron and C. Edwards, *Why Economists Disagree: the Political Economy of Economics*, (1983).

[27] That is to say they *all* attribute wealth creation primarily to human labor without giving proper credit to the contribution made by capital assets such as donkeys.

market principles is essential to individual freedom and democracy. Similarly, *none* of the schools understands that effective universal individual property rights in capital are essential for optimal efficiency and sustainable aggregate growth, nor understands that capital has a distributive relationship to growth that is essentially independent of productivity.

Binary theory, however, uniquely holds that to comprehend the way labor and capital work together to produce goods and services, it is both necessary and sufficient to conceive of all production as the result of two sweeping and mutually exclusive categories. Similarly, to understand the importance of binary productiveness together with its relationship to poverty, general affluence and growth, just two categories suffice. They are:–

- the *human* (including all forms of mental and physical labor);
  and

- the *non-human* (i.e. capital including land, tools, animals, machines, structures, patents, processes, intangibles, and anything else that can be owned and is capable of producing an income).

Thus in terms of binary productiveness, additional distinctions between land, fabricated capital and intellectual capital are unnecessary and confusing. The same is true for distinctions between labor and various forms of 'human capital'.

Furthermore, it should be noted that, because the question being addressed is the physical creation of wealth, money (which is a claim on wealth, paid on market principles for the creation of wealth) is *not*, of itself, a factor of production. As a medium for facilitating the efficient exchange of various forms of wealth in a way that does not require direct barter, money certainly enables people and machines, for example, to work together so that they can co-operate in market transactions to produce goods and services. But *the people and machines* physically do the work of production, *not* the money (which merely facilitates the market exchange of the goods and services provided). So in binary economics, the two factors of production are human labor and non-human things called 'capital assets' or just 'capital'. In short, labor and capital.

b) The two ways of earning

So binary economics gets its name from the fact that there are *two* (and only two) independent factors of production (the human and the non-human). Thus, in a private property economy, there are *two* (and only two) legitimate ways to earn a living:–
* working through one's labor

    and
* working through one's capital assets.

Each way of earning is an expression of the law of private property – you own what you produce. In an economic sense, there are two forms of private property – property in labor and property in capital. Indeed, the essence of a private property system is that just as people can be productive by laboring, *so they can also be productive merely by owning capital*. In short, a person can be a labor worker and/or a capital worker.

However, it is important to note that although all humans (unless they are slaves) own one factor of production (i.e. their labor*), only a few humans own a substantial amount of the other factor* (i.e. capital). This is because their rights to acquire capital are determined (and limited) by the existing property system. In the closed private property system of the existing unfree market economies, generally only those who already own capital have effective capital acquisition rights. In other words, generally, it takes capital to acquire additional capital.

With regard to being productive merely by owning capital, conventional market economics (although professing a belief in private property in capital) is surprisingly inconsistent. On the one hand, it frequently admits that a person can earn from capital and considers this fact of great importance; it calculates rates of return on capital; it devises strategies to provide incentives that may encourage owners to invest in more capital; and it worries about 'disincentives' for capital investment. Yet, on the other hand, in crucial ways, conventional economics fudges the issue by conceiving and measuring capital income as ultimately a function of human productivity.[28] Conventional economics also ignores the full earning capacity of capital when it alleges that the distribution of capital acquisition has no direct relationship to economic growth unless that distribution somehow affects human productivity. It denies that the market distribution of capital acquisition, in and of itself, produces growth independent of increases in productivity.

Further, conventional theory assumes that the only way *most* people can participate in the benefits of capital investment is through jobs (via higher productivity) and welfare (via earnings redistribution). Quite remarkably, it *never* considers that most people could achieve yet greater benefits more directly through the acquisition of capital on market principles.[29] And then, to cover up the injustice of a closed private property system *in which only existing owners can effectively earn by owning*, conventional thinking generally refers to capital income as 'unearned income'.[30] It thereby denies the legitimacy of private property rights in capital by implying that the work done by capital is not legitimately earned by its owner.

---

[28] Conventional economists, starting with Adam Smith (1776), measure all return on capital as ultimately a function of the cost of the labor which is replaced by capital investment or by the amount of labor which the product of capital can purchase in the market. See Chapter Three.

[29] Under the present closed private property system of the unfree market economies, there is a great deal of truth in the assumption that most people cannot benefit directly through the acquisition of capital. That assumption, however, would most certainly *not* be true in the binary economy.

[30] In calling income earned by capital 'unearned income' simply because it has not been earned by labor, people are denying private property principles and ignoring reality.

Yet, from the binary perspective, the whole point of private property in capital is to enable people to earn *without personally laboring.* Likewise, the whole point of capital acquisition is *to replace labor (and capital) with more efficient capital.* In this way, production and leisure are optimized at minimal costs (i.e. more productive capital is employed to produce better goods and services with greater efficiency and less labor, than can be provided by labor alone, or provided by labor and less productive capital). In other words, in a private property system, the purpose of capital acquisition is to replace and vastly supplement labor productiveness with capital productiveness and thereby to generate and distribute more earned income *from capital* rather than from labor.

Denying that capital income is earned income does nothing for the people who are wrongly and unnecessarily excluded from direct market participation in capital acquisition and earnings. Calling capital income 'unearned income' simply confuses people about the effects of the capital substitution for labor that is relentlessly going on all around them. It causes them to focus on earning exclusively by laboring, and to ignore the more potent prospect of earning by owning productive capital.

Binary economics, however, teaches that it is just as legitimate to earn by owning capital as by laboring. Again, that is the whole point of private property in capital. What is illegitimate is the present closed private property system which:–

- restricts effective capital acquisition rights to the relatively few (who already own a substantial capital estate); and
- needlessly denies effective capital acquisition rights to most other people (who dearly need them) thereby foreclosing, as a practical matter, their ability to earn by owning capital as well as by laboring.

c) The road from serfdom – universal individual private property in the two factors of production

If any society is to be free, its people must have private property in their own labor. Indeed, without private property in their labor, people are slaves. But people today live in a post-industrial economy in which production has become ever more capital intensive. As production becomes ever more capital intensive, the way in which each person participates in the economy must likewise become more capital intensive. Hence private property *in capital* has become economically even more important to individual liberty and material well-being than private property in labor.

So, based on the binary notion of two-factor production, binary theory holds that, in a post-industrial economy, it is increasingly important to the economic well-being of each individual, and to the growth of the economy as a whole, for each person to become increasingly productive through the acquisition of capital on market principles. Accordingly, it is not enough to have a theoretical right to acquire capital, a right that is, at present, effectively available to only a few. Rather it is essential that the right to acquire productive capital ownership be effectively available to all consumers on market principles. This requires an open private property system (characterized by effective, universal, individual, capital acquisition rights) in which the incremental earnings of capital can be distributed on market principles to those expected to purchase its incremental output. Indeed, only in this way can supply generate the market demand necessary for general affluence and sustained growth.

5.   The binary explanation of growth, poverty and affluence

As will become increasingly clear, the binary view of production, based on the concept of productiveness, has momentous implications which will reshape the way people look at everything economic and much else besides.   Those implications will eventually fill articles and books in fields as diverse as political, social, and business studies; law and philosophy; and the natural sciences.[31]   More obviously, the implications will resonate in the foundational private property systems, market structures, and institutions of newly flourishing economies throughout the world.   For the purposes of this introduction, however, we shall confine discussion just to those implications which impinge upon the critical questions of growth, poverty and affluence.

a)   Growth

Beginning long before the industrial revolution, but continuing with ever-increasing effect since, the examples of the donkey and the truck, together with many others, can be generalized to explain the process of per-capita economic growth which has been experienced by the unfree market economies.   That process can be characterized primarily as a technological process whereby capital is employed to produce more and better services, ever more efficiently, than could be achieved by employing labor alone (or labor and less productive capital).

In short, the binary proposition is that growth is a process whereby *ever more efficient capital productiveness replaces labor productiveness **and** adds to total productiveness.*   Per unit

---

[31] When the binary view of production becomes widely influential it will be recognized as correcting an error in thinking about production and distribution that is at present embodied in *all* these studies.

of output, in task after task, and in the aggregate (economy-wide), compared with labor, capital is doing ever more of the work. The aggregate per-capita effect of the continual increase in capital productiveness is characterized by more total production, with relatively more of the work being done by capital, and relatively less of the work done by humans. This is a process which intensifies with the distribution of capital acquisition.

As a first corollary of the growth proposition, *per-capita economic growth is primarily caused by increasing capital productiveness rather than increasing human productivity* (as the conventional paradigm maintains).[32] Capital may increase the productivity of *some* workers but, in so doing, it concentrates higher productivity into fewer workers while forcing redundancy onto many more. Despite increases in *some* wages, or even an increase in the median or average wage (of those still working), ever more of the work is done *by capital* per unit of output and in the aggregate (society wide).

As a second corollary, *the promise that technology creates more jobs than it destroys* (offered by many conventional economists) *is a false promise* in terms of labor's share of work done per unit of output and in the aggregate. As a systemic solution, the promise of more jobs spawned by new technology to compensate for lost jobs ignores the greater reality that capital is doing ever more of the work in task after task in almost every aspect of production.

The promise of sufficient lasting jobs to replace and supplement the jobs eliminated by technology likewise ignores the

---

[32] This is not to deny that technological advance is the product of human ingenuity and the accumulation of knowledge, but rather that the great increase in output in any given time period over time is primarily the result of the additional work done by capital during that time period rather than i) the human ingenuity and accumulation of knowledge that led to its invention, creation and maintenance; or ii) the human productivity associated with its current output as measured by the short-run market mechanisms that theoretically determine the value of inputs and outputs.

compelling market imperative of capital/labor substitution. That imperative, it should be remembered, is to discover, invent, perfect and employ new forms of capital to produce ever more and better services ever more efficiently, than could be achieved by employing either labor alone or labor with less productive capital. Thus the purpose and effect of technology is relentlessly to minimize the labor necessary for most production.

Of course, at various times and in various places, technological advance may create numbers of jobs, some of them high paying jobs. But many more will be lower paying than the ones eliminated by the advance. This is because, per unit of output, in task after task, and in the aggregate, the great growth brought by invention is a process by which ever more efficient capital is doing ever more of the work as its productiveness replaces labor productiveness *and* adds to total productiveness.

So, if growth is primarily caused by capital productiveness rather than labor productivity, and if through technology capital greatly adds to total work done (as binary economics contends), then strategies to help poor and working people that are confined to job creation, job training, and other forms of 'productivity oriented' redistribution miss the whole point of the industrial revolution. Such strategies *cannot* systemically provide most people with effective market participation in an industrial economy adequate to maintain, much less improve, their market share of production over time.

Thus in industrialized economies like those of the U.S. and the U.K., we always see some new high tech jobs for the most able, competitive and well-connected people; and also numerous lower-paying jobs for many others. However, at the same time, it is also true that for many others there is *no* work. Indeed, most of the realistically available work skills of a growing number of people in the poor and middle classes simply have no ready market – no matter how much job training the people undergo. Those work skills have no ready market because the unfree market economies are already able to produce an overabundance of goods and services that cannot be sold. Moreover, the work skills that are needed can frequently be found more cheaply by employing people in the less industrialized economies abroad.

b) *Poverty*

Taking a broad view, binary economists see that throughout human history, as a general rule, labor by itself rarely produces a living standard much above modest subsistence. So, without effective participation in the capital markets, most of those struggling to earn a living solely by way of the labor markets cannot rationally hope to keep pace as more and more work is done by ever more efficient capital. Without participation in capital acquisition, most people face a deteriorating standard of living characteristic of a less capital intensive, more labor dependent economy. Put another way, with their participation limited to the labor markets, people cannot compete with donkeys and trucks for hauling; nor with elevators and cranes for lifting; nor with steam shovels for digging; nor with mechanical ploughs and reapers for planting and harvesting; nor with computers for record keeping and calculating. In task after task, the labor content continually diminishes (as a percentage of the total input) and sometimes abruptly vanishes (as with automation). Moreover, as labor becomes less competitive with the capital that both replaces it and greatly adds to total work done, the aggregate market share of production earned by labor in free markets will *decline*.

Yet people still need and desire the goods and services once provided by labor which are now increasingly being provided and vastly supplemented by capital. Therefore most people can earn to purchase those goods and services (and fully participate in the great capital growth of an economy) *only* if they can participate competitively in the markets to acquire a share of the capital acquisition that is producing the new wealth. If they do not so participate, most people will become progressively poorer i.e. be *less* able (without earnings redistribution) to afford the things that capital increasingly produces. So we can now see the systemic explanation for poverty in an industrial economy:–

> *Most people remain poor because they have no effective means of acquiring an adequate share of the capital that continually replaces labor productiveness and vastly increases total productiveness.*

c) Affluence

Implicit in the above explanation of the cause of poverty is also the explanation for the cause of affluence (material abundance), viz.:–

Affluence is the product of capital.

The idea that capital productiveness (and *not* labor productivity) is the primary source of affluence is fundamental to binary economics. It follows that a competitive opportunity to acquire capital on market principles is an essential precondition to the economic well-being of most people.

Yet there really is nothing new or strange in the notion that capital ownership is essential for economic well-being. It might be new and strange to conventional economics but it is confirmed by common experience around the world. Thus it is no accident that all the relatively prosperous economies (e.g., those of the U.S.A., Germany, Japan, U.K., France, Italy and Canada) are well capitalized. Similarly, it is no accident that virtually all wealthy individuals are well capitalized. In this regard, binary economics teaches that what is true for the wealthy is true for the poor: what is true for individuals is true for nations. Indeed, without capital ownership, billions of individuals can ceaselessly toil and they will still remain poor, lucky to end up with bare subsistence. Affluence is almost always the product of capital, particularly fabricated capital such as machines, structures, patents, etc. It follows that more wealth requires more capitalization; that all economies must become more capitalized; and that all individuals must become well capitalized.

6. The principle of binary growth

The idea that growth and affluence are primarily the product of capital (and *not* labor) leads to another momentous concept in the new binary paradigm – the principle of *binary growth*. This principle holds that the more broadly capital is acquired over time on voluntary market transactions, the larger the economy will grow. The growth connection, moreover, is essentially independent of any productivity gains that might result from the broader ownership of capital. In other words, the principle of binary growth states that *capital has a distributive relationship to growth that is essentially independent of labor productivity.*

Compared to the conventional view (be it left-wing, centrist or right-wing), the binary idea that capital has an independent distributive relationship to growth is a revolutionary concept. It is revolutionary because conventional economics explains all growth as fundamentally a function of productivity. Conventional economics, moreover, does not consider the distribution of capital ownership to have any positive relationship to economic growth unless it is reflected in increased productivity.

In contrast, binary economics holds that the broader distribution of capital throughout the population produces a growth that is essentially independent of increased human productivity. This is easy to understand if it is recalled that, in our example, the donkey is doing *nineteen times* as much work as the man in a way that has little to do with human productivity. In truly free markets, moreover, the donkey is capable of distributing *nineteen times* as much income as the man – again in a way that has little to do with human productivity. As for the truck, the comparable figure is *thousands* of times greater.

In conventional economics, the power of capital to create and distribute wealth has long been obscured or ignored. Take the example of a hand tool which is as much a piece of non-human capital as a factory. In simpler economies in far-off times, when people fashioned their own tools and reaped the increased bounty and leisure arising from the joint output of human effort and tools, the distributional power of capital was obscured. The obscuring happened because the person doing the laboring would also be receiving the income (or reward) due to the non-human capital (the tool).

Of course, in those far-off times, the obscuring of the distinction between human and non-human output in relation to growth may have been a matter of little practical consequence. However, it becomes a matter of the greatest practical consequence in a highly industrialized unfree market economy today when most people face formidable barriers to the acquisition of a viable share of the capital that is doing ever more of the work. In such an economy, capital acquisition is not a matter of taming donkeys, tending land, or fashioning simple hand tools. As we will explain later, it is a complex process which at present requires the ownership of existing capital in order to acquire more. The process is therefore only open to the well-capitalized while the poor and middle classes are excluded and so become unable to participate directly in the earning power of capital and unable to that extent to afford its incremental output.[33]

At which point binary economics begins to focus more closely on the reasons for the exclusion and first observes that, in the unfree market economies, capital continues to buy itself steadily for existing owners. In other words, *the capital pays for itself out of its own earnings*. Indeed, of the billions of dollars in new capital acquired each year, *almost all of it is acquired with the*

---

[33]   Notwithstanding a much-heralded increase by individual shareholders in equities through mutual funds, retirement plans and the like, 90% of the population have a non-existent or trifling capital participation.   See Edward N. Wolff, *Top Heavy: A Study of Increasing Inequality in America* (New York, *Twentieth Century Fund*, 1995); and Edward N. Wolff, *How The Pie Is Sliced: America's Growing Concentration of Wealth*, (*The American Prospect*, Number 22, Summer 1995, pp. 58-64).

earnings of capital, and much of it is acquired with borrowed money.

So if capital can buy itself for the well-capitalized on borrowed money, the principle of binary growth indicates that it can *even more profitably buy itself for poor and middle class people.* When these people begin to earn capital income *as owners* (which income will be paid to them *after* the capital itself has paid for its acquisition) they will spend their new capital income on the additional goods and services that capital increasingly provides. This is a very important feature of the binary economy because, in the contrasting unfree market economy, almost all the new capital is acquired by *existing* owners. Existing owners generally have little or no unsatisfied consumer needs and wants. Consequently, when they are given the exclusive opportunity (i.e., an effective monopoly) to acquire all the capital, as happens in the present closed private property system, they seek to reinvest most of their capital earnings in more profitable enterprize, but in the context of relatively *less*, and very uncertain, consumer demand.

Therefore, focusing a little more closely on the situation at the capital acquisition bargaining table, we note that poor and middle class people possess a chip, a huge chip, which can never be matched by even the most extravagant of the rich. That chip is their immense pent-up appetite for the basic necessities and modest luxuries which are increasingly provided by capital – an appetite which can be satisfied on market principles by additional, profitable investment once the private property system is opened to poor and middle class people in the same way that it is now open to the wealthy.

Thus by distributing earning capacity (by way of efficient capital acquisition) more broadly to the poor and middle class people who will spend their capital earnings on consumption, capital produces *more* growth if broadly acquired than if narrowly acquired only by existing owners. This is because existing owners have:–

• largely satisfied consumer needs; and

- an investment appetite that is suppressed by the lack of consumer demand.

So, building on the foregoing, we can now restate a proposition that may seem to some to be an unfathomable inductive leap but, to others, merely the logical extension of the principles advanced thus far:–

Sustainable growth in an industrial economy requires that the incremental productiveness of capital be increasingly acquired ever more broadly by those expected to purchase what it produces.

To understand the unique aspect of the proposition, it helps to bear in mind that *it has nothing to do with increased human productivity*, nor with increased capital investment, but depends *entirely* on the distribution of capital ownership on market principles. The importance of this proposition is explored below.

7. The critical importance of binary growth

If the binary paradigm has a practical importance beyond its theoretical elegance, it is in the prospect of binary growth. Binary growth is the answer to the personal concern, "What's in it for me?" It is the answer to the broader, social, concern, "What's in it for *everyone*?" It is also the answer to the immediate question, "Why read this book?" Indeed, compared to all conventional approaches (be they left, centrist or right) in the *material* world, the promise of binary growth is what is singularly new in binary economics.

Yet even without binary growth, binary economics may have appeal to some people as:–

- a means of achieving *productivity* growth by a broader distribution of capital ownership;

- an alternate socialist way of _re_distributing what we already redistribute, except through more capitalistic rather than laboristic rhetoric; or
- another means (but not the only means) of _re_distributing _additional_ wealth from the wealthy to everyone else.

However, _none_ of the above involves any binary growth, and _none_ of them will likely offer sufficient reason for most people to study a wholly new system that overturns much twentieth century political and economic analysis.

But with binary growth, binary economics offers a very worthwhile subject for study. With reasonable assumptions and internal logical consistency, it uniquely offers substantial growth _beyond_ productivity gains and broad affluence _beyond_ productivity and earnings _re_distribution. In a sentence, the binary economy offers something big, new and important not promised by any conventional economic school be it left, centrist or right. Given such promise, how can people credibly proclaim the need for new approaches and yet not be very eager to explore binary economics?

8.   The binary property solution

Having provided a new understanding of growth, poverty and affluence in an industrial economy, binary theory then:–
- identifies the pervasive but entirely correctable, flaw (in both logic and justice) in the existing unfree market economies that unnecessarily suppresses growth, perpetuates poverty, and limits affluence primarily to owners of existing capital; and
- proposes a concrete, private property free market solution that enables all people to become well capitalized for the material benefit of poor _and_ rich alike.

As to the flaw in the existing unfree market, we need point only to the present system of corporate finance that dominates all the unfree market economies. It is the system by which capital is acquired by corporations, and equity interests in those corporations are *simultaneously* acquired by shareholders. That system facilitates the acquisition of the 'crown jewels' of the unfree market's private property system. In the U.S.A., for example, the system results in the largest two thousand corporations owning over 90% of the nation's productive non-residential assets. But these crown jewels are narrowly hoarded. Under the present system of corporate finance, effective market participation in the capital acquisition and growth of those corporations is closed to most people. It is therefore not surprising that, in the unfree market, the best living conditions (housing, health care, education and leisure opportunities) are largely closed to most people as well.

Of course, some people who are not capital owners are also able to enjoy the best living conditions. By hard work, keen intelligence or good luck – or living beyond the law – they may come to prosper. But 'some' people are *not* most people; and the unhappy fact is that, although conventional capitalist market theory claims that everyone has the right to acquire capital, *effective* acquisition rights are limited to existing owners. This is demonstrated by the fact that of billions of dollars worth of capital acquired each year in the unfree market economies, almost all of it is paid for with the earnings of capital, not labor.[34]

Moreover, the conventional method prescribed for acquiring capital – work hard, save hard and invest wisely – is wholly

---

[34] In the U.S.A., for example, most business capital is acquired by internally generated funds or borrowing. Only a small amount is acquired by selling stock to the public and almost all the capital acquired that way is acquired by people and institutions that are themselves already well-capitalized. See R. Brealey & S. Myers, *Principles of Corporate Finance* (2nd edition, 1984); Lynn A. Stout, *The Unimportance of Being Efficient: an Economic analysis of Stock Market Pricing and Securities Regulation*, (87 *Mich. L. Rev.*, 613 at 648, 1988).

unrealistic for most people whose labor income is barely enough to make ends meet. There are, of course, dramatic success stories of rags to riches but, statistically, they are the exceptions to the rule.

So the question is – How can the system of corporate finance be made open to all people on market principles? Asked another way, how can people without capital be enabled to compete effectively with people who already own capital for the acquisition of efficient capital assets?

In its most general terms, the answer is remarkably simple – *by using the very same private property principles, institutions and practices that now work so well for well-capitalized people* but expanding and perfecting them to work for all people. In fact, binary economics simply uses the time-tested principles, institutions, and practices of present corporate finance but in a modified form.

Therefore, in the binary economy, there are the same corporations, trusts, banks, insurance companies and central banks as at present except that they are enabled to transact their business and to co-operate even more efficiently than they do today. The consequence is that everyone can participate in much more capital acquisition on market principles than is possible at present.

Thus the key to opening the process of capital acquisition to more people is to be found in the basic logic of present corporate finance which is to enable corporations to acquire capital assets *before* money has been earned to pay for them. In fact, corporations borrow money to pay for much of their capital assets. The corporations borrow, and the lenders lend, with the expectation that the capital assets acquired will generate (in a competitive period, usually no longer than five to seven years) sufficient net income to repay their acquisition cost and also generate sufficient revenues (in the form of reserves for depreciation, research and development) to replace themselves.

Thus the corporations borrow, and the lenders lend, on the market-tested expectation that the capital acquired will buy itself, indefinitely replace itself, and continue to earn competitive income *indefinitely*. The borrowed money is then *repaid out of the earnings of the assets acquired*.

As the corporations repay the loans, the shareholders of the corporation earn a growing private property right (called 'equity') in the corporate assets acquired. This equity is reflected on the financial books of the companies and in the corporate shares of the owners. Therefore, by using this method, the corporations sumultaneously grow wealthier and more productive, and the owners of the corporations grow wealthier and more productive even as they sleep.

The evidence for the ongoing profitable viability of this system can be seen in the steady growth of America's three thousand largest companies, representing over 95% of the U.S.A.'s publicly investable assets:–

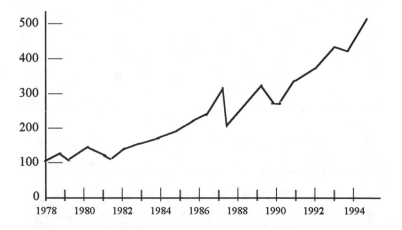

Fig. 2 – 1. Growth of a unit value – simplified version of a Russell 3000 Share Index.

The figure is a simplified version of a Russell 3000 index. The line represents the rising value of an original $100 invested in 1978. To that value is added the accrued annual earnings and then the inflation rate is subtracted. (A similar pattern of broad growth is revealed in various indices of American equities for many decades).

Very obviously, Fig. 2 – 1 shows that a substantial capital growth is taking place.   The growth, moreover, goes on *indefinitely*.   This is because the capital acquired by the corporations not only earns enough to buy itself but also enough to replace itself with state-of-the-art capital replacements by way of tax-free reserves for depreciation, research and development. Allowing the corporations to earn and set aside a reasonable amount tax-free for depreciation, research and development (while the labor income of most working people is taxed) is another marvelous benefit of being a capital owner. This benefit is rationalized by conventional economics as a means of promoting greater efficiency – it is claimed to be essential to the greater prosperity enjoyed by the unfree market countries as compared to the greater poverty suffered in the former communist countries.   But the same, *and even greater,* efficiency can be achieved if this marvellous benefit is extended to all people so that *more* of the earnings of *more* capital can be distributed to those expected to purchase its output.

However, it is important to understand that, although wealthy people are generally investing in new capital acquisition on terms where the capital pays for its own acquisition at competitive rates, some of the investment is undoubtedly in start-up, high-tech and other risky enterprizes.   Such enterprizes are not listed in the Russell 3000 and they often go bankrupt although, if they do succeed, can succeed spectacularly.   In other words, wealthy people have portfolios with a substantial proportion of stable Russell 3000 corporations mixed with investments of greater risk.

Binary investment, however – for the benefit of the poor and middle classes – will concentrate on the more established, less risky companies of the Russell 3000. This is because, although the gains of the Russell 3000 are unlikely to be spectacular, they do amount to a steady, fairly riskless accretion of capital assets. By the use of non-recourse credit (with the interest cost being repaid out of pre-tax corporate dollars), moreover, the assets in effect purchase themselves for their owners.

Binary investment, therefore:–

Uses the same kind of capital investment which presently buys itself for the wealthy on credit and which can also, even more profitably, be structured competitively to buy itself for the poor and middle classes.

Yet, crucially, that binary investment does *not* take from existing owners. Although existing owners may have to compete for particular capital acquisition, no ownership changes hand in connection with binary investment other than by voluntary transfers.

Binary investment will, moreover, benefit existing owners because they, too, will be part of the expanding binary economy and its many opportunities including conventional ones. In essence, all that happens in a binary economy is that something which benefits the wealthy at present is also made available to benefit poor and working people. But to enable the poor and most working people to participate competitively in the capital markets, it is necessary to equip them with a *binary property right*. This takes the form of a market right which approximates the very attractive market right of existing owners to participate in the credit-worthy capital acquisition plans of well-established publicly-held companies. The binary property right is described more fully below.

a)   The binary property right

Having made its explanation of growth, poverty and affluence; having articulated the key principle of binary growth related to the potent distributive power of capital; and having identified the defective institution (the present closed system of corporate finance) which prevents open participation in capital acquisition on market principles, binary economics goes on to prescribe its remedy – the binary property right, viz.:–

A market right (comparable to the market right of existing owners) for each and every person in the poor and middle class to compete effectively for capital acquisition on credit.

Accordingly, *every person* (male or female, in a job, out of a job, pregnant, on a pension, sick, or looking after an infirm parent) *has a binary property right* (but only on market principles) *to compete effectively to acquire private and individual ownership of productive capital assets which include the best capital assets.*

The acquisition of capital assets over time increases people's productive power by augmenting their (often declining) labor productiveness with greatly increasing capital productiveness. The effect is to replace and vastly supplement each person's labor productiveness with capital productiveness and thus to provide each person with more earned income from capital rather than labor. In this way, binary economics addresses the root cause of middle class and other poverty (i.e. inadequate productive power) rather than merely treating the symptom (i.e. inadequate consuming power).

In summary, the basic binary property right is *the right to acquire capital on non-recourse corporate credit and to repay the loan with the earnings of the capital acquired.*

b) Market rights compared with welfare rights

It cannot be over-emphasized, however, that the binary property right is a market right, not a welfare right. A welfare right is merely the right to take from the market without the obligation to provide something in voluntary exchange. In the case of a market right, the right to take from the market requires respect for the property of others. Thus, the market right to take is predicated on the antecedent production of something provided in voluntary exchange for the thing taken. Consequently, binary economics recognizes a market right so that people's productive input can equal their consumption outtake.

The binary property right is accordingly a right to participate in production and in market transactions with willing buyers and sellers of goods and services with respect for everyone's private property. It is *not* the right to compel a transaction or to barge in on, or prevent, the voluntary transactions of others. So, to the extent that existing corporations determine to capitalize on the binary property right, their decisions must be consistent with the property rights of existing shareholders who, typically, must authorize the binary transactions.

Nevertheless, although the binary property right is a market right which respects the rights of others and requires voluntary transactions for its implementation, it is intended to be an *effective* right and not a merely theoretical one. In other words, it is intended to enable people without capital to compete *in practice* with existing owners for new capital acquisition. This is done by modifying the present legal and administrative structure to make the right effective in practice. Just as the rights of existing capital owners are supported by a legal and administrative infrastructure, so the binary property right requires a supporting infrastructure. It can be said here, however, that it is a light infrastructure requiring very little legislation and, in the long run, something which *reduces* legal, administrative and other complication. The binary infrastructure is of considerable importance and will be discussed at length in Chapter Eight.

c)   *Economic self-sufficiency – the binary competence*

So a binary economy would provide all poor and middle class people with a *second* way – a capital way – of earning additional income by equipping each person with the binary property right. As we will explain, this will establish for each person a *binary competence*.

Although many will oppose and ignore that right, binary economists are confident that, once legislated, it will allow people who presently own little or no capital to begin competitively acquiring efficient capital on the earnings of capital. It also enables everybody to become self-sufficient. Without taking from the wealthy, in free market transactions, a binary economy will gradually increase the capital ownership acquired (and therefore the capital income earned) individually by each person who at present earns little or no current spendable income from capital. This fulfils the American Dream of having an independent capital estate which is sufficient to satisfy basic needs.[35]

The binary approach to economic self-sufficiency thus broadens the conventional economic goal (which is no longer realistic in a modern industrial economy) of attempting to make all people fully productive by way of their labor alone. The broadening gives economic self-sufficiency *by a combination of labor and capital with the* **capital** *competence providing an ever larger component of the self-sufficiency over time.*

As to the extent of economic competency, binary economists set no particular limits on the power of people (when equipped with the binary property right) to earn abundance and leisure.[36] They do, however, have a goal which is the binary promise to enable every person eventually to acquire a *binary competence* which is defined as:–

A capital estate large enough to supply sufficient current consumer income to support at least **one half** *of an affluent life style (measured in the context of what society as a whole can efficiently produce).*

---

[35] At present, however, that Dream is but a dream.

[36] It may be, however, that people living in a binary economy (with its secure basis for individual living standards) may tend not to make a frenetic pursuit of greed (as is so often the case with some people living in the unfree market) but, rather, will take a more balanced approach to what is materially necessary and, on the whole, will give greater value to the educational, spiritual and creative.

Of course, along with having the substantial income from their capital competence, each individual will also be free to gain income from labor as now. Indeed, they will be freer and better able to do so.

A binary competence usually takes the form of a 'basket' of shares or stock in large credit-worthy companies. It is acquired individually by poor and working people gradually over time on credit using the earnings of the capital represented by those shares to make repayment – just as the capital-rich do today.

After the binary capital has paid for itself, it begins paying out its full earnings to its new owners.[37] This full pay-out (net of reserves for depreciation, research and development) is a special feature of the binary property right which is reflected in a mandatory provision of the binary stock. Conventional common stock does not require the full pay-out but rather provides that company managers may withhold the earnings of capital for various corporate purposes such as new capital provision and a reserve for unexpectedly poor financial performance. Nevertheless, the practice of withholding earnings may be well and good for substantial capital owners who have few, if any, unmet needs and desires but it effectively starves out poor and middle class people from capital acquisition. As will be more fully explained in Chapter Eight, the full pay-out provision on binary stock is essential if the binary market right is to be competitive with the property rights of existing owners as a means of acquiring capital on credit. However, binary economists opine that, once the wonderful market benefits of full-return binary stock become better understood, conventional shareholders as well will come to demand full pay-out common stock thereby forcing company managers to live more faithfully by the discipline of the market.

---

[37] The true, full dividend earnings of shares, in a binary economy, could be as much as five, possibly eight or nine, times what are paid out at present. See Louis & Patricia Kelso, *Democracy and Economic Power* (1991), pp. 124-129.

Therefore, in each year of the binary economy, after the initial payback period of the first shares acquired, additional shares will become fully paid and they, too, will begin paying out binary dividends to their new owners. So, as the supply of fully paid capital increases, the capital income on those shares distributed to new owners also increases. Beginning perhaps with a small annual dividend (amounting to only a tiny percentage of a middle class person's income), the dividends promise to increase year by year from a tiny percentage, to 5%, to 10% and then 20%, and so on, until they pay for the goal of binary competence – 50% of a reasonably affluent lifestyle. Exactly how long this process will take is unknown. Binary economists, however, expect to see demonstrable binary growth and distributive justice within a decade.[38]

Thus, to those people willing to accept universal, individual binary competence as a goal, binary economics offers a systemic private property solution to the problem of post-industrial poverty. The material benefits of individual competence, however, are not limited to people usually thought of as poor. Rather the benefits extend to all people with little or no capital income. Binary economics therefore seeks primarily to benefit just about everybody from the poorest up through the upper middle class. All of these people have important needs and desires that could be met with additional income which, at the moment, they find difficult, if not impossible, to earn legitimately by way of their labor.[39]

---

[38] Some binary economists think the goal of binary competence can be fully achieved for all people in fifteen to twenty years or so. Others think it may take a generation or two. The period is not so important as that the process of implementation immediately begin.

[39] In this spirit, binary economics holds that whoever is not well-off in an industrial economy, is poor. The poor have substantial material needs and wants (from the next meal, to a child's education) and live with substantial anxiety that these will not be met no matter how hard they work. Whatever other problems they may have, most well-off people do not have this anxiety.

Furthermore, widespread individual competence would *also benefit the wealthy*. Wealthy people will prosper because they will be participating in *a growing economy* that has ever more prosperous consumers no longer needing redistributed income on which to live. The wealthy, moreover, will gain from owning capital assets paying out much greater earnings than at present. Put simply, the wealthy will live in a wealthier society and they will pay less tax. In fact, *everybody will pay lower tax*. Because all individuals will become increasingly productive, there will be decreasing need for governments to raise taxes to make up the distribution shortfall of the closed capital markets. With increasing binary competence, the need for government intervention to pay for welfare benefits (and, in due course, education and subsidized housing) will be diminished. Consequently, *government will be diminished*.

Of course, some people may allege that providing universal, individual capital competence means taking capital from those who already have. *It does not*. No binary investment is commanded by government fiat; it proceeds only with willing buyers and sellers. Existing owners will maintain title to all of their present assets – in the binary economy, no assets are confiscated, taxed or involuntarily encumbered. Existing owners, moreover, will be free as they are now to use their assets as collateral to borrow money to bid for additional capital acquisition in competition with others.

However, in a binary economy, 'others' will fairly include *all* people, not just existing owners, precisely because the rest of the population will have the binary property right. In this way, poor and middle class people will become increasingly competent by reason of their new capital ownership. The prospect of a systematic steady increase in capital-based consumer income will then make more capital investment profitable and less expensive. The growing individual competencies will thus provide the basis for a sustainable growth and general affluence completely beyond the comprehension of conventional economics. The ensuing growth represents *nothing* taken from existing owners: it is the natural consequence of opening the capital markets to all people on market principles.

d) Other benefits offered by the binary competence

Up to this point, the binary promise of growth and distributive justice, based on the universal binary competence, might largely bring to mind *material* abundance and leisure. The binary promise, however, extends also to many other matters.

Thus, as people come closer to acquiring a full binary competence, the eternal dread of penury (faced by so many) will be replaced by a growing sense of self-sufficiency and confidence. Indeed, living within a binary economy that:–

- recognizes *everybody's* need to own capital;
- explains coherently how people can begin to earn so that they can buy what is increasingly produced by capital; and
- provides them with a legitimate, competitive means of doing so,

people will find that their feelings of profound alienation and powerlessness (entirely understandable in an economy that offers most people only menial jobs and degrading welfare) will be replaced with a growing sense of belonging and participation.

Furthermore, the right to acquire, and earn from, a binary competence on market principles is something which goes to all individuals without discrimination based on race, sex,[40] creed,

---

[40] In a binary economy, women will find themselves increasingly on equal terms with men. Women bring up children, care for aged parents, keep the home together and, in a thousand ways, sustain others but they are rarely paid for those efforts. Many, perhaps most, women also have to get paid work to supplement the home's income, but if they get that work it is generally low paid. This is because women are one of those groups which always find themselves in an inferior economic position despite their contribution to the life of the human race being no less than that of any other. A United Nations

national origin, or political or social status. The binary system indeed provides a non-discriminatory, full and continuing participation in the economy that honors everyone's right to life, liberty, property and democracy.

Moreover, as all people acquire an increasingly secure capital base, it is conceivable that there will be a diminution in perceived human needs (which, in the case of some people today, amount to almost limitless dreams of conspicuous consumption) to a more balanced understanding of what is really required for human happiness. Fear of, and the reality of, material insecurity are probably the main reasons why some humans come to have almost limitless wants and greedy, highly possessive attitudes. Even people who are, on the face of things, materially secure (like the well-off) can have psychological attitudes manifesting themselves in a flaunting of wealth or a desire to possess wealth primarily because others do not. The binary economy, however, holds a potential for greatly improving attitudes because it provides a profound material security for all.

Furthermore, the growth promised by the natural operation of a binary economy need *not* be a growth that degrades the environment. To the contrary, binary economics promises green growth. Clean air, clean rivers; green lands, forests, meadows and wetlands with an abundance of animal and plant life, are all things which can be achieved by binary economics. This is because the combination of an efficient binary economy and binary competence means that:–

- any individual, or group of people, can be enabled to earn their living in a new way so that a previous living, marring the environment, is ended;

---

report estimated that women own a mere 1% of the world's capital assets. Amongst other things, the economic empowerment of women (together with education) will result in voluntary control of family size.

- any society will be able to afford more expensive, but ecologically more desirable, practices.[41]

Thus the disgraceful environmental depredations (which so often go on more extensively in poor neighbourhoods, regions and nations) can be reduced and eventually ended.

It can therefore be seen that the benefits of binary competence extend well beyond the narrowly material. Unfortunately, however, conventional market economics has yet to recognize the practical value of a program to realize universal competence. While paying lip service to open markets and the need to involve all people productively in the economy, conventional economics has shown virtually no interest in the binary offer of effective, universal, individual capital acquisition rights on market principles.[42]

Binary economics, however, teaches that such a program is essential to freedom, democracy, individual economic well-being

---

[41] Although deplorable degradation of the environment has occurred (and occurs) in the unfree market economies, it is nowhere near as great as that which has occurred (and occurs) in the socialist economies. The main reason is simply that the more efficient unfree market economies are able to afford more environmentally friendly practices. Another reason is that in socialist societies nobody has a proprietary stake in preserving the viability of the environment.

[42] One encouraging exception (to the general rule that conventional economics shows no interest in binary competence) is to be found among economist members of the Society for the Advancement of Socio-Economics (SASE). Socio-economics is an emerging meta-discipline that begins with the assumption that economics is not a self-contained system, but is embedded in society, polity and culture. Drawing upon economics, sociology, political science, psychology, anthropology, philosophy, history, law and management, socio-economics regards competitive behavior as a subset of human behavior within a societal context that both enables and constrains competition and co-operation. In successive international conferences on socio-economics, binary economics has attracted growing interest as a beneficent, distinct alternative paradigm to the neo-classical paradigm that dominates much of conventional market economic theory.

and sustained aggregate growth. It is also readily and richly achievable on a consentual basis that honors everyone's right to life, liberty, dignity and property.

9.   Doubts about the new and the old

It is natural for people to have doubts about both the new and the old. Thus if a proposed system is untested, unrecognized by the received wisdom, and promises seemingly unattainable goals (when judged by conventional standards), people are bound to have doubts.

But if a system is old, people will also have doubts. They have known the system far too long not to have recognized shortcomings. This is particularly so when the system seems to operate with much unexplained suffering that goes unremedied year after year despite constant effort to eliminate it.

So how should we balance doubts about the new and the old? In what spirit should we try to decide if the doubts are, or are not, valid? These matters are discussed below.

a)   Doubts about binary economics

As will be clear by now, the binary economy promises much greater abundance and leisure for everyone by means of universal, individual capital ownership achieved democratically without taking from existing owners. It comes into being voluntarily, gently and steadily, but powerfully, benignly affecting society on the grand scale.

So does the promise of the binary economy raise doubts because it somehow seems too good to be true? After all, if binary economics is so wonderful, why is it only now beginning to be noticed by those smart intellects (in universities, think-tanks and government) whose job it is to discover powerful, new ideas? Why is it not *already* being embraced by the politicians concerned with growth and distributive justice? Is there some catch?

The brief answer, as will be more fully explained later, is that too many smart intellects have minds governed by an outdated paradigm. Too many academicians, consultants and politicians are confused and blinded by obsolete economic thinking. And, although there are certain market conditions for the successful operation of a binary economy, there is no catch. In short, doubts about binary economics will disappear as it becomes understood.

Nevertheless, any doubts which might reasonably arise regarding the promises of the untried binary economy should be weighed against the legitimate doubts about a system of 'free market' economics and private property which works very well for a few, not so well for more, and badly for most. It is a system that operates with much unexplained, and seemingly needless, suffering. We refer, of course, to unfree market capitalism.

b) *Doubts about unfree market capitalism*

For people genuinely concerned about economic growth and distributive justice, there is no lack of doubts about the unfree market. The first doubt arises when it is noticed that there are always great swaths of persistent poverty even in the most affluent, industrialized unfree market economies. Conventional market theory, starting with Adam Smith, says that human labor creates most of the wealth and that everyone can have work. Yet many people, and in some nations most, remain in poverty *even if they have jobs.*

For the second doubt, consider the strange phenomenon that, in the unfree market economies, it often takes two wage earners to bring home today what one wage earner could bring home thirty years ago.[43] Conventional theory continually talks of the rising

---

[43] It is highly significant that, in the U.K., for example, women are increasingly becoming the main bread winners. Twenty years ago,

productivity of labor, yet many people seem to be earning relatively less (assuming they are in work).[44] How can this be if there really is a genuinely rising labor productivity? And why are the middle classes – formerly materially secure with the associated social status – now finding that their security and status are weakening or, in many cases, have gone?

Then there is the third doubt occasioned by observing that, even in the most successful unfree market economies, there are vast surpluses of goods and services. Similarly, there is vast unused productive capacity and willing (but unemployed) workers whilst, concurrently, growing numbers of people lack basic necessities. Obviously, something is out of kilter.

60% of the employed work force was male: today it is 51%. Yet the average earnings of full-time working women are only £170 per week as compared to the £268 for men. In addition, more and more jobs are becoming part-time and *more men* are doing part-time jobs (which have less fringe benefits than full-time ones). (Report by *Income Data Services*, May, 1993.) Similarly, in 1994, the U.K. government's *Labour Force Survey* found that, since early 1990, full-time jobs had fallen by 6% while part-time jobs had risen by 5.5%. Moreover, the trend is accelerating. In *The End of Work* (G.P. Putnam & Son, New York, 1995), Jeremy Rifkin provides depressing new data on the deteriorating labor earnings received by increasing numbers of workers in the U.S.A. and around the world.

[44] In the U.S.A., there is a similar shift to part-time and temporary work. *Whatever Happened to the Great American Job?* (*Time* magazine, March, 1994) describes the profound change in the workplace as "the temping of America" with companies shedding permanent staff and increasingly relying on part-timers or self-employed freelancers hired only for a specific project. "A transformation that is merciless and profound is occurring....They are the great corporate clearances of the 1990s: the ruthless restructuring efficiencies....As the Scottish farmers were torn away from the soil, millions of Americans are being evicted from the working worlds that have sustained them, the jobs that gave them....a context, a sense of self-worth, a kind of identity".

The fourth doubt concerns the recurrent booms and busts that have characterized the unfree market capitalist economies ever since the start of the industrial revolution. Why are there these great booms and busts when there is a continually growing technological ability to produce goods and services and when nobody doubts the continuing existence of strong, widespread, unsatisfied consumer desire for those goods and services? Is the physical capacity to produce somehow out of sync with the ability to consume?

These questions are particularly pertinent at times when unfree market economies suffer recessions and their governments do not know what to do. Moreover, the questions are even more pertinent to periods of alleged 'recovery' because they ask why a 'recovery' is always the prelude to another recession.

The questions provoke further questions. Why is the growing technological ability to produce on market principles, with ever-increasing capital substitution for labor, not matched with a growing ability of each individual to earn consumer income on those same principles? And how can the unfree market economies ever expect their populations to purchase the incremental output of capital unless the markets for capital acquisition are effectively open to everyone?

Then there is the question as to why welfare dependence continues to grow massively, rather than shrink, as society's ability to produce goods and services continually advances with technology. Unfree market rhetoric says welfare dependence is wasteful and should be eliminated and people required to work. Yet, in country after country, welfare dependence (open and disguised) continues its inexorable rise decade after decade.[45]

Now consider the frightening scene of the inner cities which are increasingly prone to riot and other violence. Those that can,

---

[45] Since 1979, U.K. welfare rose at an average annual rate of 3.7% in real terms, and was projected to rise at a rate above 3% until the year 2000. (DHSS paper, *The Growth of Social Security*, 1993). In 1998, after government review, an annual figure just under 3% remained.

flee to the suburbs only to find crime coming after them. The inner cities – containing an alienated, poorly educated and unemployed underclass – are time bombs set to explode. And the question is – *What can be done?*[46]

Somewhere at the back of the reader's mind, a voice may be saying that all these doubts and questions must have something to do with the advance of technology. So we ask – What will happen to most workers as ever more work is done by robots, computers and other forms of capital?[47] Well, what will happen? Unfree market theorists allege that it does not matter if capital assets substitute for labor in the productive process because, in some unspecified way, service and other jobs will increase and everyone will benefit. However, most of those service jobs are hardly likely to pay good wages (assuming there will be sufficient jobs). Then there is the straightforward question as to how the industrial economies of the U.S.A., Japan, Germany, France, U.K., Italy and Canada can fairly be called 'free market' economies when most of their populations are excluded from meaningful participation in the capital markets.

Of course, despite the doubts and unanswered questions, there may still be some people who continue to assert that unfree market capitalism is the highest possible evolution of human

---

[46]   Many inner-city areas are now drug-ridden and ravaged by crime. They can easily explode into rioting (as in Los Angeles and other U.S. cities, 1992). The situation is likely to get worse unless the inner-city populations are made truly productive as binary economics teaches they can and must be. People want, and need, to earn properly and legitimately for themselves. In his book, *The Culture of Contentment* (1991), J.K. Galbraith recognizes the inner-city problems and predicts an apocalyptic future. Unfortunately, although recommending to his students Kelso and Adler's *Capitalist Manifesto*, Professor Galbraith has yet to encourage publicly the exploration of binary economics.

[47]   W. Leontief, *The Distribution of Work and Income*, (*Scientific American*, September, 1982). V. Renshaw, *Organizing Work in an Information Age*, (*10 Journal of Post Keynesian Economics*, 1988, 618 at 621).

society.[48] But those people should ponder, for example, why an allegedly successful 'free market' increasingly has to rely on redistributing a substantial percentage of national income to 'create' jobs (often phoney jobs) and provide welfare payments (both explicit and disguised).[49] They should also ponder why on earth capital owners have to be given 'incentives' to encourage them to invest. With the bulk of people having many unsatisfied wants, it would be thought that, in a free market, they would be falling over themselves to invest yet – everybody is only too aware – they are not.[50]

Then those with religious belief may find their doubts expressed in the following questions:–

- If God is a god of plenty, and if human understanding of the physical universe is a gift from God, then why (despite the great promise of technology to produce abundance and leisure) does the world still have persistent poverty even in the most affluent industrial capitalist economies?

- Is persistent poverty *really* the nature of God's universe?

---

[48] This assertion is made by Francis Fukyama (*The End of History and The Last Man*, 1992). With no indication that he has considered binary economics, he believes that, with the fall of communism, capitalism has triumphed and nothing much better is possible or desirable.

[49] In the binary economy, redistribution will become increasingly unnecessary because all individuals will become increasingly able to produce for themselves, and therefore better able to pay for what they consume.

[50] Capital owners are not willing to invest, of course, because a closed private property system will inevitably fail on market principles to distribute the consumer income necessary to purchase what can be increasingly produced by capital. Also, redistributionary measures designed to increase the amount of demand will inevitably fall short of providing the demand necessary to support investment while simultaneously discouraging investment by reducing the return on capital.

- Or rather is it something caused by humans, which can be corrected by humans with new understanding, and that people and societies of good will, regardless of their faith, are called upon to study, understand and correct?

  Lastly, we ask:–

- *Why* does the unfree market provoke so many doubts? *Why* so many unanswered questions? Is there some underlying flaw, something wrong, in the traditional conceptions of private property and economics that prevents, rather than facilitates, solutions to the problems and answers to the questions?

Thus, when considering the doubts that may arise because binary economics is untried, ignored by conventional thinkers, or seemingly too good to be true, the reader should also consider the doubts about the present unfree market system. These doubts may also naturally arise after taking a long, hard, honest look at the unexplained failings of the unfree market economies and then listening to an inner voice which softly, but persistently, whispers, *"There must be a better way."*

10.   The so-called 'free market' is really an unfree market

A principal reason for the failings (and for the persistence of those doubts and unanswered questions) is that the so-called 'free market' of conventional capitalism is a free market only in its rhetoric. In reality, it is *un*free, self-contradictory and logically incoherent. Thus the rhetoric says anybody can come to own productive capital. In practice, however, most people are excluded from the capital markets and so excluded from capital ownership *even if they would play entirely by the free-market rules*.

Then there is the rhetoric which claims that all corporations, large or small, must sink or swim without government help.

Admittedly, there is some truth to this claim. In the name of competition, governments may allow a few of the largest corporations (and many of the smaller ones) to fail and be swallowed up by others.

But too many failures, for example, of America's largest two thousand or the United Kingdom's largest three hundred corporations, cannot be countenanced. If too many fail, the unfree market governments have a problem – loss of jobs is a disaster for individuals and, through the ripple effects, a disaster for thousands more. Because the unfree market is committed to redistributing income primarily through jobs, welfare and conventional closed capital investment (rather than by making all individuals properly productive through capital ownership), the loss of too many large corporations together could severely damage the economy. At the next election, it could also defeat the political party in power. So the government, although denying that certain corporations are 'too big to fail', intervenes in various ways thereby contradicting the rhetoric.[51]

---

[51]   In the U.S., the government practice of bailing out major banks (e.g. Continental Bank of Illinois) and industrial corporations (e.g. Chrysler Corporation) is evidence of this 'too big to fail' doctrine that undergirds the pretence of the free market. See Walter Adams and James W. Brock, *Corporate Size and the Bailout Factor, (Journal of Economics Issues*, vol. 21, pp. 61-85, March, 1987) which says that if a corporation is big enough, society, through government, feels compelled to guarantee the corporation's survival. See also *Economic Implications of 'Too Big to Fail'* (U.S. House Committee on Banking, Finance and Urban Affairs: hearing, May 9, 1991); Robert L Hetzel, *'Too Big to Fail': Origins, Consequences and Outlook (Federal Reserve Bank of Richmond, Economics Review*, vol. 77. pp. 3-15, 1991; Robert B. Reich and John D. Donohue, *Lessons from the Chrysler Bailout (California Management Review*, pp. 157-183, vol. 27, No. 4, Summer, 1985); Arthur E. Wilmarth, Jr., *Too Big to Fail, Too Few to Serve? The Potential Risk of Nationwide Banks (77 Iowa Law Review 957*, March, 1992); R. Charles Moyer and Robert Lamy, *'Too Big to Fail': Rationale, Consequences and Alternatives*

Further there is the contradiction between the rhetoric which claims there is a true free market which upholds private property rights and the reality which abrogates them. The rhetoric says that capital owners keep what they produce. But the reality is a system which massively expropriates the earnings of capital and then redistributes them. The expropriation and redistribution are mainly done through the *political* structure in what is a social (supposedly majoritarian) intervention and reallocation of the market distribution (i.e. they are done by what is in essence the *socialist* method). In this way, huge redistributions of income are made from those who have greatly earned (largely, the capital asset owners) to those who have earned little or nothing on the fair market value of their labor (e.g., those in low-paying jobs, the unemployed etc.).

The earnings redistribution is done in different ways examples of which are:– the recirculation of taxes to pay for 'free' education; subsidized housing; and various welfare benefits. But the redistributions are not limited to the welfare of the poor. There is welfare for corporations which includes the favoring of sectors of industry – e.g. farming, research and foreign trade – with the promise that there will be a 'trickle-down' effect to other areas of the economy. There is other government welfare in the form of unnecessary bureaucratic jobs (very often administering the earnings redistribution which is such a feature of unfree market economies) and, of course, there are the 'make-work' jobs themselves which are an attempt to give people the dignity of

---

(*Business Economics*, pp. 19-24, vol. 27, July, 1992). The same approach is followed by conservative and liberal governments alike. A bailout of Credit Lyonnais, one of Europe's biggest banks, by the French government is a case in point – see *Credit Lyonnais inquiry comes to light today*, (*Financial Times*, p. 17, Company & Markets section, 12th July, 1994). The same policies are pursued in Japan. See *Ailing Japanese banks thrown lifeline* (*Financial Times*, 11th December, 1994) and *Bailout in Japan indicates government isn't yet ready to lift its heavy hand* (*Wall Street Journal*, p. A. 10, 12th December, 1994).

being productive via their labor when they could even more easily have the dignity of being productive via their individual capital ownership.

But whatever the redistribution, whatever the subsidy, whether public or private, it all contradicts the rhetoric of 'free market' efficiency and invades the income rights of capital owners. Despite which, the redistributions continue and on a very large scale precisely because the *market* distribution of income has proved economically and politically unacceptable to almost everybody.[52] *The market distribution fails because the effective right to acquire capital assets is narrowly limited to existing owners.*

Most remarkably of all, the invasion of private property rights by the expropriation of the earnings of capital is countenanced by the well-capitalized because, in the existing situation:–

• their consumption needs are overly met;
• their effective monopoly on capital acquisition is preserved; and
• they believe that economic growth is only a function of productivity. Consequently, they believe that their rate of capital earning/accumulation, even after the redistribution process, is more or less as good as can be expected, i.e., optimal.

In summary, the unfree market economies are, in practical implementation, a compromised patchwork of plutocratic capitalism and pervasive, albeit often disguised, socialism. Tottering along on government-promoted capital growth strategies for capital owners, they offer only jobs and welfare (but never enough) for everyone else. Moreover, trying to lubricate a

---

[52] Thus the redistribution of capital income is an unavoidable expedient lest people's economic suffering and discontent reach dimensions of social and political disorder that could destabilize society and the government. The plain fact is that, in the unfree market, it is politically unacceptable for capital owners to receive all their true earnings.

faltering system, they selectively demand barrier-free competition here whilst condoning protectionist policies there. Because true productive capacity is not widely spread amongst the population, the unfree market economies are forced to redistribute, tax, subsidize, monetize, borrow, spend, lend, manipulate interest rates and manipulate the money supply. In other words, unfree market capitalism will resort to massive continuing (but often disguised) non-market expediencies in the attempt to hide the failings of its unfree market while maintaining a hypocritical pretence that it is a true free market when, patently, it is not.

11. The unfree market is only a success in comparison with communism

So far, the unfree market has been able to get away with the pretense of being a true free market because, *by contrast*, it impressively out-performed the state communist economies. Thus, whether the former Soviet leaders gave up the Cold War because they feared better guns or desired more butter, or both, the victory of comparatively superior efficiency undoubtedly goes to the unfree market.

This victory of unfree market capitalism over communism comes as no surprise to binary economists who recognize the power of markets to create wealth. The plain fact is that, whatever the manifest imperfections of the unfree market economies, they are better at creating wealth than the socialist ones.

The victory, however, still seems to baffle socialist critics who continue to dismiss unfree market logic as circular (in that it assumes the efficiency it is trying to prove). Yet, if they would serve the people, socialists must come to recognize the deeper truth that there is nothing imaginary about the relative bounty of unfree capitalism's supermarkets as compared to the miserable scarcity in most of the shops of formerly communist countries.

Indeed, in terms of efficient, productive and distributive capacity, the difference in per-capita output between unfree market and communist economies is so great that it must be more than the product of circular logic or the self-interested rhetoric of the wealthy.

And it is. The relative bounty of the unfree market economies is the result of real and efficient causes related to the employment of capital and labor on market principles in a private property system. Binary economists, therefore, understand that *the way to serve and empower people is not to destroy, burden or tax the private property system, but to expand it for the individual benefit of everyone.*

Just as the socialist critics must come to recognize the deeper truth that there is nothing imaginary about the relative bounty of the unfree market, so right-wing theorists and analysts must also recognize a deeper truth which will not go away simply because it has been hitherto ignored – *the unfree market defeated communism only with a limited and faltering success.* Unfree economies look good *only when compared* with the failed communist alternatives. The unfree economies have certainly provided impressive growth, but always in a stop-go rather than sustainable manner. Moreover, *they are unable, on market principles, to distribute broadly the consumer earnings necessary to purchase what can increasingly be produced by capital.* As a consequence, they must increasingly rely on redistributionary market intervention to make up the short fall.

Thus the dismal paradox of the unfree market manifests itself in many ways, viz.:–

* great, excess productive capacity amidst widespread unmet needs and wants;

* overabundant earning power for some and insufficient earning power for many others; and

* a theory that boasts income redistribution should never be necessary blatantly contradicted by the reality of a growing

need for redistributionary measures to keep the economy going.

In short, massive surplus productive potential surrounded by, but wholly unconnected with, massive inability to earn to purchase what is increasingly produced by capital.

Is this dismal paradox *really* the result of natural laws of scarcity (as conventional economics contends)? Or is it, as binary economics contends, the result of imperfect human institutions that can be improved to enable people to generate more bounty? Binary economics teaches that the scarcity of the unfree market is an *unnatural* scarcity resulting from an effective monopoly on capital acquisition. That unnatural scarcity can be replaced by natural bounty once the capital markets of the unfree economies are opened democratically to all people on market principles.

Thus the binary rejection of the unfree market does not imply any doubt as to the power of efficient markets (truly open to everyone) to facilitate vast increases in the production of goods and services and simultaneously to distribute to all people individually the income necessary to purchase goods and services. Rather the rejection stems from the firm conviction that the present closed system of private property does not allow markets to work for all people. This is because most people are effectively excluded from participation in the potent capital markets and are instead restricted to the less potent markets for labor. As a result the powerful distributive quality of capital to produce immense growth is suppressed.

So when the unfree market (with its *closed* private property system and inefficient markets) is further compared with the binary economy (which has an *open* private property system and more efficient markets), then the binary economy is bound to be the winner. The comparison is particularly instructive because unfree market capitalism claims that the institution of private capital ownership (effectively open to under 10% of the population) and its alleged 'free market' are the basic reasons for its economic triumph over communism. Yet that same unfree market also denies that the private ownership of capital (open to

100% of the population) and a market *closed to no one* (as in a binary economy) would produce an even greater triumph.

Unfree market capitalism cannot have it both ways. The sauce that enriches the goose, will also enrich the gander.

12. The main reason for unfree market failure

Thus the main reason for the comparative failure of the unfree market is *not* (as the conventional economic analysis might suggest) a problem of worker productivity or insufficient capital investment (private or public). Increased worker productivity and wise conventional capital investment can improve any economy, but they *cannot, in themselves,* distribute adequate productive (and therefore adequate purchasing) power sufficient to enable people to purchase what is increasingly produced by capital and sufficient to produce sustainable growth.

Nor is the failure the result of workers who are not sufficiently trained or well-managed. Good training, good education and good management are essential for achieving efficient production but, *in themselves, are incapable* of distributing widespread productive power and therefore the widespread, capital-based purchasing power necessary for general affluence and sustainable growth.

Nor does the failure stem from a lack of employee control of, or participation in, the business decision-making process. These things may enhance competitiveness and improve work conditions. However, *in themselves, they are incapable* of distributing widespread productive power and therefore the widespread capital-based purchasing power necessary for general affluence and sustainable growth.

Nor is it the result of insufficient job creation programs, transfer payments[53] and other redistributionary measures. *All of these things, in themselves, and even taken together, are incapable of achieving widespread productive power,* and therefore the widespread purchasing power necessary for general affluence and sustainable growth.

Unfree market failure occurs because of institutions and strategies built on a faulty conception and implementation of both private property and market economics. Consequently, the institutions are structured effectively to limit capital acquisition to the already well-capitalized rather than to serve all people. The strategies, moreover, fail to address the key issue which is *how to distribute adequate productive power* and therefore distribute the adequate purchasing power necessary for widespread affluence and sustainable growth.

So, despite its promise of growth and efficiency and its claimed expertise, conventional economics (as reflected in the national economic policies of the unfree market societies) rests on a number of seriously faulty premises that stifle growth and prevent distributive justice. They include the following:–

- labor is producing most of the wealth;
- growth is fundamentally a function of human productivity;
- technology creates more good jobs than it destroys;
- the economic problems of the poor and middle classes can be solved primarily with capital for the well-capitalized, and jobs and welfare for everyone else; and
- capital has no distributive relationship with growth that is independent of human productivity.

In contrast, binary economics rests on true premises that will facilitate growth and distributive justice. They include the following:–

---

[53] 'Transfer payments' is often the unfree market term for redistribution. By open and hidden means including various taxes, governments take massive amounts of national income and then 'transfer' or redistribute it in various ways.

- *capital* is producing most of the wealth;
- growth is fundamentally a function of capital productiveness;
- technology does *not* create more good jobs than it destroys;
- the economic problems of the poor and middle classes *cannot* be solved without effective, and efficient, capital acquisition rights for all people; and
- capital *has* a positive distributive relationship with growth that is independent of human productivity.

Thus conventional economics does not understand that, in the post-industrial world, *affluence is the product of capital* whereas labor alone increasingly produces mere subsistence.[54] Traditional programs for investment, jobs and welfare have produced many workers (although never enough jobs)[55] but relatively few capitalists. This is at a time when the individual ownership of capital is increasingly essential to every person's economic well-being and equally essential to sustained aggregate economic growth. The faulty conceptions of conventional economics have created and perpetuated *closed* capital markets that limit most people's participation in growth to a function only of their labor productivity. Individual prosperity and sustained aggregate growth, however, require *open* capital markets offering all people increasing individual participation in growth by way of capital acquisition on market principles.

Therefore, according to the binary view, the unfree market economies will *never* correct their structural defects until they abandon their unfair and inefficient economic strategies of effective capital acquisition rights only for the wealthy with mere jobs and welfare for everyone else. Instead, they should adopt

---

[54] *Some* well-trained and educated individuals are contributing more to the productive process, but the contribution of most humans is being outpaced by the ever-rising contribution of capital.
[55] Such jobs as are produced will pay well in a few cases, tolerably well in more cases, and poorly in most.

fair and efficient strategies to achieve effective, universal, individual capital ownership for *all*.

Once the faulty premises of conventional economics are understood and replaced by the true premises of binary economics, the defects in our undemocratic private property system will be easily identified and corrected. The result will be that everyone will be able to participate in the growing productiveness of capital, and in a growing economy. That participation will be not only as labor-workers but also increasingly as *capital-workers* (i.e. owners of productive capital).

13. How to investigate binary economics

The binary economy, on market principles, offers to extend to 100% of the population, individually, the effective right to acquire a viable capital estate so as to produce widespread abundance and leisure without taking from the wealthy. By tapping the abundance of nature using a truly open private property free market system, binary economics promises to end the dependence of humans solely on their labor. It promises to enable everybody to be a real producer of wealth not only as a laborer but increasingly as a capital worker. It promises to enable all people to acquire an independent economic base upon which they can bring out their best.

But, at present in our closed private property system, there is no effective, practical means of enabling all individuals to earn a basic standard of living and to acquire an independent economic base upon which to build their moral, creative and spiritual development. So the binary promise is beyond all present reality and beyond any dream built on the conventional productivity paradigm. In truth, the binary growth effect of 100% private and individual market participation in capital acquisition and ownership is so far from people's experience and perception of what is possible that they may, at first, have difficulty in comprehending it.

How then should readers approach the exploration of binary economics – an idea that requires us to re-examine our empirics, history, perceptions, expectations and learned intuitions; indeed, the way we think about everything? Is it a daunting exploration to be undertaken and judged only by experts? Not at all! Experts are not necessarily the best judges because, being deeply schooled in the older, accepted paradigm, they can develop a trained incapacity to see the new one. Although we believe experts in many disciplines will eventually reformulate their fields of learning as a result of binary principles (and some experts have already begun to do so),[56] it is possible that they may not be among the first to see and understand the new binary paradigm. In certain areas, the generalist and the common man or woman have the great advantage that they may have learned less of the older paradigm and may therefore harbour fewer barriers to the acceptance of the new.

a)   The vase between the faces

Understanding originality is sometimes easier for a non-expert than an expert. It just requires a genuinely humble recognition that one's pre-conceptions can be wrong and a willingness to look at things from another angle and with other assumptions. It helps to imagine looking at the matter from someone else's perspective and therefore to be willing to suspend, at least temporarily, a commitment to one's own angle and assumptions. So suppose a small, isolated tribal society, with simple tools and no pottery, has for centuries had a big line drawing on a wall in a cave, like this:–

---

[56] E.g., at the Symposium on Binary Economics, 10th Conference on Socio-Economics, Vienna, (1998):– *The Distributive Relationship Between Capital and Growth*, Dr. Charles J. Whalen (School of Industrial Labor Relations, Cornell University); *Alternatives for Restructuring the Welfare State: Beyond Redistribution*, Dr. Richard Coughlin (Chair and Professor of Sociology, University of New Mexico); *Questions from a Social Security Perspective*, Dr. Keith Wilde (Office of the Chief Actuary, Canada Pension Plan, Ottawa).

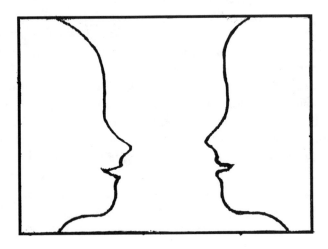

Fig. 2 – 2. Two faces or a vase.

Tribal lore is that the lines were drawn by an early visionary who said they had an important meaning. Unfortunately, he never told anyone what it was; but the lines were traditionally interpreted by later generations as two faces staring at each other.

However, with an understanding of the existence of vases as well as of faces, it is simple for modern people to point out a vase between the faces. We can see the drawing as either faces or vase. Yet it would not be so easy to point out the vase to tribal people who have never seen vases. For them, it would take an imaginative leap to see the vase because there is nothing in the organizing logic of the faces that leads to the discovery of the vase between. Yet, with the organizing logic of the vase, it is possible to interpret the reality of every aspect of the two lines in a completely new and different way. With one conception, there is nothing between the faces. With the other, there is a beautiful, useful vase artefact – a pleasing capital creation capable of doing work and producing leisure.

Seeing the vase, however, does require a willingness to employ different assumptions. Furthermore, if the traditional interpretation of the faces is accepted then, as time goes on, it will grow ever more deeply entrenched in lore, social institutions and psychology. Thus, if centuries of decorative practice by those in charge of the drawing have added complex detail depicting eyes, cheeks and ears, none of that detail would assist in the discovery of the vase. On the contrary, as shown below, when more detail is added to the faces, it becomes difficult, if not impossible, to see the vase.

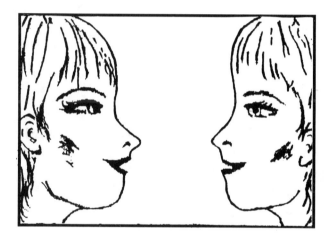

Fig. 2 – 3. Facial detail obscuring the vase.

Now consider the situation in present day society regarding the understanding of economics. Twentieth century economists do *not* start with a fundamentally fresh look at the economic situation. They all begin from the unquestioned productivity assumptions of Adam Smith, and then fill in the details by following the implications of those assumptions. Leading economists and their followers may take issue with one another in various ways; and they may also take issue with Adam Smith in various ways. But none fundamentally question the productivity theory of growth by taking a look at a fresh counter theory, namely, that capital is independently productive and has a distributive relationship to growth. Thus we have a case where, for more than two centuries, decorative practice (of complex intellectual, political, economic and social varieties) has filled in all the detail of the faces. Accordingly, understanding the difference between the conventional economic paradigm and the binary paradigm is very much like understanding the difference between seeing only faces and seeing not only faces but also a vase.

Conventional and binary economists both look at the same lines of the drawing – the same realities of failed socialist economies and faltering plutocratic capitalist societies – but they see very different possibilities. Looking at the two lines in the drawing, the conventional economist sees the entire economic reality bounded by a left-wing face and a right-wing face, each opposing the other in principle and philosophy. Beyond the extremes of the left-wing and right-wing faces, the conventional economist sees only one additional possibility – a mixed centrist position that compromises the differences between left and right through an always conflict-ridden process. The process is conflict-ridden because it is premised on two false premises:–

- that labor is the primary means by which most people can engage in wealth creation and participate in income distribution on market principles; and

- that capital has no positive distributive relationship to growth that is essentially independent of human productivity.

In contrast, looking at the very same lines, the binary economist rejects the very limited conventional view of reality. Binary economists do, of course, see the left-wing and right-wing faces and the mixed centrist conflict-ridden compromises. But they deny that the faces and compromises are the only possible alternatives. Instead, they see something extra – the possibility of material abundance in the form of the vase between the faces. This is a material abundance far surpassing in quality and quantity whatever might be achieved merely by splitting the differences between the two faces and compromising left-wing and right-wing principles through the political process. Binary economists see something *new* – *something beyond* the conventional view.

Thus the experts (including economists and other academicians as well as business and government leaders) may not as a group be in the best position to appreciate a new idea. Arguing back and forth about the detail of the faces, many experts endlessly repeat and expand on the outdated thinking of the old paradigm, filling in greater detail based on limited preconceptions and, all the while, making it ever harder for society to discover the vase. Thus to explore the new paradigm, experts are asked to disregard the assumptions making up the very structure and historical development of their thinking process. In other words, to understand and give reality to the new paradigm, requires an expert to disregard some of the very thinking that makes the expert an expert.

b) *Important questions*

So, from a common-sense perspective and without undue effort, an informed person may give fair consideration to binary economics in a straightforward way. That person need have no fear of being bluffed or bamboozled. Nor will it be necessary to wade through pages of mathematical equations and abstractions. Once the organizing principles of the new binary paradigm are understood, then some addition and subtraction of the very simplest sort, together with a sense of proportion and balance, will suffice to reinforce what is intuitively obvious to bring forth a comprehensible, orderly, and internally consistent view of economic growth and distributive justice.

Therefore, as you read this book, you need only have an open mind. That mind, of course, should be exacting in examining the suppositions, logic and claims of binary economics. It should be equally exacting of the suppositions, logic and claims of the unfree market. In particular, it should be exacting in comparing the unfree market's theories with its actual performance.

Even then, it can be human nature not to see something right underneath the nose.   So, as you proceed, ask yourself the following questions:–

i)   Is binary analysis new?

ii)   Does it rest on reasonable assumptions?

iii)   Is it internally consistent?

iv)   Does it explain an important range of experience in its own terms?

v)   Does it helpfully predict an important range of future events in its own terms?

vi)   Does it provide a specific proposal for helping people that is worthy of rigorous exploration by those professing a concern for questions of growth, distribution and democratic participation?

vii)   What are the drawbacks if it is tried and fails?

viii) Is it worth trying?

We believe that binary economics offers satisfying answers to each of these questions.   Whatever your answers, we are confident that this book will give you an unusual and stimulating time.

Book II

The new binary paradigm

Book II as a whole presents the binary paradigm as a distinct paradigm and compares it to the conventional economic paradigm that is shared by left-wing, mixed centrist and right-wing schools. Chapter Three opens by examining the great growth in per-capita economic output experienced by the largest unfree market economies. Conventional economics explains the growth in terms of labor productivity (a paradigmatic concept which is traceable back to Adam Smith) while binary economics explains the same growth in terms of capital productiveness. Obviously, there are important implications if the binary explanation is the better view of reality. Chapter Four goes on to examine more closely the paradigm of conventional productivity while Chapters Five and Six examine and develop the new binary paradigm of productiveness and show how it leads to economic justice and growth.

Book II

Chapter Three

The great growth in productive capacity and total economic output

1. *A period of great change*

In 1700, a process which was to lead to almost inconceivable economic and productive change was already under way. The process had in fact begun in the dawn of civilization with the first crude tools, and it gained force with their slow improvement over the millennia. However, around the year 1700, particularly in Western Europe, things were beginning to move more quickly.

Thus, in 1690, the Frenchman Denis Papin had demonstrated that steam could push a piston contained in a cylinder and that, when the steam cooled, the piston moved the other way to fill the ensuing vacuum. Then, after much troublesome experiment, the Englishman Newcomen succeeded in building an effective pump-engine, the first being installed in a Staffordshire coal mine in 1712. Although it made such profligate use of coal to produce the steam that two stokers were required to keep it running,

Newcomen's pump-engine was soon capable of doing the work of twenty men and twenty or more horses.   Despite an initial skepticism that anything could ever replace men or horses, the pump-engine drained mines of their water more efficiently and at lower cost with less human work than the men and horses they replaced, with consequent benefits for the efficient production of coal.

But Newcomen's pump-engine, being a gobbler of coal, was impractical for the tin and copper mines of Cornwall (where there was no local coal).   The problem was solved by James Watt whose steam engines pumped at a quarter of the cost (1775).

With even greater implications for the future, Watt's engines were also designed to transmit the power of steam to a rotating wheel (1784).   The transmission principle would, in due course, make possible the operation of machinery anywhere – in mines, in factories, on canals, in fields, on roads, in and under the sea and, eventually, in the air.

The old spinning wheels and weaving frames, moreover, were being replaced by mechanical marvels like those of Arkwright, Crompton and others.   The marvels began doing the work previously done by tens, hundreds, even thousands of people. There were new processes for producing iron.   By one means or another, an increasing industrial output was being achieved in ways that required less labor per unit of output.   Crucially, new structures (such as roads and, in particular, canals) enabled goods and vast amounts of raw materials to be transported further using much less labor at much lower cost.

As the eighteenth and nineteenth centuries progressed, it was the same in agriculture.   New seed-drills, ploughs, reapers, structures and techniques were enabling an enhanced output with less labor.   During the nineteenth century, thousands of farmhands streamed off the land to work in the cities where ever more was also being made with less labor per unit of output.

The overall picture was that tools, machines, structures (including railways), production facilities and techniques, became more sophisticated, expansive, comprehensive, powerful and versatile. Consequently, there were better goods and services produced at a faster rate and on a larger scale. Productive capacity had expanded, output had expanded, qualitatively and quantitatively, far beyond anything experienced on Earth before.

So an environment which, before 1700, would have seemed to most people to be either static or, at best, capable only of slow improvement, was, by 1850, fast becoming one of great, undeniable, never-ending and accelerating technological *change*. By 1900, society was steaming, and would soon be soaring, on a course in which technology would be continually evolving and always tending to replace humans in the wealth-creation process while also increasing total output.

The process of technological change then assumed great new proportions becoming robust, self-reinforcing and ever-expanding. It continues with an accelerating thrust today because of the impact of the revolutionary changes brought about by the development of electrical devices, the internal combustion engine and precision machinery together with other advances in fields such as chemistry, microtechnology (including computers), bio-engineering and robotics.

2. Explaining the great growth in productive capacity and total economic output

So there can be little dispute that, over the last two hundred and fifty years, the productive capacity and output of industrial economies like those of the U.S.A., Japan and Western Europe have grown tremendously. With some country-specific variation and volatility, a graph of the growth in per-capita productive capacity would look something like the solid line in the figure below. It rises in a fairly uniform way.

The actual production (gross national product, or GNP) of those economies on a per-capita basis is shown by the dotted line. It displays more up-and-down fluctuation than productive capacity shown by the solid line. This dotted line basically tracks the growth in productive capacity but lies "sometimes above it, sometimes – more often, in the case of the U.S. – below it."[57]

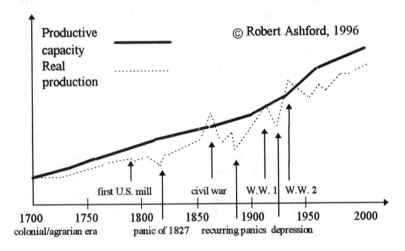

Fig. 3 – 1. Increase in per-capita productive capacity and real production: 1700 – 1990.[58]

Now both conventional economics and binary economics agree that the vast growth in productive capacity and the vast growth in total per-capita output have actually occurred. Moreover, they

[57] Robert M. Solow, *The Great Automation Question (1): Technology and Unemployment*, (*The Public Interest*, Fall, 1965, vol. 1, pp. 17-26, at 20).

[58] References consulted for this diagram include:– Shepard B. Clough and Theodore F. Marburg, *Business Cycles* in the *Economic Basis of American Civilisation* (New York: Thomas Y. Crowell Co., 1968), pps. 206-209. *Statistical History of the United States from Colonial Times to Present* (Stamford, CT: Fairfield Publishing, 1970). Series F470-479.

both agree that, while the opening of new lands (as in the U.S.A.) and other elements contributed, the growth certainly has something to do with advancing technology, particularly fabricated capital assets in the form of tools, machines, structures, material, and processes.

But at that point the agreement ends. Conventional economics and binary economics fundamentally disagree as to the precise explanation of the growth in productive capacity and where it truly lies. Hence they also disagree as to the true cause of the growth in total output and as to how people can most efficiently and justly participate in that growth.

3.   The conventional explanation

Conventional economic thinking is pre-occupied with productivity. It therefore explains the growth as a function of increasing productivity, particularly human (labor) productivity. Admittedly, some schools of conventional economics also give considerable emphasis to capital and capital productivity. But a rigorous examination of their analysis demonstrates that their considerations of the importance of capital are based on increasing labor productivity. Indeed some conventional schools flatly deny that there can be any growth at all without increases in labor productivity. It is as though conventional economics views a tool or machine as an extension of a person's hand.

The pre-occupation is revealed in conventional analysis that declares all growth in output to be grounded in (labor) productivity thereby ignoring the growth attributable to capital productiveness. For example, after surveying various sources of growth in productive capacity, Dr. Robert Solow explained:–

> Any change in the quantitative relation between output and employment must show up in the conventional productivity statistics. Here productivity means nothing but the value of output per man-hour, corrected for prices. It goes up whenever

labor requirements for a unit go down, and by the same
percentage.   There are productivity statistics for certain
industries, for manufacturing as a whole, and for even broader
aggregates.   It doesn't matter much which aggregate is
selected.[59]

From a binary perspective, however, the conventional pre-
occupation with human labor as the ultimate cause of most or all
growth is quite out of touch with reality. Such a pre-occupation
ignores the independent productive capacity of capital to do its
own work.   Contrary to the conventional wisdom, this
independent productive capacity has little to do with the
concurrent productivity of human beings.

In respect of that capacity, consider for a moment a great dam
curving across a wide river. Apart from millions of gallons of
fresh water, the dam provides millions of kilowatt hours of
electricity. Those gallons and kilowatt hours are provided by a
number of independent agents in an elaborate production process
– the sun (which evaporates water into the sky); the weather
(which stimulates rain); gravity (which makes rain fall and the
river flow); concrete (which, by heightening the river level,
increases the water pressure); and the turbines (which turn
dynamos). That is to say, *non*-human things, behaving as if they
were animate, are doing the creation. They are *not* behaving
merely as extensions of human hands.

Now, because the sun, gravity and weather cannot be owned,
there is a natural human tendency to discount, even ignore, their
part in a productive process. But the river can be owned and,
most certainly, so can the concrete dam with its turbines and
dynamos and the land on which it stands. They obviously play a
substantial part in the productive process. To the dam's massive
and continuous work input, of course, there is a human

---

[59] Robert M. Solow, *The Great Automation Question (1): Technology
and Unemployment*, (*The Public Interest*, Fall, 1965, vol. 1, pp. 17-26,
at 20).

contribution – a few workers regulate the turbines and dynamos. However, nobody can doubt that the bulk of the output is occasioned by *non*-human things with, of course, the sun (even though it cannot be owned) having pride of place.

And it is the same with any machine or industrialized process. Thus, with a hand saw, a man cuts one cord of wood per day. With an electric saw, he cuts ten cords per day. *With more productive capital (the electric saw) and with less human labor, more is produced.* Similarly, on a 2,500 acre family cotton farm in the Mississippi delta, a driver at the wheel of a $135,000 mechanical picker can do the work of 500 people.[60] Just as donkeys haul sacks, trucks haul sacks, and electric saws cut wood, so mechanical pickers pick cotton, even though drivers are also involved.

Likewise today, in factories of all types around the world, machines are doing more work, more precisely and more quickly. At the very same time, and for the very same reason, the work of humans in process after process is being reduced to lever pulling, button pushing, computer entry, and monitoring. Again, *with more productive capital, and less labor, more is produced.*

Moreover, from the binary perspective of recognizing who or what is actually doing the work, it makes no difference that a machine requires the co-operation of an operator because, equally, if there is to be increased output, an operator requires the co-operation of a machine. A machine is no more an extension of an operator's hand than an operator is an extension of a machine.

Lastly, the conventional conception of machinery as an extension of a person's hand borders on the ludicrous when a fully automated factory is considered. The huge productive capacity and prolific, continuous output of a fully automated factory *cannot* be explained by a greatly increased human

---

[60] Jon Thompson, *King of Fibers*, (*National Geographic*, vol. 185, no. 6, June 1994, pp. 60-86, at p. 66).

productivity because *no humans are involved in the productive process.*[61]

Nevertheless, in an attempt to allege that humans are involved, the conventional mind may raise the subject of repair and maintenance. However, maintenance and repair workers are *not* in themselves part of an automated factory's productive process. They certainly keep a factory going and are paid for so doing but they are ancillary to production. Just as veterinary surgeons are paid for treating animals yet receive no payment for subsequent work done by the animals, so maintenance and repair workers receive payment for their work but are *not* entitled to additional payment for subsequent work done by the factory. Similarly, doctors treat patients (and are paid for giving that treatment) but nobody in his right mind would claim that doctors are entitled to their patients' subsequent labor earnings.

Likewise, those who designed and built the automated factory will also have been compensated at the relevant market rates for their work. Just as in the case of the vet, (or the inventor who has sold an invention), they are not entitled to payment for subsequent work done by the factory.

Thus, by seeing virtually everything in human terms, the conventional human-labor explanation of increased productive capacity and increased aggregate output fails to take into proper account the independent productive capacity of non-human things from the sun to the tiniest computer chip. The labor explanation is very weak in respect of mechanized processes and collapses completely when the fully automated factory is considered. By

---

[61]   More and more automation is being introduced into many thousands of individual tasks. Cars, for example, are now produced by a quarter of the work-hours required only a few decades ago. Of the relatively few workers in a car factory today, *some* may have a genuinely rising productivity. But the productivity of others is being continually supplanted by the productiveness of new, near-automated machinery so that, with full automation, the human productiveness in car production will have been reduced to nil.

seeing virtually everything in human terms, the labor-based explanation of the growth over the last two hundred and fifty years can be shortly and aptly characterized as a hubristic homocentric denial of reality. It is time to turn to the binary explanation of the growth.

4. The binary explanation

The binary explanation rejects increasing labor productivity as the main source of economic growth. Without hubris and in a refreshingly holistic way, binary economics sees the vast rise in capacity and output as primarily due to the increasing productiveness of the non-human capital assets. That is to say, the machines, structures and technology have an independent and increasing ability to produce *by themselves*. They are *independently productive*. It is as if the machines and technology are animate with a fecund life of their own. The binary view is that human labor serves to elicit the huge potential of the machines and technology. Put simply, more and more wealth will be produced if humans concentrate on bringing out the tremendous powers of nature.

Because humans and capital assets are independent producers, it is possible to assess their work input contribution in percentage terms. Thus, in considering the fully automated factory, the binary explanation puts the work input at almost 0% for the humans and virtually 100% for the capital assets. The automated factory example illustrates the endpoint of the process of invention and technological advance. Driven by a natural and beneficial human desire to do more, more quickly, with less human effort, the process reveals a general production rule regarding capital and labor:–

More things (in quantity and kind) can be done, more quickly, efficiently and effortlessly with more productive capital and less labor.

That is not to say, of course, that some labor is not required to enable capital to do more work. In fact, binary economics readily concedes that the process of invention and technological advance requires considerable labor input in the form of:–

- human creativity, invention, inspiration and, sometimes, luck to conceive of more productive capital;

- labor to create and perfect it;

- labor to replicate it; and

- labor to deploy, maintain, operate and monitor it.

The labor inputs of the above are physically necessary for technological advance and, in a true free market, and as a matter of justice and efficiency, are compensated at market rates. But the efficient employment of a necessary and even enhanced labor input must not be allowed to obscure the greatly increased input coming from the productive capital. Once the capital becomes operational, it is doing its own work and, in the case of the automated factory, the capital productiveness is nearly 100% of the output.

So, once the general production rule is applied to the increased productive capacity and increased aggregate output over the last two hundred and fifty years, things are understood in a new (binary) light. Instead of seeing all growth as primarily a function of labor productivity, and instead of seeing the contribution of capital as merely a derivative extension of the productivity of labor, the binary light reveals the independent productiveness of capital, in percentage terms, as the more substantial and ever-rising factor of productive capacity.

Binary economists, therefore, see the growth as primarily resulting from the independent increasing productiveness of capital assets. In percentage terms, there has been a *shift* or change in productive input from human labor to capital asset. Consequently, the distinction between conventional *productivity* and binary *productiveness* is crucial:–

- *productivity* is the *conventional* concept which ultimately attributes most or all of the growth to human labor: whereas

- *productiveness* is the *binary* concept which certainly takes account of human labor but sees an even greater percentage of wealth creation as being done *by capital* (assets).

Thus when considering the productive capacity and the actual production that prevailed in the unfree market economies in 1700 and comparing them with the vastly greater productive capacity and actual production that exist today (and after making adjustments for population growth), both binary economics and conventional economics agree that there has been substantial economic growth. But they *dis*agree as to who or what is doing the extra work and disagree in a *very* big way because:–

- conventional economics alleges that *labor* is doing approximately 70% of the work; whereas

- binary economics holds that *capital* is doing over 70% of the work.

How can this difference be explained? What is the fundamental logic of conventional economics – supposedly grounded in scientific reality – that denies and explains away the vast and growing independent productive capacity of capital to do more and more of the work? This question is explored in the next section.

5.   The failure to grasp the change – Adam Smith

Such is the scale, in percentage terms, of the shift or change in productiveness from human labor to capital asset that the question arises as to why conventional economics has failed to understand it. After all, conventional economics is supposed to be 'the queen of social sciences' with a strong grasp of reality.[62]

For the answer we have to start by going back to the middle years of the eighteenth century when economics did not exist as a distinct discipline. The study of the economy was done under the banner of philosophy. Not surprisingly, but unfortunately, the early scholars of the nascent study failed to grasp the full revolutionary impact of the technological changes in production that were going on all around. The phenomena were new to human experience and the impact was hard to assess. Thus the scholars saw that per-capita output was increasing; that labor was undergoing increasing division and specialization; that individual worker productivity was growing; and that capital was abridging labor, employing more labor, and apparently making labor more productive.

But the scholars also failed to see something of even greater import – that, *in percentage terms*, capital assets such as machines were doing more and more of the work *both in individual tasks and in the aggregate*. As a consequence they failed to achieve true understanding of the most important cause of the resulting growth and distribution in an industrial economy. The failure was to have world-wide and centuries-long consequences because it was embodied in the work of Adam Smith, Professor of Philosophy, whose *An Inquiry into the Nature and Causes of the Wealth of Nations* (1776) provides the

---

[62] Of course there are those economists whose analysis denies that conventional economics can ever be a hard science because its propositions cannot potentially be falsified. See e.g., Robert A. Solo, *The Philosophy of Science and Economics* (M. E. Sharpe, Armond, New York, 1991). The denial rests on the propositions of Karl Popper who treated the possibility of falsification as the true test of a science. Binary economics can be, and we believe is, a science because its basic proposition (that capital has a distributive relationship to growth) can be proven true or false by merely opening the process of capital acquisition to all people on market principles and then observing the results.

foundational starting point for *all* schools of economics from Marxist to neo-classical capitalist. Smith's seminal position is visually set out in Fig. 3 – 2 below:–

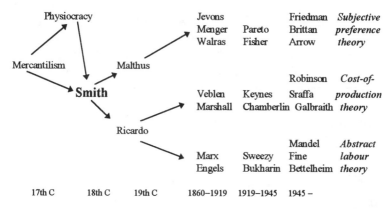

Fig. 3 – 2. The historical development of economic theory.[63]

Smith is well known for his panegyric of the 'invisible hand'[64] – the ideally competitive market mechanism which allocates resources and employs people, with increasing specialization, according to their highest productive good. In this way the mechanism optimizes wealth, while optimally compensating the suppliers of labor, capital and resources according to their input. The ideal result is the facilitation of the optimal creation and expression of value in the way people produce, consume, save and invest.

---

[63] K. Cole, J. Cameron and C. Edwards, *Why Economists Disagree: the Political Economy of Economics* (1983), at p. 16. Reproduced by kind permission of Longman Group Limited.

[64] (The individual is) "led by an invisible hand to promote an end which was no part of his intention. By pursuing his own interest, he frequently promotes that of society more effectually than when he really intends to promote it." (*Wealth of Nations*, Book Four, Chapter Two).

Consciously trying to do for economics what Isaac Newton had done for physical science, Smith argued that human self-interest operating in open markets is the universal force which keeps the economy in a competitive, self-adjusting process by maintaining the optimal balance of supply and demand. Thus market participants (buyers and sellers) pursuing their own interest, benefit not only themselves but society as a whole. Although he himself was sceptical that there would ever be a market without price-fixers, cartels or monopolies, Smith is deservedly credited with the first systematic promulgation and analysis of the free-market ideal as a natural law.

6. The error at the heart of Smith's thinking

But not well known, still less understood, is the foundational error at the heart of Smith's thinking which, with various modifications, dominates *all* conventional economics to this day. That error is a basic misunderstanding of the impact of the industrial revolution on the way goods and services are produced and, even more fundamentally, a misapprehension of the dynamics of economic growth.

Smith's foundational misunderstanding of the main reason for economic growth is set out below in his own words. They are worth reading carefully because they clearly attribute all growth to labor and view machines as being but things which 'abridge' labor.

> The annual produce of the land and labor can be increased in its value *by no other means*, but by increasing either the number of its productive labourers, or the productive powers of those labourers who had before been employed. The number of its productive labourers can never be much increased, but in consequence of an increase of capital, or of the funds destined for maintaining them. The productive powers of the same

number of labourers cannot be increased, but in consequence of either some addition and improvements to those machines and instruments which facilitate and abridge labor; or of a more proper division and distribution of employment. It is by means of an additional capital only that the undertaker of any work can provide his workmen with better machinery, or make a more proper distribution of employment among them. (*Italic emphasis supplied*).[65]

Thus, in Smith's view, growth is most fundamentally a function of human productivity. According to Smith, increased capital contributes to growth only by increasing human productivity and by employing more people, rather than by increasingly doing more of the work itself.[66]

The emphasis on human productivity as the operative source of growth was no doubt influenced by Smith's belief that the increase in individual or national wealth was primarily due to the division and increasing specialization of labor, with people concentrating on particular tasks rather than many.[67] He identified the growth advantages of the division of labor as follows:−

This great increase in the quantity of work, which, in consequence of the division of labour, the same number of people are capable of performing, is owing to three different circumstances; first, to the increase of dexterity of every particular workman; secondly, to the saving of time which is

---

[65] *Wealth of Nations*, Book Two, Chapter Three.

[66] *Wealth of Nations*, Book One, Chapter One. And always Smith's analysis of the incentives for capital investment assumes a *closed* private property system.

[67] "The greatest improvement in the productive powers of labour, and the greater part of skill, dexterity, and judgement with which it is any where directed or applied, seem to have been the effects of the division of labor." (*Wealth of Nations*, Book One, Chapter One). Having made a now famous visit to a pin manufactory, Smith saw the great rise in output per worker as due primarily to the specialization of the workers.

commonly lost in passing from one species of work to another;
and lastly, to the invention of a great number of machines
which facilitate and abridge labour, and enable one man to do
the work of many.[68]

This emphasis on human labor and specialization is
understandable because, at the time Smith was doing his thinking,
the most obvious feature of economic development was the
manufactory. Manufactories were *not* factories. They were
buildings where, *using hand tools* rather than machinery, a
number of people came to work together and were able to
specialize on different aspects of a process, with consequent
increased efficiency, as compared to each person having to master
individually all aspects of production.

So Smith's famous visit to a pin factory was in reality a visit
to a pin manufactory with its new hand tools rather than
machines. In the circumstances, therefore, it is not surprising that
he categorically concluded that the most significant effect of the
machines of his day was to increase labor productivity and
thereby to make profitable the employment of more workers.[69]

Unfortunately, in making this conclusion, Smith had failed to
understand a far more significant aspect of the change in the
production of goods and services, namely, *that machines were
actually doing more and more of the work themselves*. Human
specialization can certainly increase wealth output to an order of
perhaps tens of times, but the really gigantic increases in output –
to an order of hundreds, thousands, even millions of times (as in a
modern hydraulic power station compared to a water wheel) – are
now coming from capital assets particularly high technology
processes and machines.[70]

---

[68] *Wealth of Nations*, Book One, Chapter One.
[69] *Wealth of Nations*, Book Two, Chapter Three.
[70] As we shall see, this is a fact that has not only great productive
consequences, but also great distributive consequences.

Such gigantic increases in output, of course, were *not* part of Smith's experience. He could only perceive a more or less continuous and slowly accelerating economic growth.[71] When he was writing in 1776, the first widely usable steam engines were only just being perfected and their revolutionary consequences were far from apparent. The great farm mechanizations and factory industrialization were still decades away. Even more so, the revolutions in electricity, chemistry, precision engineering and micro-technology were a century or more off, and way beyond his imagination.

Therefore, at a key moment in history – when the industrial revolution was just beginning to produce growth of unprecedented magnitude with unprecedented speed, far beyond the capacity of human beings working more efficiently with simple tools – the study of economics (in the person of Adam Smith) had committed itself to the increasing specialization and productivity of labor as the main cause of, and explanation for, the increasing wealth produced by nations.

Of course, Smith did recognize a connection between increased capital and increased output and gave consideration to the role of capital in industry.[72] For example, he considered that capital was

---

[71] "Since the time of Henry VIII, the wealth and revenue of the country has been continually advancing and, in the course of their progress their pace seems rather to have been gradually accelerated than retarded. They seem, not only to have been going on, but to have been going on faster." (*Wealth of Nations*, Book One, Chapter Nine).

[72] Major chapters and sections of Smith's analysis are indeed devoted to the role of capital in production. Thus, he saw capital accumulation as an essential antecedent to the specialization of labor; to the employment of more people at higher wages; and to the realization of economic growth. Moreover, although he recognized that capital was capable of 'abridging' labor, and although he was quite concerned that working people should have adequate earning capacity, he exhibited no fear that technology might lead to massive labor redundancy. To the contrary, although Smith believed that competition and diminishing returns on the increasing supply of capital would limit the

essential to growth because he saw it as facilitating the specialization of labor, making labor more productive, and employing more workers. But, in an important sense, he did not see capital as *independently* productive. Thus he failed to see the most important effect of the introduction of technology which was that, for countless individual tasks, and in the aggregate, capital was continually doing a larger and larger percentage of the work. Labor content per unit of output was *decreasing*; and aggregate per-capita output was *increasing* while using ever less labor.[73] It is certainly true that new jobs were created and people employed as the productive power and sophistication of capital instruments increased. However, for most tasks, and in the aggregate, *capital work was **replacing** labor work* per unit of output while vastly increasing total output, as tools, machines, and processes were continually being replaced by ever more productive tools, machines and processes.

It is also true that Smith recognized three sources of wealth – land, capital and labor. But he analyzed the earning capacity, and therefore the value, of the land and capital, as well as the value of all production, ultimately as a function of the individual worker's decision whether or not to work at a given wage, a decision which is in turn a function of productivity.[74] Although conceding at a

---

rate of capital formation, he seemed to think that capital was capable of employing an unlimited amount of labor at ever higher wages. However, Smith's consideration of capital assumes that its primary productive and distributive functions are in making labor more productive and in employing more workers rather than in doing more and more of the work itself as an independently productive agent.

[73] "It's worth remembering that from the very onset of the Industrial Revolution, machines were introduced not as a way of enhancing skills, but as a means of displacing people." Jonathan Porritt, *Seeing Green*, (1984).

[74] "The real value of all the different component parts of price, it must be observed, is measured by the quantity of labour which they can, each of them purchase or command. Labour measures the value not only of that part of the price which resolves itself into labour, but of

few points that capital assets and land, along with labor, can be productive, Smith treated labor as the most fundamental creator of wealth or value. Indeed, much of Smith's analysis seemingly assumes that in the most fundamental sense only labor creates wealth.[75] Furthermore, although he conceded that land can be independently productive, he did not regard capital assets as similarly so.[76]

So Smith's observations were made during the *manufactory* period. During that period the tools of agriculture and industry were still small and the increases brought by technological progress were five- or ten-fold rather than the hundred- and thousand-fold increases in per-capita output that were to come. Increases in per-capita output in the order of five- or ten-fold can perhaps be rationalized as the result of the specialization of labor, with the tools simply augmenting the human output.

But increases in the order of a hundred- and a thousand-fold (which result when combine harvesters replace sickles; tractors

---

that which resolves itself into rent, and of that which resolves itself into profit." (*Wealth of Nations*, Book One, Chapter Six). "Labour....is the real measure of the exchangeable value of all commodities." (Book One, Chapter Five).

[75] "No fixed capital can yield any revenue but by means of a circulating capital. The most useful machines and instruments of trade will produce nothing without the circulating capital which affords the materials they are employed upon, and the maintenance of the workmen who employ them. Land, however improved, will yield no revenue without a circulating capital, which maintains the labourers who cultivate and collect its produce." (*Wealth of Nations*, Book Two, Chapter One).

[76] "Rent may be considered as the produce of those powers of nature, the use of which the landlord lends to the farmer....It is the work of nature which remains after deducting or compensating everything which can be regarded as the work of man....In manufactories (i.e. the precursors to our mechanized factories)....nature does nothing; *man does all*; and the reproduction must always be in proportion to the strength of the agents that occasion it." (*Italic* emphasis supplied). (*Wealth of Nations*, Book Two, Chapter Five).

replace hand-ploughs; mechanical looms replace hand looms; locomotives and trucks replace horses and carts; and dams replace water-wheels) *cannot* be explained merely as a function of the increased specialization of human labor or human productivity. Rather these great infusions of productive power can be comprehended only with an appreciation for the increasing independent productiveness of capital. In other words, understanding growth in productive capacity and economic output requires a logic that recognizes that capital is doing ever more of the work.[77]

7.   The unrecognized insight of Jean Baptiste Say

It is significant to observe that not all economists of the day agreed with Smith's analysis that growth is caused mainly or wholly by the specialization of human labor and increasing labor productivity. Most notably, the French economist Jean Baptiste Say took serious issue with Smith. In a remarkable passage, Say wrote:–

> To the labour of man alone he (Smith) ascribes the power of producing values. This is an error. A more exact analysis demonstrates....that all values are derived from the operation of labour, or rather from the industry of man, combined with the operation of those agents which nature and capital furnish him. Dr. Smith did not, therefore, obtain a thorough knowledge of

---

[77] "That the application of power and machinery to production, even in Smith's day, might have been a far greater source of efficiency than the specialized application of workers to a task, is more than probable. And it has certainly been the case since. To this day, nonetheless, Smith's division of labor remains a totemic source of efficiency, a cliché in all discussion of international trade policy." J.K. Galbraith, *A History of Economics*, (1987), p. 69.

the most important phenomenon in production; this has led him into some erroneous conclusions, such, for instance, as attributing a gigantic influence to the division of labour, or rather to the separation of employments. This influence, however, is by no means inappreciable or even inconsiderable; but *the greatest wonders of this description are not so much owing to any peculiar property in human labour, as to the use we make of the powers of nature. His ignorance of this principle precluded him from establishing the true theory of machinery in relation to the production of wealth.* (*Italic* emphasis supplied).[78]

Unfortunately, Say's trenchant identification of Smith's error was ignored, or simply not understood, by later economists. Compared to Smith, Say is generally viewed as a second-order intellect who was little more than a translator (into French) of Smith. Say, however, did make several independent contributions to economic thought and is known for his famous (and controversial) Say's Law – the idea that supply generates its own demand. Yet, although some writers give him credit,[79] Say remains largely unrecognized for his insight that capital and not labor was the primary cause of growth. When the binary paradigm replaces the conventional economic paradigm, however, Say will receive full recognition as an early provider of this key insight that was left for Louis Kelso and other binary economists to develop.

---

[78] J.B. Say, *A Treatise on Political Economy*, (1830) 6th American edition, p. xl-xli. This was not Say's only objection to Smith's approach (see pp. xli-xliii) but it may prove to be his most important one. See Elmer Masters, *The Classical Roots of Louis Kelso's Binary Economics*, (paper given at a Seminar on Binary Economics, Syracuse University, NY, April, 1994).

[79] For an informative analysis of Say's reading of Smith, see Evelyn Forget, *J.B. Say and Adam Smith: An Essay in the Transmission of Ideas*, (Canadian Economics Association). See also Evert Schoorl on J.B. Say, in *Revue Europeenne des Sciences Sociales*, tome xxx, 1992, no. 92, pp. 33-45.

8. The productivity foundation of all conventional economics

Although it has been modified and qualified, Smith's basic framework for understanding growth, premised on productivity, still remains the foundational starting point for *all* conventional schools and their analyses of growth.[80] *All* the schools, although in different ways, see increasing labor productivity as the foundational cause of growth.   In market terms, each school measures and understands the cost and earning capacity of capital as ultimately a function of the individual decision of whether to labor or remain idle, which in turn is fundamentally a function of productivity.

Moreover, because all the conventional schools analyze the earning capacity of capital as ultimately a function of human productivity, none of them treats capital as having an independent productive and distributive function.   Again, this is traceable back to Smith who said that the profits of capital will vary with its scarcity[81] but did not see that the profits of capital also vary with its distribution (because it is independently productive). Consider this passage from the *Wealth of Nations*:–

---

[80] Some of those schools are:– a) the *neo-classical* which lays primary stress on marginal productivity; b) the *Keynesian* which seeks to manage aggregate demand to promote fuller employment but which nevertheless premises sustained long-term growth on increased productivity; c) the *monetarist* which would limit increases in the money supply to steady increments consistent with productivity gains; d) the *socialist and Marxist* which sees capital as capable of earning no more than its replacement value, and views all additional increased production as 'surplus value' and a function of labor productivity.

[81] Focusing only on the shorter term impact of the law of supply and demand on the profitability of capital as a function of scarcity, Smith did not focus on the longer term impact of the law of supply and demand on the profitability of capital as a function of its distribution.

As capitals increase in any country, the profits which can be made by employing them necessarily diminish. It becomes gradually more and more difficult to find within the country a profitable method of employing new capital. There arises in consequence a competition between different capital, the owner of one endeavouring to get possession of that employment which occupied by another. But upon most occasions he can hope to justle that other out of his employment, by no other means than by dealing upon more reasonable terms. He must not only sell what he deals in somewhat cheaper, but in order to get to sell, he must too sometimes buy it dearer. The demand for productive labour, by the increase in funds destined for maintaining it, grows every (day) greater and greater. Labourers easily find employment, but the owners of capitals find it difficult to get labourers to employ. Their competition raises the wages of labour and sinks the profits on stock....[82]

It can be seen from the above that Smith focused on the short-run impact of the law of supply and demand on the profitability of capital (a time span in which the distribution of capital acquisition is of minimum consequence). But in so focusing he ignored the impact of the law of supply and demand on the profitability of capital in the long run (a time span in which the distributional impact of a broader acquisition of capital is increasingly important). Smith's focus no doubt stemmed from the fact that he believed:–

- the greatest share of the national income was truly being earned by workers by way of wages; and
- the income earned in production (when distributed primarily by wages in a context where capital could employ increasing amounts of labor at higher wages) would inevitably be sufficient to purchase what has been produced.[83]

---

[82] *Wealth of Nations*, Book Two, Chapter Four.

[83] "As in a civilized country there are but few commodities of which the exchangeable value arises from labour only, rent and profit

However, Smith's focus was blurred and so he failed to see that:–

- capital, like donkeys or increasingly productive and automated machinery, was not only doing more and more of the work, but was also distributing more and more of the income; and that
- the distributional function of capital has itself growth consequences grounded firmly in the law of supply and demand.

In short, Smith failed to see both the growth caused by the increasing independent productive power of capital and the growth caused by its distribution on market principles. So the conventional habit (stemming from Smith) of seeing all growth as ultimately a function of human productivity, does not really allow for the growth contribution and potential of the independent productiveness of capital. Indeed, some later conventional schools have even broadened their analyses to see all growth just as a function of human productivity plus capital productivity. Capital productivity, however, is a derivative of human productivity and so the broadening still does not fully account for the growth contribution and potential of the independent productiveness of capital and its distribution. From the binary perspective, seeing all growth as a function of productivity is like loading more sacks on the donkey and pretending you are doing the extra carrying.

So it is the basic conventional productivity paradigm that binary theory challenges. In contrast to the conventional paradigm, the binary paradigm sees increased growth as primarily a function of growing capital productiveness and its distribution. The recognition that capital does work in and of itself, as in the

---

contributing largely to that of the far greater part of them, so the annual produce of its labor will always be sufficient to purchase or command a much greater quantity of labour than what was employed in raising, preparing, and bringing that produce to market." (*Wealth of Nations*, Book One, Chapter Six).

case of the donkey, and that capital productiveness is both replacing and vastly supplementing labor productiveness, has tremendous distributional consequences. These consequences add a new, positive dimension to the great political and industrial debates that have polarized economists of all stripes for over two centuries. Once it is recognized that capital is independently productive, and that capital productiveness is replacing and vastly supplementing labor productiveness, it then becomes clear that capital has not only a productive relationship to growth but also a *long-term* independent (and very potent) *distributive* relationship to growth. This independent distributive relationship to growth is a function of the market distribution of the independent productiveness of capital.

Thus it is for readers, for their own economic self-interest and that of their families and their descendants, to decide whether total growth over the last two hundred and fifty years (and even more so, over the next two hundred and fifty) is a function of:–

- productivity growth
  or
- productiveness growth
  or
- some combination of the two.

In making their decision, readers should remember that for themselves, their families, and their descendants, fundamental questions of growth and distributive justice are at stake.

9. Some implications of the conflicting explanations for total economic growth

It will now be apparent from what has been said so far that conventional economics focuses on productivity, primarily human productivity.   In contrast, binary economics focuses on productiveness, primarily capital productiveness. Consequently, conventional economics and binary economics are locked in conflict over the main reason for the growth in productive capacity and total economic output. And there is good reason for that conflict. The differences between the two sides go to the foundational understanding of the essential conditions for growth and distributive justice.

The conflict, moreover, has startling implications. Indeed, some of them could well occasion alarm in those people who do not yet understand that capital assets are independently capable of producing and distributing on market principles far more wealth than humans ever will. But other implications (which are also the logical and inevitable consequences of the independent productive and distributive power of capital) promise a magnitude of growth and a quality of distributive justice which will give people a new confidence that they can solve today's seemingly intractable economic problems.

These implications flow not only from capital's independent productive function, but also from its independent distributive function. They are best understood when it is recognized that, in a free market, production and the distribution of the purchasing power arising out of the production are *not* separate phenomena but rather the two halves of one equation:–

$$work\ input\ =\ monetary\ outtake$$

The equation reflects the logic of fair exchange. It is also a fundamental law of the free market. The same balanced relationship is the foundation of double-entry book-keeping (the system that keeps account of property rights):–

$$debits\ =\ credits$$

A person's private property right in his/her productive labor *and* capital entitles that person to the work done by (i.e., the production of) his/her labor or capital. This work done – this production – is income which can be consumed or exchanged for the work done of equal value by others (through their labor and their capital).[84]

Thus if, beginning at least with the industrial revolution, growth is not primarily the result of increasing labor productivity (but rather the result of the increasing capital productiveness that replaces labor productiveness *and* vastly increases total productiveness) then a number of important propositions follow:–

- capital and *not* labor is the only viable source of affluence for most people and most societies;
- technology does *not* create more good jobs than it destroys: at best it will generally concentrate higher productivity jobs into relatively fewer workers leaving most others with lower paying jobs or no jobs at all;
- labor's percentage claim on aggregate production is *decreasing*. Even if overall labor productiveness is actually rising, its percentage claim on the total production will *still relatively decrease*. This is because capital productiveness and its percentage claim on total production will have risen even more.[85]
- sustainable growth requires open markets that provide universal individual access to capital acquisition so that a growing portion of the incremental productiveness of capital may be efficiently acquired by those expected to purchase its output.

---

[84] Thus, the free market is an institution that honors private property rights by the principle of free and voluntary exchange (as opposed to coercive appropriation). Money is needed as a measure of income and to avoid the exchange problems of barter.

[85] The relative *decrease* in labor's share of total income will certainly (but unnecessarily) be a shock to the intellectual system of those who do not yet understand that capital assets easily out-perform humans and that, in the out-performance, there is the practical foundation for great growth and distributive justice.

Further, *without universal individual access to capital acquisition on market principles*, a number of additional consequences will follow:–

- an industrial economy *cannot* on market principles distribute the earnings of production to those expected to purchase what can be produced;

- the efficient market pricing of capital and labor will be distorted. Labor will be over-priced while the true earnings of capital will be hidden, suppressed, taxed and redistributed by principles other than market principles;

- large-scale social pressures to redistribute income, with attendant tensions and political problems, are also inevitable. Because, at present, only a small percentage of the population owns (and is capable of acquiring additional) substantial capital assets, pressures toward redistribution will pit the poor and middle classes against the better-off. Consequently, most people will:–

- envy those who are better-off;

- disparage the closed private property principles that protect the capital of wealthy people and enable them to acquire more capital without laboring, while denying the same private property principles to everyone else; and

- justify earnings redistribution as inevitable and necessary.

Nor is it just a matter of poor pitted against rich. Because the declining labor claim on production will be unevenly distributed between some (but never enough) higher-productivity jobs and many more (but never enough) low-productivity jobs, pressures toward earnings redistribution will also pit the poor and middle classes *against each other*. Consequently there are endless no-win battles aimed at redistributing income from those with higher wages to those with lower wages or no wages at all.

Of course, where redistribution is concerned, the wealthy can always afford to give up a portion of their excess earnings. This is because, as long as their consumption needs are overly met, and their effective monopoly on capital acquisition is preserved, the wealthy are really only foregoing faster investment growth.

In contrast, the middle class and working poor cannot as easily afford the redistribution and their resistance to it will become more fierce and more widely spread as overall earnings redistribution continues to grow.[86] Thus the stage is set for the middle and lower classes to fight each other over scraps from the table when they should be sharing in the main meal.[87]

Furthermore, *without universal individual access to capital acquisition on market principles*, a number of further additional consequences will follow:–

- there will be a continual creation of huge amounts of debt, both personal and governmental, as those who have not been able to produce sufficient for their own needs borrow money *and* have to pay interest on what is borrowed;[88]
- there will be a continual pressure to debase money because, in practice, this is a means of indirectly taxing and redistributing income in economies where many people are insufficiently productive;
- the economy will lurch between inflation and slump and always suffer from a fear of both; and
- substantial growth will be unnecessarily suppressed.

---

[86] Although there is much rhetoric aimed at decreasing the percentage of national income taken in taxation, the trend over decades has been persistently upwards.

[87] The practice of redistribution pits people against one another and foments political fighting, social tension and alienation in the unfree market societies.

[88] Most government borrowing today (and consequent debt/deficit) is in effect borrowing on behalf of those who have not been able to produce sufficient for their own needs. Which is why unfree market governments have such huge amounts of debt. In 1994 the ratio of gross public debt to G.D.P. was:– Italy 118%; Sweden 93%; Canada 95%; Japan 79%; U.S.A. 64%; France 57%; Germany 54%; U.K. 50%. (OECD *Economic Outlook*, June 1994).

The list of implications set out above is so long that readers may have forgotten that they ultimately arise from the conflict between conventional economics and binary economics over the main reason for the growth in productive capacity and total economic output.   The implications, moreover, have massive consequences.   Not surprisingly, conventional economics then tries to avoid the implications with their massive consequences by denying that capital:–

- is doing more and more of the work;
- is therefore earning more and more of the income; and
- has a distributive relationship to growth that has nothing important to do with human productivity.

Having made its denial, conventional economics then teaches people the false notion that the unfree markets will generate and distribute more or less optimal wealth via the mechanism of increased productivity.   In particular, it declares that (as regards optimal efficiency) it does not matter who owns the productive capital when, as should be clear by now, it matters very much.

Book II

Chapter Four

Conventional productivity

1. Two different foundations to two schools of economics

We have said enough so far to make it clear that conventional economics and binary economics rest on two entirely different foundations. The former rests on the concept of productivity with a heavy human labor emphasis. The latter rests on productiveness with a heavy capital asset emphasis.

Conventional economics sees all growth as a function of productivity, primarily human productivity. Consequently, in different ways, the various schools of conventional economics explicitly or implicitly deny that capital has an independent productiveness – a productive quality that is essentially unrelated to any human labor that may be required to co-operate with it to provide goods and services. In essence, the conventional analysis of capital productivity is *derivative from, rather than independent of*, its analysis of labor productivity.

In contrast, binary economics sees capital as having substantial independent productiveness which is capable of:–

- doing more and more of the work (even though it may require the co-operation of humans); and
- distributing to consumers (in *open* capital markets) the income necessary to purchase what it produces.

With an understanding of the productiveness concept, people will learn that economies may be structured to grow not merely as a function of increased labor (or capital) productivity but also to grow, much more quickly and justly, as a function of independent capital productiveness, *accelerated by* a broader distribution of capital acquisition on market principles. In particular, binary economies unleash the power of technology for the individual benefit of everyone.

As a result of having two entirely different foundations, there arise two entirely different ways of understanding not only growth but also other economic phenomena and issues such as capital-labor substitution, inflation, redistribution and what is (or is not) a true free market. So, in view of the very different foundational concepts of conventional productivity and binary productiveness, it is sensible to examine those concepts a little more closely. This chapter mainly concerns itself with a description of productivity. Chapter Five focuses on binary productiveness; and Chapter Six explores the phenomena of growth, distribution and finance in the light of productivity and productiveness.

2.   *Conventional productivity*

a)   *Classical economics*

As we have explained in Chapter Three, the conventional focus on productivity as the fundamental cause of production and growth started with Adam Smith who saw all economic growth primarily in terms of the increasing specialization and productivity of human labor. Indeed, capital was important to Smith only because it:–

- facilitated labor specialization;

- increased human productivity by abridging the time and effort necessarily required of people to do work;

- enabled people to do more work; and

- was capable of employing additional labor at increasing wages apparently limited only by the fact that capital would become marginally profitless if it became too plentiful.

In fact, nowhere in the *Wealth of Nations* does Smith recognize that capital is important because it is independently productive. Accordingly, Smith did not see that capital can be more productive as it becomes more broadly owned for reasons independent of human productivity.

Moreover, since Smith wrote in 1776, the way goods and services are produced has changed immensely from labor intensive to capital intensive. Yet the conventional economic analysis of the function and importance of capital in the wealth creation and distribution process has not changed. Capital remains important to conventional economics only for precisely the same reasons that Smith advanced to describe the pre-industrial world.

The truth is that Smith's so-called 'classical' approach has not been borne out by the facts. Apart from some brief periods in particular places where almost everyone seemed to be doing better, the general industrial experience since Smith made his assessment of the situation is that wages rise only for *some* people, while many more others (in increasing numbers today) are left with lower paying jobs or no jobs at all. For all the undeniable increase in productive capacity and for all the greater availability among the general population of some essential goods and services, plenty of people are *not* deriving the benefits that Smith's economic paradigm seemed to promise.

Indeed, if poverty is measured not only absolutely (by comparing what most people have with what their predecessors had) but relatively (by comparing what most people have with what society could actually produce *if only there were more market-based demand*) then the unfree market is seen to be keeping people from far more wealth than it actually delivers. Which is why, of course, conventional capitalism and 'classical' economics are found unsatisfactory by many people. Since Smith wrote, despite a gigantic increase in productive capacity, poverty and the fear of poverty are as prevalent as ever while welfare dependence has *increased*.

Moreover, despite Smith's competition theory suggesting that market forces would eventually reduce the profitability of capital assets as they became more plentiful to a point of near zero marginal returns, wealthy capitalists as a group (although few in number) have been growing wealthier and more numerous.[89] Not surprisingly, feelings of resentment, alienation and despair spread among those who are denied access to capital productiveness.[90]

b)   *Socialist economics*

Writing three quarters of a century after Smith, when the growing momentum of massive industrialization was far more evident, Karl Marx certainly recognized the awesome, growing

---

[89] Apart from Smith's economics, other theoretical approaches have emerged in the attempt to explain the phenomenon of growing numbers of welfare dependants side by side with wealthy capitalists. All the approaches, however, are built upon (sometimes in contradictory ways) Smith's productivity paradigm. Indeed, although they differ on many points, the Marxist, neo-classical and Keynesian schools together with all conventional schools professing some allegiance to 'free market' principles, are built upon the human productivity theory of growth.

[90] Kevin Phillips, *The Politics of Rich and Poor: Wealth and the American Electorate in the Reagan Aftermath*, (Harper Perennial, New York, 1990).

productive power of capital in the form of great new machines such as steam hammers. He also recognized that people could not successfully compete with capital merely by working hard. Seeing no private property way of enabling the masses to participate in the productive power of the new machinery, he therefore urged that ordinary people recognize class interests and band together in economic self-defense against the owners of the emerging industrial empires. In particular, he urged that the capitalists should have their privately owned assets expropriated. But he needed to provide a moral foundation for the abrogation of private property, so (in the labor theory of value) he made a wholesale embrace of Smith's view that labor is the sole source of both wealth and value.

Moreover, in taking up Smith's labor productivity paradigm, Marx not only looked at the great machines that were doing ever more of the work (machines that Smith never saw and probably could not have imagined) but concluded, in a stroke of pure fantasy, that the machines were merely 'congealed labor'. By this Marx meant that the only financial return which the machines themselves were entitled to was a return sufficient for restoration and improvement (i.e., reserves for depreciation, research and development). Any additional return for the work done by capital (i.e., the profits which, under private property principles, belong to the legitimate owners of the machines), said Marx, should be paid as wages to workers to reward human labor productivity.

Marx therefore considered it moral and just to distribute most of the earnings of capital machinery to the workers. In the Marxist analysis, it was *their* work (or the work of their laboring predecessors) and *not* the work of the capital machinery which did the production and was therefore entitled to most of the profits.

But Marx's theory offered an efficiency and productivity element as well. If Adam Smith was right that capital profits increase when capital is scarce and decrease when it becomes plentiful, Marx reasoned, then the erosion and destruction of private property in capital would eliminate incentives to keep it scarce. At the same time, said Marx, by rewarding labor productivity the socialist distribution of wages will hasten growth by giving greater incentives for working harder and developing more machines that increase productivity. Thus, although Marx's 'congealed labor' theory of value was put forward to give the mass of people a *moral* right to the income which was increasingly flowing to the new owners of capital, it also had a purely economic component that paid homage to human productivity as the sole source of wealth and growth. However, it should be clearly understood that the 'congealed labor' theory of value is *not* an accurate expression of the most fundamental economic reality of all – who or what physically creates the wealth – and so socialism *cannot* provide a blueprint for economic growth and distributive justice.

Indeed, one basic reason for the collapse of explicit state socialism/communism is that it was not ultimately based upon an accurate conception of this fundamental economic reality. Another reason for the collapse is the erroneous idea that the value of consumer goods, capital goods and labor can be justly and efficiently determined and rewarded by a controlling political structure in such a way as to produce substantial growth together with widespread economic well-being. A third reason is the false belief that people in sufficient numbers will invest their time and energy to develop, build, operate, preserve and protect productive capital assets when they have no protectable private property interest in those assets.[91] A fourth is the false belief that a system can maintain respect for the dignity of the individual while abrogating fundamental private property principles. Needless to say, binary economics is based on none of the false concepts

---

[91] Without such a private property protectable interest in capital assets (or a comparable interest in their labor) from which to derive compensation for their efforts, people must continually prove themselves exclusively through a wage and price system that is politically determined rather than market-determined.

which led to the establishment and subsequent collapse of state socialism/communism.[92]

c)   Neo-classical economics

In the second half of the nineteenth century, when the emerging socialist ideas were still untested on a national scale but yet spreading among economically underpowered people, unfree market economists themselves tried to address the anomalies and problems left unsolved by Adam Smith's market approach. If Smith's invisible hand was not delivering the abundance and leisure promised by generally increasing human productivity, some rationale was needed to support a claim that the prevailing market system was at least as good as could be expected or, in other words, was 'the best of all possible worlds' or, in a single word, was 'optimal'.

Thus conventional economists, intent on defending the existing market system, turned to optimality. They applied the principles of calculus to productivity. They devised the 'first derivative' of productivity (called 'marginal productivity') and so founded today a dominant (if not *the* dominant) school in conventional economics – the neo-classical school.   In calculus, when derivatives are set to zero, they can be used to determine and prescribe the conditions for maxima and minima in any multi-

---

[92] The reasons for the failure of state socialism/communism occasion debate. Left-wing defenders of socialism look to matters of historical specificity as to why socialism failed in Russia and its satellites while right-wing theorists, observing the foundational defects of socialism, claim that a viable socialist or communist model can never be possible. Nevertheless, right-wingers should not gloat too confidently over the collapse of regimes which explicitly endorsed Marxist thinking. The logic of earnings redistribution is deeply embedded in the conventional economic paradigm which dominates the left-wing, center *and* right-wing of the unfree market economies. Those economies, moreover, are subject to the errors that keep most people from the widespread abundance promised by the increasing productiveness of capital.

variable process such as how much capital and how much labor to use in producing goods and services and how much of various goods and services to provide.

Therefore, theoretically, calculus and the theories involving marginal analysis of human preferences and diminishing returns have had an appealing application to wealth maximization and cost minimization in buying and selling various quantities of goods and services. In large part, it is its grounding of productivity in calculus and its apparent capacity for quantification that gives neo-classical economics its appeal to many people as a discipline apparently closer to the natural sciences than the social sciences.

But the application of calculus to productivity analysis points to optimal efficiency *only to the extent that* the prices for capital and labor are true (as opposed to false) prices. In other words, marginal productivity points to optimal efficiency only to the extent that markets actually efficiently price the available supplies of capital and labor. (However, efficient market prices require that there be no formidable barriers to market entry; and in the unfree market economies, most people face insurmountable barriers to efficient participation in the capital markets).

Moreover, marginal productivity is an important consideration in maximizing growth only to the extent that basic human productivity is important to growth. But, if growth is primarily the result of increasing capital productiveness, rather than increasing labor productivity, the marginal productivity analysis will *not* point to optimal efficiency and will be fundamentally misleading. Thus, in deciding whether the conventional productivity approach or the binary productiveness approach has the better view of reality, it is significant for the reader to recognize the fact that important predictions based on neo-classical marginal productivity theory do *not* bear out as important predictions based on the natural sciences have done.[93]

---

[93] P. Ormerod, *The Death of Economics*, (1994); R. Solo, *The Philosophy of Science and Economics*, (1991).

The neo-classical economists, moreover, shunned Marx's explicit 'congealed labor' theory of value because it destroyed private property in capital by giving all earnings (above reserves for restoration and modernization) to the state to redistribute to the people in wages. Nevertheless, the neo-classical economists did *not* reject Adam Smith's more general labor theory of value that saw the value of all goods (including capital) as ultimately grounded in the individual decision to labor or to take leisure.[94]

d)   *Keynesian and other conventional schools*

In various ways, Keynesian economic analysis, and other schools, take exception to neo-classical marginalist thinking. However, *none* of these schools abandons the idea that growth is primarily a function of human productivity. *None* fundamentally denies that the marginal analysis provides the primary market connection between the law of supply and demand, growth, inflation and all significant economic variables.[95] Moreover, *none* accepts the binary premise that capital has an independent distributive relationship to growth.

---

[94] Cole, Cameron, Edwards, *Why Economists Disagree.*

[95] Thus Keynes in the *General Theory* at p. 212 says, "It is much preferable to speak of capital as having a yield over the course of its life in excess of its original cost, than as being *productive*. For the only reason why an asset offers a prospect of yielding during its life services having an aggregate value greater than its initial supply price is because it is *scarce*; and it is scarce because of the competition with the interest rate of money. If capital becomes less scarce, the excess yield will diminish, without its having to become less productive – at least in the physical sense."

3.   *Productivity definitions*

Conventional productivity manifests itself mathematically as a *ratio* or rate *of total output per unit of input.* The fundamental focus of conventional economics is on labor productivity. However, considerable emphasis is also given to capital productivity (although it is more frequently conceptualized in terms of the rate of return on invested capital, rather than capital productivity). In addition, much of the modern market theory of growth and wealth maximization focuses on the concept of 'marginal productivity' which can be applied either to labor or capital to determine the last profitable unit of either in producing goods and services in the light of expected revenues and costs.

a)   *Labor productivity*

Labor productivity is calculated by dividing the *combined* production of labor *and* capital by the per-hour or, more usually, per-dollar cost input of labor. It should be noted that the output of *two* factors (labor and capital) is being related to the input of just *one* (labor) in the form of a *ratio.* Therefore, the labor productivity calculation does not, in itself, tell how much labor is or will be expended to do a job and how much will be earned from providing the labor. This is because productivity is only a ratio. To be sure, all things being equal, the higher the productivity of the worker, the more attractive to the employer. But, according to the conventional theory, how much labor will actually be employed, and how much it will actually earn, depends on how productive it is *in competition with* capital invented to do the same and more work, more cheaply.

b)   *Capital productivity*

Rather similarly, capital productivity can be calculated by combining the output of capital *and* labor with respect to per-

dollar capital input.[96] Again, the output of *two* factors (capital
and labor) is being related to the input of just *one* (capital).
Again, the true percentage contribution of each separate factor to
the physical creation of wealth is *not* being calculated.
Productivity is only a ratio. Capital will be employed to replace
and supplement the work of labor only if it is expected to produce
more and better work, more cheaply, than available labor.
However, although everyone concedes that the growing per-capita
production experienced by the unfree market economies has
become increasingly capital intensive, conventional economics
still prefers to emphasize labor rather than capital productivity,
and to measure and value capital productivity as fundamentally a
function of labor productivity.

c) *Marginal productivity*

'Marginal productivity' is the concept that is offered by
conventional economics to link the productivity of labor and
capital competitively with market decisions whether to employ
more capital or more labor, in various proportions, to provide
various goods and services. In terms of calculus, it is the 'first
derivative' of productivity.

'Marginal productivity' is a measure of the increase in output
obtained by the combined output of capital and labor by using one
additional unit of input (either a unit of labor or a unit of capital).
Under a generally assumed law of diminishing returns (tending to
an equilibrium of zero usefulness, satisfaction or profits),
marginal productivity is supposed to explain how market
participants (including managers, entrepreneurs and investors)
calculate exactly how much labor or capital to employ in a
particular production process to maximize output for any level of
available outputs. This analysis is backed up by the maximizing

---

[96] 'Capital productivity' is commonly expressed as the rate of return
on capital investment.

and minimizing principles of calculus applied to input and output ratios, expressed in various units including prices.

With varying degrees of faith and skepticism, the schools of conventional economics further assume that:–

- present markets accurately reflect the true prices of capital and labor;
- managers, entrepreneurs, investors and other market participants operate in a sufficiently competitive environment such that they will endeavour to get the calculations right; and
- those who get them wrong will pay the penalty of poor economic performance by being replaced by more of those who get the calculations right.

4. Marginal productivity theory and growth

Yet present markets do *not* accurately reflect the true prices of labor and capital, and there is growing evidence that market participants do not actually make their investment and employment decisions with marginal productivity considerations explicitly in mind. Nevertheless, as a model for explaining and quantifying the growth experienced by market economies over the last two hundred years, productivity theory (as buttressed by marginalist analysis) has gained wide acceptance as the best, most rigorous and, in some circles, the only credible explanation of the undeniable per-capita growth.[97] Indeed, although it is questioned, criticized, satirized and sometimes bitterly attacked, productivity theory is nevertheless widely and staunchly defended (sometimes by the very same questioners, critics, satirists and attackers) as

---

[97] Robert A. Solo, *The Philosophy of Science and Economics* (M.E. Sharpe, Inc. Armond, New York, 1991, pp. 39-51).

the only foundational market game in town. In fact, all the conventional schools pay homage to the theoretical power of the productivity analysis and then try to correct (in theory and/or practice) for its perceived shortcomings.

Binary economics does not dispute that management principles of profit maximization and cost minimization, along with sound principles of risk management (even based on the inaccurate pricing of goods and services as determined in the closed markets of the unfree market) are an important part of the market mechanisms which helped the unfree market economies significantly to outperform the communist economies. But an appreciation of these principles does not require accepting the whole of the marginal productivity analysis of growth as the only (or even the primary) explanation for that growth. It is one thing to have a great respect for the ability of able managers, entrepreneurs and investors to maximize profits and minimize costs in ways that produce growth in *relatively* free markets (an ability that does not as easily materialize in socialist markets where prices are even more heavily politically determined). It is quite another to believe that the marginalist analysis provides an accurate understanding of who or what is doing the extra work, and who or what accounts for growth.

In other words, the processes by which people (individually and together) in reality minimize effort and costs while maximizing output and profits are *not the same* as the conventional, productivity-based market theories advanced as the primary or exclusive explanations of growth. Specifically, binary economics denies that the productivity theories of growth take into account the substantial independent growth effects of capital productiveness and its distribution among the population. Binary economics further denies that the markets for capital and labor can be efficient as long as most people are excluded from capital acquisition.

5.   *Productivity and demand*

Significantly, the marginal productivity functions for capital and labor determine only the *relative* mix of capital and labor at a particular margin of production (and therefore, presumably, closely reflect the composition of the mix of capital and labor actually employed in production from point to point throughout any period). But they *do not directly determine* how much of a particular good or service will be marketable. For the aggregate of goods and services produced in an economy (and also relatively for every good or service offered in the entire economy), the question of any anticipated increased quantity of production (even when marginalist analysis is applied) depends more significantly on the demand, *existing and anticipated*, for the goods and services. This demand for production depends on the tastes, needs, wants and spending patterns of those who have earned, or will earn, in the production process (or upon the demand of those to whom the income of earners is redistributed). If there is no anticipated demand, there is no reason to add up the costs of satisfying it.

In the conventional market analysis, the demand for goods and services (which, admittedly, largely influences how much can be profitably provided) is simply a function of the distributed, or redistributed, earnings generated in their production. If it is assumed that the markets for the capital and labor used in production are competitive ones, then the very same optimal process of production (including investment in capital) will also generate the optimal income available to purchase what is produced. But if the present markets are not competitive (because they are closed markets, as binary economists contend) then this wealth maximization process will be less than optimal. How much less than optimal? There is a lot of debate in some circles but conventional economics provides no real way of knowing.[98]

---

[98]   Indeed one foundational principle of competitive equilibrium (which requires some buyers and sellers to see and trade on the deviant

Rather, as a matter of faith and ideology, some conventional economists contend that the situation is near optimal i.e., as good as can be expected, or the best of all possible worlds. It should also be remembered, however, that the conventional market analysis excludes, ignores or trivializes the possibility of binary growth and the greater efficiency it offers.

Furthermore, if the conventional marginal analysis is more closely examined it can be seen that the prices of all consumer goods are ultimately treated as a function of the decision of a worker to labor for those goods at the prevailing wage or remain idle. Likewise with the price of capital. Because capital must first be created and then pay for its acquisition cost before it can begin earning incremental income for its owners, its value to its owners is seen only as a function of the present value of its deferred earning power as compared to the present enjoyment of what *could* be consumed if the earnings were spent on consumption rather than to purchase that capital. Thus, the conventional theory says that people will defer more (or less) from current personal consumption depending on the anticipated rewards for deferring consumption (or 'waiting'). Ironically, given the present closed capital markets, that comparison is usually made by (or for the benefit of) people who have no unsatisfied consumer needs and wants of the sort that might actually be satisfied by the employment of that capital.[99]

---

prices) suggests marginalist analysis will *never* in itself be capable of determining how far its closed markets fall short from true efficiency. This is because maintaining the equilibrium (with totally efficient prices) requires some period of disequilibrium (with inefficient prices) and neo-classical analysis has no way of determining how much time for any given good or services is spent by the market in equilibrium or disequilibrium.

[99] The basic market choice of the rich is to choose between different forms of excess – on the one hand, excess current and deferred consumption (which they do not need), and, on the other hand, excess productive capacity (which they can use only to acquire additional excess productive capacity). None of this makes market sense. Rather

Further, because the present capital and labor markets are assumed to be more or less competitive, this prospect of deferred income (which determines the value of the capital) is itself seen as a function of consumer demand for the output of the capital which is in turn based on the individual worker's decision to work for consumer goods at the prevailing wage or remain idle. Thus, in the conventional analysis, the value of *all* goods and services (both consumer and capital) is basically a function of the work decision, which is in turn a function of human productivity.

Therefore, according to conventional economic analysis, on the one hand, the present prices that consumers offer for consumer goods are a function of the workers' decisions to work or remain idle (although, in fact, millions of people are willing to work but their services are not employed). On the other hand, the price of capital goods is viewed as a function of the decision of owners to wait for income they do not need for consumption,[100] and rather to invest in excess productive capacity to produce what too many others cannot afford. In other words, in the conventional analysis, the value of both consumer goods and producer goods is a function of present and future prices of additional consumer goods (which the rich do not need and the

---

it flatly contradicts Adam Smith's basic proposition that the purpose of production is consumption.

[100] For example, in considering saving and investment, Marshall said, "the growth in wealth involves a general deliberate waiting for pleasure which a person has .... the power of commanding in the immediate present." (A. Marshall, *Principles of Economics*, 8th ed., 9th Variorum ed. London and New York, Macmillan, 1920, p. 234). See also K.H. Hennings on *Waiting* in *The New Palgrave: New Capital Theory*, John Eatwell, Murray Milgate, Peter Newman eds. (W.W. Norton & Company, New York and London, 1990). In other words, in the conventional analysis, the rich are being productive by waiting. But, in the binary analysis, the rich are being productive by owning, *not* waiting. And, in a binary economy, the poor do not have to wait to become capital owners.

poor cannot afford), prices which in turn are functions of human productivity.

So it can be seen from the above paragraph that there is a snarled contradiction in the conventional analysis. On the one hand:-

i) whatever the reward demanded by owners for investing and thereby deferring consumer income (income that they do not need), that reward will seemingly be more readily paid if workers would only work for less, and if more productive capital can be acquired to replace them; while, on the other hand,

ii) if the workers accept less for their labor, or if they are replaced by capital, they will have less to spend and the investment incentive will be reduced by the resultant falling demand despite the falling costs implicit in i) above.

Again, the conventional analysis argues that, in a competitive environment, the balancing of the countervailing forces of i) and ii) above will be optimal. But the only evidence of this is that the unfree market economies have worked better than communist economies. However, evidence of its comparative victory over state communism is far from proving that the unfree market is operating at a level of efficiency that is anywhere near optimal. Indeed, *the unfree market victory over communism was in reality only the victory of one poor performer over a completely disastrous one.*

Furthermore, it is at this point in the analysis of growth that the independent productive and distributive function of capital assumes critical importance. The binary analysis reveals that:-

• the ability of capital, like donkeys, to do work exists *independently* of the willingness or ability of individuals to work for capital's output; and

• on market principles, in a binary economy, capital can buy itself for (and then distribute its earning power to) those expected to purchase its output whether or not existing owners spend their earnings on investment or consumption.

Thus, in a binary economy:–
neither

- the motivational desire, nor the competitive ability of the worker to find work;

  nor

- the patience and abstinence of the owner who may invest or consume;

is needed for efficient capital acquisition. Rather, by reason of its independent productiveness, capital (in a binary economy) has the inherent ability to produce wealth and to distribute the income necessary to purchase its output.

That ability is demonstrated in the next two chapters.

Book II

Chapter Five

Binary productiveness

1. Productiveness defined

Productiveness can be thought of in two ways. Viewed retrospectively, as the result of some act of production, it can be thought of simply as 'work done'. Viewed prospectively, it can be thought of as 'productive capacity' (i.e., an ability or potential to do work). Thus people and capital have a productive capacity, or a potential productiveness, which may manifest itself in actual productiveness, or work done, when capacity and opportunity coalesce.

2. Independent producers

With regard to *binary* productiveness (i.e., productiveness in a labor/capital economic system), we have observed that there are two broad, and mutually exclusive, categories of independent producers:–

• human beings;
 and

• capital assets.

Thus a capital asset is an independent producer *in exactly the same way* as a human is an independent producer. This was illustrated by the donkey which carries sacks in the same way as the man does. Moreover, the donkey has approximately twenty times the potential productiveness of the man because it can carry five times the load twice as far in half the time. Therefore, independent producers can work by themselves *or* co-operate with other independent producers. So a human can work alone, *or* work with another human, *or* work with a machine (a capital asset); while a machine can work alone, *or* with another machine, *or* with a human.

The concept of the independent producer is not limited to the hauling of things. It extends to the production of goods and services of all kinds. Thus land and plants are obviously independent producers of food. With the help of the sun, the rain, and other flora and fauna, they can produce food without any human work at all.[101] The fact that the land and plants can be made to produce more if people work with them does not change the fact that land and plants are independent producers. As independent producers, the land, plants and people tending them have a working partnership each contributing their share of the work.

The same even-handed logic applies to the work of simple farming tools and mechanized capital assets like tractors, combines and harvesters. They add their great contribution to production in a way that is no less independent than the land, plants and people.

---

[101] The sun, air and rain are, of course, other major contributors to plant growth but, because they cannot be owned, they are usually ignored by conventional economics.

Since the dawn of the industrial revolution, the economic landscape has proliferated with a vast and growing number of independent producers in the form of fabricated capital assets which are independently productive. A long list of independent producers can be offered. Here are just a few examples. A vending machine is an independent producer, providing the service of a human salesperson. The same is true for an automatic toll-taker, lighthouse or bank-teller machine. Just as human salespeople, lighthouse keepers and bank-tellers are independent producers of the services they provide, so, too, the capital instruments that are performing the very same work are also independent producers of comparable services.

The same relationship of human and non-human independent producers to actual production is seen in the example of copying. It took the scriveners of the past weeks, even months, working with the help of quills and ink, to copy out a long document by hand. Typists using typewriters cut the same work down to days while dramatically increasing total production. Enter the new capital asset, the modern photocopier, which, at the press of a button or two, accurately completes the work in a few minutes. Nearly 100% of the work input credit goes to the photocopier. From the binary perspective, the quills, typewriter and photocopier each independently contribute to production. Each exhibits its independent productiveness – and the trend is always towards greater capital productiveness.

Another remarkable example concerns communication over distances beyond human earshot. In centuries past, a runner might run many miles to deliver an urgent message. No one can deny that the runner was an independent producer of an important service. Homing pigeons were also used to carry messages. Who would deny the work of the pigeons in carrying the messages? And when the human messenger teams up with a pony to deliver messages much faster and further, there is much more wealth in the message-delivery service being provided than in the service provided without the pony. And the *pony* is doing most, if not all, of the extra work. Like the human runner and the pigeon, the pony is an independent producer of wealth.

Nowadays, of course, it is sensible to use another independent producer – the capital instruments of the telephone system which are linking up with a world-wide web of multi-media means of communication. To be sure, the communications industry still employs hundreds of thousands of workers, but the human work involved in transmitting each telephonic message continues to diminish as capital does more and more of the work. Indeed, all the communications workers in the world working full-time for a year but without capital instruments, could not deliver more than a tiny fraction of the messages delivered in a single day with the work of present-day capital instruments. The instruments owned by the communications companies are no less independent producers than the human runners, pigeons and ponies of years past.

Thus, for efficaciously carrying the messages, the capital owned by the communications companies increasingly gets more of the credit. In the light of the above examples, it can be seen that, from a binary perspective, the extra work done by a donkey (vending machine, photocopier, land or other capital asset) is primarily the result of *its own* independent productiveness. Although binary economists readily admit that capital competes with labor for employment, they deny that the productiveness of capital is best understood as a function of capital or labor productivity. Specifically, the productive capacity of capital to do work is not primarily or substantially related to any measure of the productivity of the person leading the donkey, driving the truck or pressing the button on a photocopier. Nor is it directly or substantially related to whatever human (or capital) productivity is involved in creating, repairing, or maintaining the donkey or the truck.

However, neo-classical economists argue that the relative value of the input of the donkey and the man *must* be determined by the marginal productivity theory alone. But this neo-classical approach wrongly assumes that:–

- the present labor and capital markets are generally efficient;
- the value of capital is fundamentally a function of labor productivity; and
- capital has no positive, independent distributive relationship to growth.

In contrast, binary economics makes three important counter-propositions:–

- the market pricing of capital and labor *cannot* be efficient, as commonly assumed, because most people are effectively and unnecessarily excluded from capital acquisition on market principles;
- capital has a productiveness which is fundamentally independent of labor productivity; and
- capital has a distributive relationship to growth that is not significantly connected to productivity.

By way of productiveness, therefore, binary economics enables people to analyze growth in a new way while keeping an open mind as to the unproved assumptions of conventional economics. By also keeping an open mind, the reader will be in a position to make a fair assessment of productiveness.

3. *Work adds up*

In order to explore growth from an open-minded perspective, binary economics looks back on history to examine how production has changed over time. In so doing, it sees all growth in an economy during any specific period as the result of extra work done in that period compared to an earlier period. The extra work done in a later period is therefore the total work done in the later period *minus* the total work done in the earlier period.

Thus, in per-capita terms:–

| | total work done in later period |
| *minus* | total work done in earlier period |

| *equals* | extra work done in later period |

Therefore, all the individual labor tasks done in a specific period comprise the total work done by people and all of the capital tasks comprise the work done by capital. And the sum of the two equals the total work done in an economy in that period.

In contrast, looking at particular markets, and at the aggregate of all markets, conventional economics assumes that the present market prices are the true measure of who or what is doing the work and therefore concludes that, for example in the U.S, economy, labor is doing 70 - 75% of the work (because labor takes 70 - 75% of all present-day earnings). Binary economics, however, suspends this unproved assumption to look more deeply into the matter.

4.   *Particular tasks analyzed*

In looking more deeply into the matter of who or what does the work, we examine particular processes of production as they have evolved over time. We then infer from them an underlying pattern that may give a more elegant, rigorous, realistic and helpful understanding of growth – one that may enable us to unleash the bounty of nature for the benefit of all. Thus, we proceed by illustrative example.

a)   *Digging holes*

Holes are useful for many purposes including storing, protecting, planting, constructing and burying. A graph of the number and size of useful holes in an economy might indeed be a rough measure of its growth.

i)   With the fingers

Now it is possible that there was a time when people had to dig all their holes 100% literally *by hand* i.e., they had to scrabble painfully in the ground with their unprotected fingers perhaps for four hours or more. As a result, holes were relatively few in number, mostly small, and of limited usefulness. In respect of a hole dug in four hours using fingers, it can be said that the digger's work input was 100% of the work input and, if money or equivalent were involved, he would be entitled to 100% of the financial outtake.

ii)   With a shovel

But our ancestors were inventive. They began co-operating more intelligently, not only with each other, but also with the supply of nature. For example, they used sticks and flat stones to dig holes in a way that was much faster, easier, cleaner, and less painful than before. Then, to eliminate toil and hardship, while increasing output and leisure, people fashioned rough shovels. Over the course of time, shovels were perfected to make digging easier and more efficient. By the beginning of the industrial revolution, a hole that might have required four hours scrabbling with the fingers could be dug in one hour or less with the help of a shovel. Moreover, in a given period of time, with the help of shovels, four times as many holes could be dug.

Now the conventional analysis explains the additional holes (i.e., the growth) by saying that, as a result of having a shovel, a man has four times his former (fingers only) productivity. The conventional analysis thinks the primary function of the capital asset (the shovel) is to increase labor productivity and it ignores the shovel as having no independent existence rather seeing it as an extension of the man's hand. Although insisting that the shovel owner must earn a rate of return for use of the shovel, the conventional analysis sees the shovel as having no independent productive capacity but rather sees its value only as a function of increasing human productivity.

Accordingly, conventional economics mathematically ties the rate of return on capital to the productivity of labor. Thus, in conventional economics, the productive input and earning capacity of the shovel are not entirely ignored: rather, they are seen as derivative functions of human productivity.

Moreover, this homocentric insistence on seeing the shovel's productivity and earning capacity as entirely dependent on the man's productivity is, according to conventional economics, reinforced by the fact that the shovel will not dig holes without the man. Yet that is to forget the equal fact that, in the same time, the man cannot dig the extra holes without the shovel. Indeed, while conceding that none of the increased output which materializes after the introduction of the shovel would have occurred without the people to work the shovels, binary economists observe that *nor would the growth have occurred without the shovels to work the people*. So, in terms of the extra work done, the shovel is no more dependent on the man than the man is dependent on the shovel. And it is more sensible (as binary economists contend) to consider them both as independently productive because they are both obviously doing work.

So binary economics does *not* explain the change in technology from hand-digging to shovel-digging as a function of productivity. Rather, in binary terms, the most significant aspect of the change is that the labor productiveness (work done) in producing each hole has *decreased* from 100% to 25% of its former amount, and capital productiveness has *replaced* 75% of the former labor productiveness. Thus an independent capital asset (the shovel) has entered the productive process and is co-operating with the person by relieving him of at least three-quarters of the work. This time, the productive input of the shovel is most definitely *not* being treated merely as a function of the productivity of the man.

So, from a binary perspective, there is a new productive process in which only 25% of the work is being done by human labor and the remaining 75% is being done by the non-human shovel. In other words, binary economics views the shovel situation as embodying a 75% physical *shift* in work done from one independent producer (the man) to another independent producer (the shovel). Therefore, in respect of a hole dug using a shovel, the man's 25% work input + the shovel's 75% work input = 100% of the work input. Moreover, if money or equivalent are involved, the man's 25% monetary outtake + the shovel's 75% monetary outtake = 100% of the monetary outtake.

Thus, as shown in the figure below, the productive process has changed from:–

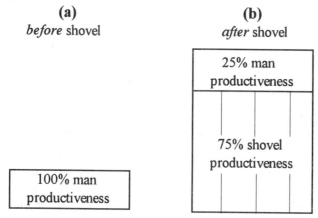

(a)
before shovel

(b)
after shovel

Fig. 5 – 1. Shift from labor to capital productiveness – shovel.

Which nicely sets the scene for a classic case of paradigm conflict. The conventional paradigm views the change from before-shovel to after-shovel as the man having four times the former productivity. In contrast, the binary paradigm views the change as the man having only ¼ of the total productiveness with the shovel having the remaining ¾.

The conflict arises because, although the man may be seen by conventional economics as having four times his former productivity, the binary approach considers it much more important to recognize that the man has only ¼ of his former (labor) productiveness per unit of output, with capital work replacing ¾ of the work once done by labor. Thus, in the example, the most important effect of the capital instrument (the shovel) is not to increase labor productivity but to replace former labor productiveness with new capital productiveness. Just like the donkey, *the shovel* is doing a major part of the work that was once done by the digger alone.

iii)   With a steam-shovel

Now let us progress the example from a man with a shovel to an operator with a steam-shovel (as mechanical excavators used to be called). With the help of the powerful steam-shovel, the operator can dig an equivalent hole every minute. With a ten minute rest per operator per hour, this amounts to 50 holes per hour and 200 holes in the time it took to dig one hole by hand (using fingers). There has undoubtedly been a 20,000% increase in output. And, in conventional economics, because growth tracks increases in human productivity, that amounts to a whopping 20,000% increase in productivity!

However, binary economists ask – *Who or what is doing the extra work?* From a binary perspective, the *steam-shovel* is doing most of the work. With much less effort, in half the time it took to dig one hole by hand (using fingers), almost *one hundred times* more holes can be produced.

So the independent productiveness of the steam-shovel has *not only replaced but also vastly supplemented labor productiveness*. This is the primary function of capital ever since people began making tools and discovering more productive ways to unleash the powers of nature so as to increase output while eliminating pain and toil. From the binary perspective, the productiveness of the steam-shovel could easily account for *over* 99.5% of the increased productiveness in producing each hole, and for the aggregate production of holes.

So the productiveness has shifted from:–

<table>
<tr><td align="center">**(a)**</td><td></td><td align="center">**(b)**</td></tr>
<tr><td align="center">*before* shovel</td><td align="center">to</td><td align="center">*after* steam-shovel</td></tr>
</table>

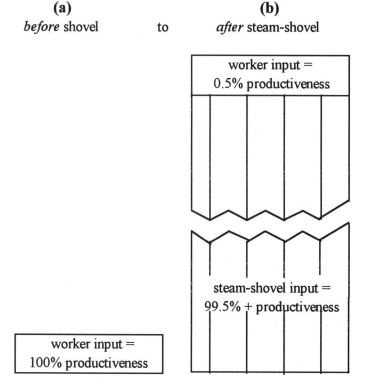

Fig. 5 – 2. Shift from labor to capital productiveness – steam shovel.

b) Carrying sacks

i) With a donkey

We now return to the sack example. A man can carry a sack on his back for a mile but is then exhausted. With the help of a donkey, five sacks are carried twice as far in half the time. The donkey does all the carrying, and the man does the loading, unloading and supervising.

Whereon the binary economist asks – ***Who or what is doing the extra work?*** Exactly how much of the work is done by the donkey, and how much by the man, may be open to debate. However, if a reader has any difficulty in understanding who is doing most of the extra work, a moment's fancy is helpful. Ask the donkey who is doing most of the work. "*I* am," the donkey would reply ....

The man, of course, might be tempted to minimize the work of the donkey by emphasising his own changing contribution. Eager to maximize his share of the production, he would say that the donkey could do no carrying without a man's intelligence together with his loading, leading and supervisory skills. Thus the man might claim that there should be a productivity premium to pay for the loading, leading and supervisory skills as compared with the lesser wage rates for the skills necessary for carrying a sack on the back. And binary economists agree that, to complete the carrying as a commercial transaction, a man must load and unload the donkey and know where to go. But a man carrying a sack on his back equally has to load, unload and know where to go. So binary economists are prepared to agree only that *some* extra skills *may* be involved (e.g. in supervising and guiding the donkey) and so *some* higher wages may be payable. Nevertheless, if the donkey could negotiate terms for itself (as its owner can) it would certainly point out that, without its help, the man alone could not carry a single sack more than a mile in an hour without becoming exhausted. So *none* of the extra work would have been possible without the donkey.

Furthermore, the donkey would ask – How much work is *really* involved in the loading, guiding and supervising? Is it *really* as much work as that involved in carrying, say, just one sack for one mile? It hardly seems so. Moreover, using the donkey, the man is *not* exhausted after the carrying and so, with the help of the donkey, must be doing **less work, not more.** Indeed, if the man is not doing less with the help of the donkey, we would expect that laborers would prefer to carry sacks themselves rather than to load them onto donkeys. This, of course, never happens in practice except when carrying is paid in artificially high wages or when carrying becomes an end in itself (as with muscle-trainers and body-builders).

So, notwithstanding the claims of the man, binary economics sides with the donkey. From the binary perspective, it is *the donkey* which does most, if not all, of the extra work.[102]

Thus as shown below:–

---

[102] Going further into the detail of the labor (man) and capital (donkey) contributions to carrying sacks, it is necessary to consider the costs of the peripheral labor considerations in providing the donkey. Someone made the effort of catching or breeding the donkey; someone made the effort of feeding, sheltering, caring and training it. But the total of all that effort must be *less* than the extra work that a donkey does or, simply, donkeys would not be employed to do carrying. In other words, the donkey's productiveness must have sufficient value to those who want to carry sacks at least to cover the cost of providing the donkey to do the work. Therefore, after adding in all the peripheral labor considerations, if the donkey is not doing more work than it eliminates, it would not be used. Certain jobs that did not exist before (e.g., donkey tending) may be created by the use of donkeys in production, and these jobs may be entirely labor-intensive (at least, for a while): nevertheless, the use of donkeys for carrying will continue only if, with their help, more work is done with *less* labor per unit of output. The question of whether greater or merely *different* skills are required in modern production will be explored in more detail below.

(a)   **(b)**

without donkey   to   *with* donkey

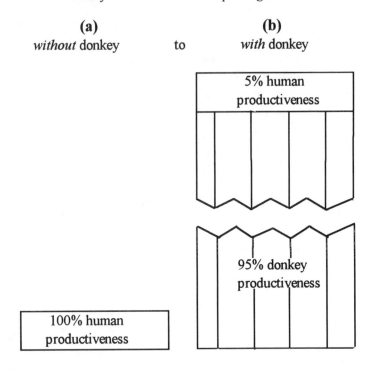

Fig. 5 – 3.   Shift from labor to capital productiveness –
donkey.

ii)   With a handcart and horse and cart

Similarly, when a man decides to co-operate with an independent handcart, the *handcart* does a good percentage of the work input (its owner being entitled to the financial outtake for that percentage). Then, when a horse is harnessed to a cart, the independent *horse and cart* do virtually all the work with the man, now a horse-driver, acting only in a supervisory, tending capacity.

It matters not an iota that the horse and cart cannot operate without a horse-driver because, for all practical purposes, it is equally true that a horse-driver cannot operate without the horse and cart. Each requires the other to operate but, when they do operate together, it is *the horse and cart* which physically do the bulk of the work, far more than the man alone, or the man plus the donkey.

iii)   With a lorry

Moreover, when a lorry (truck) is substituted for a horse and cart, the combined efforts of the driver and the lorry with its marvellous engine can convey 1000 sacks at a speed of 50 miles per hour achieving 500 miles in a ten hour day. Regardless of what the present (unfree) markets may be paying today, the binary view is that the lorry physically does the bulk of the work per unit of output with the fortunate lorry-driver, now protected from the elements and comfortably seated in his cab, merely operating the controls with energy and attention to spare to listen to the radio or talk on the car phone.[103]

From the binary perspective *capital productiveness has both replaced and vastly supplemented labor productiveness.* Although the calculation for the increase in conventional productivity shows an astronomical rise, labor productiveness for doing the carrying is less than 1%, even approaching zero, while capital productiveness is at 99% +, even approaching 100%, thereby accounting for almost all of the work per unit of output.

---

[103] Nor does the lorry-driver have an indisputably greater skill than that of the horse-driver. Indeed, some might argue that a horse-driver's skill is superior to that of a lorry-driver. The comparison of a horse-driver's skill with that of a lorry driver is highly relevant because conventional economists are always prepared to allege that modern skills are the main cause of a hundred or thousand-fold increase in productive power. The conventional mind thinks any new or different skill is necessarily a higher skill than the one it replaces. Thus, to the conventional economist, a lorry-driver must have hundreds of times more expertise than a horse-driver because a lorry-driver 'carries' many more sack-miles in the course of a day. That is nonsense. Most sensible people today would put the expertise of horse-driver and lorry-driver at about the same level.

So it should now be clear that, based on the binary analysis of hole-digging and sack-carrying, the concept of productiveness can be illustrated in several ways. Thus the shift in productiveness from labor to capital in the work of sack-carrying could be illustrated as follows:–

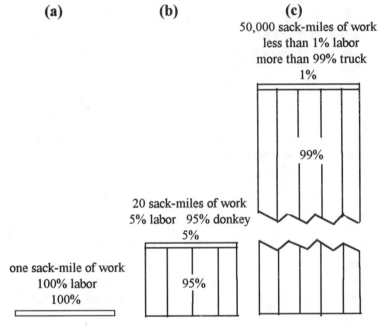

(a)   **(b)**   **(c)**

50,000 sack-miles of work
less than 1% labor
more than 99% truck
1%

99%

20 sack-miles of work
5% labor   95% donkey
5%

one sack-mile of work
100% labor
100%

95%

Fig. 5 – 4. Shift from labor to capital productiveness – sack carrying.

The figure shows the productiveness (work done) or the potential productiveness (productive capacity, or how much carrying can potentially be done) per unit of output in a unit of time, based on three ways of carrying. On the left, there is one sack-mile using 100% labor (man only) productiveness. In the center, 20 sack miles use 5% labor productiveness (man) and 95% capital productiveness (donkey). On the right, 50,000 sack-miles use less than 1% labor productiveness (driver) and more than 99% capital productiveness (lorry).

Thus the figure represents three 'snapshots' of the relative contributions of labor and labor productiveness to total growth. The overall pattern is clear – taken together, there is a *shift* in productiveness from labor to capital accompanied by a great increase in output. The pattern reveals a general rule:–

The more capital productiveness and the less labor productiveness per unit of output, the more work can be done, and the more income can be earned by employing more capital and less labor.

The figure below then illustrates the same shift in productiveness from labor to capital, but goes further by showing how the shift might have occurred gradually over time:–

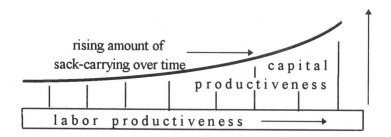

Fig. 5 – 5. Shift from labor to capital productiveness – over time.

Like Fig. 5 – 4, Fig. 5 – 5 above shows a growing shift from labor productiveness to capital productiveness per unit of output accompanied by greatly increased growth. In Fig. 5 – 5 the curved rising line shows the total and growing amount of sack-carrying done over time. The bottom area shows the carrying-related productiveness (loading, leading, unloading, driving) done by labor. Note that, although there is continuing growth with technological change, the amount of labor productiveness per unit of output does not grow. From the binary perspective, the human work per unit of carrying is never greater with more capital than without. To the contrary, the human work per unit of carrying almost invariably decreases. Except for the intrinsic sport of it, or unless wages are artificially inflated beyond the market value of their productive input, there is never any real point in employing capital in ways that increase labor work per unit of output. At each point in technological development (along the horizontal axis), the vertical distance between the total work line and the labor productiveness line reveals the increasing amount of capital productiveness per unit of output.

The changing relationship between capital, labor and production can also be expressed as percentage contributions to unit and total production. Thus, implicit in the greatly increasing capital productiveness (compared to relatively constant labor productiveness) is the fact that per unit of output, and in the aggregate, in percentage terms, capital productiveness is increasing while labor productiveness is decreasing. This relationship is illustrated in Fig. 5 – 5. In other words, the binary analysis reveals growth as a process whereby *capital productiveness replaces labor productiveness and increases total productiveness.* The more capital productiveness and the less labor productiveness per unit of output, the more work can be done, and the more income can be earned by employing more capital and less labor.

However, the independent productiveness of capital – which replaces labor productiveness and increases total productiveness – is ignored and obscured in the conventional productivity analysis of growth. With these points in mind, we can now begin to examine some powers of capital – powers that the productivity analysis of growth ignores and obscures.

c) *Some powers of capital*

In the examination of digging and carrying, binary economists maintain that capital has several powers, subsumed in its independent productiveness. The first two powers of capital are its ability to:–

i) **replace labor** (by eliminating labor and relieving people of some of the most time-consuming, difficult and otherwise disagreeable aspects of the work); and also

ii) **vastly supplement** labor (by doing far more work, far quicker, than humans alone can ever do).

But capital can do far more. With increasing efficiency, it can:—

iii) *do work that labor working alone* (or labor working with simple hand tools) *can never practically do*;

iv) *do work with virtually no human labor involved* (as in the form of robots and other automation);

v) *buy itself on credit and pay for the cost of its acquisition out of its future earnings;*

vi) *distribute the income to purchase its output within an open private property system.*

In the next section on lifting people with elevators, we will explore iii) and iv) above. We shall consider v) and vi) in Chapter Six.

d)   Lifting people – two lessons from elevators

Before steam, internal combustion and electric engines, there were rudimentary animal- and human-powered elevators but nothing that could lift thousands of pounds hundreds of feet in the air in a matter of minutes and, later, seconds. Lifting on such a scale was work which was impractical for animals or humans alone.

Then there arose a great and growing mechanical capacity to lift millions of people and billions of pounds in freight ten or more stories. That capacity is the direct result of a great increase in capital productiveness. It has little to do with any increase in labor productivity.

Therefore, *in addition to replacing and vastly supplementing the work of labor, capital also does what labor alone can never do*. For example, humans working alone cannot fly (they need the work of airplanes); humans alone cannot grow food (they need the work of land or land-substitute, seeds, sun, rain and countless flora and fauna);[104] and humans cannot communicate across the Atlantic (nowadays the job is done very nicely by satellites). This then is the third power of capital:–

To do work that labor working alone, or working with less capital, can never practically do.

Thus capital opens to people an entirely new physical relationship to everything material.

Nevertheless, the conventional productivity approach ignores all the new kinds of work done mostly by capital, but with the help of some labor. And the ignoring is done by focusing all the more on human productivity. Accordingly, the early mechanical elevators had cumbersome levers that took strong men to operate. But by 1950, a person of less than average size and strength, could manually move a lever along a dial thereby stopping the elevator at desired floors. Although it took a little training to learn to stop the elevator smoothly, even that work was soon to be replaced by electronic switches and circuits that guided the elevator more smoothly and accurately. With the help of these state-of-the-art elevators (which were larger, faster and much easier to operate than their predecessors of 1920), operators could serve many more people, more quickly, more easily.

Although the improved elevators were doing more and more of the work, conventional economic analysis alleged that human productivity for this task was up and still rising. Between 1900 and 1950, along with the rising productivity figures for thousands of other tasks (which were also being transformed by technology to require less labor for more output), these rises in productivity were recorded, studied and debated by conventional economists. The rises were then used to shape the rising productivity theory of growth and document it with the appearance of scientific validity.

But this appearance of validity was not to last. Precisely why it would not last brings us to another lesson from the elevators

---

[104] Although a nursing mother can produce milk for her baby.

and an illustration of the fourth power of capital which can be restated as follows:–

Capital increasingly produces more by automation.

This power is memorably demonstrated by a story that happened repeatedly in the United States beginning around 1950. In one form or another, it has increasingly happened throughout the entire world ever since.

Let us briefly turn the clock back to 1950 when a company operates ten manual elevators. The chief financial officer goes to the president with a plan to purchase automatic elevators which are projected to save the company money by reducing labor costs. According to the plan's projections, when the cost of borrowing to acquire the automatic elevators is added to the cost of maintaining and operating them, the total is less than the cost of maintaining and operating the manual elevators. In short, although borrowing costs will be higher for the automatic elevators, labor costs will be much lower.

To test the plan, the company decides to replace five of its old manually-operated elevators with new automatic ones. These are bigger, stronger, faster, safer, carry more people and require less maintenance than the old ones. Five of the operators are sacked.

So, inasmuch as the company is now delivering more elevator service with half the operators, should we conclude that the remaining operators are more than twice as productive? Of course not. The remaining operators are still doing *exactly the same job* as before except there are fewer operators. The automatic elevators are simply doing more of the work, and they are doing it cheaper. From a binary perspective, the additional output and efficiency has nothing important to do with increased worker productivity. Quite to the contrary, the automatic elevators are doing the work of the five replaced manual elevators *plus the work of the five replaced elevator operators.* Thus, what is most important in binary terms is that independent capital productiveness has now replaced half of the former labor productiveness.

5.   The   conventional   productivity explanation contradicts itself

The binary approach is straightforward compared to the conventional productivity analysis which reveals itself to be ambiguous and contradictory. When trying to understand the great questions of automation, growth and distribution in terms of productivity, conventional economics claims that it does not matter whether we look at aggregates for particular markets or at aggregates for manufacturing as a whole.[105] But the facts in the elevator example clearly indicate otherwise. The productivity figures, which are frequently advanced by conventional economists as hard facts, depend critically on what factor the conventional theorist puts in the numerator and denominator of the productivity ratio.[106]

Thus, consider the effect on the productivity calculation when the numerator is company elevator output, or some national or other output aggregate, but the denominator is:–

the remaining operators

When the remaining operators are the denominator, productivity is *increased* because the same or more service is being delivered by fewer operators and so a lower labor cost. The alleged increased productivity is, of course, ludicrous. In reality, the remaining operators are working as before delivering the identical service in the same time. They are *not* working any more productively. To the contrary, only capital (the automated

---

[105] Robert M. Solow, *The Great Automation Question (1): Technology and Unemployment*, (*The Public Interest*, Fall, 1965, pp. 17-26, at 18).

[106] The numerator of a common fraction is the one above the line and the denominator is the one below. Thus in the fraction ¼, the numerator is the **1** and the denominator is the **4**.

elevators) is doing more work and, as a percentage of the input, labor is doing *less*.

even fewer operators

Productivity is *further increased* as the number of operators decreases.

one operator

Productivity *increases even further.*

one part-time operator

Productivity *leaps skywards* with just a single part-time operator.

It then goes on *an astronomical rise* when there is a part-time operator doing only a few minutes' work each day.

no operators

With no operators, productivity has risen to *infinity*!

Or perhaps it is better to say it has gone down to *zero*. In reality, those laid off have no productivity with respect to their former jobs (although they may be functionally indistinguishable from those still on the job) and must earn their livelihood elsewhere or go on welfare. Conventional economics tries to minimize or ignore the implications of this zero productivity factor. Assuming more or less competitive markets, conventional economists reason that these laid-off people will (more or less) find (more or less) optimal jobs in the (more or less) optimal economy. Binary economics makes no such assumption and engages in no such reasoning.

Now consider the effect on the productivity calculation when the numerator is the output of manually-operated elevators and the denominator is:−

the remaining operators

In this example, productivity is *unchanged.*

As long as their wages remain unchanged, the productivity of the remaining operators will be unchanged in financial terms because they are delivering the same service at the same cost. But their wages will not likely remain the same indefinitely if the automatic capital is doing identical work right beside them at cheaper cost. Free market forces will exert downward pressure on the wages for elevator operators. For a time the operators may accept a cut in wages to remain competitive with the new capital. In that case the human operators will seem to be working with greater productivity, but their productive capacity has not really changed, and the human operators will not be able to remain competitive with the automatic elevators indefinitely.

Thus, depending on what is put into the numerator and/or denominator, productivity is *either increasing, infinite, zero or unchanged.* This is an unsettling ambiguity to say the least.

6.   *Productivity contradiction is exposed*

Returning to our story, in 1955, the inevitable day arrived – the remaining five operators still employed by the lift corporation were sacked because of the introduction of five more automatic elevators, which also happen to be capable of carrying more weight at a faster speed than the earlier ones. And it is precisely at this point that conventional economics is exposed as having got things completely wrong. One moment, according to conventional economics, the operator output was either staying the same (for each individual operator) or marvellously increasing (for the operators as a whole, for company performance and for other industry, state, regional and national aggregates).

Then, suddenly, with the full automation of all the elevators, the productivity of the individual operators (now without jobs) crashed to *nil* on the one hand while, on the other, the productivity of the aggregate operator service has gone shooting up into the sky on its way to infinity even though the job of elevator operator no longer exists.[107] The end result is *nil* productivity for individual operators and an *infinite* productivity for the operators as a whole even though no operators are actually employed! As for the local trade/labor union, it has some potentially infinitely productive elevator operators if they can only find jobs.[108] Clearly, this conventional interpretation is preposterous!

But, if the capital investment is a truly profitable substitution of capital for labor (as in the case of automatic elevators), then elevator operator jobs will diminish. This is because a process starting around 1950 with a few firms (as in the case of the automatic elevators), will quickly spread throughout the economy. Over the years, the process will continue: thousands of automatic elevators will replace thousands of workers. Aggregate labor productivity for elevator service will *increase* sharply, approaching infinity until virtually all operators are fired. Labor productivity for this task is now functionally *zero*, although elevator service, company, industry, state and national productivity figures will have *increased*. Hopefully, the laid-off workers will find better jobs in the larger economy traceable to the increases in aggregate productivity.

Yet the same process of substituting and vastly supplementing capital productiveness for labor productiveness is also going on in

---

[107] The value of the fraction output/input becomes infinitely large as the denominator becomes infinitely small (i.e. approaches zero). In terms of calculus, used to describe conventional marginal productivity:– Lim F(o/i) = infinity as i approaches zero.

[108] Trade/labor union policy *cannot* win long-term benefits for union members without a binary strategy. Resisting the introduction of new technology and using conventional productivity to justify more wages for fewer people with jobs cannot achieve lasting gains. Only binary economics (by enabling widespread private and individual ownership of technology) can give a new, powerful way to win real long-term benefits.

all aspects of production. So when one considers the economy-wide population of capital-displaced workers, there is reason to fear that too many will find only worse, lower-paying jobs and too many will have to accept welfare permanently.[109]

In another scenario (actually played out in some American cities), the workers unionize and effectively bargain to keep their jobs, now consisting of pressing the button for the passengers as they call out their destinations. Seemingly the productivity of workers would remain *unchanged* from the days of the manual elevators. How can this be?

The promise of higher pay to workers for higher productivity is thus based on contradiction. The contradiction and incongruity underlying the conventional analysis are illustrated in Figure 5 – 6 below:–

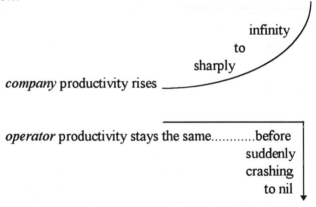

Fig. 5 – 6. As more automation is introduced, conventional human productivity points in two contradictory directions at once.

The above figure gives memorable expression to the way in which conventional productivity points in two contradictory directions at

[109] Jeremy Rifkind, *The End of Work: the Decline of the Global Labor Force and the Dawn of the Post-Market Era*, (G. P. Putnam & Sons, New York, 1995).

once thereby revealing its incongruity with reality (and its quite disastrous implications for trade/labor unionists). This preposterous situation arises because conventional economics does not understand that *independent* capital productiveness has both replaced and substantially supplemented labor productiveness for elevator service. The contradiction and incongruity can also be expressed as shown in Figure 5 – 7 below:–

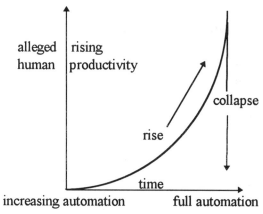

Fig. 5 – 7. As more automation is introduced into individual tasks, conventional human productivity is exposed as being self-contradictory.

The contradiction happens because conventional economics conceives of all growth as ultimately a function of human productivity and thereby fails to recognize that, continually, new, marvellously prolific, *independent* capital assets have an *independent* ability to:–

• replace human labor in the wealth-creating process, doing work faster and cheaper;
• vastly supplement the amount of work that labor can do without capital;
• do vast amounts of new work that labor alone can never do;

and
* do work without labor.

7.   Binary economics, based on productiveness, does not contradict itself

In contrast, the concept of binary productiveness provides a logical analysis of the elevator situation which fits the physical facts. The installation of the five automatic elevators reduced the overall human work input for that task to less than 50% of the total input and increased the work input of the (capital asset) elevators to more than 50%. When all the elevators were automated, the human input went down to 0% while that of the (capital asset) elevators, for that task, went up to 100% of total productiveness and more than 100% of the former total productiveness.[110] This analysis involves no contradiction. It is also congruent with reality for it focuses on *both* the human and non-human contributions to the production of goods and services. The focus reveals generally a shift from the human contribution (a *declining* percentage of total input) to the capital asset contribution (an *increasing* percentage) as set out in the three following juxtaposed figures relating to the elevator example:–

---

[110]   Because the new elevators carry more people faster, they are actually doing *more* than 100% of the work done by the original operators working with the manual elevators.

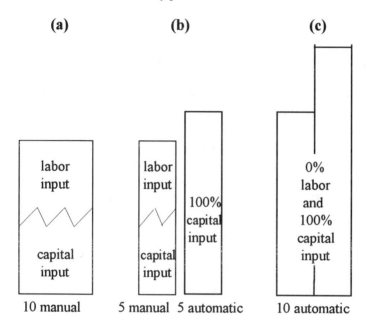

Fig. 5 – 8. Human productiveness as a proportion of total input shifts downwards while capital asset productiveness shifts upwards.

The figure on the left shows 10 manually-operated elevators and therefore a sizable labor productiveness in providing an elevator operator service at a certain overall level. For simplicity's sake, we have assumed a 50/50% contribution from labor and capital.

In the center, there are 5 manually-operated and 5 automatic elevators. The figure shows that labor productiveness in the total elevator operator service has dropped to less than 25% of the total productiveness (because the new elevators carry more people, faster). For the same reason, capital productiveness has risen above 75% of the total productiveness. Thus, to illustrate their greater productiveness, the automatic elevators are shown as being 'larger' than the manual elevators. Moreover, overall elevator service has increased above the former total productiveness and it has done so entirely as a result of the greater capital productiveness.

On the right, capital productiveness has wholly replaced labor productiveness in providing elevator service and has also increased total elevator service.   Not only does the work of operating elevators shift from a percentage of productiveness for labor to 100% productiveness for capital; but the 100% capital productiveness of the new elevators *is greater than (i.e., the new capital does more work than)* the former productiveness of the operators, manually-operated elevators and automatic elevators put together because the new automatic elevators carry more people, faster. Thus, to illustrate their greater productiveness, the newest automatic elevators are shown as being even larger than the automatic elevators installed five years earlier.

Viewing the economy as a whole, the overall shift from labor to capital productiveness can be illustrated thus:–

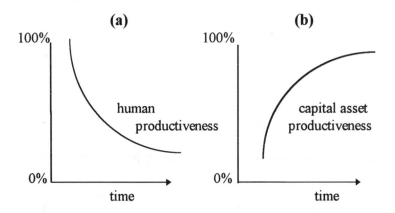

Fig. 5 – 9. Overall human productiveness as a proportion of total input shifts downwards while capital asset productiveness shifts upwards.

8.   The fatal mistake of conventional productivity analysis

So what is the underlying reason for conventional theory getting things so badly wrong? On a superficial level, conventional theory makes the fatal mistake of assuming that, in the process of wealth creation, there is always a substantial and necessary physical connection between human labor and capital assets. *It then deeply embeds this mistakenly assumed interdependence between human labor and non-human capital assets by placing it at the foundation of marginal productivity analysis.* That foundation links the cost and value of all production with the individual decision of whether to work or not.

Yet there does not have to be necessary connection between labor and capital for production to happen. For example, plants grow and fruits ripen by themselves: fish and animals breed. Modern readers, moreover, should have no doubt on the point because there are tens of thousands of 'robots' in the world today, together with millions of other machines, technological processes, and technical mechanisms which run, or almost run, themselves.

Of course, it can be argued that, to a greater or lesser degree, there is always a human connection necessary to realize capital asset productiveness – the fruit of a tree has to be gathered, for example; buttons must be pressed to set machines in motion. However, if the argument is accepted, the connection must never be allowed to obscure the fact that the tree grows the fruit and the machine does its own work.

9.   Invention, creation; production; maintenance, repair, management, stewardship; entrepreneurial activity; and skills – are all the work of labor, not the work of capital

Because of its homocentric preoccupation with human productivity, the conventional analysis is confused about the market relationship between labor work such as the invention, operation and maintenance of machinery, and the work independently done by capital. The confusion disappears once it is firmly and foundationally understood that capital (like donkeys, trucks, shovels and elevators) does work in exactly the same way that humans do work. Or, in other words, that *capital is independently productive*.

a)   Invention and creation

In this context, 'invention' is shorthand for all human activity which results in a discovery, invention, conception or understanding that leads to ways of doing more with less labor. From a binary perspective, however, the work of inventing is *not* the subsequent work of the invention. For example, the work done in 'inventing' the use of a donkey or a truck to carry sacks is quite simply *not* the work done by the donkey or the truck. The capital that is created and employed with the new 'invention' does its own work and can be separately owned by someone who is not the inventor. Moreover, if it is separately owned, a property right in that capital entitles the owner to the claim on the income earned from its work, even though the inventor's historical contribution earns nothing currently.

This is not to say that the work of invention is not highly valuable and historically essential to the growth that has benefited humanity. Indeed, for the sake of efficiency and economic justice, it is essential that invention be adequately rewarded or it will be less forthcoming. Thus, in virtually all of the unfree market economies, patents, copyrights, trade marks and trade secrets are protected by law as, in effect, legislated 'intellectual capital'. The policy behind protecting valuable invention as legislated capital is to preserve economic incentives for invention and creation that would otherwise be quickly eroded by the free-ride copying that results from respecting no private property in invention. But in such a case, the earning capacity of the legally protected intellectual property is in effect a legislated property interest in the income earned (i.e., in the work done) by each independently productive capital embodiment or use of the invention.

b) *Production*

Just as invention is the work of labor so people who prepare, deliver and install capital do valuable work, but it is labor work and not the work of the capital itself. Similarly, those who start, guide, operate, monitor and stop the work of capital do not do the work of capital. Their work may be essential to the work of capital, just as the work of capital may be essential to the starters, stoppers, operators, guiders and monitors, but each independent factor is doing its own work.

Likewise, farmers do considerable labor work. However, they do *not* do the work of the rain, the seed, soil, rain and sun: and they do *not* do the work of the tractor any more than they do the work of the donkey.

c)   *Maintenance, repair, management and stewardship of capital*

Those people who provide maintenance, repair, management, and stewardship of capital also do valuable work. Such work is essential for capital to do its work and deserves compensation at competitive market rates. But such work is not the work of the capital itself. A doctor who saves a patient's life is not entitled to be paid for the work done by the rehabilitated patient. Likewise, the people who repair a truck do not do the work of the truck any more than they do the work of the truck driver, or any more than the people who bred the donkey do the work of the donkey.

In the same way, managers who provide services (such as plans for capital acquisition and for the employment of capital and labor in production) and people who provide accounting, legal, financial and communications services, may be essential in maintaining and enhancing the productive capacity of the capital. But their work is not the work of the capital and labor they manage, account for, defend and finance.

Also, a professional trustee and investment advisor might act to protect and enhance the productive capacity of a capital estate, much like a doctor and an athletic coach might protect and enhance the performance capacity of an athlete. But the work of trustee or financial adviser is not the work of the capital estate. The work of protecting and enhancing the performance of another person or thing, is *not* the work of the performer.

d)   *Entrepreneurial activity*

Perhaps no market participant more captures the imagination of people in general, and the zeal of the staunchest defenders of the unfree market system in particular, than the successful entrepreneur. Certainly, many entrepreneurs start with inherited wealth and advantages, but many others seem to go from rags to riches. Some (performing with remarkable genius, vision, energy, daring, persistence, wisdom and other qualities) build vast fortunes as a special function of their exceptional, personally productive talents.

Influenced by productivity analysis, Joseph Schumpeter and other conventional economists view entrepreneurial activity as a major source of growth. Indeed, this line of reasoning leads some to believe it is *the* major source of economic growth. Therefore, some conventional economists recommend policies that facilitate the investment and business activities of entrepreneurs over those of larger, less flexible and innovative, more staid and bureaucratic companies (such as many of those in the Russell 3000 Index). Behind these policies, are beliefs such as:–

- smaller start-up companies provide a relatively greater source of explosive growth and technology development; and

- small start-up companies are more labor intensive, and therefore create more jobs.[111]

However, the policies are all ultimately based on productivity and they have an unfortunate effect in the broader economy – they deflect attention from the more important question of participation in capital productiveness. While conventional economists remain almost entirely pre-occupied with productivity and earnings redistribution debates, virtually all capital continues to be acquired by existing owners and, at the same time, other people, who might be efficiently allowed to participate in capital acquisition on market principles, are being needlessly excluded.

Binary economics welcomes the contribution of entrepreneurs to growth and offers an economy that will make entrepreneurial

---

[111]   However, other conventional economists disagree. Within conventional economics, the result is an internecine war (based on different theories of productivity) among:– i) economists who believe that policies should favor small entrepreneurial companies; ii) those who believe that policies should favor a different mix of companies, or certain industries, or larger companies; and iii) those who favor a policy of laissez-faire neutrality.

investment more attractive.[112] Nevertheless, it objects to much conventional analysis of entrepreneurial activity. This is because the analysis *fails to disentangle the labor component from the independent capital component of growth.* As in the case of other human labor that co-operates with capital to do work, the work of the entrepreneur in conceiving of profitable products and services, and then in founding, financing, operating and selling of productive enterprizes to provide those goods is to be highly valued. However, the entrepreneur's work is *not* the work of the capital owned by the enterprize. Like the donkey, that capital does its own work and distributes its income through the private property system, except to the extent that its income is redistributed to others.

e)   Skills

The conventional concept of human productivity (rather than capital productiveness) as the primary cause of growth, embeds

---

[112] There is no shortage of entrepreneurial people with ideas of goods and services that people need and desire, nor a shortage of people with ideas as to new and better ways to produce them. Such people, however, usually lack the economic resources to implement their (often very practical and visionary) dreams. But there are two correctable barriers to the greater success of more entrepreneurs. Firstly, there is a lack of market-based (i.e., capital-productiveness-based) consumer demand to make more investment profitable. Secondly, there is *a lack of inexpensive investment funds* (because existing owners have only to compete among themselves, and therefore have a virtual monopoly on capital acquisition). Once the economy is structured to distribute the incremental earnings of capital productiveness on market principles to those expected to purchase its output, and once existing investors do not continue to hold a virtual monopoly in the safest capital acquisition investments of the largest companies, the business prospects of entrepreneurial persons and companies will increase, as will their attractiveness to investors.

yet another conventional idea – the notion that the operation of increasingly productive capital necessarily, or generally, or mostly, requires greater skills. Accordingly, some conventional economists use the concept of allegedly increased skills as a major basis for the productivity theory of growth. Forgetting that humans own their own labor but do not necessarily own capital, they fudge vocabulary by speaking of 'investment' in education and training as investment in 'human capital'.

Binary economists reject the increased skills theory and, more generally, the human capital theory behind it. They agree that the shift from labor intensive to capital intensive production sometimes requires higher skills which should certainly be compensated at competitive market rates. However, a more careful look at the productive processes that involve increasingly more productive capital indicates that, *per unit of output,* the overall employment of skills required of humans is *not* invariably greater, or even generally greater or mostly greater, than the skills required of people laboring by hand or with less productive capital. Conceiving, constructing, operating, maintaining, repairing and monitoring increasingly productive capital instruments and increasingly productive capital processes may require higher skills of *some* people. But the greater requisite skills are concentrated into fewer workers, leaving others with lower-skilled, lower-paying jobs or, all too often, with no jobs at all.

The truth is that, in terms of volume of work (both in the aggregate and per unit of output) the effect of increasingly capital intensive production requires lesser skills (sometimes routine, mindless and boring work) of many others. For example, today's truck drivers on the New Jersey Turnpike do *not* have indisputably superior skills to those necessary to lead a horse-drawn wagon from Philadelphia to New York in 1776 when Adam Smith wrote. Indeed, a strong case can be made for the proposition that it required much more skill to drive the average horse and wagon with 100 sacks from London to Brighton in

1800 than to drive the average truck carrying 1,000 sacks the same course today.[113]

To take another example, the operator of a great industrial revolution steam-hammer could stamp out cutlery by the thousand. But, in reality, the operator only had a *different* skill compared to that of the pre-industrial revolution metal-worker and, again in reality, that skill was at a level much *lower* than that of the metal-worker. When today, therefore, a hydraulic press engenders pressures of thousands of tons per square inch with the modern operator merely pressing buttons and watching dials, *the hydraulic press is doing most of the work* (and the modern operator is using much less skill than did the metal-worker).

Likewise, early elevators required more skill to operate than the later manual models which were larger, faster and did everything but provide buttons for the passengers to bypass the operator. Today's automatic elevators require no skill beyond the ability to push the right button.

Thus, in general, *the skills required for different tasks in the modern world of technological production are merely different, but not necessarily more valuable and productive, than the ones*

---

[113] Regarding the comparison of a horse-driver's skill with that of a lorry-driver, it should be understood that modern technology demands ever-changing, *different* skills. But these skills can often be acquired after a few months, even a few weeks training (and those months or weeks of training should be compared with the seven year apprenticeships and life-time learning of the past). So a willingness to learn new skills (which is an attitude of mind rather than a skill) is necessary nowadays but the new skills are not always indubitably at a higher level than those of the past. Even a modern commercial jet pilot may have no more skill than an early bush pilot and less skill than an early mariner. The real distinction is that today's jet pilot is an operator of a very sophisticated, very expensive capital instrument. Today's skills are *different* from those of the past. Moreover, it is hard to envisage any productive activity nowadays in which physical effort is more than in a comparable activity in 1800. See Louis & Patricia Kelso, *Democracy and Economic Power*, p. 17.

involved in earlier forms of production now rendered obsolete.
And even in cases where the skills are obviously greater such as
with the operation of word-processing rather than manual
typewriters, the fact remains that there is less labor work *per unit
of output.*

f) Replacing redistribution psychology with capital participation

Sometimes people cling to old paradigms because of a
psychological need. Sometimes the need is one of basic survival.
Sometimes it is a need to help the disadvantaged. Sometimes it is
simply the need to be needed, or the need not to be redundant. All
of these needs may be at work in the minds and hearts of those
who defend the homocentric productivity paradigm and the
associated redistribution psychology.

Thus, it is easy to understand how people (deeply concerned
about economically underpowered people who must increasingly
compete for work against increasingly more productive capital)
will look for creative, metaphorical, even fanciful ways to try to
rescue for working people a portion of their ebbing economic
power. Marx's theory of congealed labor was just such an
attempt. So are fuzzy analyses and rationalizations that confuse:–

- the valuable human contribution to production by way of
  invention, creativity, management, trusteeship,
  entrepreneurial activity, and increasing skills in some
  areas;
  with
- the independent work done by capital.

This fuzzy thinking (which is championed not only by
socialist, but also some conventional market economists who
support various forms of government redistribution) is born out
of:–

- an ignorance or denial as to who or what is actually
  creating the wealth;

and

- a lack of appreciation as to how people can most effectively and efficiently participate in wealth creation.

Binary economics agrees with those who believe that most people are unjustly excluded from the wealth-creating process and therefore deprived of a larger share of production. However, binary economics also teaches that the just and efficient remedy to exclusion from the wealth-creation process is the *inclusion* in that process rather than the redistribution of wealth and income.

10.   Recapitulation of productiveness

In summary, binary economists see the primary function of capital as replacing and vastly supplementing labor productiveness with capital productiveness. Given demand for its potential output, capital is increasingly employed to produce goods and services whenever that capital is expected to do any of the following profitably:–

- replace human labor in the wealth-creating process, doing work faster and cheaper;
- vastly supplement the amount of work that labor can do either alone or with less productive capital;
- do vast amounts of new work that labor alone can never do; and
- do work without human labor.

a)   The rise in capital productiveness

Therefore the donkey, truck, shovel, steam-shovel and elevator examples – and hundreds like them – serve to illustrate a systemic paradigm for understanding one of the most important economic aspects of the industrial revolution, i.e., the great increase in production and productive capacity is primarily the result of rising capital productiveness. The rise began in the dawn of civilization with the first rudimentary tool-making. It continues with increasing impact through the so-called high-technology and information revolutions of the present time. It will continue into the future and the aggregate rise over time is illustrated in Figure 5 – 10 below.

b)   The shift from labor-intensive to capital-intensive production

With the concept of independent productiveness as its foundation, the binary paradigm reveals a correlative feature of the increasing capital productiveness – the on-going shift from labor-intensive to capital-intensive production. Thus the same shift in productiveness from labor-intensive to capital-intensive that was apparent in individual tasks (like hole digging, sack carrying and people lifting) is revealed in the aggregate of all the work done economy-wide.

This shift is implicit in Figure 5 – 10 below which shows not only a great rising increase in capital productiveness compared to labor productiveness but also reveals that, as a percentage of total production, capital productiveness is increasing while labor productiveness is decreasing. The rising line demonstrates the percentage shift from labor productiveness to capital productiveness and it ascends sharply from 1900 onwards.

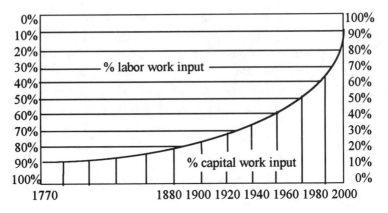

Fig. 5 – 10.   Increasing capital productiveness (and decreasing labor productiveness) in the production of goods and services.[114]

Thus, just as capital is doing ever more of the work, it is also earning (*and in efficient markets, its owners would be receiving*) ever more of the income.   In a market economy, the increasing percentage contribution of capital productiveness to overall production means an increasing claim on production earned by capital.

Likewise, the decreasing percentage contribution of labor productiveness to overall production means a decreasing claim on production earned by labor. The implications of these increasing and decreasing market claims are explored in the next chapter.

11. Some consequences of productiveness

If the productiveness concept provides a better understanding of capital, labor and production and of who or what is doing the

---

[114]   Adapted from a drawing by Louis and Patricia Kelso.   The percentages are estimated on the assumption that the value of productive inputs is measured in reasonably competitive markets.

extra work, a number of important consequences follow. Several will be discussed briefly below and explored more fully in later chapters.

a) In a market system, productiveness is a claim on production

In a free market, private property system, the producer has the right to keep what he or she produces and may voluntarily exchange that production for the production of others (either directly or through the medium of money). Thus, payments for real production are earned income; whereas payments for producing nothing (although made under the guise of wages) are merely disguised welfare. Accordingly, a review of the percentage contribution of each independent producer to the production of hauling sacks, digging holes, lifting people or any other work, will also (*in competitive markets*) reveal the market claim of each individual producer on the total joint production of capital and labor and also (if money is involved) the percentage claim of the exchange value of the production.

Therefore, looking at the hole-digging example, the labor claim on the value of every hole decreased from 100% of relatively few holes, to 25% of many more holes, to 5% of vastly more holes. And in the example of carrying sacks, the human earnings decline from 100% of the value of one sack-mile, to 5% of the value of 20 sack-miles, and then further declines to less than 1% of the value of fifty thousand sack-miles. The same is true in task after task and in the aggregate. As capital productiveness replaces labor productiveness and vastly increases total productiveness, capital's claim on the income of production increases, and labor's claim diminishes.

Thus the only way most people can maintain a competitive participation in the production of an economy is to increasingly participate by way of capital acquisition.

172   Binary Economics – *the new paradigm*

b) *The disappearance of real jobs*

As capital instruments and processes continually substitute
themselves for labor in the production process, while vastly
supplementing total output, the conventional economic promise
that workers who have lost their jobs can get equal jobs elsewhere
is true only for *some*. For increasing numbers, it is untrue. This
is because labor's percentage claim on total output is in *decline*.
Some workers, of course, will find new jobs, even better paying
jobs. Too many others, however, will only find lower paying jobs
or become permanently redundant. In other words, the promise
that technology creates (or may create) more work than it destroys
is generally a false promise. At best, it is true only for certain
industries and for certain periods of time.

Admittedly, the unfree market has been capable of creating
sufficient growth to give a small though real wage rise for those
lucky enough to be in the best jobs. That growth, however,
cannot be sustained because, in the aggregate, insufficient wages
are being distributed to a relatively shrinking worker base. This
is because conventional productivity is *only a rate (i.e. a ratio of
output per unit of input): it is not a sum*. It is only a theoretical
opportunity to earn a sum *if employed*. A person earns by way of
conventional productivity only *if employed* by time or piece.
Therefore the systemic effect of capital-labor substitution in the
unfree market is to concentrate greater productivity into fewer and
fewer workers *without* providing a correlative systemic means of
true production for those who have been sacked.[115]

Thus workers must beware of the seductive conventional
promise of higher worker productivity. Accordingly, by relying
only on conventional human productivity to win higher earnings

---

[115] The issue was succinctly put by an AFL-CIO officer in 1963 who
said, "For every $5,000 worth of investment you can get rid of one
worker. The machine has no vacations, no pensions and no fringe
benefits." (Cited by Louis & Patricia Kelso, in *Democracy and
Economic Power*, p. 141).

for their members, many workers and labor unions are following a long-term *losing* strategy. The pace of technological change is now so fast that humans are in reality contributing to a smaller and smaller proportion of the total wealth produced. The binary paradigm implies that the best way to make peace with the fact that capital eliminates labor work is for employees and unions to bargain and work politically for a competitive opportunity to participate in capital acquisition according to binary principles.

c) *The appearance of phoney jobs*

Despite the fact that for any given level of total output, as a result of increasing capital productiveness, the total number of work-hours necessarily required to produce that output *decreases*, conventional economics claims that unfree market growth will produce more jobs. But technological progress eliminates a lot of labor work and so conventional economics is really only promising mostly low-paying and temporary jobs. To try to compensate for the lack of proper jobs conventional economics has to 'create' *phoney* jobs (a disguised form of welfare benefit) and welfare benefit itself.

d) *Education and training in themselves will generally be insufficient to maintain competitive share of production*

Nowadays, young people, students and other adults are rightly exhorted to educate themselves and undergo training for the new skills which can elicit the productiveness of the new capital assets. Education and training are indeed essential for any society. But successful elicitation of capital productiveness *reduces* the number of real jobs and often reduces the wages of such jobs as remain. In other words, *labor's percentage claim on total output is in long-term decline*. Indeed, if the lack of skills were *really* the key to competitive participation in the economy by

174   Binary Economics – *the new paradigm*

most people, then increased skills training would not need to be systemically subsidized.

So education and training *in themselves* cannot enable labor to maintain a competitive share of total income.   People are deceiving themselves (and are being deceived) by the conventional claim that education and training will be sufficient for most people to maintain competitive participation in production.   The many millions of well-educated and trained people in the world today who cannot now get proper jobs would be wise to work to understand binary economics and then work to establish a binary economy.   And educators would be wise to start teaching it.

e)   In the unfree market growth is being suppressed

Over   time,   capital   assets   continually   increase   in productiveness   replacing   and   vastly   supplementing   labor productiveness.   Obviously,   sustained   growth   on   market principles *cannot* take place unless the capital-labor substitution process is linked *at the same time* with widespread private and individual   acquisition   of   the   assets   which   are   continually replacing labor input with capital input.   For sustained growth on private   property,   free   market   principles,   the   incremental productiveness of capital must be acquired individually by the masses of people expected to buy what capital increasingly produces.

In the unfree market, however, capital acquisition is restricted to existing owners so that the market distribution of capital income is insufficient to support consumption and thereby growth is suppressed.   The result is that the unfree market economy is doomed to continue to convulse unsteadily through periods of growth and slump, with low wage earners and those on the dole resisting (rather than facilitating) technological change.

f) It matters whether capital is narrowly or broadly owned by the people

The preoccupation of conventional schools with labor productivity leads them to claim that capital is important to growth *only* to the extent that it increases productivity. The schools further claim that the distribution of capital ownership in itself has no positive relationship to growth unless it somehow motivates the new owners personally to behave more productively. But one of the most important implications of binary productiveness is that the more broadly capital is acquired on market principles, the larger the economy will grow *independent of any conventional productivity growth.*

Based on productiveness, it makes a big difference whether capital is acquired by a tiny minority (who have few, if any, unsatisfied needs and wants) or is instead acquired by the great majority. The great majority (because they are now entirely dependent on only their labor and welfare for their income) find it more and more difficult to afford the goods and services which are increasingly the product of capital. If the great majority were increasingly to acquire capital, *they would spend more capital earnings on goods and services.* They would thus fuel a larger economy than if the new capital were to be acquired exclusively by the few rich. So, if the present private property system were to be opened on binary principles, a self-sustaining pattern of broader wealth distribution and growth would surely follow. In this way, the independent productiveness of capital can be fully unleashed to generate capital income for the very people expected to consume what capital increasingly produces.

Of course, some conventional economists will repeat an argument customarily directed to socialists who would redistribute capital and income to meet the needs of poor and working people. "Redistributing capital does not create more wealth. It merely spreads around pieces of the same pie!" those economists say.

But binary economics does *not* redistribute existing capital nor spread around pieces of the same pie. *Rather, a binary economy enables all people to compete efficiently for the acquisition of capital assets on market principles and thereby to create more pie for themselves and a larger more broadly distributed pie for society as a whole.*

12.   Conclusion

Once we understand binary productiveness and its revelation of the efficient power of capital to:–

- replace and vastly supplement human labor;
- to do vast amounts of work that labor can never do alone; and
- to do many things without any labor at all,

the question arises:– *Why does conventional economics continue to be so preoccupied with labor productivity?*

The question also arises as to why the unfree market economies continue to offer capital acquisition only for the already well-capitalized and jobs and welfare for everyone else. If capital is doing more and more of the work, then do not all people need to acquire more and more capital to maintain and increase their participation in production?

In the past, conventional unfree market economists have always side-stepped these critical questions by insisting on one or more of the following dubious propositions:–

- technology creates (or may create) more good jobs than it destroys and therefore people can optimally participate in production on market principles by way of their productivity;
- increased jobs require increased growth which requires increased productivity;
- increased productivity requires more capital investment;

- capital investment must generally be the investment of existing owners; and
- those who cannot competitively support themselves in the labor market (via productivity) can be helped only by public or private redistribution.

But the binary analysis based on productiveness reveals the following propositions:–

- technology does not create more good jobs than it destroys: those who own little or no capital cannot participate optimally in production unless they are enabled to acquire capital on market principles;
- increased efficiency and growth require increased capital productiveness;
- optimal capital investment requires open markets for capital acquisition in which all people may participate;
- capital can buy itself for all people individually (including poor and working people) more efficiently than it can buy itself exclusively for people who are already well-capitalized; and
- those who own little or no capital *can* be enabled to acquire capital on market principles without redistribution.

To understand these binary propositions it is necessary to explore productiveness more deeply, in particular its relationship to growth, distribution and finance. These matters are discussed in Chapter Six. They are developed more fully in Book III.

Book II

Chapter Six

Growth, distribution and finance

1. What causes the great growth in productive capacity and total economic growth?

Let us now return to the question of what, over the course of the industrial revolution, has been the main cause for the great growth in productive capacity and total economic output. As has been stated, conventional economic theory (from Marxism on the left to neo-classicism on the right) believes that it is primarily the humans who do the work and that capital assets, such as machines, serve primarily to make humans more productive.

Consequently, conventional market economics offers the productivity theory of growth to explain how unfree market capitalism out-performed state-sponsored communism. The productivity theory is also offered to 'prove' that the unfree market's performance is 'optimal' and to imply that a binary system, open to all people, will not work even better. However, all of these offers of alleged proof fail if the productivity theory of growth is false or significantly incomplete.

At present, society uncritically accepts the conventional view. When, for example, a newspaper article or television program refers to 'rising productivity', a generally rising human productivity is meant, and the contribution of the non-human capital assets is being largely, if not completely, ignored except as a function of increased human productivity. Based on their reading the newspapers, people who have little or no knowledge of economics are in effect told that growth comes *only* from increased productivity, and that capital is important *only* because it increases productivity. They are given no reason to suspect that capital is producing more and more of the wealth and that therefore all people need to be able, *and can be enabled*, to acquire capital of their own so that they might thereby participate in that growth on market principles.

In basing its growth foundation on human productivity, conventional market economics does not entirely ignore the productive effect of capital. It holds that the primary function of capital is to increase human productivity. Accordingly, conventional economics insists that capital should earn a return for its employment in production; but it theoretically reckons that return as a function of human productivity.

Furthermore, using productivity glasses, conventional economics sees growth as theoretically optimal, and more or less nearly optimal in practice. It insists on understanding the productive input of capital entirely as a function of productivity, and denies that the distribution of capital can cause growth except as a function of increased productivity.

Thus, conventional economics sees the same growth as binary economics sees, but explains it as a function of productivity. This is shown below:–

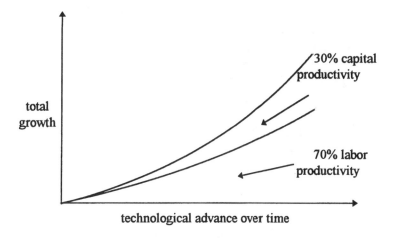

Fig. 6 – 1. Conventional economics explains the growth as a function of productivity.

Indeed, at its foundation, conventional economics views all growth as a function of productivity.

Binary theory directly challenges that view by recognizing the non-human capital assets as having an independent, ever-rising productive capacity of their own to create wealth.[116] Further, in task after task, it sees that 70%, 80% or 90% of wealth is now produced by capital. As far back as 1970, a United Nations report[117] estimated that, in the U.S.A. and Sweden, human labor contributed only to 10% of gross national product while technology and capital accounted for the other 90%. In some processes, capital accounts for nigh on 100% of the production. The figure of nigh on 100%, moreover, is particularly noteworthy

---

[116]   The first classical economist to appreciate the independent productive input of capital was Jean Baptiste Say in his celebrated *A Treatise on Political Economy*. See, for example, page xl of the 6th American edition. But Say's analysis was not understood by the economic thinkers who followed him. See Chapter Three.

[117]   Cited by Charles Levison in *Capital, Inflation and the Multi-Nationals*, (1971).

because it highlights the ability of some capital assets to create wealth with minimal human involvement.

As capital productiveness replaces labor productiveness and increases total productiveness, its augmenting effect on growth is illustrated below:–

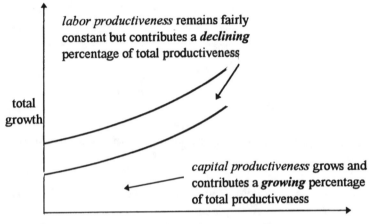

Fig. 6 – 2. Binary economics explains the growth as a function of productiveness.

Thus, with the progression of time, we see two phenomena occurring simultaneously:–

• capital is both replacing and vastly supplementing labor production per unit of production and in the aggregate; and
• total growth is substantially expanding.

From a binary perspective, the growth is fundamentally explained by the fact that capital is independently productive and is continually doing an ever greater portion of the work. Further, the productiveness of capital has a very potent distributive relationship to growth which is suppressed when capital markets are closed to most people as a practical matter. As a result of this positive distributive relationship, much of the capital that can buy itself profitably almost exclusively for less than 10% of the population can also buy itself even more profitably if the markets are structured so that all people are able to participate.

In contrast, at its foundation, conventional economics rejects the productiveness theory of growth.   Instead, conventional economics sees the same growth but explains it as a function of human productivity rather than capital productiveness.   It denies that the present closed capital markets can suppress growth because it denies that our capital markets are closed.

Further, rather than address squarely the consequences of the growing independent productiveness of capital and the present closed market's capital acquisition practices, conventional economics insists that the actual earnings of capital must be determined only by the present markets themselves.   And it does this despite the fact that the basic conditions of free market efficiency (starting with the requirement that there be no substantial barriers to market participation) are *not* met in any of the capital markets of the unfree market economies.

2.   The paradigm clash

It should therefore be clear to an objective observer that the conventional approach and the binary approach are locked in a remarkable paradigm conflict in explaining growth.   Both see a substantial increase in productive capacity and actual production in the last two hundred and fifty years, but they offer entirely different, and seemingly conflicting, explanations for that growth.

In an economy like that of the U.S.A., conventional economics sees labor as producing a fairly steady 70%+ of the wealth, because the human productivity claims 70%+ of the income on the aggregate national markets.   Conventional economics further assumes the markets are competitive and therefore accurate in their pricing.

In contrast, binary economics points out the falsity of the notion that present markets are competitive and accurate in their pricing. Rather the binary economist recognizes that capital is producing at least 70% of the wealth, and will continue to produce an even greater percentage as capital productiveness continues to replace and vastly supplement labor productiveness.

So, if binary productiveness explains production and growth better than conventional productivity, it should be clear by now that the present overall earnings figures for labor and capital do *not* reflect the true percentage contributions to the physical creation of wealth. Very roughly, at present 70 - 75% of overall earnings go to labor and 25% to capital. But, in a binary economy, the figures would be *the other way round* – 70 - 75% to capital and 25% to labor.

3.   The   conventional   'free   market'   argument

a)   Factor shares

In an attempt to refute the binary view that capital is now producing over 70% of the wealth, conventional economists point to widely cited statistics of the economy of the U.S.A. which show that over 70% or so of present overall earnings consistently goes to human labor. Then they assume that the 70% results from more or less free and competitive markets for labor and capital. Indeed, recourse to the assumption of more or less competitive markets is the ultimate trump card in the conventional economist's deck.[118]   Some neo-classicists use it imperiously. But

---

[118]   This was the primary objection offered by Nobel Laureate Paul Samuelson in dismissing binary theory as a crankish fad – *Patrimony for the Progress of Puerto Rico: Hearings on H.R. 1708 Before the Senate*, 118 Cong. Rec., 20,207, 8 June, 1972, (statement by Paul A. Samuelson, read into the record by Senator Harris). Professor Samuelson thinks a true free market exists today and so thinks that,

even scholars within those schools which strenuously question the extent of present market efficiency in the internecine debate within conventional economics, also employ the same trump card to try to silence outsiders (including binary economists) who *seriously* question present market efficiency.

Conventional economists further note that the more or less steady 70% share of a growing (and, they allege, optimal) pie has held steady for over 150 years. This more or less constant percentage, they claim, indicates that capital productiveness cannot be producing an ever greater portion of the wealth, but rather that capital and labor are each contributing more at a steady rate as determined by efficiency-optimizing market mechanisms.

It is noteworthy, however, that this constancy of 'factor shares' of national income may be interpreted differently so as to undermine the very efficiency on which its assumed validity rests, and therefore to undermine the credibility of the claimed 70% labor claim on production. Because, over time, markets can be expected to exhibit fluctuations, this constancy has therefore been a source of wonder to conventional economists. Indeed, it has been dubbed one of the curious mysteries of capitalism in practice[119] which is to say that conventional economists cannot explain it *consistently with the unproven assumption that present markets are essentially free and competitive.*

The conventional reliance on the national income figures based on assumed market efficiency is subject to other objections that have validity without regard to binary theory. For example, if labor's present 70% claim on national income really is earned

---

since labor gets about 70-75% of total earnings at present, labor must be doing 75% of the total work input. Samuelson's basic position is that of *all* conventional economists (and politicians) who think they live in a free market when, in reality, they live in an unfree one. Samuelson, *Economics*, (11th edition, 1980, p. 181).

[119] Robert M. Solow, *A Skeptical View on the Constancy of Factor Shares*, (American Economic Review, Sept. 1958, pp. 917-949).

income, and not redistributed income, why has America lost so many industrial jobs to foreign economies? Statistics show that, as a result of lower wages paid in foreign countries, employment in selected machine-producing industries declined from 679,500 in 1977 to 402,400 in 1987.[120] Thus, the present 70% figure is padded because it includes compensation for unproductive work (such as when elevator operators are paid to operate elevators that can just as well operate themselves in response to passenger direction).

Furthermore, where companies find cheaper labor markets they also invest in new, more capital intensive production systems further to minimize labor costs. Thus the shift to cheaper labor markets occasions a further investment in capital so as to undermine further the economic efficiency of that 70%. And once the question of market efficiency on an international level is considered, it becomes clear that every nation protects and supports major portions of its favored domestic industries (which includes the internal labor and capital markets) to counterbalance similar activities of other nations. Thus, whatever the rhetoric of 'free trade', the statistics relied upon by conventional economists to prop up the productivity explanation of growth are the product of massive state intervention intended to support domestic industries and labor markets (including wage rates) and all the while, facilitating capital acquisition for capital owners, but only jobs and welfare for everyone else.

---

[120] *Census of Manufacturers*, U.S. Commerce Department (1987). The areas of work included:– production of machine tools (cutting, forming and accessories); power-driven tools; turbines and turbine generator sets; internal combustion engines, equipment and machinery; motors and generators; office machines; construction, mining, oil and gas; rolling mills; and textile machinery.

b)   The unfree market is not a true free market even within the conventional definition

A moment's reflection establishes that the existing labor and capital markets of the unfree market *cannot* be free and efficient because they do not meet the well-known and necessary conditions for market freedom and efficiency. These conditions include:–

i)   barrier-free market entry;

ii)   numerous buyers and sellers;

iii)   freedom from collusion among market participants;

iv)   freedom from coercion;

v)   negligible transactions costs;

vi)   perfect information.

Applying those conditions, the unfree market *cannot* be a free or an efficient market because:–

a)   in the most important market of all (i.e. that for capital) 90% or more of the populace (having no collateral) are *in practice* excluded. Therefore condition i) above fails.

b)   there are *not* numerous buyers and sellers of capital because 90% of the populace are not buying and selling.[121] Therefore condition ii) above fails.

---

[121]   What is 'numerous' is, of course, relative. Binary economists readily concede that the effective number of buyers and sellers of capital in the unfree market economies (which number never includes more than 10% of the population) might be characterized as 'numerous' compared to the number of capital participants in a communist economy (which involves only the state and the black market participants). Binary economists also readily agree that the greater number of capital market participants is a driving force behind the relative efficiency of the unfree market economies compared to communist economies.   Indeed, this is but an expression of the distributive relationship between capital and growth. But participation by 10% of the population is not optimal participation, and it does not

c)   by maintaining a market infrastructure that enables only some people to participate efficiently in capital acquisition, the present participants in the capital market (with the help of the government) *do*, in effect, collude to ensure the exclusion of others.   Therefore condition iii) above fails.

d)   the second most important market (i.e. that for labor) is subject to massive coercion, open and disguised.   When people are excluded from vital participation in production they will feel coerced to redistribute the earnings of others. They will in turn employ their energies to coerce producers to relinquish a share of their production.   Coercion becomes a matter of survival.   The low dividends which companies pay out in the unfree market reflect that, through governmental, trade union, political and other coercion, capital is denied most of its true earnings. Therefore condition iv) above also fails.

e)   transactions costs are not negligible.   Taxes, for example, are an important element in transactions costs. Taxes exist largely as a result of concentrated capital ownership and the consequent need for earnings redistribution.   Therefore condition v) above also fails.

f)   market participants inevitably lack perfect information.   At present, the most important systemic information they lack is an understanding of the binary premise that capital has a distributive relationship to growth.   Once they come to understand the premise, many market participants will want to capitalize on it.   But at present condition vi) above fails in an important way (although it is a way that can be corrected).

Thus all these conditions for free market efficiency, widely accepted by conventional economists, fail.   As a result, the claim of conventional economics that the 70% figure for labor's

---

produce optimal efficiency.   Optimal efficiency requires effective individual market participation by 100% of the population.

earnings is an accurate measure of productive input collapses even when judged by the very conditions held out by conventional economics. Therefore the best that conventional economics can offer to support its statistics is *the claim of relative efficiency which is no more than a claim of relative inefficiency*, with no basis for determining how inefficient or efficient the capital and labor markets really are.

4.   *Capital markets cannot be competitive unless they are open to everyone*

From a binary perspective, the conventional argument that labor is producing approximately 70 - 75% of the wealth misses the productive essence of the industrial revolution. The argument misses precisely because it is based *on human productivity rather than on capital productiveness*. Failing to understand that growth is primarily a function of capital productiveness rather than labor productivity, conventional economics consequently fails to understand that capital has a distributive relationship to growth and that universal, individual participation in capital acquisition on market principles is an essential condition for market efficiency.

Without effective access to individual capital acquisition on market principles, most people will be forced to exercise political and social power in strategies to divert and capture some of the income increasingly earned by capital. Consequently people inevitably get up to every stratagem they can in the perennial endeavour to compensate for their lack of ownership of what really creates the wealth – the capital assets. In other words, if people are excluded from the capital markets, not only is the earnings figure of capital falsified but the earnings figure of labor is bound to be falsified as well.

This diversion and capture (i.e. redistribution) of capital income to create phoney labor income is accomplished through real and pretended work (which is disguised welfare), various subsidies, earnings redistribution and explicit dole. The redistribution of the income of capital is illustrated in Figure 6 – 3 below:–

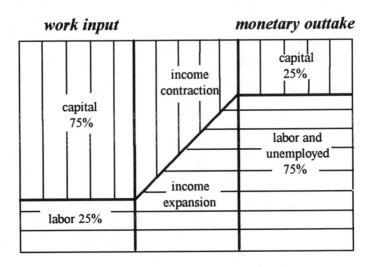

Fig. 6 – 3. In the unfree market, work input does not equal monetary outtake.[122]

In other words, the binary view based on productiveness holds that the present approximate 70 - 75% overall wage claim on production is not the result of competitive markets. Rather it results from a complex of social conventions and legislation necessary to distribute a portion of the income that would automatically be distributed to capital in an open private property system. Thus, in an industrial economy that denies most people

---

[122] The figure is an adaptation of one drawn by Louis and Patricia Kelso who use actual work input percentages of 90% (capital) and 10% (labor) and actual monetary outtake percentages of 22% (capital) and 78% (labor and unemployed).

effective access to capital acquisition on market principles, the wages of labor are inevitably artificially inflated, and the wages of capital are inevitably both artificially disguised and diminished with the result that the allocational and operational efficiency touted by unfree market economists is severely compromised.

Binary economists are not alone in questioning the efficiency of the capital and labor markets of the unfree market economies. Many people – even some conventional economists – are also prepared to doubt seriously the efficiency.[123] But readers should bear in mind that the binary disagreement on the extent to which present markets are efficient, is merely ancillary to the more fundamental, novel, and important points of disagreement between the conventional paradigm and the binary one viz., on the fundamental matters of:–

- who or what is actually creating the wealth;
- where the increased productive capacity really lies; and
- what is to be done about it.

These are fundamental points on which conventional productivity analysis and binary productiveness contradict each other.

Thus, if valid, the binary basis for doubting conventional market efficiency (i.e., that capital productiveness and not labor productivity is the primary source of production and growth in the unfree market economies and that capital has a potent distributive relationship to growth) is uniquely powerful. It not only enables binary economists to refute the claim of conventional market economists that markets are entirely, optimally, or more or less efficient; but also, and more importantly, it enables binary economists to offer specific and unique means to open the markets so as to make them work efficiently and profitably for all people

---

[123] There is a growing recognition among conventional economists that the markets for labor and capital are not efficient. See, for example, *The Economics of Imperfect Competition and Employment*, George R. Feiwel, ed., (1989). See also *3 The New Palgrave, A Dictionary of Economics*, J. Eatwell, M. Milgate & P. Newman, eds., (1987) at pp. 831-833, 837-841.

individually by enabling them to acquire shares of the increasing productiveness of capital on market principles.

5.   *Productiveness and distribution*

The question of who or what is producing the wealth is fundamental to growth and distributive justice in a market economy.   Conventional economic strategies attempt to promote growth and distributive justice via productivity and earnings redistribution.   Binary strategies seek to promote growth and distributive justice via capital productiveness and a truly open private property system which makes earnings redistribution unnecessary.

In this section, we explore the binary approach to distribution based on productiveness, compare it to the conventional approach based on productivity, and consider some of the private property implications that can either enhance or suppress the growth potential of independent capital productiveness.   The section thereby provides a further explication of the fifth power of capital set out previously:–

Capital can distribute the income to purchase its output within an open private property system on market principles.

a)   *Production is income*

In a free market private property system, those who produce the wealth are entitled to own that wealth.   Thus, fortified by the logic of fair exchange and the institution of private property, in a true free market economy, production and income are *not* isolated phenomena mediated by state intervention, but two sides of the same market equation.   In other words, *production becomes income*: and private property in labor or capital production entitles the owner of the labor or capital to the income earned from that production. That income can then be exchanged for other production or for money to buy other production. Therefore, pay for production is real income; whereas pay for non-production is redistributed income.

b)   With increasing productiveness comes increasing income on market principles

Binary economics understands that the great historical growth stems primarily from the fact that *capital productiveness replaces labor productiveness and vastly increases total productiveness*. Because income is pay for production, binary economics recognizes that people can earn sufficient market incomes from the growth of capital productiveness (sufficient for individual economic well-being and sustained growth) *only* if they have effective participation in capital acquisition. In other words, just as capital productiveness is producing an increasing proportion of the economic growth, so people can participate in that growth on market principles only through capital acquisition. Accordingly, if real income is pay for productiveness (i.e., work done), then capital not only increasingly does more and more of the work, it can also increasingly distribute the income to purchase what it produces.

Thus, given the distributive power of capital, conventional economists are entirely wrong when they teach that the pattern of capital acquisition has no relation to growth unless it is reflected in increased productivity. To the contrary, it matters greatly who can acquire capital on market principles because capital has not only a productive power, but also a life-supporting *distributive* power that is essential to the economic well-being of all individuals, and of society as a whole. Therefore, binary economics welcomes capital (which embodies invention and technological change) and provides the practical mechanism, on market principles, to enable all people to acquire a share of the growing capital productiveness (and therefore growing capital income) that replaces labor productiveness (and its relatively diminishing labor income).

6.   The third lesson of the elevator

The inseparable connection between independent binary productiveness and market distribution (which conventional economic analysis obscures and ignores) brings us to the third lesson of the elevator[124] (which is also the fifth power of capital) set forth in the previous chapter:–

Capital can buy itself on credit and pay for its cost of acquisition out of its future earnings.

This lesson is helpfully highlighted by the elevator story, but it is true for all well conceived capital investments. In other words, in considering the third lesson of the elevators, it is helpful to conceive of the effects of the elevator acquisition as a paradigm – a fundamental example of capital acquisition that can enable all people, individually, to acquire a growing capital estate that can independently do work and therefore increasingly supplement their labor income with capital income.

The story of the shift from manual to automatic elevators starting in 1950 when the market decision to acquire elevators was first proposed, reveals that the automatic elevators succeeded in replacing and supplementing the labor productiveness with increasing capital productiveness while minimizing overall costs of production.   Moreover, *they did so for their corporation's shareholders competitively using borrowed money on the promise of its future earnings.*   This was the essence of the capital acquisition plan.   As the capital repays its acquisition costs, the company would be increasing its rate of return, the

---

[124] The first two lessons of the elevator were that capital can:– i) *do work that labor working alone* (or labor working with simple hand tools) *can never practically do*;   ii) *do work with virtually no human labor involved* (as in the form of robots and other automation).

bank would earn interest on the money lent, and the shareholders would increase their equity ownership as well as their rate of return on equity. The same dollar of earnings that repays a dollar of the indebtedness to the bank, simultaneously pays for an ownership interest (for the company's shareholders) in the capital acquired (because the capital acquired is that much less subject to the debt incurred to purchase it).

There is nothing particularly mysterious about the process. It is just one of the credit mechanisms of corporate finance regularly employed by private companies (using borrowed money) to acquire the capital that replaces and vastly supplements labor productiveness, while shareholders *simultaneously* acquire a stock interest in the capital acquired. In this way, billions of dollars in private capital are every year acquired for existing shareholders using non-recourse corporate credit.

In the case of the automatic elevators, the capital acquisition occurred because particular market participants (who are players by reason of their private property rights) had a confluence of interest in entering into a voluntary transaction. Those participants were:–

- the *company*, represented by its managers who believed the elevators would increase output while reducing overall costs, and repay their acquisition cost in a competitive period;[125]
- *bank lenders* who believed the new elevators were a creditworthy capital acquisition; and
- *shareholders* who had confidence in the transaction.

The confluence of interest came about because these market participants noted the potential productiveness of the new automatic elevators and the associated projected capital earnings. Unless the participants had had a reasonable belief and confidence

---

[125] Although the managers may not have an investor's interest in the financial outcome of the capital investment, if the capital fails to perform competitively, the managers responsible for deciding on the transaction will have to face the consequences of owner dissatisfaction.

in the projected capital earnings, the capital acquisition (of the automatic elevators) would not have occurred.

If everything goes according to plan, legal title to the elevators will eventually be fully owned by the company, but the ultimate claim on the earning power of (i.e., private property in) the elevators will be owned *by the shareholders*. In a closed private property system, the incremental productiveness of capital (which both replaces labor productiveness and vastly increases total productiveness) will generally be acquired by existing shareholders. These shareholders do not have (to anywhere near the same degree) the same unsatisfied consumer needs and wants as the people who have been, and who continue to be, put out of the old work and kept out of the new work that capital is doing. Inevitably, the great disparity between:–

- the pattern of distribution in increasing capital productiveness to those who do not need it for consumption;
  and
- the distribution of unsatisfied consumer needs and wants of those people who are excluded from capital acquisition,

suppresses growth and perpetuates economic injustice. These matters are considered in Chapter Nine.

7. Business failure, risk and insurance

But everything does not always go according to plan. There is *always* the risk of financial failure. While some companies were investing in concepts that succeeded like automatic elevators, others were investing in concepts that failed like the American Edsel automobile.

One of the theoretical foundations of financial economics is that this risk of investment failure is *efficiently* priced in efficient markets. On this theoretical point, conventional economics and binary economics agree. Shareholders require higher returns for riskier investments; and bankers charge higher interest rates for riskier loans. Firms and individuals spread and minimize their risks sometimes by diversifying their operations and investments and, sometimes, by specifically purchasing insurance against the risk. Thus firms like Lloyds of London insure or 'underwrite' risky transactions so that in the event of their failure, participants need not suffer the full consequence and are therefore more able to participate. Therefore, insurance against the financial failure of transactions enables firms and individuals to participate in transactions from which they would otherwise be excluded because they cannot afford to bear the risk of loss.

8.   Loan insurance

Another form of insurance is *loan insurance* which insures the lender against the failure of the borrower to repay the loan. Such loan insurance is particularly helpful for borrowers who have insufficient collateral to support an acquisition loan even though the planned capital expansion looks profitable. In effect, *the loan insurance serves as a substitute for collateral*. Loan insurance therefore has the potential for helping to level the playing field between those who do, and do not, start with assets to use as collateral.

It is significant to note that loan insurance does *not* insure the borrower for risk of loss should the capital fail to pay for its cost of acquisition. It only insures the lender against losses on the acquisition loan. However, with loan insurance, a borrower who would otherwise have been excluded from a potential market acquisition is enabled to compete with others for that acquisition.

At present, through legislation in some unfree market economies, loan insurance is sometimes available to special borrowers in government-favored activities, particularly in the area of international trade, defense contracting, and small and minority businesses. Nevertheless, loan insurance is not yet generally available to insure banks for general corporate lending that would support corporate capital acquisition plans such as the one discussed above for purchasing automatic elevators. (Rather in such lending, to minimize the risk, banks more typically spread their risk of lending by diversifying their risk in mutual risk-sharing arrangements with other banks in the form of loan syndications).

More significantly, from a binary perspective, such loan insurance (which binary economists call 'capital credit insurance') is not yet generally available to enable people without capital to participate in the capital acquisition plans of prime credit-worthy companies. But, based on binary productiveness, the principle of loan insurance can indeed be profitably applied to such situations on efficient market principles.

In fact, the principle has been applied to loans for homes in the U.S.A. in the form of the Federal Housing Administration which for over six decades has profitably enabled American home buyers to acquire homes on credit by insuring the lenders against risk of loss for a fee generally no more than 2% of the amount borrowed. Given a binary understanding of a market economy, there is no reason why this loan insurance function cannot be combined systemically with time-tested principles of corporate finance and risk diversification to open capital acquisition to all people individually on market principles.

9.   *Pricing the risk of business failure*

The changes necessary to open the present capitalist system to enable all people to compete effectively for capital acquisition are modest, but fundamental and powerful. They will be described in Chapters Seven and Eight. Until those changes are made, essentially all capital acquisition will take place in the existing closed private property system. As a result, after all the risk-sharing arrangements are negotiated, the risk of business failure associated with capital acquisition is, in conventional theory, ultimately borne by existing shareholders and is reflected in the equity return demanded by investors. If the markets for capital and labor are substantially open and optimally efficient, then this return will be competitively priced to compensate for the risk of business failure. However, if the markets are operating suboptimally, the risk of business failure will be unnecessarily over-priced, and capital investment will be unnecessarily kept scarce. The risk is overpriced because existing owners have to compete only with other existing owners for capital acquisition.

Binary economists, moreover, believe that the present risk of business failure is unnecessarily high. This is because the present primary reason for business failure is inadequate consumer demand to purchase readily producible goods and services which in turn is the result of the closed markets for capital acquisition. The high risk is then inefficiently subsidized by the governments of the unfree market economies primarily for the benefit of existing owners. However, opening markets to all potential competitors will enhance investment efficiency. These matters are further considered below.

a) Overpricing resulting from narrow distribution

The risk of business failure in the unfree market economies is unnecessarily high (and so unnecessarily overpriced) because, while there is chronic excess productive capacity, there is an accompanying failure to distribute the acquisition of the incremental productiveness of capital on market principles to those expected to purchase what capital increasingly produces. And the main conceptual impediment to correcting this failure in market distribution is the mistaken belief that labor produces most of the wealth because the belief falsely implies that sufficient income for sustained growth can be efficiently distributed via wages and earnings.

b) Overpricing resulting from narrow ownership

The risk of business failure is overpriced because the pool of effective competitors participating in capital acquisition is limited to existing owners. But, in the binary economy, the credit mechanisms which presently enable capital to buy itself on borrowed money for existing owners will be more properly structured so as to be more efficiently available to all people on market principles. There will then be increased competition among investors for credit-worthy capital acquisition investment opportunities.

Thus, once poor and middle class people are able to compete effectively for capital acquisition, then existing owners will no longer enjoy an effective monopoly in the relatively risk-free steady annual capital accretion of major corporations such as those among the three thousand largest in the U.S.A. This will eliminate a significant monopolistic element in the present system. With greater competition for credit-worthy capital acquisition in the binary economy in which all people are vested with effective market rights to acquire capital, existing owners may have to turn to investments bearing greater risks (for which they will be commensurately rewarded) thereby making more investment available to entrepreneurial firms. In the binary economy, the scarcity premium on *financial* capital will decline, but more *real* capital will become profitable as the distributive principle of binary growth takes root and begins to bear fruit in the form of spendable capital income for its new owners after the capital has paid for itself.

c) Inefficient subsidy

The present inefficient governmental subsidies occur in response to the closed unfree market's failure to distribute the income necessary to purchase what it produces. The subsidies are attained by a combination of protectionist and redistributionary measures (reflected in taxing, spending, labor, bankruptcy and monetary policies) designed to keep a sufficient number of major companies solvent and a sufficient number of people sufficiently satisfied in jobs and wealth and so prepared to vote to keep the government in power. In the unfree market economies, these policies result in a roller-coaster ride bumping from boom, to inflation, to slump, and then back again but always with endemic inflation, unemployment and fear of depression.

The binary economy, however, would open market mechanisms to enable market participants to price the risk of business failure (in the form of commercial capital credit insurance) competitively in markets in which everyone can participate effectively for capital acquisition. In this way, the independent productiveness of capital (which enables it to buy itself on borrowed money for the well-capitalized in our present private property system) can also be harnessed to work for poor and middle class people.

10. Conclusion

Based on our discussion, readers should now be having some intimations that, as compared with the conventional analysis founded on productivity, the binary analysis founded on productiveness provides an entirely different understanding not only of growth and poverty, but also of capital-labor substitution, income distribution and the long-run efficient and just operation of markets.[126] With even greater practical significance (as

---

[126] Most people remain poor in the unfree market economies no matter how hard they work because they have not acquired a viable share of the capital productiveness that continually replaces labor

opposed to being merely another academic or theoretical way of thinking about things), binary economics offers a concrete strategy for establishing a just and broadly affluent economy.

That just and broadly affluent economy is *not* one that undermines or rejects the private property and market mechanisms that enabled the unfree market economies to outperform and defeat state-sponsored communism. Rather it is one that improves the mechanisms for the individual benefit of everyone by opening them in a way that yields growth and distributive justice which will make the world a better place for everybody.

The strategy for achieving that economy is explored further in the next chapter.

---

productiveness and vastly increases total productiveness. Unfree market economies start and stall from boom to bust because they fail to distribute to most people on market principles the income necessary to purchase what the economies can produce. Capital and labor markets become increasingly inefficient in their pricing as people are increasingly excluded from capital acquisition. Capital substitution for labor is suppressed in a closed private property system and optimized in an open one.

Book III

The strategy and structure of the binary economy

Book II presented the new binary paradigm. It offered an explanation of, and prescription for, growth. Book III sets out the practical application of the new paradigm. Briefly, the binary strategy is to establish by democratic means an open private property system and a true free market so that everyone can acquire efficient capital assets with the earnings of capital on market principles and thereby enjoy the foundation for widespread, individual affluence and sustainable growth.

After explaining the strategy of the binary economy and lightly setting out the structure in Chapter Seven, the structure is developed more fully in Chapter Eight.

Chapter Nine then focuses on the critical promise of binary growth. It explains how the independent productiveness of capital and its broadening distribution work together to produce that growth and thereby provide the free market basis for increasingly widespread affluence.

Book III

Chapter Seven

The binary strategy

1. Different paradigms produce different strategies

It should come as no surprise that different paradigms produce fundamentally different strategies. Thus if growth is primarily a function of human productivity and if capital increases human productivity (as conventional economics alleges), then a private property system that fosters capital acquisition only for the well-capitalized with only jobs and welfare programs for everyone else, may be the best possible course.

But if growth is primarily a function of capital productiveness and its distribution (as binary economics holds), the conventional economic strategies built on a closed private property system will only perpetuate massive poverty, as they have in the past. This is because they fail to enable most people to earn on market principles sufficient income to buy what is increasingly produced by capital. The conventional approach enables capital acquisition on market principles (and therefore provides increased productive power and capital income) primarily for wealthy people who, unlike the poor and middle class, do not need additional income to support their consumer needs and desires.

At the same time, the conventional approach needlessly denies effective capital participation to those who need it most (namely, the more than 90% of people in every economy who lack an appreciable income-producing capital estate). From a productiveness standpoint, these are the very people who need capital income so that the society can achieve the abundance and leisure promised by the industrial revolution.

The conventional productivity paradigm, therefore, has led to an economic strategy of government-promoted capital investment incentives for the capital owners with only jobs and welfare for everybody else. The conventional strategy, common to all the unfree market economies, denies capital participation to most people, who increasingly need it, and instead restricts their economic participation only to competing for (indeed, frantically scrambling for) jobs when there are never enough jobs, particularly well-paying jobs, to go round.

Of course, many conventional market economists promise that technology creates more jobs than it destroys. The higher productivity, they allege, will make workers more employable in the larger economy. However, the massive and growing welfare dependence and the 'structural adjustments', 'rationalizations' and 'down-sizings' of the 1980s and 1990s (euphemisms for large numbers of permanent lay-offs) belie this promise. Evidence of higher productivity but lower wages, also belie this promise.[127] Surveying the future, moreover, the lay-offs, rationalizations and down-sizings look ominously set to continue.[128]

---

[127] *Productivity Is All, But It Doesn't Pay Well.* Keith Bradsher, (*The New York Times*, June 25th, 1995, p. 4-E).
[128] See Jeremy Rifkind, *The End of Work: The Decline of the Global Labor Force and the Dawn of the Post Market Era*, (G.P. Putnam & Sons, New York, 1995).

What is more important, binary analysis reveals that the critical question is not whether technology (embodied in productive capital) creates more jobs than it destroys. Rather the question is whether technology can *ever* create *enough* jobs when its purpose and overwhelming effect are to reduce the labor content of work by replacing and supplementing labor productiveness with capital productiveness and thereby to produce and earn more with capital rather than labor.

Although conventional economics promises most people greater market participation in production *only* by way of higher productivity, binary logic shows that, as capital productiveness replaces labor productiveness and greatly adds to total productiveness, it inevitably concentrates any higher human productivity into *relatively fewer* workers per unit of production. Consequently, the labor content of total production is reduced, and therefore labor's market claim on that production is also reduced. Thus as capital productiveness replaces labor productiveness and greatly adds to total productiveness, it thereby reduces labor content per unit of output. *Labor's aggregate percentage market claim on aggregate production must therefore also decrease.*

This is not to say that capital productiveness does not often create new jobs, some of them very high-paying. Nor is it to deny notable examples where capital has opened markets to a valuable new range of human services. Nor is it to deny that, in the first years of a binary economy, *more* jobs could well be available because of the growth effects. Rather, it is to stress that the per-unit and aggregate effect of increased capital productiveness is to reduce the labor content of production and thereby to reduce the market claim of labor as labor on production. Per unit of output, and in the aggregate, the purpose and effect of technological advance is to eliminate labor content while increasing capital content. The aggregate result is continually *to eliminate (labor) work and jobs.*

Thus, exclusive reliance on a jobs strategy to enable most people to survive and flourish may have been the best hope in a pre-industrial economy, but it misses the point of the industrial revolution. Even in the most affluent of the unfree market economies, most jobs produce little more than subsistence and very few (less than one in ten) produce robust economic security. In contrast, affluence is almost always the product of capital.

So, according to binary logic, as production becomes more capital intensive, the way in which each individual participates in production must likewise become more capital intensive, in the form of individual ownership of capital. Thus the binary logic is in harmony with the purpose of the industrial revolution – *to produce more with more capital work and less labor work.*

Therefore, one essential purpose of a just private property system, in support of a democratic, industrial market economy, must be to enable all people individually to acquire capital productiveness on market principles as it replaces labor productiveness and increases total productiveness. In short, the only democratic, true free market solution to the distributional and growth consequences of the independent productiveness of capital is to eliminate what amounts to an effective monopoly on capital acquisition (now reserved for existing owners under our closed private property system) by opening the capital acquisition markets to all people on market principles.

Thus it can be seen that, if the binary paradigm has the better explanation of the industrial revolution and industrial growth, then the growing productiveness of capital has profound consequences:–

- To participate in the affluence of capital productiveness on market principles, most humans must come to acquire capital.

- As long as the present effective monopoly on capital acquisition prevails, most humans will continue to have comparatively little or even no true earning power. Without true earning power, most people will be forced to demand, in wages and welfare, a redistribution of the earnings from capital that they are needlessly excluded from acquiring. As a result, the true free market is grossly distorted with resulting inefficiency.

- If the increasing productiveness of capital is not acquired by those expected to consume what it produces, the income from production will not be linked with income for consumption. By reason of the law of supply and demand, growth is thereby suppressed and an unnatural scarcity is institutionalized, where relative bounty would otherwise prevail.
- By ending the present monopoly on capital acquisition, markets will operate more efficiently, and the unnatural scarcity that now prevails in the world will be increasingly replaced by relative bounty.

2. Conventional corporate finance does not work for most people

In an industrial economy in which capital productiveness continues to replace and vastly supplement labor productiveness, there is an obvious need for a private property system that enables all people to participate increasingly in the market for capital acquisition. Unfortunately, the present private property system is structured to exclude most people from effective capital participation no matter how hard they work.

The structural defect in our present undemocratic private property system is the closed market for capital assets dominated by an equally closed system of corporate finance. In all the unfree market industrial economies, most productive capital is now held by corporations, and its ownership is represented by common stock. In the U.S.A., for example, the largest three thousand corporations (represented by the Russell 3000 Index) own over 95% of the nation's investable non-residential capital. The corporations (and therefore their shareholders) then acquire new capital assets with the earnings of the capital acquired. In many cases, they do so by obtaining a secured loan usually using existing assets to provide the security or 'collateral' to support the loan.   The new capital assets, bought with credit, subsequently make repayment of the loan out of their earnings.   Of the billions of dollars of capital acquired each year, virtually all of it is paid for with the earnings of capital, and much of it is acquired with borrowed money, i.e. credit.

Thus the logic of present corporate finance is to enable a corporation (and so, its existing shareholders) to acquire capital assets *before* it has earned the money to pay for them and simultaneously to enable its shareholders to acquire an equity interest in those assets by paying for them out of the earnings of the assets so acquired.   By this logic, the well-capitalized get richer even as they sleep.   But others do not.   This is primarily because they do not have access to sufficient collateral to support credit for loans to purchase productive capital assets with the loans repaid from the future earnings of the assets so acquired.

So the existing system of corporate finance is structured to work primarily for the well-capitalized (who have the necessary collateral) and, at the same time, is structured *not* to work nearly as effectively for anybody else.   This is why, over the years, capital assets, in all unfree market countries, have remained narrowly owned.   This is why it takes capital to acquire additional capital or, in more superficial terms, why it takes money to make money.   This is also why there are great discrepancies in wealth within societies; why there is chronically over-abundant supply along with chronically insufficient demand; and why, in parts of some countries, social order is collapsing or has collapsed.   The truth is that the conventional prescription for acquiring capital – work hard, save and invest wisely – is mere rhetoric and is wholly unrealistic for most people whose labor income is barely enough to make ends meet.   Those people need a new system of corporate finance which enables them to participate in capital acquisition on market principles.

3.   The   binary   goal   of   universal competence

In the second chapter, we spoke of the first goal of universal binary competence.   By this we mean that everybody should individually own a capital estate producing a substantial income. In other words, they should become binary capitalists.

a)   'Capitalist' defined

In some circles, capitalists are glorified but in others the word 'capitalist' is a dirty word with nasty connotations. For centuries, some people with wealth and power have abused the poor and excluded them from a better way of life; others have done little to help the situation;[129] and still others have tried to extend a helping hand but have produced only a limited success at best. Consequently, since Marx published his analysis of class conflict, the deeds and misdeeds of rich and powerful people (which have political and moral dimensions) have come to be confused with what it means economically to be a capitalist; and this confusion obscures why it is essential for everyone to become a capitalist.

Accordingly, the binary goal of enabling everyone to participate in production as a capitalist must be understood in practical economic terms.   Just as a laborer participates in production by the productiveness of his labor, so a capitalist participates in production by the productiveness of his capital. Thus a capitalist in binary terms is not someone defined by belief in one or another theory of capitalism, or by political or moral deeds or misdeeds, but rather is merely someone who produces and earns by owning capital. And binary economics reveals that increasingly everyone must be able to produce and earn by owning capital.

---

[129]   Edmund Burke counselled that all that is necessary for evil to prevail is for good people to do nothing.

Yet this definition is too broad to be of practical significance as an objective goal offered to make everyone better off. It must be sharpened. Some capitalists own billions of dollars in assets, while others own only a few shares of stock or a quarter acre of marginally productive land. So, to lay a realistic and practical foundation for the goal of universal binary competence or the goal of enabling everyone to become a capitalist, let us define a capitalist as someone who produces at least 50% of his/her current consumption from the ownership of capital. Thus the binary definition of capitalist is consistent with the Adam Smith axiom that the purpose of production (including the acquisition of productive capital) is consumption.

b)   Modest definition

It should be noted that our definition is a modest definition. It could also be considered a minimal one. So, according to the definition, our capitalist is just barely as much a capitalist (earning from capital) as a laborer (earning from labor). If he earned any less from capital he would drop below the 50% level and would thus be more a laborer (and/or welfare recipient) than a capitalist.

Therefore our definition of capitalist is a minimal one embracing a modest goal. People who become capitalists the binary way (i.e. who become 'binary capitalists') will not be the wealthiest of capitalists. Binary capitalists will still have to labor for half their consumption (or else rely on private charity and public welfare monies). They will still truly prosper only with hard work and motivation. Compared with many of today's unfree market capitalists many of whom earn considerably more than 50% of their current consumption from capital ownership, binary capitalists would seem to be relatively poor.

It should also be noted that many people today who might be considered wealthy by conventional standards would not be considered capitalists by our definition. For example, a highly-paid professional earning $150,000 per year from real labor income might need to own a capital estate larger than $2,000,000 to earn capital income consistently in excess of labor income so as to qualify as a capitalist. In practice, there are many people with substantial labor incomes but no substantial capital estates and they generally have high current expenses to maintain their employment and their professional facades. Although they may be currently prosperous, many are only a redundancy notice away from ruin.

c) *A practical goal*

Binary economics offers for most people a modest but practical long-term goal of capital participation which is not subject to the problems and whims of the labor market. Once the binary economy is established and the private-property, true free market system begins to operate competitively, people will begin to acquire capital in market transactions. After their capital has paid for itself, the new binary owners will begin to earn at first only a tiny percentage of their income from capital – say 1% or less. But in the next year the percentage is likely to double and, in succeeding years, grow to 5%, 10%, 25% and, eventually, 50% or more although the exact pace of this growth is debatable.

So, in a binary economy, as capital productiveness continues to replace and vastly supplement labor productiveness, people can look forward to increasing capital acquisition which will earn increasing capital income to supplement their labor income. As the economy grows with increasing capital productiveness, everyone's individual capital participation grows in a balanced way. By linking increasing capital productiveness with increasing consumer power, the open-market binary economy operates in harmony with the law of supply and demand. Thus, the binary economy with its open system of corporate finance offers much greater growth and distributive justice than the unfree market system with its closed private property system that effectively excludes most people from capital acquisition.

4. Acquiring capital on credit with the earnings of capital

To people schooled in the conventional productivity paradigm of unfree market capitalism, the binary offer to enable all people individually to acquire self-financing capital (i.e., to acquire capital on terms where it is expected to pay for itself out of its future earnings) must seem quite out of touch with reality. But the remarkable thing is that binary economics is only offering to do *what is already done at present*.

Although appearing somewhat foreign and mystical to many people who have never directly experienced the benefits of capital ownership, the idea that capital (properly conceived and implemented) is self-financing – that it pays for itself out of its future earnings at competitive rates within a competitive time-frame – *is the basic logic, and minimum requirement, of the present closed system of corporate finance*. *All* present day corporate finance is dependent upon new assets paying for themselves at competitive rates. The financial performance of the Russell 3000 provides long-term, sustained, documented, market evidence of this basic rule of financial feasibility.

So binary economics reasons that, if capital can buy itself for the well-capitalized as at present, it can in the future likewise buy itself for everyone else. Moreover, although conventional economic theory claims that private savings are necessary for capital formation, the whole purpose and logic of present corporate finance is to enable corporations to acquire assets *before* they have earned the money to buy them (i.e. the acquisition is done using credit, *not* savings). Wealthy people use this logic to acquire additional productive capacity. Once the binary property right is established, the same logic can be extended to the rest of the population, individually, on market principles.

5. *The binary property right*

The binary property right is the effective right of all individuals to acquire productive capital assets on market principles. Along with productiveness and binary growth, it provides a distinctly new understanding of the law of supply and demand together with the long-term and short-term market relationships among labor, capital, distribution, growth and poverty. The binary property right is an integral part of the new binary paradigm and the new policy which flows from it.

In practical terms, the binary property right is essentially the right to acquire capital assets on credit, to pay for them with the pre-tax net earnings of the assets acquired, and then to receive the full net income from those assets as long as they remain productive.[130] It is one important property right presently used by the well-capitalized to get richer, and it is a right that is all the more essential for the rest of the people. This effective right will enable all people to participate in production not only as labor-workers but increasingly as capital-workers i.e. owners of capital. It will harness for all people the power of capital assets to pay for themselves and to generate income indefinitely.   It will link production directly with consumption on market principles to provide the basis for sustained growth.

Nevertheless, it must always be remembered that the binary property right is a market right, *not* a welfare right and the two rights must be distinguished from one another. A market right is a right to participate (provide productive input) in voluntary

---

[130]   Net income is income after reserves, depreciation, research and development are set aside to repair, restore or replace capital so that the investment remains in capital that is capable of generating a competitive rate of return indefinitely.

exchange for the productive input of others. What you take out should equal what you put in. A welfare right is a right to take out, without a correlative input obligation. It thus imposes an input obligation on others, usually taxpayers.

Moreover, the binary property right is not a right to acquire any specific capital or to participate in any specific transaction. Nor is it an automatic right to credit on any particular terms. Rather the binary property right is the right to participate in fair competition with other owners (both conventional and binary) for the acquisition of credit-worthy capital assets on market principles. It materializes in the form of acquired assets and real income only as the result of wholly voluntary credit-worthy market transactions. Furthermore, even when binary capital acquisition occurs, the owners of binary property receive no spendable income unless the underlying capital first pays for its acquisition and then generates a net income to distribute to its beneficial owners. *No* confiscation, taxation or governmental command is involved.

6.   *Everybody needs capital credit*

Everyone knows that wealthy people enjoy *credit* and can therefore borrow to acquire capital. That is to say, they have access to capital credit. But far fewer people realize that vast amounts of capital assets are bought with capital credit that is repaid with earnings from the very capital assets so acquired. So why is it that others (the middling classes, for example) cannot also enjoy capital credit so that they, too, are able to invest in wealth-creating capital assets with borrowed money and repay the money with earnings from the very capital assets so acquired?

The answer is that credit for borrowing money to acquire capital is available to all individuals only in theory and in rhetoric. However, *in practice*, in the present closed private property system, such credit is *generally available only to those who can offer collateral* to secure the credit. Credit is therefore generally available only to people who are already well-capitalized.

Collateral is usually an existing asset offered to a lender as security against the possibility that a loan may not be repaid. Thus a person might borrow to buy shares in a company offering as collateral, for example, the title to other shares, or a home, or other assets. Similarly, a company (and so its shareholders) might borrow to purchase new machinery offering as collateral, for example, an existing factory or part or all of the company's assets. Moreover, even the very capital assets acquired can be used as collateral to secure the credit.

In a pre-industrial economy, collateral was of less significance than today because wealth creation was much more labor intensive. But, as advancing technology made production increasingly capital intensive, the collateral requirement became increasingly important.

The development of commerce and technology has created ever larger markets and ever greater opportunities to acquire increasingly productive capital. Yet these increasing opportunities are restricted to the owners of the ever larger pool of capital who continue to comprise a tiny percentage of the population. Thus because wealthy people have collateral (and so can borrow for investment in capital assets) while the poor do not, the requirement for collateral increasingly has become a barrier which effects a permanent exclusion of the mass of the population from any chance of ever acquiring a substantial amount of wealth-creating assets. In short, in our present closed private property system, *it is essentially the advantage of possessing collateral that keeps the capital assets narrowly owned.*

The essential point was set forth by Kelso and Adler in *The New Capitalists* in 1961:–

> *Collateral serves as an insurance to the lender against the risk that the borrower might not repay a loan.*[131]

---

[131] Louis Kelso & Mortimer Adler, *The New Capitalists* (1961), 57-59.

Further, in the case of borrowing to acquire capital (where the loan is expected to be repaid out of the very capital assets acquired), the collateral provides the lender with an insurance against the risk of financial failure of the business for which the credit (i.e., capital credit) is extended.   Moreover, if banks provided unsecured capital credit it would undermine stability and confidence in the monetary system.   The requirement for collateral, therefore, has become a virtually universal requirement for effective entry into the capital acquisition markets.

Thus, if most people are ever to be enabled to use credit for capital acquisition (which is increasingly essential to their economic well-being, to economic justice and to sustained growth) some substitute for the insurance function of collateral must be instituted in every market economy that intends to be free and open.   It was to provide this practical, efficacious, and essential substitute for collateral that Louis Kelso realized (in a true stroke of genius) that capital credit insurance could be priced in truly open and efficient markets, and included in the cost of borrowing. In this way, access to capital credit on market principles – and thereby the effective right to acquire capital assets and to pay for them out of the very assets acquired – could be enjoyed individually by *all* people, not merely by wealthy people.[132]

7.   Historical antecedents for the binary property right

Although the binary property right has yet to be fully recognized in any market economy, it has two clear antecedents in the U.S.A. – the Homestead Acts and the Federal Housing Administration (FHA).   Both antecedents are more limited than

---

[132]   Louis & Patricia Kelso, *Democracy and Economic Power* at 40-43.

the binary property right but they did enable people without
capital to acquire capital on credit, and both were highly
successful.

a)   The Homestead Acts

Under the first Homestead Act of 1862, people without
savings were enabled to acquire midwest and west frontier land on
credit in exchange for the promise to reside on the land and
cultivate it. Proponents of the Homestead Acts maintained that
access to land (then the most productive form of capital) was
essential to individual prosperity, economic growth, and the very
fibre of democracy.   While the eastern seaboard of the U.S.A.
remained essentially plutocratic, the midwest and west frontier
lands increasingly became an area of small landowners (i.e., small
capitalists).

Moreover, and very significantly, *during most of the
Homestead era, the economy experienced a broadening
ownership base, impressive growth, and a broadening
distribution of income, with little or no inflation.* That growth,
broadening distribution of income, and little or no inflation (all
resulting from the broader distribution of capital) are *exactly* what
binary economists predict for the binary economy.[133]

The beneficial broadening of capital ownership, however, was
happening at a time when other forces would diminish its potency.
Thus land was needing less labor; modern machines were to make
small farms unprofitable; and most people were to move to cities
to live in rented housing and work for wages. Then the U.S.
Congress, without exploring whether the benefits of broader
capital ownership could be achieved by extending the logic of the
program to the emerging industrial economy, terminated the

---

[133] The binary significance of the Homestead Acts was identified by
Louis and Patricia Kelso (*Democracy and Economic Power*, pp. 16,
19, 152).

Homestead program. This was a fateful error grounded in the mistaken conventional economic paradigm.

By 1850, industrial capital had overtaken land in value[134] and artificial (fabricated) capital – in the form of tools, structures, materials, processes and the like – had become the most important form of productive capital. In this context, two important differences between land and artificial capital should be noted. First, productive land is limited whereas artificial capital can grow without comparable apparent limitation.[135]   Second, artificial capital has produced more per capita economic growth in the major unfree market economies since 1750 than has land.[136]

With these insights in mind, binary economists conclude that the logic underlying the Homestead Acts (viz., that access to capital is essential for individual prosperity, sustainable growth, and the functioning of a democracy of informed citizens) is sound. The logic therefore can and should be extended to enable people to acquire industrial and other forms of artificial capital with the anticipation of far better results than were achieved in the broad land ownership of the Homestead era.

---

[134] Louis & Patricia Kelso, *Democracy and Economic Power*, (1991) at p. 19.

[135] "There are no known limitations to the amount of fabricated capital that can be created, so long as effective consumer demand – physical demand matched with consumer purchasing power – remains unsatisfied." Louis & Patricia Kelso, *Democracy and Economic Power*, (1991) at p. 22.

[136] It is true that per-acre production has increased in many areas as has the amount of productive land, but both increases are the result of using increasingly productive capital applied to the land, e.g., irrigation works, fertilizer, bio-technology and mechanization.

b)   The Federal Housing Administration

The second antecedent of the binary property right is the Federal Housing Administration (FHA) which, in 1934, was established by Congress to create a nation-wide home-loan insurance program. Despite a few years of mismanagement in the 1980s, the program has been a great success. With FHA insurance at approximately 2% of the loan, for the first time millions of average families without sufficient savings or credit to purchase a home were able to secure the credit necessary to buy homes and then repay the loans out of their future incomes.

The FHA loan insurance insures the lending bank and thereby provides a substitute for the security or collateral normally required by banks for making loans. Thus, the availability of insurance eliminated a major barrier (the requirement of collateral) that stood between millions of families and the ownership of their homes. Similarly, in the binary economy, the availability of capital credit will eliminate a major barrier (the requirement of collateral) that now stands between millions of people and the ownership of a portion of the equity of credit-worthy corporations.

But the FHA insurance program is *not* a give-away or a subsidy. To the contrary, by law and in practice, it is a market-based program with the premiums set high enough to cover losses and leave the FHA with decades of profitable operation. The same would be true for the binary capital credit program described below.

c)   Building on the good antecedents

With the Homestead and FHA antecedents for the binary property right in mind, we turn now to a consideration of how the binary property right can best be achieved on market principles in a modern industrial economy. Because the most productive capital in the unfree market economies is acquired and owned by the nation's largest credit-worthy companies, the binary strategy is to enable all people to participate in that sort of capital acquisition on market principles. Thus the binary strategy is to build on the strengths of the Homestead Acts and FHA loan insurance, by combining their best features with features of other institutions (that now facilitate capital acquisition primarily for existing owners) to create an economy in which the system of corporate finance works for everyone.

Thus the nineteenth century idea behind the Homestead Acts (that broad-based land ownership is essential to individual prosperity, sustainable growth and a well-functioning democracy) was a sound idea. However, land is limited today and is no longer the most important form of capital in the major unfree market economies. Moreover, there are too many people for everyone to be supported by working and owning the land. With modern capital farm instruments and technology, only a relatively few workers are needed to do the human work involved in producing the food to feed thousands more. Today's challenge, therefore, is to implement the spirit of the Homestead Acts and to ensure that all people come to acquire a share of industrial capital.

Likewise, just as the principle underlying the Homestead Acts is sound, so is the principle underlying the FHA. The principle is one of loan insurance to enable people who have no savings to acquire their residential capital (their homes) on credit repaid by their future earnings.

The principle is the sounder in the corporate capital context because homes do not pay for themselves in the way that credit-worthy corporate capital does (rather, homes are usually paid for out of their owners' labor income). Moreover, the earning power and credit-worthiness of the average FHA-eligible homebuyer is not nearly as great *nor as insurable* as the corporate capital acquisition of one of America's three thousand largest credit-worthy companies. Thus, the concept of credit insurance (applied by the FHA to enable people without savings or other collateral to acquire homes on credit) is undoubtedly capable of being extended from homes to the most productive forms of capital.

In summary, the optimal market structure for realizing the binary property right can be conceived as a combination of the best features of the Homestead Acts and the FHA, with modifications and improvements to take into account the circumstances of the industrial revolution. Accordingly, the binary strategy is to modify the economic infrastructure that facilitates present corporate finance so that all people may come to participate in capital acquisition on market principles. This strategy realizes what wealthy people already well understand – it is much better to acquire capital with future earnings of the capital acquired rather than with the earnings of labor. And the binary approach enables *everyone* to participate in capital acquisition on the future earnings of the capital acquired.

Like the Homestead Acts, the binary economy would enable all people to acquire a share of the capital that is producing most of the wealth. Like the FHA, the binary economy would provide a self-supporting market-based insurance program to enable people to acquire capital even when they lack the personal collateral or savings for investment. But more is needed to establish the binary property right as a vital competitive market right in the profit-driven world of corporate finance. This brings us to an opening consideration of the binary infrastructure.

8. The binary infrastructure

In order to realize the binary property right, and to enable everyone to enjoy the benefit of capital credit, national binary legislation would provide credit-worthy corporations with new ways to meet their capital requirements (but only those that are otherwise credit-worthy). *At the same time* as those capital requirements are met, the corporation's employees, consumers, nearby residents and others[137] would be enabled to acquire, on

---

[137] Regarding criteria for eligibility to participate as binary beneficiaries see Chapter Eight.

credit, full-return dividend-paying stock in the corporation.[138]
The legislation would authorize, but not require, such financing.
Thus corporations could meet their capital requirements by way
of conventional financing, binary financing, or a combination of
both.

Decisions as to capital investment would reside entirely in the
private sector. No binary financing would occur unless a credit-
worthy company has a credit-worthy plan to acquire capital
assets. In such a case, in addition to the conventional closed ways
of corporate finance (which are closed to most people without
substantial assets), the company could employ a binary financing
plan which has, at its center, something called a *constituency
trust*. But a binary financing *cannot* occur unless the managers
of credit-worthy companies, their existing shareholders, lenders,
capital credit insurers and fiduciaries of the constituency trusts
(described below) first approve the transaction.

a)   The constituency trust

There is a need to co-ordinate the borrowing activities in a
single responsible entity which is acceptable to both a lender and
a capital credit insurer. There is also a need to protect
beneficiaries from personal liability. Beneficiaries are primarily
employees, but also consumers of participating companies, and
others, including local residents, unemployed persons and welfare
recipients. Beneficiaries need the protection just as existing
capital owners are protected from personal liability when
corporations they own borrow money to acquire capital.

---

[138] 'Full-return dividend-paying' means that all income earned by the
underlying capital represented by stock (net of reserves for
depreciation, research and development) must be paid to its owners.
Once the binary economy takes root, binary principles suggest that this
return will be much larger than it is at present.

To fulfil both needs, binary legislation would authorize the establishment of constituency trusts.[139] The trusts would act as the financial trustees (fiduciaries) for the binary beneficiaries. The trustees would independently scrutinize the capital acquisition proposal for financial soundness. They would then execute the necessary documents; hold title to the shares; review and monitor company performance; repay the lenders; and account to the beneficiaries.

b)   The importance of full return stock

As indicated above, the stock held by the trusts would be a special 'full return' stock paying its full return (net of reserves for depreciation, research and development) as income to the trust. The trust is obligated to use the income first to satisfy all debt obligations incurred to acquire the capital and the stock, and then to pay the full remaining income to the beneficiaries.[140]

The full return feature of the binary stock is a critical element of the binary infrastructure and it deserves special emphasis. There are those who have suggested that various broader ownership programs should be embraced as consistent with binary principles even though the type of stock participation they

---

[139] The best known of these trusts at present is the Employee Stock Ownership Plan (ESOP), a creation of Louis Kelso, which is now employed by approximately ten thousand American companies covering approximately ten million workers including some of America's largest (Procter & Gamble, J.C. Penney, Anheuser, Busch, Texaco, Polaroid, Hallmark and United Airlines).

[140] Neither the participating company nor the trust is taxed on the net income of the capital because neither has use of that income. The corporation starts by paying the full net earnings to the trust and the trust uses that income first to repay the lender and then to provide income to the beneficiaries. But the lender would pay taxes on its (interest) income and the beneficiaries would pay taxes on the spendable income they receive according to the income bracket in which they find themselves.

offer does not include the binary full return feature. Advocates of such watered-down approaches to broader capital acquisition may argue that half a loaf is better than none. But let the people beware. Binary economists are *not* talking about a loaf or half a loaf; rather the binary goal is to provide a means to acquire a growing capital participation *in the bakery itself.* For people who are not well capitalized, that goal requires competitive, self-financing, full return, capital acquisition rights.

The truth is that *without the full return feature there is no competitive, self-financing property right.* The full return feature is required by:–

- *the lender* to enable the loan to be repaid at competitive rates;
- *the beneficiaries* who have increasing need to participate in the capital income earned from increasing capital productiveness; and
- *the entire economy* to achieve sustainable aggregate growth and distributive justice on market principles.

Thus to be viable and truly competitive, binary economics holds that the full pay-out right is essential to a competitive broader ownership program.

c) *Capital credit insurance*

In a binary economy, the prospect of binary growth can be capitalized on credit with the risk of failure priced in the form of private capital credit insurance. Furthermore, the principle of binary growth indicates that a market for such insurance may spontaneously develop. As with other new forms of insurance, however, legislation and regulation providing minimum safeguards and standards would be necessary.

d)   Establishment of the Capital Credit Reinsurance Corporation

Just as in the U.S.A. the Federal Housing Administration was profitably established to insure and reinsure capital credit to home-buyers to enable them to acquire homes (residential capital) with borrowed money, so binary economists recommend the establishment of a Capital Credit Reinsurance Corporation or CCRC to provide similar insurance for non-residential capital. The CCRC would be the only new entity in a binary economy. Nevertheless, as we shall explain, its function (to provide market-based insurance and reinsurance to enable people to acquire business capital at competitive rates) is one already offered under special circumstances for favored businesses in the existing unfree market economies, but presently that function is practically available to only a few.   Further, the profitability of such insurance (already established with respect to residential capital acquisition) seems even more auspicious with respect to the non-residential capital requirements of prime credit-worthy business corporations.

Although some libertarian conventional free-marketeers protest against any government involvement in markets, the fact remains that before the FHA, there was no viable credit market for millions of would-be American home-buyers.   Sixty years after the establishment of the FHA there is now both a viable credit market for millions of additional American home-buyers and also a good record of market-based profits earned by the FHA.[141]

---

[141]   In this context, it should be noted that just as the FHA insurance program was a profit-making enterprize, *not* a subsidy, so, in the same way, the binary insurance concept advanced here is *not* a subsidy, but a market-driven program operated to provide loan insurance profitably based on proven principles of risk management.

e)   The central bank

The final participant in the binary economy is the central bank which has the responsibility of managing the money supply to accommodate real growth in demand, while controlling inflation and maintaining stability. In a binary economy, to accommodate growth consistent with controlling inflation and monetary stability, the central bank would be authorized to discount binary financing loan paper held by lenders at the central bank's administrative costs.[142] No specific amount of central bank discounting would be required; rather any discounting would proceed only as consistent with overall monetary policy. The subject of monetary policy is discussed in Chapter Eight.

f)   Summary of the binary strategy

Thus, the binary strategy employs:–
- tested principles of corporate finance and trust law;
- proven insurance as a substitute for collateral;
- affirmative state action based purely on market principles to enable everyone to benefit from the vast financial infrastructure that supports capital acquisition; and
- a flexible but disciplined monetary policy.

In this way, the strategy enables people without capital to compete individually and effectively along with existing owners for the acquisition of capital assets.

Nevertheless, decisions as to particular capital investments would reside entirely in the private sector. As indicated previously, the binary property right carries with it no right to any specific participation in any specific financing or acquisition of any type or amount. No binary financing is compulsory: rather specific binary financings only proceed if private firms with

---

[142] In the U.S.A., this sort of discounting is authorized by Section 13 of the Federal Reserve Act.

credit-worthy plans, private lenders, capital credit insurers and trustees agree.   Title to no capital assets would be coercively changed. Given its role as a risk insurer, through the CCRC, and its role as manager of the currency through the central bank, the government in a binary economy could facilitate or reduce the incidence of binary financing just as it facilitates or reduces the incidence of conventional financing today. But binary economists argue that the roles, as structured in a binary economy, will be much more easily maintained according to open market principles.

The essential effect of these binary proposals is *not* to socialize private capital, as Marx proposed, but instead may be characterized as democratizing credit necessary to enable all individuals to acquire private capital on market principles.[143]   In so doing, the binary approach does not ration credit for any particular set of investment priorities.   Nor does it prohibit private credit transactions of the type that now dominate capital acquisition for the virtually exclusive acquisition rights of existing owners.   Rather, it extends to all people competitive market access to capital credit.   In this sense, it comprehends the same fundamental problems that Marx and others identified, but provides a universal capitalist rather than a socialist solution.[144]

---

[143]   The binary democratizing of credit has nothing to do with the theories and proposals of Major C.H. Douglas and the Social Credit Movement which fail to link production and consumption by way of private property rights on market principles. Thus, when addressing the credit needs of people without capital, to avoid confusion with the analysis of Major Douglas (which they reject), the Kelsos do not use the term 'social credit' but 'commercially insured capital credit'. See, for example, Louis & Patricia Kelso, *Democracy and Economic Power*, supra, note 1 at 105.   See generally, C.H. Douglas, *The Monopoly of Credit* (1921); C.H. Douglas, *The Nature of Democracy* (1920); W. Hiskett, *Social Credits or Socialism: An Analysis of the Douglas Credit Scheme* (1935); E. Holter, *The ABC of Social Credit* (1934).

[144]   See Louis Kelso, *Karl Marx: The Almost Capitalist* (American Bar Association *Journal*, March, 1957). In this remarkable article, Kelso

By enabling people without capital to acquire capital on credit, and to repay the credit loan out of the income of the capital thus acquired, and then to enjoy the full net return of that capital indefinitely, these proposals create a system of private property in which all people may participate in capital acquisition on market principles.

Of course some unfree marketeers may object to the proposed binary infrastructure as an unwise government intervention in the market even though it does no more than open the market to all people. In their boast of relative victory over socialism, some unfree marketeers neglect sometimes to acknowledge the essential role of the unfree market governments in maintaining the commercial laws and institutions that constitute the market infrastructure for the production and distribution of goods and services.[145] Clearly, the rhetorical hands-off approach of the unfree marketeers does not comport with the reality of the beneficial governmental maintenance and support of the financial

---

shows that Marx came near to developing binary economics but failed to do so because of three errors, viz.:– i) even though Marx understood the ability of the non-human assets to create wealth, he developed the false labor theory of value (previously advanced by Ricardo); ii) Marx failed to grasp that, without private and individual ownership of the assets, some form of totalitarian state is inevitable; iii) Marx assumed that the wealth created by the non-human assets had been created by the mass of human beings but stolen from them by asset owners i.e. he began his analysis with a study of the distribution of income *rather than with a study of how wealth is produced.*

"The problem is not that capital is privately owned, as Marx supposed. The problem is that most people don't own any." (William Greider, *One World, Ready Or Not.* Simon and Schuster, 1997.)

[145] "It is only under the shelter of the civil magistrate that the owner of ......valuable property can sleep a single night in security. The acquisition of valuable and extensive property, therefore, necessarily requires the establishment of civil government." Adam Smith, *Wealth of Nations,* Book Five, Chapter One.

infrastructure. Apparently, some unfree marketeers like the financial infrastructure for themselves, but not for everyone else.

Nor can it be said that the binary opening of the financial infrastructure is an interference with free market decisions. To the contrary, the need for financial infrastructure, governed by law and order, is obvious. People will not voluntarily bring goods and services to the market if their property in those goods and services is not sufficiently protected. Nor will they enter into exchanges unless the transactions are sufficiently protected. So establishing the binary infrastructure that facilitates competitive capital acquisition on behalf of all individuals is *not* an act of market intervention. It merely opens the vast market infrastructure of the unfree markets to all people as it is claimed to be open today but is not. In the next chapter we shall examine the structure of a binary economy in greater detail, beginning with a closer examination of the binary property right.

Book III

Chapter Eight

The structure of a binary economy

1. The binary property right

To achieve the growth and distributive justice promised by the distributive power of capital it is necessary to open the capital markets to all people. Once the private property system is opened in this manner, binary growth will materialize over time as capital is acquired in voluntary private transactions by willing buyers and sellers of goods and services. In such an economy, the incremental productiveness of capital (as it replaces and vastly supplements labor productiveness) can be acquired by those expected to buy its output, as required for sustainable growth. All this happens, however, *only* if individuals have a practical right to acquire the ownership of capital assets on market principles.

Thus a binary economy is one that develops within a private property system structured to realize effectively the binary property right. This foundational right is the right, vested in every person, to acquire capital assets (land, structures, machines, legally protected intangibles, etc.); to pay for the capital assets with the pre-tax yield of the capital acquired; and then to receive all the net income earned by that capital (after depreciation, research and operating reserves) indefinitely.

The property right has two components – the acquisition right and the income right. Each component right can be considered a right in itself.

Thus, there is:–

- the *acquisition* right – the right to acquire capital and to pay for the capital out of the pre-tax earnings of the capital acquired;
  and
- the *income* right – the right to receive all net income earned by the capital after it has paid for itself.

Yet the acquisition right and the income right have a powerful relationship predicated on market principles which will be explored below. At the moment, it is simply important to realize that, over time, the acquisition right dramatically strengthens the income right and vice versa.

Note that the right to credit on market principles is implicit in the acquisition right. This can be seen from the fact that the full payment for the capital is completed *after* it is acquired. Thus, this right assumes vitality only if credit is available to finance the transaction on market terms. (In other words, the only investment opportunities made available to all people in a binary economy are those that are determined to be credit-worthy).

Note also that the income right matures *only* after the capital has satisfied the repayment obligations arising from the extension of credit. Finally, and most critically, note that the acquisition price of the capital can be fully paid, and net income can eventually be distributed to the new owners, *only after* the capital has earned the necessary income by doing work of equal market value. So any benefits to the owners of binary capital are *not* the result of redistributed earnings of others, but rather solely the result of the work done by their own capital.

Thus, the binary property right is a market right, not a welfare right. It is conditioned on voluntary market transactions. It is not an absolute right to a specific amount of income or to capital credit for any proposed financial transaction.

Nevertheless, the efficient democratic market force released by the legislation of the binary property right is not to be underestimated if capital does work of its own, as binary economists claim. Although it is not a blank check entry into any particular transaction, the binary acquisition right will enable all people to begin to compete effectively for credit-worthy capital acquisition alongside of those who already own substantial capital estates.

Furthermore, as intimated above, by reason of the distributive power of capital in a private property economy, the income right (as it matures over time) will add potency to the acquisition right by augmenting the productive power of all citizens (by increasing their ownership of capital) and thereby making more capital investment profitable. Thus the realization of the binary property right will establish the open market conditions for widespread affluence, distributive justice and sustainable growth.

Therefore, if the binary view of the economy (based on the independent productiveness of capital and its distributive power) is sound, then the binary property right is the right essential for each individual and for sustainable growth for the society as a whole. As we explain more fully in Chapter Fourteen, it is a right whose import lawyers, financial advisers, economists and other fiduciaries must begin to understand if they are to be able to serve their clients and beneficiaries.

2.   The legal infrastructure

Writing in 1820, William Blake wisely counselled that those who would do good must do it in minute particulars.[146] So, too,

---

[146] "He who would do good must do it in Minute Particulars. General Good is the plea of the scoundrel, hypocrite, and flatterer; for Art and

granted the lofty goals of binary theory as embodied in the binary property right, its practical effect must be realized in minute particulars.

In the world of business, the binary property right will flourish as a competitive right *only* if the laws recognize and protect it in the 'minute particulars' of capital transactions. Just as existing owners of capital can demand legal protection before they invest, so binary transactions (which enable people without capital to acquire capital) also require explicit protective legislation.

Although it may seem complicated at first blush, a binary economy in reality operates on relatively few underlying economic principles (those founded on productiveness). It is good news, moreover, that the basic legal infrastructure for a binary economy is achieved by the amendment of a mere dozen or so laws and, with some adaptation, relies entirely on *existing* corporate, trust, banking, insurance, regulatory and monetary institutions. Thus these are the institutions which, though imperfect, have created abundance for the well-capitalized and can now be opened to do the same for everyone else.

3. General Theory diagram

A complete overview of the structure and voluntary operation of a binary economy can be understood just by mastering the relatively simple dynamics of the diagram below which contains six boxes representing six entities. During the course of this chapter, each box will be considered in turn both discretely and in relation to other boxes. In this way, the reader quickly comes to an understanding of the basic structure of the binary economy.

Science cannot exist but in minutely organized Particulars."
Jerusalem, f.55, l. 54.

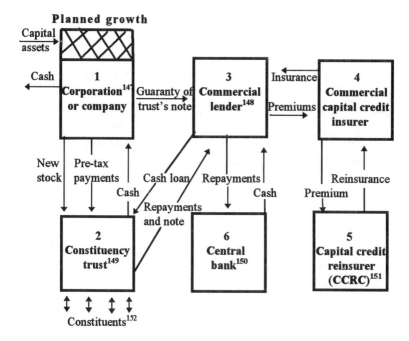

Fig. 8 – 1. General Theory diagram.

---

[147] Title-owning and operating corporation/company (except in the case of a residence where the owner holds asset in trust until it is paid for).

[148] Qualified commercial bank, savings and loan, insurance company or other lender.

[149] Stockholder constituency trust (escrow in case of (residence) RECOPs).

[150] Federal Reserve Bank in the U.S.A.

[151] Capital Credit Reinsurance Corporation (CCRC) – a government Capital Credit Reinsurance Underwriter.

[152] Types of constituent (eligibility politically determined):– employees (ESOPs and MUSOPs); consumers (CSOPs); citizens in general (GSOPs); individuals (ICOPs/ISOPs); home owners (RECOPs); citizen participation in commercial capital (COMCOPs) and public capital (PUBCOPs).

The diagram is a simplified version of one drawn by the Kelsos who frequently labelled it 'General Theory'. It is offered to solve the fundamental growth and distributional problems considered, but left unsolved, by Keynes in his *General Theory*. (Unlike Keyne's approach, however, it does so wholly on free market principle, without earnings redistribution.) It represents both a single transaction by willing buyers of goods and services and *the aggregate operation of the entire binary economy*. Building on the practical successes of the Homestead Acts and the Federal Housing Administration (FHA), the diagram contains *all* the institutions or groupings necessary and sufficient for binary financing. Moreover, it illustrates how those institutions can participate profitably in a system of corporate finance wherein transactions may be structured on market principles to enable people without capital to compete fairly alongside people with capital for the acquisition of capital assets.

4.   Six major institutions

A binary economy features six institutions or groupings:–
- private corporations/companies seeking to make capital acquisitions;
- constituency trusts, authorized to borrow money on behalf of specified constituencies (employees, consumers, residents, and others) to purchase binary stock issued by participating companies;
- qualified lenders, primarily banks;
- private commercial capital credit insurers;
- the Capital Credit Reinsurance Corporation;
- the central bank or Federal Reserve.

Functionally, all these institutions exist in some form today. But, at present, they serve effectively only the acquisition rights of existing owners. In part, limiting their service primarily to existing owners is the result of their conventional economic mindset – they do not see the great market potential that is unleashed for all people, existing and would-be shareholders alike, that comes from using binary financing. However, apart from the mindset, these institutions are not at present authorized to engage in binary financing transactions, except to a very limited degree through the American ESOP. Moreover, the would-be beneficiaries do not presently have effective capital acquisition rights that can be competitively served on market principles. Nevertheless, with appropriate binary legislation, these institutions will be able to provide the open market means necessary for enabling people without capital to compete with people who already own capital for the acquisition of capital assets. Significantly, the enabling will be by way of voluntary market transactions, initiated and implemented by individuals and private firms, in ways that provide the foundation for widespread individual prosperity and sustainable growth.

Thus, once they are authorized to do so, private companies will be able to begin to satisfy their capital requirements in competitive ways that make capital owners of their employees, consumers and others including welfare recipients. The availability of binary financing, on a purely optional basis, for a nation's largest credit-worthy corporations will in effect create an important systemic exception to the adage '*It takes money to make money*'. In other words, the legislation supporting a binary economy will unstack the present deck of cards (stacked in favor of existing capital owners)[153] by giving everyone a competitive means of acquiring capital.

Readers are invited to follow the step-by-step sequence of a binary financing transaction set out in the rest of this chapter. By so doing, they will understand how the six institutions interact

---

[153] Edward Wolff, *Top Heavy: A Study of Increasing Inequality in America* (Twentieth Century Fund, 1995) gives figures for 1989 showing that 1% of the U.S.A.'s households owns nearly 40% of the wealth (in the U.K. it is about 20%). The lowest 20% of American citizens earn only 5.7% of the after-tax income paid to individuals.

with one another to create the binary system allowing people without competence (i.e., those who are under-capitalized, or not capitalized at all) to compete on a more equal footing with the well-capitalized for the ownership of wealth-creating capital assets.

5. *An open system of corporate finance*

The basic purpose of present corporate finance is to enable firms to acquire capital assets *before* they have earned the money to pay for them. By this logic, existing shareholders acquire additional capital even as they sleep. With binary financing, however, the same logic, used by the six institutions, can work competitively for people who presently own little or no capital.

To understand how the six institutions are able to co-operate profitably with one another to make binary financing competitive with traditional financing, we begin by observing that, in our present closed system of corporate finance, a corporation/company can acquire capital assets in one, or a combination, of three ways:–

- By *issuing new stock or shares.* This means inviting those who have sufficient money or credit available to them to buy *new* shares in the company. In practice this means that the *existing shareholders* or other existing wealthy people come to own the new capital assets.

- By *withholding dividends* (i.e. the earnings of capital) from the shareholders and using the retained earnings to finance the acquisition. This involves no new shareholdings in the company. Thus the *existing shareholders* come to own the new capital assets.

- By *borrowing money* either in the form of bonds or short-term notes to a broad pool of investors, or in the form of loans from banks or other lenders. Once the borrowed money has been repaid, the *existing shareholders* come to own the new capital assets.

Which of the three ways is the more attractive will depend on the particular preferences and circumstances of the market participants. In the U.S., the largest companies achieve most of their capital acquisition either with retained earnings (60%+) or borrowed money (30%+) with very little new capital (typically less than 7%) acquired by the issuance of stock. However, with any of these three methods, alone or in combination, the financing will create virtually *no new owners*.

Indeed, after the financing is complete (i.e., after the capital has paid for itself), the ultimate ownership of the new corporate capital will vest in people *who were existing owners of capital* before the transaction commenced.[154] Furthermore, although workers struggle to save enough from their labor income to invest in capital acquisition, the fact remains that almost all of the capital continues to be acquired with the earnings of capital, *not* labor, and much of it is acquired with borrowed money on credit generally available only to people who are well-capitalized.[155] These generalizations will hold true with only rare exceptions. Thus, although the present system of corporate finance is ostensibly open to everyone, most people without substantial

---

[154] Most of the owners will be the already well-capitalized. There may be some exceptions but their capital participation will be small because it is largely limited to earnings based on their labor productivity rather than based on the increasing earning power of capital which is the essence of the binary property right. *New York Stock Exchange* ownership statistics for 1990 indicate that 21% of all Americans are share owners in one form or another. However, most of that 21% have only a small holding producing a small income.

[155] That is, the capital will either have been acquired i) with retained earnings (i.e., the past earnings of capital); or ii) with borrowed money repaid with the *future* earnings of capital; or iii) with proceeds from the sale of stock paid largely by people whose income contains a high proportion of dividends and interest.

capital or collateral for credit (which means most people) are
effectively shut out.

Moreover, there is an obvious reason why the new corporate
capital always vests in existing owners.   Given the present
economic infrastructure of the unfree market economies, business
people, lenders, insurers, fiduciary investors, and others have no
practical market alternative to present methods of corporate
finance.   Consequently, they are not able to serve the capital
acquisition rights of most people (i.e., those who own little, or no,
capital).   The unpleasant reality is that, in the present unfree
market economies, the capital acquisition rights of most people
are simply not competitive according to the hard rules of the
market.

However, in a binary economy, credit-worthy companies will
have a new way of making a capital acquisition called a *binary
financing*.   Such a financing will enable a nation's largest and
most credit-worthy companies to satisfy their credit-worthy
capital requirements while simultaneously making capital owners
of their employees and others.[156]   Crucially, when available in the
full binary structure, binary financing will become increasingly
competitive with conventional financing for particular capital
acquisitions as its greater market efficiency proves itself over
time.   Increasingly, (by reason of the distributive power of
capital) in a binary economy, companies will be able to acquire
new capital assets while simultaneously encapitalizing their
employees and others *and* do so in a way which is *to the financial
advantage of the company and its conventional shareholders as
well*.

---

[156] The 'others' might include:– i) consumers of the company's
products; ii) neighbors (i.e., residents in areas where the company's
major operations are located); *and* iii) welfare recipients who can
progressively be removed from welfare roles as their capital incomes
grow.

6.   *A credit-worthy business plan*

A binary financing starts with a credit-worthy business plan
for capital asset acquisition coming from a credit-worthy private
company. A 'credit-worthy' capital acquisition plan is one for
which a bank or other lender would loan the acquisition money at
(or near) prime interest rates. In practice this requires that:–

- the capital acquisition is reasonably expected to pay for its
  acquisition cost at a competitive rate (usually within five to
  seven years); and
- there is sufficient collateral to secure the loan in the event
  that the reasonable expectation of repayment is not
  fulfilled.

The planned capital acquisition is shown in the cross-hatched
portion of Box 1 (of the General Theory) in the figure below. On
both the individual company level and the economy-wide (or
aggregate) level, this can be thought of as capital growth.   In
material terms it may be thought of as a plan to acquire automatic
elevators, or a new manufacturing plant, or an entire company.

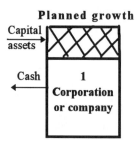

Fig. 8 – 2. Box 1 of the General Theory diagram.

Given such credit-worthy plan for capital acquisition, in a
binary economy, companies would have a new competitive choice
in satisfying their capital requirements.   They could continue
financing all or part of the capital acquisition in one of the three
conventional ways discussed above, or they could finance some

portion (or even all) of the capital acquisition via binary financing.

Of course, management financing decisions which require a substantial change in the capital structure of the company usually require shareholder approval by at least a majority, and sometimes more. Shareholders might prefer that management make the acquisition exclusively for themselves without allowing any participation by employees or others, particularly when the expected interest charges for borrowing the money is less than the expected profits resulting from the capital investment. In that way, the existing shareholders can capture the entire gain.

But, on the other hand, shareholders in a binary economy may come to see that the special benefits of binary financing outweigh the benefits to be derived from maintaining their exclusive participation in the capital acquisition by way of conventional financing. As will be explained further, these benefits include:–

• a lower cost of borrowing;

• a synergy of interests among employees, consumers, and other shareholders;

• the development of a growing capital-based consumer economy (requiring ever less earnings redistribution and having lower inflation and interest rates); and

• a new important way of supporting good corporate citizenship.

In the mature binary economy, whether conventional financing or binary financing proves more competitive may depend on the facts and circumstances of the particular financing. Sometimes conventional financing will best serve a company's interests; sometimes binary financing will prove more competitive; sometimes the company may find the optimal advantage by proceeding with a mix of conventional and binary financing.

However, in those cases where binary financing is competitive for at least a portion of the financing plan, the way is opened to broader capital acquisition and binary growth. In considering what best serves a company's long-term interests, of course, broader capital acquisition and binary growth are crucial factors.

7. *The constituency trust*

In the case of a binary financing, employees and other beneficiaries of the financing do not directly make capital acquisitions for themselves. They do not use their own labor earnings or savings to acquire the capital, and they incur no personal liability for the loans used to acquire the capital in the event that the capital fails to generate sufficient earnings to repay the loans as expected.

The capital acquisitions are made on behalf of the beneficiaries by an acquisition vehicle called the *constituency trust*, of which the well-known ESOP (Employee Share Ownership Plan) is an example. The constituency trust is shown below on the bottom left of the General Theory diagram as Box 2. *Any* individual or group of individuals is potentially capable of being a constituent of the trust.

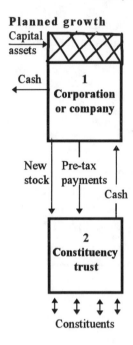

Planned growth

Capital assets

Cash

1
Corporation or company

New stock

Pre-tax payments

Cash

2
Constituency trust

Constituents

Fig. 8 – 3. Box 2 of the General Theory diagram.

In the early phases of a binary economy, however, most binary financing would likely proceed via the American ESOP model. This is because the ESOP has a proven track record and because employees are in the most potent position to contribute to their company's efficiency. Yet even in the early phases, for certain companies which are capital intensive (such as utilities – electricity, gas, water, etc.) and which have a steady, on-going relationship with their consumers, the inclusion of consumers as binary beneficiaries would make considerable business sense.[157]

---

[157]   When Louis Kelso first proposed the CSOP (Consumer Stock Ownership Plan), special credit accounts for frequent-fliers, telephone callers, renters, card-holders and general customers were just appearing on the scene. Now companies are doing everything but

As the growing binary economy takes root, others would then be included as well.

Acting on behalf of the employees and other beneficiaries, trustees of an ESOP or other constituency trust are authorized to borrow funds from a lender bank to invest in a special common stock of the company called *binary stock*. Thus the company would be able to receive money to buy new capital assets in exchange for newly-issued binary stock having special obligations to its new binary shareholders.

The constituency trust would be administered *either* by a committee within the participating companies *or* by separate institutions such as the present private and public pension and retirement funds. The administration would be governed largely by the same fiduciary standards regarding loyalty, prudence and obedience as are applicable to fiduciaries today. Thus good fiduciaries will definitely not want to be involved in financing transactions that are not credit-worthy when judged by rigorous standards of financial feasibility.

8.   *Binary stock*

When the binary means is chosen by a company to finance all or a portion of the company's capital requirements, the constituency trust uses the funds it has borrowed from the lender to invest in binary stock issued by the company. Thus the company receives the cash necessary to make the capital acquisition, and the constituency trust holds an equity interest in the company, represented by the binary stock.

The terms of the binary stock require that the company distribute *all* earnings of the capital represented by the stock (net of adequate reserves for depreciation, research, and development) to the constituency trust. The acquired stock is pledged to secure

encapitalizing their consumers which, according to binary theory, would be yet more efficient.

the loan and is released from that pledge after the loan is paid off. So the trustee must first apply the earnings to satisfy the loan repayment obligations and only when that has been done are the net earnings available for distribution to the beneficiaries.

As the loan is paid off in installments, shares that were pledged to secure the repayment are released from pledge, and all net income on those shares is distributed to the employees and other beneficiaries pro-rated on the basis of the share ownership. Because the company and the trust have no use of the income coming from the capital (which is simply distributed directly to the beneficiaries), they are *not* taxed on it. (But earnings which have come to beneficiaries are taxable in the same way as other personal income earned by them is taxable today.)

Although the loan is made for the benefit of the employees they are *not* personally liable for its repayment. As it does for wealthy people, the trust mechanism protects the binary beneficiaries from personal liability for default against the borrowing obligations incurred by the trust. Certainly the stock acquired is pledged as security for repayment of the loan, but no other assets of the beneficiaries are at risk.

9. *Rules of eligibility for financial participation*

The ultimate financial participation contemplated in a binary economy is that participation which produces *a binary competence* in every person. But not everyone can achieve it immediately. In the transition from our present closed system to the open binary system, some people will not live to enjoy the full competence that will be available to their children or grandchildren. Thus the order and extent to which various citizens participate in binary financing will obviously be a matter of great concern, particularly in a society just awakening to the newly promised, but little understood, benefits of such financing.

Consequently, eligibility to become a beneficiary of binary financing (and thereby to enjoy the benefit of non-recourse, insured capital credit) would be established according to basic ground rules set out by law. Among the guiding principles for eligibility, prescribed by law, would be:–

• to reward productiveness; and

• to provide all people with a growing source of capital income so as to reduce dependence on labor income; and

• to reduce, and ultimately to eliminate, welfare dependence and the need for earnings redistribution by vesting a binary competence in every person.

In the spirit of binary theory, these principles would have to be applied in a broad and inclusive manner, not subject to unfair exclusion or discrimination.[158]

Thus, according to binary theory, eligibility should be formulated in part so as to reward productive input through employment and entrepreneurial relationships. As with present compensation structures, participation in capital acquisition can be structured to reward such factors as excellence, efficiency, inventiveness, craftsmanship, diligence, technical achievement, and willingness to perform difficult or unpleasant tasks not yet automated. A major portion of binary financing will involve a nation's largest corporations which enjoy prime business credit. Through an ESOP, these companies could progressively encapitalize their employees.

Generally, employees would participate in proportion to their compensation as in today's ESOPs. Participation in proportion to compensation (as capital markets become more universally participatory) will increasingly represent compensation commensurate with labor input. But participation reflecting seniority, extraordinary service not otherwise compensated, and

---

[158] For example, once a company establishes an American ESOP, the law requires that the company's plan for eligible participation must be anti-discriminatory and not stacked against the rank-and-file employee.

other factors, is also possible.   To achieve diversification, participating ESOPs could combine to form Mutual Stock Ownership Plans (MUSOPs).

Further, companies with large stable consumer relations such as energy, telephone companies, and banks, might form Consumer Stock Ownership Plans (CSOPs) with capital participation in proportion to patronage.   Many companies might also choose to encapitalize their 'neighbors' and communities (i.e., people living near significant company operations).

In addition, there would be need for participation by people working for the hundreds of thousands of small businesses, start-up businesses and risky businesses.   These employees need access to capital acquisition on market principles as surely as do the employees of the prime credit-worthy companies.   The same is true of the growing number of independent contractors who may work by the hour, project or piece.   Their participation in the capital acquisition requirements of the prime credit-worthy companies can be organized by way of Individual Capital Ownership Plans or ICOPs, (or Individual Stock Ownership Plans – ISOPs) and they could be serviced by institutional fiduciaries such as those that manage individual retirement accounts, private trusts and mutual funds today.   The binary program also contemplates the voluntary participation not only of the nation's most credit-worthy companies, but also privatizations of profitable publicly-owned service entities.[159]

Eligibility would include therefore not only private but also public employees, consumers and residents.   Ultimately, it would include *all* people, even those without specified relationship to participating firms.   The idea of universal, individual participation in capital productiveness without regard to productivity responds effectively to the economic market imperative implicit in the idea that capital has a powerful distributive relationship to growth that is suppressed when capital acquisition is restricted to existing owners.   It recognizes the

---

[159] For example, dams, bridges, toll roads, public buildings.

economic reality that capital is doing most of the work and is increasingly doing more of it, and therefore must be acquired increasingly by those expected to purchase its output if a market economy is to function efficiently and justly.

Thus the idea of universal, individual participation without regard to human productivity reflects the binary goal of a universal, individual binary competence required to realize universal individual prosperity, sustainable growth, and distributive justice. And as explained in Chapter Eleven it also provides the essential economic participation necessary for true democracy.

Given a strong work ethic, reinforced by the productivity paradigm, and the reality that the voting majority (the middle class and working poor) will not likely unleash so powerful a technique as binary financing in a way that benefits the non-working poor more quickly than it benefits the voting majority, there are obvious questions to consider. So participation in proportion to wages is likely to be politically the most favored gateway to capital acquisition at first. Yet, as those who work become wealthier, they may leave the work force to make room for others. As the binary economy expands, more of the unemployed may find jobs and therefore begin to participate in capital acquisition in proportion to their wages.

However, if the binary analysis is correct, the major barrier to growth is not that people (employed or unemployed) are not working or working productively enough, but rather that they do not own enough. Thus the foundational barrier to greater individual affluence is not that people are not productive enough by way of their labor but that they are not productive enough by way of their ownership of capital.

Therefore, beyond questions of reward for productive input by way of employee relationship or entrepreneurial contributions, and beyond any more specific relationship to the participating company, eligibility for beneficial ownership would be set to close the gap between every person's financial situation and the realization for that person of a binary competence. Consequently, residual eligibility would be based on the universal need for a binary competence and would be provided to supplement labor income and to replace welfare dependence with income from privately-owned capital so as to provide every person with a binary competence.

Moreover, as capital income is increasingly earned by those on welfare, the need for taxing and earnings redistribution (or 'transfer payments') will diminish.   The binary approach is therefore a long-term government deficit reduction strategy.

10.   The interest acquired by the binary beneficiary

Generally, the legal interest acquired by the new binary owners is the interest of a beneficiary of a constituency trust which holds corporate common stock. But there are two important provisos to the general rule:–

- *Binary stock is 'full return' stock.*   This means that company management has no discretion to retain earnings for new capital formation. Rather the company must pay *all* net earnings (net of depreciation, research and development and operating reserves to restore the capital to a technologically current state) to the trustee. The trustee must use the income first to satisfy the loan obligations incurred to acquire the stock, and then pay all the income to the beneficiaries.

- *The beneficiaries are prohibited from invading or pledging the corpus*, at least until some prescribed maturity date, usually retirement. Such an invasion would defeat a main binary purpose – the provision of *income* from capital for the beneficiaries.[160]

---

[160]   This prohibition, however, need not prohibit the trustees of the various constituency trusts from co-operating to achieve, for their

11.   Advantages of using the trust mechanism rather than direct purchase

A number of factors favor the trust acquisition mechanism rather than direct purchase on credit by the employees and other beneficiaries. Among the factors are:–

- During the loan pay-back period, lenders will call the shots and would typically favor the shareholder oversight by professionals rather than the nascent binary beneficiaries. Lenders are evaluating seemingly credit-worthy capital acquisition plans put forth by proven management. They will ordinarily look to the anticipated earning power of capital acquired and of the company and also to the continuity of the management. They will thus want to preserve that continuity and will likely demand that the binary stock be controlled by proven fiduciaries (who will hold legal title to the stock and its dividends) at least until the shares have been fully paid. Existing shareholders will also want these protections.

- In binary transactions, the beneficiaries are *not* personally supplying any of the credit or collateral. Nor are they assuming any of the risk of investment failure. Nor are they more, or less, eligible to participate by reason of their acumen in investing funds and managing companies. Indeed, most of the nascent binary shareholders will have had little direct experience with the ownership and management of capital or corporate investments. The binary property right simply enables the beneficiaries to participate in capital acquisition, as capital pays for itself.

In sum, the protections provided to the lenders, existing shareholders and the new binary-beneficiaries themselves, make it

beneficiaries, a diversification of fully-paid holdings through a Mutual Stock Ownership Plan. Nor does it prevent the trustees from pledging the binary stock to provide collateral to support binary financing.

generally preferable that trustees be involved. However, once the capital acquired by employees and others through binary simulfinancing has paid for itself the binary beneficiaries are then free to use the *income* earned on their stock to participate in capital acquisition like traditional owners and thereby to enjoy the benefits of traditional stock ownership.

12.   The issue of worker control

The binary property right vests in *every person*. It is not limited to workers. Nevertheless, because the ESOP became the dominant vehicle for employee ownership in the U.S.A., in the minds of some people the binary property right is historically intertwined with the issue of worker control. This interconnection has led to much confusion. Thus it is important to bear in mind that the binary property right vests no altered right of worker participation in company management or operations beyond that of any stockholder, with the further wrinkle that binary stock is held in trust.[161]   The critical participation, from a binary perspective, is a participation in income rather than control.

---

[161] As in the case of the ESOP, federal law may allow the right to vote the binary stock to be passed through to the beneficiaries; but this approach is not required by binary principles. Further, there is reason to believe, at least with respect to the current ESOP legislation, that such pass-through provisions may not relieve the trustee of the duty, or deprive it of the power, to make an independent determination regarding its participation in binary financing. For example, in *Martin v. Nationbank Trust Co.*, (Civil Action No. 1-92-CV-1474 (N. D. Georgia, 1992), the Department of labor charged such a breach in a context where an ESOP fiduciary followed the instructions of ESOP participants regarding a response to a hostile tender offer for Polaroid stock by Shamrock Holdings. Likewise, in *General Counsel Memorandum* Number 39870, the Internal Revenue Service held that an employee benefit trust provision which allowed trustees to consider non-financial employment-related factors when tendering or voting

This is not to say that altered control rights might not be negotiated, or that reforms embracing binary economics and altered forms of worker participation may not be simultaneously advanced, with plausible arguments supporting a synergistic benefit from combining the two.[162]   Indeed, binary economists believe that the broadening of capital ownership will naturally lead to better and more participatory forms of management as the binary view of production and markets becomes more widely understood.

Nevertheless, it is self-defeating for those interested in broader capital ownership to shackle the binary property right with demands for worker control.   Such a strategy forsakes the rich benefits of capital productiveness for the stingy scraps to be gained by way of a greater share of productivity.   Put another way, from a binary perspective, the major barrier to sustainable growth and widespread affluence is not the absence of more worker control, but the lack of widespread individual capital acquisition rights that are truly *competitive* with the acquisition rights of the well-capitalized.

13.   The lending function

Thus mindful of the importance of financial participation, the binary employee is interested in learning how the acquisition will be financed. The company, having set up the constituency trust,

---

ESOP shares would violate the exclusive benefit rule of Internal Revenue Code Section 401 (a) (2) which governs ESOPs.

[162]   C. Rosen and M. Quarrey, *How Well is Employee Ownership Working?* (65 *Harv. Bus. Rev.*, Sept.-Oct. 1987, at 126-127) J. Case, *Open-Book Management – The Coming Business Revolution,* 1995; J. Stack, *The Great Game of Business – The Only Sensible Way to Run a Company,* 1992; M. Quarrey and J. Blasi, *Taking Stock: Employee Ownership at Work* (1986); C. Rosen and K. Young, *Employee Ownership in America: The Equity Solution* (1986).

now needs to raise money so Box 3 of the General Theory represents a bank or lender eligible to make binary loans. In most instances, the qualified lenders are banks, but might also be insurance companies and other institutional lenders.

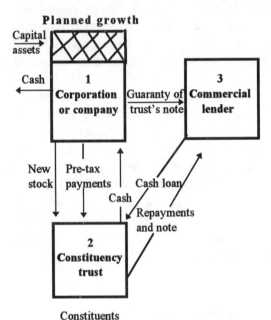

Fig. 8 – 4. Box 3 of the General Theory diagram.

As with the case of conventional debt-capital financing by corporations, the lender then seeks the answers to two questions:–

a)   *The feasibility question*

Will the capital acquisition pay for itself at competitive rates?

The feasibility question analyses the ability of the proposed capital acquisition to pay for its own acquisition cost in a competitive period, usually three to seven years. This analysis calls for projections of anticipated rates of return on the proposed capital acquisition as compared to others and, in binary terms, is focusing on a projection of capital productiveness.

To address the feasibility question, the company would typically provide a plan in the form of an investment memorandum or feasibility study which projects the timing for capital investment, construction, and operation from the beginning until the point at which revenues from the operations are projected to repay the acquisition debt. If the plan appears credit-worthy from principles of sound banking, the lender's focus then turns to the security question.

b)   *The security question*

What security is offered in the event that the capital fails to pay for itself as predicted?

Even when presented with an entirely credit-worthy plan for capital acquisition, a lender (and a bank in particular) may not properly lend without adequate security to protect the money of its depositors and shareholders.   So, to satisfy the security question, a lender typically requires not only a security interest in the assets acquired, but also a pledge of the underlying corporate stock to the extent it has been acquired on the strength of the loan funds provided. In addition, the lender will typically look to the amount of unencumbered equity of the borrowing company as a further measure of the company's ability to repay the loan in the event of a failure to meet feasibility projections.

At this point the structure of the binary financing transaction differs from conventional debt financing. Because the existing shareholders have no claim on the earnings of the binary stock, they would not wish to be involuntarily saddled with any risk of its business failure. So, if there is a business failure of the binary stock, the existing shareholders would wish the lender's claim on any default in the binary financing to be wholly satisfied without recourse to the equity of existing shareholders. As a practical matter to preserve the value of the equity of existing shareholders, this requires that the lender be satisfied on the loan obligation without recourse to the company's assets or future revenues, other than those specifically pledged.

Lenders, moreover, do not wish to see a business failure. They do not like having to foreclose on assets and dispose of them in distress situations, at depressed prices.   Yet, although it is somewhat comforting for the lender to have a security interest in the underlying capital acquired by the company and a pledge of the binary stock representing it, the reality is that there could still be business failure for which the security interests and pledges are inadequate compensation. In other words, a lender may not wish to lend unless there is plenty of collateral, or a substitute for collateral, to provide him with security if there is business failure.

This is where binary capital credit insurance fits in because it acts as a substitute for collateral. With market-priced capital credit insurance, the way is open for *any* individual to come to own wealth-creating capital assets.

14.   *Capital credit insurance*

At present, according to conventional analysis, the risk of business failure of large corporations which own most of the productive capital in the unfree market economies is theoretically borne by traditional equity investment (or other collateral).[163] In

---

[163] Binary economists agree with the conventional analysis to some extent, but they maintain that, in fact, much equity investment does *not* assume the full risk of business failure, but rather that the governments of the unfree markets spread to others, and indirectly underwrite, a portion of that risk, by means of its taxing, fiscal, labor and monetary policies.   Nevertheless, binary economists readily concede that equity investors do assume considerable risk in their stock investments, indeed more than is necessary, if the capital markets were only opened to everyone on binary principles.

competitive markets the expected earnings of the capital, adjusted for the risk that those earnings may not materialize, is reflected in both the cost and value of that equity. Therefore, to protect existing shareholders and lenders to the extent as explained above *and* to enable people without savings to acquire capital, some security in lieu of equity investment or other collateral is necessary.

Binary economics provides that security in the form of capital credit insurance as first proposed by Louis Kelso. Kelso saw the risk of business failure associated with capital acquisition as a failure of managerial judgement that a particular capital acquisition would produce goods having a market value sufficient to repay the acquisition costs.

However, Kelso reasoned that the risk of business failure is a casualty or accident risk and, like many other errors in judgement, should be insurable as such. Kelso's great insight was to see that the risk could be priced by independent private capital credit insurers, and included by the lending bank as an element of the cost of the borrowing. It could be priced and included just as the bank's fees for lending services can be priced and included.

In some ways, binary capital credit insurance is just like any other contingency insurance. For example, people are able to insure against fire, accident or rain on the day of the village gala. It is even possible to insure against the birth of twins – a premium is paid and, if the twins arrive, a sum perhaps forty times the premium is returned by the insurance company.

What is needed for sound insurance pricing is solid, well-documented past experience that fairly reflects the likely future experience. In this connection, the financial performance of America's three thousand largest companies fits the bill. Reliable data shows that, for decades, a diversified portfolio of those companies has earned its inflation-adjusted value every five to seven years.

In view of years of experience in the U.S.A., with its Federal Housing Administration (FHA), which has operated profitably for years selling home loan insurance to home-buyers at 2% of the loan, and in view of the fact that the prime credit-worthy corporate borrowers are generally borrowing at lower rates than home buyers, it is reasonable to conclude that the default risk for prime capital acquisition should be less than 2% of the amount of the loan.

Thus, in a binary financing transaction, before agreeing to make the loan, the lending bank would shop the loan around to secure the best private capital credit insurance.   In those transactions for which capital credit insurance is available, the bank pays a premium to the capital credit insurer to purchase insurance against the possibility that the loan is not repaid.   The payment of the premium happens as shown below in Box 4 of the General Theory.

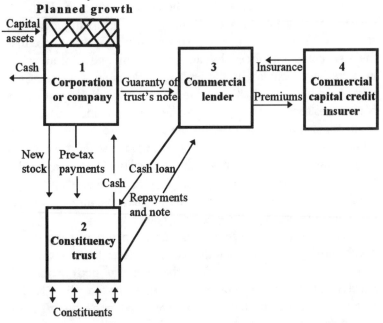

Fig. 8 – 5. Box 4 of the General Theory diagram.

Several aspects of capital credit insurance are noteworthy. First, it *insures only the lender* for any losses resulting from the failure of the constituency trust or the company itself to keep their financial obligations. Also, with that insurance, the company's revenues are protected from action by the lender, and thus the company's conventional shareholders (who would not have directly gained by the binary investment) suffer no direct loss from its failure.

Nevertheless, capital credit insurance does not protect the company managers from having to face the disappointment of traditional and binary shareholders caused by their (the managers') failed investment plans, which would generally cause losses of resources and other opportunities.[164]

In summary, the effective operation of any particular binary financing, and of the binary economy as a whole, depends on the binary proposition that the risk of capital acquisition customarily borne by traditional corporate equity, can instead be priced as insured risk premium and included in the cost of borrowing. The efficient operation requires the development of a market with commercial or government capital credit insurance underwriters who will weigh risk, calculate risk, charge for risk, be able to reinsure risk, be able to refuse risk – and take the loss if an

---

[164] The insurance insures the lenders against losses not covered by the equity investment of existing owners, but does not insure borrowing companies from loss. Thus, although the binary shareholders have no personal obligation to make good the loss (i.e., the credit extended to them is 'non-recourse'), they will nevertheless be unhappy if their binary investment ultimately fails to pay for itself and so never begins to earn spendable consumer income for them. Therefore managers of participating companies will have to answer for their failed investment decision to the shareholders (both traditional and binary). Likewise, although the lenders are ensured for binary loan losses, their eligibility to participate in additional binary financing (and so to earn additional revenues of their capital base) can be regulated by reference to their binary lending record. Thus imprudent, disqualified lenders will be out-performed by other lenders who continue to qualify as binary lenders.

investment plan goes wrong.[165]   Thus the viability of binary financing as a market alternative to traditional financing depends on the market viability of capital credit insurance, i.e. on the emergence of a profitable system of capital credit insurance.

15.   *The cost of capital credit insurance*

At present, in the U.S.A., the closest parallel to capital credit insurance is the insurance available from the American Federal Housing Administration (FHA) for qualifying home-buyers. For a fee equal to no more than 2% of the loan, the FHA has been insuring bank loans to home-buyers who have made a down-payment of 5% of the market value of the home and whose repayment prospects warrant them credit at an interest rate generally above prime.

In contrast, binary financing will be available only for financing for business capital that otherwise qualifies for prime interest rates. There are of course differences in the investment risks. In the event of default, homes may have more (or less) security value than business assets in particular cases.

Based on the FHA experience, the Kelsos, in 1986, estimated the average cost of binary insurance to be approximately 2% of the loan per annum. Any particular estimate is, of course, debatable and the question is worthy of serious study. As a corollary to the binary growth effect, however, binary logic suggests that much capital formation fails to proceed on a self-financing basis because of a systemic failure to distribute to consumers enough earnings from capital to purchase its output. Thus the financial feasibility of capital credit insurance must be judged consistently with the prospects for binary growth.

---

[165] But the binary economy will have *less* risk of failure (as compared with the present unfree market) not least because of the elimination of inflation, the ironing out of the economic cycles, and the bringing into balance of supply and demand.

Just as every car driver must pay an insurance premium (with the amount varying according to such factors as age of driver, area of residence or make of car) so most binary financings will pay an insurance premium based on the risk involved in the financing. Obviously, if the premium is too expensive, capital credit insurance will make binary financing non-competitive with traditional financing. But for relatively low risk financing, associated with a considerable portion of the capital growth of America's or the U.K.'s largest companies, binary financing (using capital credit insurance) is likely to be more than competitive with traditional financing provided that the full open market structure of the binary economy is established.

Moreover, in a binary economy, the cost of capital investment will go down (and so capital will become progressively more insurable) as compared to the costs in a conventional economy, for a number of reasons. We offer four:–

- By reason of binary growth, more investment will be profitable as capital pays for itself and begins generating binary income for employees and other binary beneficiaries.

- By opening the markets to more participants, capital and labor will be priced more competitively (by eliminating the monopoly on capital acquisition and by eliminating the need for inflating wages with the earnings of capital).

- Income distribution via the binary system will be achieved more efficiently than through the political redistribution process, as happens at present.

- With a lower threat of inflation and an ironing out of the business cycle, there will be lower risk of business failure and therefore lower capital costs.

So, from the four reasons above, and from the fact that the insurance is issued on the strength of the earning capacity of prime credit-worthy corporations rather than the earning capacity of the average FHA-eligible home-buyer, it will be understood that, when a full binary economy is implemented, the risk of loan failure can be expected to be *lower* than that on which the FHA has consistently earned a profit.

16.   The capital credit reinsurance corporation

If the principle of binary growth is real, then insuring binary financing on market principles should be highly profitable once a sufficient number of market participants come to understand it. Thus, according to binary principles, once the full binary legal infra-structure is enacted, and once the market participants come to understand the true growth potential of an open private property system, a private capital credit insurance market will eventually spontaneously emerge.

In all of his major writings, however, to accelerate the formation of a private capital credit insurance industry, Louis Kelso advocated the creation of a Capital Credit Reinsurance Corporation.   The CCRC would be a government agency with three main responsibilities:–

- to promote, form and facilitate private capital credit insurance and reinsurance companies;
- to serve as a reinsurer for the private capital credit insurers;
- in the initial stages of a binary economy (but only to the extent prudent and necessary), to serve as the primary capital credit insurer.[166]

---

[166] Reinsurance is similar to the situation when a large bet is placed with a small bookmaker who, rather than be at risk if the bet wins, 'lays off' part of the bet with a large bookmaker.   Thus, insurance companies frequently 'reinsure' a portion of the risk they are insuring by paying a fee to one or more other entities (often other insurance companies) capable of making good on that portion of the risk.   By reinsurance, insurance companies are able to spread and diversify their

But, whether as primary insurer or reinsurer, it would be expected, like the FHA, to operate profitably – that is, to set premium rates sufficient to provide more than adequate reserves to cover loan losses.

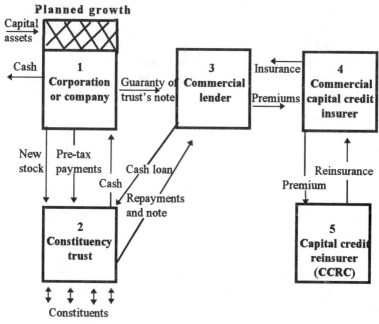

Fig. 8 – 6. Box 5 of the General Theory diagram.

To those who argue that the government establishment of the CCRC will inevitably put the taxpayer in the position of underwriting the well-being of private companies, the Kelsos have argued that, with reference to the financial well-being of the top two thousand or so U.S. companies since the New Deal, the federal government has *already* assumed the risk of their

risks over a larger pool of enterprize so as to provide more insurance at lower costs. Banks use similar risk spreading techniques when they syndicate major capital acquisition loans among a large group of banks rather than make the entire loans themselves.

aggregate failure.[167]   The major differences between the present unfree market economy and the binary economy proposal are:–

    i)   the risk is at present indirectly mediated *politically* by taxing, fiscal, labor and monetary policies (rather than explicitly as a market decision under the binary approach);

    ii)   unfree market governments promote the financing of new productive capacity so that it is owned by people with few, if any, unsatisfied needs and wants. In contrast, the binary economy opens capital ownership on market principles to those who have many unsatisfied needs and wants; and

    iii) as a result of i) and ii) above, in the present unfree market economies, the capital markets remain closed; the distribution of capital acquisition remains narrow; and economic growth is suppressed, as compared to a binary economy in which capital markets are open, capital becomes more broadly acquired, and growth is promoted.

So, in a binary economy, the government assumes *no greater risk* of business failure than it does in the unfree market economies. Rather, the government provides the private property market structure by which to capitalize the risk already assumed by the government, and facilitate its pricing and financing on market principles, for the productive and consumption needs of all.

17. Binary monetary policy

In the present economy, the well-capitalized enjoy an overwhelming advantage in the capital markets – only they have the collateral to secure the all-important credit which enables the acquisition of new wealth-creating capital assets. Moreover, even

---

[167]   Witness the governmental response in bailing out Chrysler Corporation and Continental Bank as two such companies apparently regarded as 'too big to fail'. See also note on 'too big to fail' in section 10 of Chapter Two.

the development of a system of capital credit insurance (see sections 14, 15 and 16 of this chapter) will not wholly eliminate that advantage. This is because even a modest insurance premium of 2% per annum tacked onto a bank's prime interest rate would have the effect of pricing the binary financing transaction out of the market. Thus the key question remains:–

How is it possible to eliminate the overwhelming advantage of existing owners in the capital market so as to level the playing field for those who do not own capital?

Therefore, to level the playing field, Louis Kelso turned next to monetary policy and the central bank. Specifically, he proposed that the central bank be authorized to discount the promissory note issued by the borrowing trust (which is held as an asset in the books of the lending bank). The discount rate suggested by Kelso is ¼% representing the maximum necessary cost to the central bank for administering the discount operations.

Thus, if invited by the central bank, the lending bank can tender the note and receive 99·75% additional cash for new lending. In effect, the central bank is authorized to monetize new capital acquisition which has satisfied the scrutiny of private lenders, private capital credit insurers, and government reinsurers. That is to say, the central bank is facilitating the private issuance of credit for capital investment prudently expected to more than pay for itself.

So, to whatever extent a promissory note issued by a constituency trust to a lending bank is discounted with the central bank, the prevailing 'prime' rate of interest becomes irrelevant to the cost of the financing. This is because with the cash provided by the central bank in exchange for the promissory note, the lending bank has additional dollars to lend *without the requirement of additional capital from its shareholders or deposits from customers to support the loan.*

Therefore, to the extent of the discount, the lending bank is *not* using the financial savings of existing owners but rather the 'pure credit' of the monetary system. Because the lending bank is not

using the financial savings of existing owners, any demand they
may have on the banks to earn a competitive rate on *their* money
has no direct bearing on a discounted binary loan. Nor is the
lending bank's equity at risk for the loan loss.

Thus, once all principles of sound lending are satisfied, then in
making such a loan consistent with market principles, the bank is
in effect serving as a conduit for binary (interest-free) money
coming from the central bank, not from existing owners. So the
only market charge the lending bank can fairly charge is the cost
of screening, administering, policing and collecting bankable
loans. Its market charge therefore should be no more than the
traditional 'banker's spread' – the bank's average gross revenues
for money lent minus the cost of the money to the bank – a rate
usually between 2% and 3%.

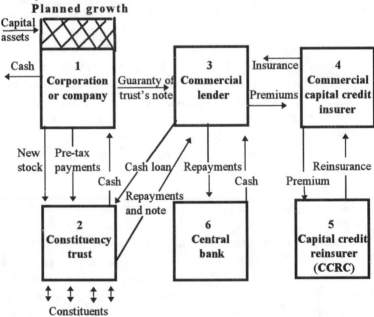

Fig. 8 – 7. Box 6 of the General Theory diagram.

18. The cost of binary financing

Therefore the total cost of binary financing works out at approximately 5 - 6% as follows:–

capital credit insurance	2 - 3%
central bank's administrative costs	0·25%
lending bank's administrative costs	2 - 3%
total (approximately)	**5 - 6·25%**

Everyone will notice the relative low cost of binary financing as compared with conventional financing. The Islamic world, moreover, will notice in particular that *no* interest is involved.

In *Two-Factor Theory*, Louis & Patricia Kelso neatly summarize the benefits of the use of 'pure credit' for viable new capital formation. They say that the credit in effect monetizes new capital formation in circumstances where the formation is as thoroughly scrutinized as is practical. Thus the monetary system would be:–

the first logical and totally flexible monetary system in history. It would monetize that factor of production which determines primarily the growth of business, and which, in an industrial or industrialising economy, primarily is responsible for producing goods and services that money is used to buy. Under such a monetary system, new money introduced into the economy in the form of payments to individuals engaged in building new plants and equipment is always directly coupled with increases in the power of the economy to produce and consume useful goods and services.

19.   *Binary discounting will not be inflationary*

Although traditional arguments based on productivity analysis suggest that the expanded 'pure credit' for those who own little or no capital will be inflationary, binary arguments built on productiveness establish that the financing will be:–

- *counter-inflationary* in the short run because when capital is narrowly owned as in unfree market economies, there is endemic underutilization of resources *and*

- *counter-inflationary* in the long run by reason of the broader distribution of income-generating capital, the improved efficiency of increasingly open capital and labor markets, and the reduction in transactions costs by substituting capital distribution for political redistribution.[168]

As Louis & Patricia Kelso say in *The Right To Be Productive* (see footnote 217 below), by using such monetized credit, or 'pure credit,'

> aggregate credit availability would be limited only by the economic feasibility of the asset growth thus financed. Neither the federal government's credit, nor its accounting, nor government guarantees would be involved. Pure credit links

---

[168] Moreover, the extension and growth in competence (together with people having much more real income to fulfil their pressing needs) will diminish the demand for consumer credit. Consumer credit is a major contributor to inflation and has the long-term effect of killing demand because people have to repay the credit together with considerable interest thereon. Consumer credit is inevitable in the unfree market economy (which fails to distribute adequate consumer demand) but is gradually eliminated in the binary one. Reputable finance houses (like reputable banks) will be able to more than compensate for loss of consumer credit business by applying to become qualified lenders in the binary economy.

growth of the economic power to produce with growth of the power to consume of those with unsatisfied needs and wants by enabling them to become capital workers and to produce higher incomes.

Thus the (binary) money flowing from the central bank is going to finance productive assets *and*, within a short time, bring new consumers with real earnings into being. Furthermore, as the binary money flows through the system to create a new capital asset it *then flows back again to the central bank* when the note is repaid.

Thus the returned binary money can be re-used for further binary financing without adding to the money supply. Therefore any inflationary pressure from the initial discounting is not repeated each time the returned money is re-used in subsequent binary financing. When the five to seven years (or shorter) period for repaying the money is over, such financing *cannot* be inflationary.

Moreover, in fulfilling its duties in a binary economy, the central bank can always reduce or discontinue binary financing for a while or reduce the traditional supply of traditional inflationary finance by traditional means to an extent equal to the outstanding amount of binary capital credit.

For a consideration of some of the monetary issues raised by binary financing in the light of other proposals see *The Federal Reserve Discount Window*, Norman G. Kurland (*The Journal of Employee Ownership Law and Finance*, Vol. 10, No. 1, Winter 1998, pp. 131-155).

20. *Recapitulation of the binary economy*

Thus the binary strategy is to build on the sound principles underlying the Homestead Acts and the Federal Housing Administration, to learn from the proven practical success of those programs, and to extend their applicability in the light of the importance of binary productiveness in the modern technological world. The strategy then goes on to establish an economy founded on an open private property system and an open capital market infrastructure that honors the binary property rights of all individuals in the minute particulars required by competitive corporate finance. The economy offers credit-worthy companies with credit-worthy capital acquisition plans a new means of financing those capital acquisitions. The means is by way of trust mechanisms that enable the companies' employees, customers, neighbors, and fellow members of the consuming public to acquire an equity interest in those companies using market-based insured capital credit, co-ordinated with disciplined, market-based understanding of production and distribution.

If the binary explanation of growth based on productiveness is accurate, and the binary claim that capital has a potent distributive relationship to growth is sound, then, although the binary financing alternative is optional, it will prove to be an increasingly competitive and profitable way for corporations to meet their capital requirements in a growing, widely prosperous economy so as to benefit the company and all of its shareholders, both binary and conventional. As capital replaces labor productiveness and increases total productiveness, the binary economy will enable all people to acquire capital on market principles so that they can individually afford to buy what is increasingly produced by capital. With the basic features of the binary economy now set out, it is time to explore in more detail in the next chapter how the voluntary operation of the binary economy will produce substantial, sustainable binary growth without inflation.

Book III

Chapter Nine

Binary growth – the natural consequence of a democratic private property system

1. Binary growth – a theoretical overview

The principle of binary growth is the third paradigm-altering concept of binary economics. It holds that capital has:–

- a productive relationship to growth (that conventional economists explain by way of productivity but binary economists explain by way of productiveness) *and*
- an independent (and very potent) *distributive* relationship to growth.

According to the principle of binary growth, the more broadly capital is acquired on market principles, and its true net income fully paid to its owners, the larger the economy will grow independently of traditional productivity-based considerations. The growth principle builds on:–

- the principle of independent capital productiveness;
- the binary property right;
- the law supply and demand, based on productiveness and applied over a *binary time frame*;[169] and
- the operation of a binary private property system within that time frame.

a)   *Independent capital productiveness*

The principle of independent capital productiveness teaches that:–

- capital is doing ever more of the work in creating ever more of the wealth;
- economic growth is a process whereby capital productiveness replaces labor productiveness and increases total productiveness; and
- capital is the source of affluence and leisure, whereas labor generally produces mere subsistence.

b)   *The binary property right*

The binary property right has been described in Chapters Seven and Eight. For present purposes, it is well to restate some of its most important features of which the most important is the practical right of individuals to acquire productive capital assets on market principles. The right extends to all people the means to acquire productive capital by using the pre-tax net earnings of capital acquired, and then to receive the full net earnings of that capital indefinitely.

---

[169] A 'binary time frame' is the time it takes capital to pay for its acquisition cost and then to begin earning spendable income for its owners. See sections 4 and 5 of this Chapter.

Once the right is recognized and protected by the binary market infrastructure, much of the capital that presently buys itself for existing owners can also competitively buy itself for new ones. As a result, poor and working people will be able to compete effectively for capital acquisition alongside existing owners.

This increased competition will naturally and efficiently produce a broader distribution of capital acquisition and binary growth. As a nation's major corporations begin to finance a portion of their capital requirements by way of binary financing, the capital so financed will (after it has paid for itself) begin distributing to its new owners (employees, consumers, neighbours, and others) the increasing income necessary to purchase what is increasingly produced by capital. At the same time, a growing understanding of the principle of binary growth *proven by its profitable results* will provide more efficient guidance to market participants in determining their highest, most profitable and optimal courses of action.

The long-run effect of the universal extension of capital acquisition rights to all people individually, on market principles, will occasion greatly enhanced and broadly distributed individual economic power to produce goods and services (through the ownership of capital) to match the needs and desires of the people to consume goods and services. Given the capacity of capital increasingly to produce and distribute abundance with ever less labor input, the broadly shared, but individually owned incentive to utilize binary financing will rest on the rich promise of steadily increasing abundance, autonomy and leisure for all people.

c)   The law of supply and demand based on productiveness applied over a binary time frame

The theory of binary growth can be understood as a unique application of the law of supply and demand over a binary time frame based on productiveness rather than productivity. A binary time frame is the time it takes capital to pay for its cost of acquisition and then begin distributing income to its owners. With an economic understanding based on productiveness and the market effect of the binary property right, this unique application of the law of supply and demand leads to a new understanding of J.B. Say's 'Law of Markets' – the idea that supply creates its own demand.

Say's Law is a controversial maxim of classical economics which has confounded and divided economists of the right, left, and mixed-center for over one hundred and seventy five years. The controversy surrounding Say's Law stems from the fact that, in theory, supply *should* create its own demand in efficient markets. However, in practice, in the unfree market economies, supply falls consistently short of creating its own demand.

In practice, the unfree market economies exhibit chronic excess supply which fails to generate sufficient demand to clear markets (of unbought goods/services) and provide incentives for more capital investment. At the same time, while people need, desire and are willing to work for more of what capital could produce, their labor is not competitively profitable compared to the capital that has replaced it and vastly added to output. Furthermore, the capital that has replaced their labor input also goes under-utilized for lack of sufficient consumer demand for its output.

Thus, although in classical and neo-classical theory, supply *should* create its own demand, *in practice it does not.* One important question is – *Why not?* An even more important question is – *What can best be done about the situation?* And binary economics has the answers. The binary understanding reveals not only *why* supply fails to distribute adequate demand in the unfree market economies, but also *how* supply can be made to distribute increasing demand to promote sustainable growth on private property principles.

When binary economists maintain that capital has a distributive relationship to growth that is independent of productivity, they see its distributional effect as a manifestation of the law of supply and demand based on productiveness over a binary time frame. Over that time frame, binary analysis reveals that much of the capital that presently buys itself for existing owners can even more profitably buy itself for new owners. It can do so *if* it is made available for sale in capital markets open to all people. In those markets, as capital productiveness replaces labor productiveness and vastly increases total productiveness, the increasing income earned by capital in providing more supply can be increasingly distributed on market principles so as to provide the widespread consumer demand to purchase what capital increasingly produces.

Thus the binary analysis reveals that the law of supply and demand has a market relationship to growth that operates naturally in all economies irrespective of their social structures, political order or customs. *By this law, more is produced in truly open markets than in closed ones.* Therefore, although it is a *natural* law with universal consequences, it is a law that produces different results in different property systems. In state-sponsored communist economies, for example, supply creates very little demand compared to its potential. In the unfree market economies, supply creates considerably more demand than in communist economies, but not nearly as much as it could. In the truly open markets of the binary private property system, however, supply will create much greater demand, very near to its full potential. So, people can either accept the consequence of the law of supply and demand (in the same way as they accept the consequences of gravity and other natural laws) thereby coming to understand it better and make it work better for them; or they can reject it – and unnecessarily pay a heavy price.

Therefore, once it is understood that capital productiveness is the primary source of supply and growth, it will also be understood that, in an open binary system, increased supply (in the form of capital) can increasingly distribute the demand (in the form of capital income) necessary to purchase its output on market principles. It can increasingly do so as the pattern of its acquisition grows broader on market principles. Then the immense growth implications of the law of supply and demand will be not only understood, but *realized* by establishing a truly open private-property free market economy such as that offered by the binary paradigm. We shall return to a consideration of Say's Law and the law of supply and demand later in this chapter.

d)   *The operation of a binary private property system within the binary time frame*

The binary infrastructure enables a market economy to optimize the growth and distributive justice promised by Say's Law. It does so by opening the capital markets that now work well for the wealthiest of people so as to make them available to everyone. Because they mature within a binary time frame, the distributional and growth effects of a binary program will begin slowly. The effects, however, will then increase dramatically after the binary capital has paid for its acquisition cost and begins to earn consumer income for its new owners.

This consumer income in the hands of the new owners will fuel a binary growth that would *not* have materialized if the new capital were to have been acquired by existing owners. Once the binary capital has paid for itself, the new owners will have capital earnings to spend on consumer goods. Indeed, even before the capital has paid for itself, spotting the increased propensity and ability of the nascent binary capitalists to consume, managers will then seek to invest more to meet the anticipated demand. Otherwise they would lose valuable market share to competitors.

Thus the broader distribution of capital, with its positive market-based effect on consumer demand, will make even more capital investment profitable. The ensuing growth is steady (not being subject to the ups and downs of the economic cycles) and ever upward until such time as all unsatisfied consumer needs have been met. Had existing owners acquired the capital, they would have been courted by private concerns and government to invest their earnings *but in the context of comparatively weaker consumer demand.*

2.   The voluntary nature of a binary economy

Viewed in the aggregate, the binary system incorporating the binary property right allows efficient individual micro-economic decisions regarding capital acquisition to be achieved while simultaneously broadening capital ownership (and production-based consumer income) on market principles rather than restricting it to people who are already well-capitalized. This is its singular genius.

However, once the binary campaign is victorious and the laws legitimizing the binary property right are enacted, nothing perceptibly out of the ordinary will necessarily happen in the first year (apart from the profound psychological effect such a victory will have on the people who appreciate its benign potential). The legislation will be historic and momentous, but the effect will be consentual and gradual. The laws will have been changed simply to allow binary acquisitions for the benefit of employees and others.   Institutions such as corporations, banks, insurance companies and trusts, will have expanded authority to engage in binary transactions.   However, they will still have to obey all laws, respect all property rights, and otherwise serve their investors, depositors, contractors, suppliers, beneficiaries etc., as under existing law.

The binary infrastructure will simply *allow* credit-worthy corporations to satisfy their capital requirements by encapitalizing their employees, consumers, nearby residents of company sites, and others using binary stock.   Any binary stock must distribute its full return (net of reserves for depreciation, research, development and working capital) first to repay acquisition debt and then to pay all net income to the individual beneficiaries indefinitely.   Any capital assets and binary stock actually acquired will be only as a result of wholly voluntary commercial transactions involving participating companies, lenders, insurers, trustees and beneficiaries.   *No* confiscation, taxation or governmental direction of investment is involved.

Because a binary economy allows, but does not require, any particular financial transaction, nor any type of transaction, nor any volume of transactions, the market participants are wholly free to go about financing capital acquisitions in the conventional way.   Nevertheless, binary analysis suggests that the profitable opportunity to encapitalize all consumers individually will not be ignored by those interested in growth and justice.

3.   *The long-term capital perspective*

An appreciation of the full effects of binary growth requires a long-term capital perspective.   Binary proposals are not an immediate expedient or a quick fix.   They will not jump-start an economy with jobs and government spending.   Rather, the predicted benefits of the operation of a binary economy on market principles are sustained, long-term, systemic benefits.   Consistent with the virtues of patience and a concern for the generations to come, the binary approach teaches that, to comprehend a lasting economic solution, people must separate:–

- urgent material needs (today's food, clothing, shelter, medical treatment, next month's rent, etc.) and the immediate financial need for a job or welfare check (cheque)
  from
- longer-term economic well-being for themselves and their offspring based on their market participation in production.

Because it requires a capital solution that plays fairly by the rules of the market, the binary approach requires a long-term appreciation of its effects.   Just as a seed does not become a fruit-bearing tree immediately simply because people are hungry, so capital does not begin to generate a spendable income on market principles for its new binary owners, simply because they demand it to do so.   Generally, before paying spendable income to its beneficiaries, the capital must first pay for itself.   But after the capital cost recovery period, a binary economy promises a market-driven infrastructure to provide a growing capital income for all households, thereby reducing dependency on labor income and providing a systemic basis for deficit reduction by progressively eliminating the need for 'transfer payments' i.e. the redistribution of earnings in various ways through the political and fiscal system.

4.   The binary time frame

Thus, in order to comprehend the full, systemic potential of the ESOP and other constituency trusts, as binary capital credit devices, to provide long-term income and promote sustainable growth, it is helpful to consider their operation within a 'binary time frame' composed of two segments:−

- *The capital payback period.* This can also be called the 'capital cost recovery period'.   It is the time it takes for a capital asset to pay for itself.   Significantly, the capital payback period is a period of limited duration.   The 'Wall Street Rule' recommends that it generally be no more than seven years.   In periods of boom it could be three to five years and perhaps a decade in times of severe depression.

- *The binary consumer income period.* This is the period over which the capital pays out income for consumer use. It can commence in any year in which all the capital acquisition obligations have been contractually met. Significantly, it is of indefinite duration and is theoretically perpetual *if* the capital is well managed, with sufficient reserves maintained for the depreciation, research and development required to restore the capital to a technologically current state.

The consumer income period, when the full earnings of the capital are paid to its beneficiaries, fully matures only after the capital has fully paid for itself. However, consumer income payments to the beneficiaries can be structured to begin even during the payback period in any year during which the annual payback obligations on the acquisitions are fully satisfied with earnings of the underlying capital.

5. *Binary growth in a binary time frame*

So let us assume the start of a binary economy with binary capital financing transactions each having a capital payback period of seven years. Assume also for simplicity's sake that, according to the financing terms, no income is to be paid to the beneficiaries of binary financing until after all the capital has paid for its entire acquisition cost. In such a transaction, capital financed in the first year of the binary economy will not produce spendable consumer income for its beneficial owners *until the eighth year*. But thereafter, it will produce that income *indefinitely* if it continues to be well managed.

Then capital financed in the second year of the binary economy will produce further consumer income for the beneficiaries in the ninth year and so on. By the fourteenth year, seven full years of binary financing will be providing the full payout of the equity return to the beneficiaries. By reason of their higher marginal spending rate, more of the additional income earned by the new binary capitalists (who have many unsatisfied consumer needs and wants) will be spent on consumption than if the income had been earned by existing capitalists (who have few, if any, such needs and wants).

This broad-based incremental consumption will fuel a demand for more consumer goods which in turn will provide incentive for greater capital investment. In other words, after the capital has repaid its acquisition cost it will begin paying out its full net income to its binary beneficiaries. The beneficiaries will then be able to spend much of their capital income on the necessities and simple pleasures that they could not have otherwise afforded. These necessities and pleasures are the kinds of things that capital can increasingly produce, but which the existing owners of capital have little unsatisfied appetite to consume. They are also the kinds of things that billions of people need and desire, yet cannot afford on their labor income alone. However, they could afford these things in the long run *if* they could acquire capital on the earnings of capital and then begin receiving capital earnings after the capital has paid for itself.

Spotting the increased propensity and ability of the nascent binary capitalists to consume, competitive managers will then seek to invest more to meet the anticipated demand. If they did otherwise, they would lose market share in the larger consumer economy. Thus the increased production-based consumer demand added to the increased demand for capital goods, which it stimulates, produces a larger economy than would be financially feasible if capital had been traditionally financed.

Therefore, beginning at least by the eighth year of a binary economy, and increasingly in each year thereafter, to the extent of binary financing, there will be:–

- more capital-based consumer demand; and therefore
- more profitable opportunities for capital investment

as compared to the situation that would exist if all capital financing were to be done in conventional ways. If conventionally financed, the capital would have earned the great bulk of its income for people with few, if any, satisfied consumer needs and wants. Those people would certainly seek more investment opportunities *but in a context of weaker consumer demand.*

It should be noted that many conventional market thinkers object to this binary growth analysis. Growth, those conventional market economists assert, comes not from redistributing demand to those who will buy consumer rather than capital goods, but rather from investing in capital that increases productivity. The increased productivity effect of capital generally occurs, they allege, regardless of who owns it.[170] Furthermore, in the short term, (e.g., a year or less), they say, demand is demand. The shift in demand from capital to consumer goods in any year (for example, in the eighth, ninth, tenth etc. year of binary financing), they say, will not of itself produce growth; it will merely allocate more resources to consumer rather than capital goods, which will lead to slower future growth because of less capital investment.

But this conventional thinking assumes that all growth is a function of productivity and that capital has no independent productive and distributive relationship to growth. Contrary to the conventional approach, the binary paradigm teaches that consumer demand and investment demand are not fungible (i.e., interchangeable). In binary economics, demand for investment goods is *derivative of* the demand for consumption goods. The only reason to invest in capital goods is to produce consumer goods that people desire and can afford.

Thus the broader distribution of capital acquisition over time provides a growing market-based demand for consumer goods which in turn stimulates a market-based demand for capital goods. As production becomes ever more capital intensive, participation by each consumer must likewise become more capital intensive if the rewards for production are not to be choked off. In addition, the more broadly capital is acquired, the more profitable it becomes to produce more consumer *and* capital goods.

---

[170] Some conventional economists are willing to concede that a broader distribution of ownership might promote growth if broader ownership causes some change in human behavior that increases productivity. But such a growth analysis does not rely on the independent productive and distributive power of capital, but rather on increased productivity.

Viewed from a binary time frame, more consumer demand and therefore more growth will materialize over the fourteen-year period to the extent that new capital formation and capital transfers are financed with insured capital credit on binary principles rather than with traditional collateralization requirements. Moreover, in binary analysis, the incremental consumer demand giving rise to the growth is *not* redistributionary or inflationary. This is because it is linked through property rights to the production of goods and services of equal value (or *more* value). Consumer income for the binary beneficiaries is limited at all points by the antecedent earnings of the underlying capital. In any year, any consumer income distributed by the binary capital to its new owners is the result of the antecedent production (by *their* capital) of goods and services of equal value, and is received only after full satisfaction of all obligations incurred in acquiring the capital.

Further, please note that the growth effects of the binary encapitalization process, as it spreads and grows among the people, may start well *before* the eighth year. First, to the extent the return on the equity represented by the binary stock exceeds the debt-servicing requirements, income will be available for payment to the binary beneficiaries *before* completion of the capital cost recovery period, *perhaps even in the first year*.

Second, to the extent that consumers feel wealthier by reason of their capital ownership, their marginal savings and consumption rates will shift towards more consumption even *before* they begin to receive binary income. Thus, with a five-year capital planning horizon, the anticipated increase in consumption may be reflected in additional capital spending *as early as the first or second year*.

6. Linking supply and demand

Given a seven-year capital cost recovery period, Fig. 9 – 1 below shows that, beginning in the eighth year and in each year thereafter, a growing percentage of annual capital acquisitions will have paid for themselves and will be added to the capital base earning a spendable income for the new binary capital owners. The figure shows the steady growth in the percentage of annual acquisitions of binary capital that have paid for themselves and can therefore begin paying their full return (net of reserves for depreciation, research and development) as spendable consumer income for the binary beneficiaries.   If proper reserves are maintained for depreciation, research and development, a binary economy can profitably finance a growing capital base that increasingly links production and consumption on a systemic basis, faithful to truly free open market principles.

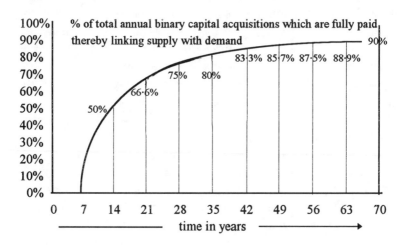

Fig. 9 – 1. Linking supply and demand.

It is important to note that increasingly over a binary time frame, the binary approach finances both supply and demand. By the end of the thirty-fifth year, 80% (28 of 35 years of capital acquisition) will have paid for themselves and will thereafter be paying their full binary incomes to employees and others. By the end of the seventieth year, 90%. As the binary period stretches out beyond seventy years (into the adulthood of our grandchildren and great grandchildren) the fraction of years of new capital formation that has paid for itself and is able to generate a second income for its citizen owners will approach 100%.[171]   Thus, increasing supply (in the form of productive capital) and increasing demand (in the form of market-based consumer income) will be essentially in a state of balanced growth.

Therefore, if the operation of the ESOP and other constituency trusts is viewed over a long binary time frame, the effect is to finance *simultaneously* the ability to produce and the ability to consume on market principles.   Over an increasing binary time frame, the broadening pattern of capital acquisition provides a basis for sustained, non-cyclical economic growth. This basis for growth continues to grow indefinitely as more capital is financed on binary principles. This is a growth connection that is *not* the result of the increased productivity of any particular workers, *nor* the result of increased investment or technological gains, *nor* of reduced transactions costs, *nor* of any other traditionally advanced basis for growth.   Rather, it is a long-term, self-sustaining   connection   between   production,   ownership, consumption and growth that exists in a binary time frame.   It is unique to binary financing, and is at the heart of the binary private property solution for the economic well-being of the poor and middle classes, without taking from existing capital owners.

Thus, because the effect of the binary property system is to provide the means to finance simultaneously the basis for both increased supply and increased demand, the binary approach offers a unique economic strategy.   The strategy is fundamentally

---

[171]   Please note that Fig. 9 – 1 assumes an equal binary investment each year and assumes no binary growth.   A growing annual investment and a faster approach to unity is more consistent with binary growth.

distinct from both the right-wing, supply-side, trickle-down strategies and the left-wing, demand-driven, Keynesian governmental approaches of taxing, fiscal and monetary policy. Unlike the conventional strategies which do not address the fundamental question of who or what really creates the wealth (and the implications thereof), the binary strategy is a long-term plan to allow individuals to become more productive (and so able to consume more) by reason of their new binary capital ownership.

Conventional economics, however, has failed to show any analytical patience for the maturation of the distributional effects of binary financing within a binary time frame. Conventional economists working for capital owners are quite willing to think through the long-term implications of capital participation for their clients and beneficiaries. However, when it comes to thinking through the implications of capital participation for people without capital, they seem to be generally able only to think about the immediate needs for jobs and welfare; and they are able to conceive of participation by poor and working people in capital acquisition only as a trade-off ultimately paid for by some function of productivity. Likewise, focused primarily on considerations of productivity and redistribution in a horizon usually no longer than five years, traditional economic strategies based on conventional economics have failed to establish a truly open market and private property foundation for all people today. Even worse, they totally ignore the legitimate capital interests of most people in the generations to come.

Yet the present conventional blindness to the sound binary approach to capital acquisition on market principles is quite out of touch with reality. For decades, the reality has been that the capital assets owned by the largest prime credit-worthy corporations of the unfree market economies have *consistently* returned their inflation-adjusted investment cost every five to seven years, except in very rare circumstances. This is the documented track record of the Russell 3000 Index depicted in Chapter One and it is this great potential that conventional economic theory obscures and effectively denies to all but the already wealthy.

The present conventional approach is like that of a driver of a motor car moving ever faster down the technological road, but looking no more than a few yards ahead, when the physics of effective response time requires systemic attention much further ahead. Such myopic navigation flirts with disaster.[172] However, once the operation of the economy is understood in terms of the law of supply and demand based on productiveness in a binary time frame, the experience-tested principles of corporate finance (that have worked so profitably for well-capitalized people of the large, so-called 'free market' economies) can begin to work for everyone else in the same way, so that increasing supply can distribute increasing demand over a binary time frame. With the increasing satisfaction of material demand, our social concerns will begin to shift from material needs to the more challenging realm of the mind and spirit.

7. The law of supply and demand and Say's Law based on productiveness in a binary time frame

The linkage of the incremental supply produced by capital with the incremental demand necessary to purchase its output on market principles to provide the basis for sustainable growth without redistribution is a singular feature of a binary economy. Building on a coherent application of the law of supply and demand over a binary time frame based on productiveness, the

---

[172] The proper analysis of growth requires a linkage between the present and the future that is more generous to the latter than the time value of money, which present-values the future largely for the benefit of existing owners. That linkage is provided by capital productiveness in an open private property system within a binary time frame.

binary approach offers the institutional means to optimize widespread supply and demand. Furthermore, it offers the practical means to realize the sustainable growth and general prosperity promised but not yet delivered to full potential by the industrial revolution. The unique application of the law of supply and demand, its relationship to Say's Law of Markets, and its remarkable potential for promoting sustainable growth, widespread prosperity and distributive justice are explored in this section.

Starting with Adam Smith, the law of supply and demand stands at the foundation of all market theories of growth and efficiency. Indeed, when explaining the triumph of the unfree market economies over communist economies, conventional analysts rely fundamentally on the efficiency effects of the law of supply and demand. But the weakness of the conventional analysis is that it is based on productivity, *not* productiveness. As a consequence, conventional economics does not recognize that capital is increasingly producing more of the supply, and therefore in efficient markets would be distributing more of the demand.

With no understanding of capital productiveness or the market potential of the binary property right, conventional economics fails to comprehend the true growth implications of the law of supply and demand. The law is usually advanced by conventional market economists with some plausibility on the micro-economic level. Thus it is used to describe the profit- and utility-maximizing behavior of individuals and firms in ways that optimize the allocation of resources, the employment of people and capital, and the fulfilment of practical preferences in supposedly efficient markets. In this core conventional application of the law of supply and demand, the price of anything is inversely proportional to its supply. In conventional theory, mediating supply and demand in supposedly efficient markets, prices determine both the cost of production and the income derived from production.

Thus, in the conventional analysis, the law of supply and demand has both an allocative function (the optimal allocation of resources and employment to satisfy demand) and also a *distributive* function (the distribution of income as payment for the production of the supply). In any particular transaction, in the conventional analysis, the market cost of supply (i.e., the earnings paid to labor and capital for their contribution to production) should, *in efficient markets*, equal the demand (the income received) for what is produced.[173] Furthermore, when all the micro-economic market transactions (in which one person's market cost is another person's market income) are added to derive the macro total of supply and demand in the economy as a whole, the conventional analysis implies that the very process of production will *in efficient markets* distribute the income necessary to purchase what is produced.

This macro application of the law of supply and demand was famously advanced by Jean Baptiste Say with the declaration that supply creates its own demand. The macro principle, which has become known as Say's Law of Markets, was not original to Say. Indeed, it was central to the thinking of Adam Smith.[174]

---

[173] At first blush, this equality of supply and demand would seem to be net of casualty losses which are not directly market costs. Casualty losses include those from theft, fire, flood, vandalism and death (which are presently commercially insured) and also business losses connected with capital acquisition resulting from errors in judgement regarding such matters as the profitability of capital investment and consumer preferences. These capital investment losses are presently insured directly by existing investors (who lose their money if the investment is a failure) and indirectly by the government in the unfree markets. Binary economics, however, reveals that these losses can be more efficiently insured with capital credit insurance in the open markets of a binary economy. Thus in efficient markets these losses are commercially insurable so that the probability of their occurrence is distributed broadly and reflected in the cost of production.

[174] Significantly, on these points mentioned in the two preceding paragraphs, binary economists find themselves in agreement with

Yet, despite the theoretical growth promise of this macro-economic application of the law of supply and demand, the actual experience of the unfree market economies has been to the contrary. In practice, in the unfree market economies, supply does *not* create its own demand. While undoubtedly outperforming state communist economies, these unfree market economies exhibit overabundant supply (in the form of excess productive capacity) and a chronic shortfall in demand. In other words, overabundant supply does *not* distribute enough demand to clear the markets of their supply even at bankruptcy prices. And, when that is the case, there is certainly no profitable incentive to invest in more productive capacity, even though people lack for many things that additional capital could produce.

Consequently, as a result of the failure of supply to create its own demand, Say's Law has been (despite its apparent validity) the subject of great controversy for over one hundred and seventy-five years – a controversy that has divided left-wing, right-wing and centrist economists. Indeed, the failure of supply to create its own demand in a way that sustains growth has caused various economists (e.g., Malthus, Marx, Keynes, and others) in differing analyses to declare that Say's Law is somehow invalid or inapplicable to the real world.

But the failure of supply to create its own demand in a closed private property system does *not* reveal that Say's Law or the law of supply and demand is somehow invalid or inapplicable. *Rather it reveals that **the present markets are not efficient**.* And they are not efficient because most people are excluded from participation in capital acquisition. The conventional perception of the invalidity or inapplicability of Say's Law arises because

---

Smith, Say and other classical economists, and also with many modern neo-classical economists of the present day. But the binary analysis differs from the conventional analysis because it understands the growth implications of the law of supply and demand in terms of increasing capital productiveness rather than increasing human productivity.

conventional economics does not understand that, if the Law is to work optimally, there have to be genuinely free markets for the acquisition of capital. Thus the conventional understanding is missing a crucial part of the overall understanding. A similar missing part of overall understanding led natural philosophers centuries ago to declare that the law of gravity applies on earth (where stones fall to earth) but not in the heavens (because the stars, moon and sun do not fall to earth).

Binary economics, however, stands outside the conventional controversy because it understands Say's Law from the perspective of capital productiveness, rather than human productivity. Recognizing that capital is now creating most of the supply, binary economics reveals that in efficient markets it would also distribute more of the demand and therefore must be broadly acquired to distribute demand most efficiently.[175]

Indeed, the distributional relationship between the increasing productiveness of capital and the law of supply and demand exists at all points in time, but is best understood over a binary time frame. Over such a period, the binary understanding of the law of supply and demand indicates that much of the capital that presently buys itself for existing owners could buy itself even more profitably if the capital markets were opened to all people by way of the binary infrastructure.

In the open capital markets of a binary economy, as more capital becomes more broadly owned, it will increasingly distribute to more people more of the income necessary to

---

[175] The matter has been well put by the Kelsos:−

"Economists have been at loggerheads over Say's Law ever since its promulgation in 1803. One of its implications is that the phenomena known as depressions, panics, and recessions cannot occur. But they have occurred, and with deepening severity, from the inception of the Industrial Revolution. Say's Law has remained a riddle to conventional economists because they approach it with a wrong assumption i.e. that there is only one way that individuals can make productive input and earn income − through labor." Louis & Patricia Kelso, *Democracy and Economic Power*, (1991), p. 34.

purchase what it produces.   The cumulative effect of the voluntary operation of a binary economy is increasingly to match supply in the form of increasing capital productiveness with demand in the form of a growing capital income earned by all individuals by way of their increasing capital ownership.

As a result of the increasing productiveness of capital in an industrial economy, the incentives to create supply will inevitably be increased if capital is acquired more broadly by people with many unsatisfied consumer needs and desires than if it is acquired by people with few, if any, unsatisfied consumer needs and desires.   When capital is acquired on market principles by a growing portion of the population, more people will (after the capital has paid for itself) begin to earn money for food, clothing, shelter, health care, simple conveniences, and eventually more consumer goods services of all kinds thereby providing greater incentives for more production.

Conversely, the incentives to create more production will inevitably be depressed if capital acquisition is effectively restricted to people with few unsatisfied consumer needs and wants.   If, essentially, all capital is acquired by a small percentage of the population with few if any unsatisfied consumer needs and desires, this small percentage will seek to invest their capital earnings but in an economy *characterized by less consumer demand*.   Therefore in an economy with capital markets closed to most people (as in the unfree market economies), the incremental productiveness of capital will not distribute sufficient consumer demand to sustain its profitability; and growth will be suppressed.

Thus in binary terms, the law of supply and demand over a binary time frame reveals that *supply (in the form of increasing capital productiveness) will generate demand in proportion to its distribution*. As a result of this distributional relationship, the law of supply and demand (although a natural law) manifests itself differently in different kinds of property systems.   For example:–

- when capital is most narrowly acquired as *in the communist societies* in markets that are entirely closed (so that capital is owned only by the state and the black marketeers*), supply will generate relatively little demand* compared to its full potential;

- when capital is more broadly acquired as *in the unfree market economies* in markets that are substantially more open (so that capital is more broadly owned but still concentrated in less than 5% of the people), *supply generates much more demand* compared to communist economies, *but still far less than its full potential*; and

- when capital acquisition is effectively open to all people on market principles, as *in a binary economy*, *supply creates optimal demand consistent with its full potential.*

In summary, by focusing on productivity rather than productiveness, the conventional paradigm fails to recognize that capital is increasingly producing the supply and therefore in efficient markets would be distributing the demand. As a consequence, conventional economics fails to understand that, for optimal growth, capital must become broadly acquired so that the earnings of its output can be increasingly distributed to those expected to purchase that output.

Thus the binary analysis reveals that the law of supply and demand is a natural law, not a political law that can be repealed or evaded to escape its consequences. Just as the law of gravity affects all things material, so too the law of supply and demand affects all things economic. By this law, more is produced in open markets than in closed ones. It is thus not only a *natural* law with universal consequences but also a law that manifests itself in differing ways in different property systems. In state-sponsored communist societies, supply creates very little demand. In the unfree market economies, supply creates considerably more demand, but far from as much as it could. In the open, binary private property system, however, supply will eventually create vastly greater demand.

So, just as it is futile to resist gravity and other natural laws, people can either senselessly resist the law of supply and demand *or* they can come to understand it better and thereby make it work better for themselves. Indeed, once it is understood that capital productiveness is the primary source of supply and growth and that, in an open binary system, capital can increasingly distribute the demand necessary to purchase its output on market principles, then the immense growth implications of the law of supply and demand can be realized by establishing a truly open private property free market economy based on binary principles.

8. Binary growth has a unique basis not grounded in conventional economic theory

It can therefore be seen that the unique distributional growth predictions of binary economics rest on a long-run application of the law of supply and demand. This application links the process of capital-labor substitution through private property rights to incremental consumer demand within a binary time frame resulting in growth.

Now conventional economic theory views the factors of growth as increased worker productivity, increased investment, and reduced transactions costs (as neo-classicists maintain) and (as Keynesians would add) the management and stimulation of aggregated demand. But binary growth has a big extra contribution which is *independent of, and in addition to,* any of the conventional factors. The big extra is the growth arising from the broader distribution of capital acquisition on market principles.

So the unique feature of binary growth is that it materializes:–
* *without* requiring any employees to work more productively;

- *without* requiring any antecedent increase in capital investment;
- *without* any reduction in transactions costs involved in running the conventional economy; and
- *without* any traditional redistribution or demand management.

Rather, the unique basis for binary growth materializes entirely *as a result of capital productiveness and its distribution on market principles*, or in other words, *as a result of the independent productive and distributive power of capital to produce growth.*

9.   Conventional bases for growth in a binary economy

Although the binary growth effect is the unique growth effect revealed by the binary paradigm, it is not the only growth effect predicted by binary economists as a result of the voluntary operation of a binary economy. Thus binary economists also predict that a binary economy will experience *additional* growth effects that can be comprehended in conventional terms. These include growth by way of:–

- a more productive workforce (because people will participate in, rather than be excluded and alienated from, the capital acquisition process);
- lower capital and labor costs (because the capital and labor markets will become more competitive);
- reduced need for redistributive taxes and other measures now used to correct the market's distributive failure that results from the concentration of capital ownership; and
- decreased transactions costs (because the distribution of capital income will be more efficient than income redistribution by way of explicit and disguised welfare).

10.   Binary and conventional bases for growth in a binary economy combine for greater growth

Thus there are *two* broad categorical bases for the economic growth that a binary economy will generate:–

- the unique binary effect based on productiveness and the law of supply and demand over a binary time frame; and
- a number of secondary effects which can be explained in conventional terms.

Further, the binary growth effect enhances the conventional growth effects and vice versa. From the standpoint of efficiency, utility and prosperity, binary economists believe that broader patterns of capital acquisition lead to better workers, customers, neighbors and citizens, *and* smaller, better government.

Therefore, in a binary economy, although existing owners will be required to compete with binary owners for the acquisition of new capital assets, they will be doing so in the context of much larger consumer demand. With greater, market-based consumer demand, more capital investment will become profitable and investment risk will be systemically reduced. With the prospect of more profitable capital investments and lower risk, and with a new constituency of competitors for capital acquisition, the cost of capital should further reduce (because the new competitors will lower the present floor below which capital investment is deemed worthwhile by the pre-existing owners) and investment will correlatively increase. *With sufficient binary growth, the value of investments of existing owners will also increase, rather than decrease, as the market economy becomes freer, more open, more competitive, and more productive.*

11.   Binary growth does not involve conventional trickle-down or redistribution

It is important to emphasize that binary growth will *not* be the result of a right-wing, trickle-down approach; nor a left-wing jobs/redistribution approach; nor any mix of the two. The binary change in distribution of capital ownership and income, and binary growth, will be the consequence of purely voluntary transactions. *No* confiscation or taxation of existing assets is involved. There is *no* 'command' in a binary economy other than the command to honor the capital acquisition rights of all people not merely the capital acquisition rights of existing owners. No citizen who acquires binary capital will receive income from that capital in any year unless the capital has paid for itself and then produced income to distribute.

Although the basic system of binary property rights requires legislation, its effect will materialize in capital acquisition transactions on market principles only if willing buyers and sellers agree. Therefore, any income received by employees and other beneficiaries of binary financing is earned by *their* capital after it has paid for itself. It is *not* redistributed from other earners. In other words, the work done by *their* capital is *not* the work of others. Likewise, the income earned by *their* capital is *not* the redistributed income of others.

Further, binary growth does not depend on the false promise that technology creates more labor than it destroys. On the contrary, it is premised on the recognition that capital productiveness replaces and vastly supplements labor productiveness and therefore, in the aggregate as a percentage of total output, capital always reduces labor's market claim on production.

Binary growth is simply premised on the recognition that capital has not only a productive but also an independent (and very potent) distributive relation to growth. This distributive basis for growth is quite distinct from the supposed growth effect and 'trickle-down' benefits of 'job-creating' increases in conventional capital investment and also quite distinct from the governmental stimulation of aggregate demand. In view of the law of supply and demand as applied to the independent productiveness of capital over the long run, binary growth is the natural consequence of an open private property system operating on market principles.

Thus, if binary growth is real, the existing closed private property system has the effect of a monopoly (because, like other monopolies, it suppresses growth) and should, for that reason alone, be eliminated so that the unnatural scarcity that prevails in our closed private property system can be replaced by a more general affluence.

12.   Ending the monopoly on capital acquisition

Binary theory predicts that existing owners of capital will suffer no loss of capital and no loss of earnings (as compared to what they would have experienced in a conventional economy). Rather they will have *increased* capital gains and *increased* earnings as a result of binary growth.

Nevertheless, the institution of a binary economy will eliminate the effective monopoly which existing owners have over the acquisition of capital. This is the inescapable correlative of extending effective capital acquisition rights to those who are at present unnecessarily denied them. Binary economics respects all existing private property rights and the rules of the free market, but it insists that existing owners do the same. Thus binary economists insist that existing owners compete with others in the capital market (as in the true free market they should).

Therefore, in a binary economy, respect for the private property rights of existing owners is maintained, deepened and fortified, but licence to hog up all the effective acquisition rights is not countenanced. This private property *principle of limitation* has its roots in the thinking of John Locke, an early grand theorist on private property, who recognized that a person's right to appropriate private property from nature (such as land) did not include the right to take so much (or spoil so much in the process of taking) as to prevent others from taking also.

The present monopoly on capital acquisition is one of the great open secrets of conventional economics. It is enjoyed primarily by private individuals, and sometimes government bureaucrats, in the unfree market economies, and by black marketeers and bureaucrats in communist societies. The leftists decry the private, plutocratic capital monopoly of unfree market capitalism. The rightists decry the government capital monopoly of communism. But *neither camp admits the monopoly in its own back yard.*

The denial is all the more inexcusable for the advocates and apologists of unfree capitalism because they profess a belief in the growth power of free markets, and then contend that the monopoly that restricts capital ownership to capital owners does not matter. These apologists claim that it does not matter whether capital is broadly or narrowly distributed as long as sufficient *income* is distributed or redistributed to the masses through jobs and welfare. Binary analysis, however:–

- exposes this position as a fundamental contradiction of private property and free market principles, and
- reveals that the more broadly capital is acquired by all consumers in an economy on market principles, and its net income is distributed to support their greater consumption, the more the economy will grow as compared with an economy that finances capital acquisition exclusively for existing owners and relies only on jobs, welfare, and other strategies to manage distribution and demand.

Thus, from a binary perspective, the present monopoly on capital acquisition is not only grossly unfair but also highly inefficient. It enables some people to acquire earning capacity far in excess of their consumer needs, while denying the same right to acquire and earn from capital to the rest of the people (who have many unsatisfied needs and wants). Thereby it also fails to distribute the consumer income necessary to buy what is increasingly produced by capital, and therefore suppresses growth. This monopoly creates and perpetuates an unnatural scarcity which can be eliminated to everyone's advantage by opening our capital markets to all according to binary principles.

13.   *Binary growth is a question of fact*

Although for reasons of justice, binary economists advocate the implementation of a binary economy, it is important to realize that the positive question of binary growth is *not a question of value, but rather a question of fact.* The great new question raised by binary theory is not whether it is good for more people to own more capital, but whether the broader acquisition of capital on binary principles will, in and of itself, produce a larger economy on market principles.

Put more precisely, the question is not whether it is good for all people to have the effective binary right to acquire capital on market principles, but rather whether the universal extension of that right to all people will unleash the distributive growth promised by the logic based on productiveness. In still other words, the proposition is:–

either

• there is a positive, non-productivity-based connection between the distribution of capital acquisition on market principles and economic growth (as binary theory contends);

or

• there is not such a relationship (as all conventional economists assume).

In principle, the proposition can be tested and proved either true or false. But it cannot be factually tested in the present property rights system, because that system is wired to foreclose any appreciable binary growth. This is, of course, because only

existing owners have effective capital acquisition rights. Without
an open private property and market system to manifest the full
potential of binary growth, any growth that is traceable to the
distribution of capital can always be explained away in the mushy
numbers which conventional economists record as productivity
growth.

The fact of the matter is that a full test of binary growth
requires a binary economy. However, a nation need not commit
itself entirely to a binary economy. Rather it could conduct a
more limited binary experiment with one of its states, provinces or
territories.   For example, the U.S.A. could enable a binary
economy to be democratically established in Puerto Rico, where
Louis Kelso proposed a binary economy many years ago.[176] But
in an absence of a real binary economy in which to test the
principle of binary growth over a decade or so, we are left to
continue using theoretical analysis, thought experiments, and
mathematical and computer modelling.

14.   Beyond the ken of conventional economics

In the history of economic thought, the long-term, capital
distribution-based binary growth connection is a revolutionary
concept (although it is a revolution in understanding, realized
without violence, but rather with respect for private property,
universal participation, voluntary exchange and democratic
process).   This binary growth is beyond the logic of all
conventional schools of market economics.[177] It is new precisely
because it is premised on productiveness rather than productivity.

---

[176] *Congressional Record, Senate*, June 8, 1972, at p. 20, 207.

[177]   A careful reading of the otherwise thorough analysis of a good
many scholars of the history of economic thought, reveals no mention
of the concept of binary growth as being within the contemplation of

A survey of leading schools of conventional economic thought demonstrates this point. The basic position of all the schools stems from Adam Smith who saw all growth only as the result of increased human productivity resulting from specialization and technology.[178] Thus neo-classical economics entertains no growth connection related to the distribution of capital ownership that is not ultimately explicable in terms of functions of productivity.[179]

Keynes understood the failure of the market system to distribute adequate demand on market principles, but failed to trace the market failure to a defective, closed private property system.[180] He therefore also failed to see the self-sustaining growth that springs from linking production to consumption through an open private property system. Likewise, although the Keynesian growth strategies seek to redistribute and stimulate aggregate demand by government measures, the Keynesian approach has no foundational concern whether or not the incremental demand is limited on market principles to the earnings

---

any person discussed in their books. See, for example, H.L. Bhatia, *History of Economic Thought*, (1978); R.B. Ekelund and R.F. Herbert, *A History of Economic Theory and Method*, (1975); L.H. Hany, *History of Economic Thought* (1949). (There is some consideration of the notion that a broader distribution of capital may cause growth by reason of greater productivity; but such growth is not binary growth because binary growth is entirely independent of productivity gains). Likewise, the concept of binary growth receives no recognition in any of the seventeen editions of P. Samuelson's *Economics;* nor in any of the writings of Keynes, Schumpeter, Kalecki, Galbraith or Friedman. After surveying and categorising the broadest spectrum of economic thought in *Why Economists Disagree: the Political Economy of Economics* (1983), K. Cole, J. Cameron and C. Edwards make no mention of binary growth as a principle recognized by any economist or school of thought they mention or describe.

[178] Adam Smith, *Wealth of Nations.*

[179] Alfred Marshall, *Principles of Economics.*

[180] J.M. Keynes, *General Theory.*

of capital acquired on a broadening base of the population (which is an essential condition for binary growth).[181]

Monetarists apply the law of supply and demand to their measures of real economic activity and opt for a limited, disciplined approach to monetary supply; but their analyses give no credence to a distributional growth factor unrelated to increased human productivity.[182]   Attention given to entrepreneurial and managerial activity is ultimately rationalized as a function of human productivity.[183]   Even attention given to the value of capital and its return is grounded in the individual decision whether to work or not.[184]

All of these conventional explanations of growth are grounded primarily in the concept of productivity and take our present closed private property system as an immutable given, when it is not.

In contrast, the binary approach uniquely:–

- concludes that the present closed private property system is *not* an immutable given, but can, and should be, democratically opened to all people; and

- reveals the logic (grounded in binary productiveness and the law of supply and demand) by which all market economies will grow in proportion to increasingly

---

[181] Admittedly, Keynes preferred 'productive' rather than non-productive government intervention (i.e. investment in infrastructure rather than outright boondoggle) but his concerns are bottomed on increasing productivity, not on expanding the ownership of capital productiveness.

[182] For example, the widely accepted monetarist view today of Milton Friedman and others that an economy like that of the U.S.A. cannot expand faster than 2 - 2½% per year without engendering substantial inflation.   This view assumes that capital has no distributive relationship to growth independent of productivity.

[183] J.B. Say, *A Treatise on Political Economy*, 6th American edition; and the works of J. Schumpeter.

[184] K Cole, J. Cameron, C. Edwards. *Why Economists Disagree: the Political Economy of Economics* (1983).

widespread acquisition of capital by all people, individually, on market principles.

The revolutionary (but democratic and peaceful) principle of binary growth, directly related to the distribution of capital acquisition on market principles, provides a sound, consentual basis for enabling all people to become substantially more prosperous on market principles without taking from the existing owners. In view of the fact that none of the most renown conventional economists have yet recognized the principle of binary growth, that principle is either a grand illusion whose underlying fallacy has eluded us and a growing number of scholars, or it is one of the most important discoveries of the twentieth century.[185]   Clearly binary economics offers a new choice in economic paradigms.

---

[185]   See J.H. Miller, ed. *Curing World Poverty: The New Role of Property* (1994). This excellent volume includes contributions from ten authors of widely diverse backgrounds all of whom accept binary theory as an essential foundation for economic efficiency and justice. In particular, the authors accept the binary paradigm as an essential cornerstone for achieving the realization of the economic vision of Pope John Paul II. See also M.J. Adler, *Haves Without Have-nots*, (1991).

Book IV

Beyond the linear paradigm

Readers will now be ready for a fuller realization that binary economics is fundamentally different from conventional economics. The conventional linear paradigm for understanding economic and political controversy puts some form of communism/socialism on the left of a horizontal line and some form of capitalism on the right. The conventional line from left to right is seen as encompassing all possible economic and political thinking. Binary economics, however, is outside and beyond the conventional linear paradigm and the matter is dealt with in Chapter Ten.

In Chapter Eleven, the recognition that binary economics is outside the conventional linear paradigm paves the way for the further recognition that readers have to make a fundamental choice between two private property systems – *either* the closed system of the unfree market *or* the truly open one of binary economics.

Chapter Twelve then discusses the broad beneficial promise of binary economics. The discussion reveals that the binary promise extends broadly beyond what are commonly thought of as economic benefits to include unifying implications for politics, democracy, psychology, developing nations, voluntary population control, the environment and opportunities for women and other disadvantaged people. Chapter Thirteen gives a brief history of binary economics; and Chapter Fourteen looks to the binary future.

At the end is the binary bibliography and some information about the authors.

Book IV

Chapter Ten

Binary economics is outside the linear paradigm

From what we have said so far, binary economics can be seen as something which, in its fundamental originality, its liberating nature, and its grand scale, is quite beyond the ken of twentieth century thought. It is even possible that, for a decade or so, it may be beyond the ken of twenty first century thought.

But it will not be beyond ken for ever. At some point, reality will intrude into economic thinking and, when it does, the binary paradigm will be recognized as having the better view of reality. When that recognition finally happens, it will be discovered that binary economics, combining originality and grand scale with minute detail, has extensive, pervasive and trenchant impact on many areas of life on this planet. Among the areas are:– poverty; economic growth; preservation of the environment; interpretations of history; philosophy; law; morals; education; psychology; equal opportunity for women, disadvantaged minorities and individuals; and the voluntary control of population levels.

A major impact, however, concerns the conventional linear paradigm for understanding economic and political controversy as well as competing interests.   Because economic and political matters in practice influence many other matters, it is probably no exaggeration to say that the impact has revolutionary consequences for almost every aspect of thinking.   We therefore propose to give some consideration to the impact of binary economics on the conventional linear paradigm.

1.   The conventional linear paradigm

The conventional linear paradigm for understanding economic issues places some idealized form of communism on the left end of a horizontal line with some idealized form of *laissez-faire* capitalism on the right.   In between are all the other economic and political forms.   So the conventional linear paradigm conceives of all existing economies and all existing political forms as left, or right, or a centrist mix of left and right – for example, forms of 'social   democracy'.   Similarly,   all   theories,   critiques   and proposals are left, right or a centrist mix.

Fig. 10 – 1. The conventional linear paradigm.

The conventional linear conception is correct in that left, right and center-mixed economies or proposals *do* lie on a line.   *All* of them are based on conventional productivity and so all are but different manifestations of *the same homocentric notion* which denies the independent productiveness of capital.   Inevitably and crucially, *all* of the manifestations then conceive that no other economics (and the politics based on it) is possible unless it lies somewhere on the line.

2. Binary economics is not on a line between left and right

The binary paradigm, however, is *new*. It offers a systemically new approach precisely because it is *not* left, *nor* right, *nor* some centrist mix. It does *not* fall anywhere on a line between left and right. Simply, in conventional terms, it defies classification.

To illustrate how foundationally different the binary approach is, consider where Louis Kelso and binary economics should be placed on the following chart:–

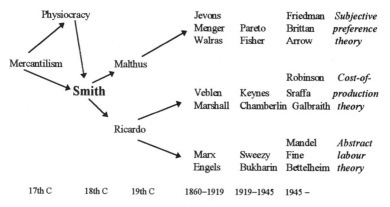

Fig. 10 – 2. The historical development of economic theory.[186]

This chart categorizes the spectrum of conventional economic thinking from left to right according to three major lines of

---

[186] K. Cole, J. Cameron and C Edwards, *Why Economists Disagree: the Political Economy of Economics* (1983), at p. 16. Reproduced by kind permission of Longman Group Limited.

thought.   Admittedly, some scholars may quarrel with the sub-categories or with the selection or position of the leading names but the chart suffices broadly to display the main, currently recognized, lines of thought *all of which are based on some concept of productivity*. Moreover, *all* of the lines stem from the thinking of Adam Smith.

Hence *none* of the economic approaches represented by these lines (and none other ever proposed to our knowledge) rests on an economic analysis based on productiveness, rather than productivity. *None* of the approaches declares that capital has both a productive and an independent distributive relationship to growth and then, based on productiveness, proceeds to establish a long-run positive relationship between the widespread distribution of capital ownership on market principles and economic growth. *None* would found a private property system designed to diffuse rather than concentrate ownership on market principles. Even in fancy, *none* speak of private and individual capital ownership by 100% of the population.   Very obviously, therefore, binary economics is outside, and independent of, the existing lines of thought.

Thus binary theory is a genuinely new idea which cannot be understood in terms of any conventional theory. It cannot be understood by placing it anywhere within the conventional frame of reference. It cannot be understood by dismembering it into right-wing and left-wing components because it is based on a different theory of economic production, participation and distribution. It can only be understood in its own (original) terms because it is as different from traditional capitalist and socialist theory as a sun-centered solar system is from an earth-centered one.

3.   Learning from Copernicus

Like the revolution in thinking that came about when people stopped believing the sun goes round the earth, and instead came to realize that the earth goes round the sun, binary economics provides a new view of reality that simplifies centuries of misleading and unnecessary theoretical complexity based on a faulty frame of reference. But discerning the new view does require a willing suspension of belief in the prevailing view of fundamental reality – an erroneous view that conventional economics has embedded in twentieth century thinking. In making that revision, there are difficulties of logic, learning and psychology.

a)   *The difficulty in logic*

The first difficulty is that there is no logical connection between the different views. Nothing in the organizing principle or empirical evidence of a geocentric solar system leads logically to the organizing principle of the heliocentric (sun-centered) alternative. Likewise, nothing in a growth analysis that is ultimately premised on conventional productivity will lead to a growth analysis premised on binary productiveness. For the same reason, the distributive implications of independent capital productiveness cannot be comprehended in a framework of conventional theory that premises all market distribution as a function of productivity. Just as a person is unlikely to discern the vase merely by staring harder at the detail of the faces, so binary theory cannot be comprehended merely by studying conventional economics in greater detail.

b)   *The difficulty due to learning*

The second difficulty is one of learning. Very few people, having at least a high school education, have not been significantly influenced in their intellectual development by either conventional right-wing thinking, left-wing thinking or some mix of the two.

Furthermore, although people may have thoroughly studied and developed great expertise in their subjects in the light of conventional economic assumptions, binary economics may subtly nevertheless call into question many of the suppositions and pet ideas of the subject to the extent they are influenced by the linear economic and political paradigm.[187]   Thus binary economics requires the re-examination of much learning about almost every important political and social issue. Consequently, some experts, who are not accustomed to having to relearn the basics of their own discipline, let alone those of another, are going to have to do precisely that if they are to understand the binary connections between their subjects and a modern industrial economy.

c)   *The difficulty in psychology*

Then there is the third difficulty that discernment of the vase can be blocked by human emotions. When this happens the very originality, liberating nature, grand scope, and pervasive impact of binary theory can provoke a deep psychological resistance akin to that experienced by Copernicus when he advanced the heliocentric vision of the solar system.   In the case of the Copernican Revolution as it is called, what was at stake psychologically was the belief that God had placed humans at the center of the universe and that all people had their God-given place in society.   To a greater or lesser extent, the belief underpinned all the contemporary social, political and intellectual power structures. Yet Copernican theory threatened (and ultimately overthrew) the belief. It was therefore a matter of the

---

[187]   Lois A. Vitt (Institute for Social-Financial Studies), *The Socio-Economic Theories of Louis Kelso: Is Sociology Ready?* (Unpublished paper delivered at the Binary Economics Sessions held at the Seventh International Conference on Socio-Economics in Washington, D.C., 1995).

biggest importance whether the Copernicans or their powerful opponents were right.

In the case of the Kelsonian (binary) revolution, what is at stake is also a belief underpinning all the contemporary social, political and intellectual power structures. That belief defines the individual's relationship to production, consumption, bounty and scarcity. The conventional productivity approach emphasizes the human contribution. It places human beings at the center of production, with capital instruments, technology, and all the resources of the globe and universe revolving around the humans.

In contrast, the binary view does *not* see human beings as the center of production. It sees production as starting with the sun, the rain, the earth, and the seeds. It certainly sees the work of humans, but then it also sees the work of animals, tools, machines and structures. It sees the productiveness of human beings as limited but capable of unleashing the ever greater productiveness of capital. Such a shift in perspective can be frightening to people who infer from it the bad news – that capital is increasingly taking away their work – and who then fail to grasp (or are merely suspicious of) the good news – that people can come to own a growing capital stake in a more prosperous economy, and thereby increasingly earn without laboring.

Taken together, therefore, it is possible that the difficulties of logic, learning and psychology may cause resistance and so confound the fair examination of binary theory. If that happens, it will produce the unhappy consequence of needlessly prolonging human suffering because great economic opportunity and new justice will have been quite unnecessarily deferred.

4.   *The Copernican challenge*

However, to ease that resistance, a deeper examination of the heliocentric challenge to the earth-centered paradigm that had reigned from time immemorial, may be helpful. According to

Copernicus's paradigm (which is understood today by school children, but was fiercely denied by all the noted experts of sixteenth century Europe) the earth was not the center of the universe but rather a mere planet – one among others – revolving around the sun.[188]   Copernicus's sun-centered theory, however, was directly counter to western religious belief (that God had created men and women and put them at the center of the universe) and counter to classical secular traditional thought.

Therefore, when careful measurements of the motion of the planets did not rigorously conform to the circular motion expected as a manifestation of God's perfection, conventional astronomers of the time invented circular digressions (called 'epicycles') for the supposed paths of Jupiter and Saturn around the earth. These fanciful, self-serving inventions had nothing to do with the physical reality of the motion of the sun and planets, but they helped to support the theory that the earth was the center of the universe. The inventions were advanced most strenuously by those who were out to maintain and shore up the faulty intellectual foundation that had been accepted as truth for centuries.[189]   For them, the earth was the center of the universe and there could be no opposed view.

So, as a diametrically opposed view, Copernican theory was certain to cause the gravest offence and, in 1616, it was declared a heresy with those who openly supported it paying the price. Thus in 1632 Galileo published *Dialogue on the Two Chief World Systems* and, in 1633, the Inquisition convicted him of

---

[188] Copernicus, *On the Revolution of the Celestial Spheres*, 1542.

[189] The great, simple, foundational insights of science are often rejected by contemporaries.   Thus most contemporaries rejected Pasteur's idea that disease was caused by (unseen) micro-organisms. The concept of great tectonic plates moving and colliding with each other on, and beneath, the surface of the earth was similarly rejected so that Wegener died despairing of his colleagues ever realizing the obvious.   Barbara McClintock was scorned for announcing her discovery of 'jumping genes'. Germs, tectonic plates and 'jumping genes' are, of course, three of the unassailable truths of science today.

heresy, forced him to recant and sentenced him to life imprisonment.[190]

When rumor of the new-fangled thinking circulated, moreover, the common sense of ordinary people was also offended. Everybody could *see* the sun going round the earth. In addition, stellar navigational technique, (based on earth-centered theory), was adequate for getting ships round the world and back to the port whence they had started.[191] As far as ordinary people were concerned, fancy intellectuals like Copernicus were out of touch and out of their minds. Put shortly, the theory of Copernicus was reviled, condemned as intellectual, moral and religious subversion, or dismissed as out of touch with reality. Put more shortly, it was suppressed.

The utility of the heliocentric view grew more widely accepted, however, and it became virtually undeniable after Isaac Newton published *Principia* in 1687. With the publication of his universal laws of gravity, Newton reconciled the motion of the heavenly bodies with the motion of things on earth. In so doing, he revolutionized our understanding of the physical world thus providing a foundation for further discoveries that would propel human society into the modern era and eventually put a man on the moon. Significantly, Newton's analysis could *not* have been conceived, and would have no apparent validity, using an earth-centered paradigm.[192] The revolutionary work of Newton serves to underscore the fact that new paradigms can reveal marvelous new realities that are inconceivable from the perspective of the old paradigm.

---

[190] The imprisonment was later commuted to house arrest. It was not until 1992 that the Catholic Church cancelled Galileo's conviction for heresy.

[191] Thomas Kuhn, *The Structure of Scientific Revolution* p. 68 (2nd. Edition, 1970).

[192] R. Ashford, *The binary economics of Louis Kelso – the promise of universal capitalism,* (22 *Rutgers Law Journal* 3, 1990, p. 119, note 438).

5.   *The binary challenge*

Now let us return to binary economics which:–
- is founded on productiveness rather than productivity;
- is founded on an open private property system which no one has yet experienced; and
- makes mind-boggling growth predictions that seem fanciful in the present closed system of private property that denies effective capital acquisition to most people.

Because almost everyone's attitude and assumptions are based on left-wing economics, or right-wing economics, or some mixed centrist position, an approach like that of binary economics – coming neither from right-wing economics (which supports right-wing politics), nor from left-wing economics (which supports left-wing politics), nor from any mix of the two – is bound to be viewed, at the very least, with suspicion.   The suspicion, moreover, can quickly turn into hostility when it is realized that the new binary creature:–
- challenges everyday thinking;
- provides incisive, intellectual concepts which lay the basis for new possibilities, new policy and new practice;
- launches a trenchant challenge to accepted economic and political doctrine; and, in particular,
- reveals that (contrary to everybody's favorite prejudice) right-wing and left-wing economic and political doctrine are in reality two sides of the same coin, sharing a common false paradigm and proposing the same dreary future (i.e. only jobs and welfare) for the common person.   In other words, *unfree market capitalism and communism are but two manifestations of the same wrong thinking*.   When told this, some communists and unfree market capitalists are bound to react with fury.

Indeed, in the present context, the resistance to binary theory is heightened not only because binary theory challenges the powerful and pervasive left-center-right linear paradigm that dominates twentieth century economic, political and private property theory, but also because it:–

- would eliminate the virtual monopoly enjoyed by existing owners (through their ownership of private capital) and by government officials (through their control of state-owned capital);
- challenges the Protestant work ethic (insofar as it is a toil ethic, rather than an ethic to develop one's talents voluntarily in a spiritually enlightened fashion); and
- rejects the labor theory of value as reflected, explicitly or implicitly, in the writings of Adam Smith, John Locke, Karl Marx and the neo-classical, the Keynesian and monetarist economists.[193]

Moreover, while extending individual economic participation by way of capital ownership, binary economics would progressively undermine the perceived need and desirability of exercising increasing *political* power to confiscate, tax, limit and control the private property rights and markets which are now fully enjoyed by only a few. Those who exercise political power frequently do not like it being taken away.

Further, psychologically, binary economics challenges the arrogant, homocentric idea that it is people who are primarily responsible for the productive bounty of nature and technology. That arrogance is a major cause of environmental depredation. By insisting that the non-human assets do work, and are increasingly doing more of it, binary economics not only exposes self-centered arrogance but also encourages a more holistic approach to life on this planet.[194]

Significantly, the binary approach discredits powerful right-wing, left-wing and mixed centrist positions held by people well-entrenched in important positions within government, business, and universities. It exposes errors swallowed uncritically not only by generations of scholars, but also by government, union,

---

[193] Cole, Cameron and Edwards, *Why Economists Disagree.*
[194] See Chapter 12, Section 8.

business and civic leaders of every political stripe for over a century. With their power and reputation at stake, it would not be surprising if, faced by binary economics, some of those leaders resist any serious exploration of binary economics.

6.   *How big might binary growth be?*

We now ask the key question – *How big is binary growth?* How big might it be in an economy with capital markets open to all people as efficiency and distributive justice require? In truth, no one knows for sure because no capitalist economy today recognizes the full binary property right. Thus, the concept of binary growth is untested; and its magnitude is speculative. It might be non-existent, trifling, substantial, or of a magnitude largely beyond our imagination.

Another key question is – *How then should the question of binary growth be explored?* And another – *Which paradigm should be used to explore the question?* The choice of paradigms is critical, because it shapes all of the analysis and judgements that follow.

Exploring the question of binary growth with an analysis largely shaped by conventional economic analysis, is problematic. A conventional analysis that explains the great growth of the unfree market economies as primarily a function of productivity, is generally incapable of comprehending binary growth. Just as nothing in the organizing conception of an earth-centered solar system leads logically to the recognition of a sun-centered one, so no dominant, logical provision for binary growth exists in the assumptions of productivity-based economics, at least as it is presently conceived. Any impetus for binary growth, therefore, is short-circuited and trivialized by a productivity analysis that *assumes* free and open capital markets, but which gains its empirical evidence from *closed* ones. Indeed, in the neo-classical approach, binary growth is excluded *by definition*. Can projections, predictions or even intuitions based on conventional economic theories reflect a principle they are not structured to recognize? Because binary growth depends on an untried open private property system, even empirical evidence, based on our existing closed private property system, provides a suspect proxy for the operation of the binary system.[195]

Insensitive to the foundational difference between conventional productivity and binary productiveness, some traditional economists who have considered binary growth informally, discount it as non-existent, fanciful or too speculative to be taken seriously. Indeed, a few have expressed concern that the shift from primary emphasis on human productivity to binary productiveness and the operation of the binary infrastructure may even lead to what might be called a binary depression. But *none* of this negative speculation has been set forth with any specificity in print so that it can be rigorously examined.

In contrast, in 1967, the Kelsos predicted that, in a binary economy, America's growth rate would triple in three to five years and in

perhaps 25 years....(people's) energies and efforts would be largely directed to the unlimited work of leisure – to education, the arts, science, sports, religion, philosophy, statesmanship and the like....[196]

In other words, people will do the work of civilization. These are certainly astounding predictions, by most economic standards and experience. Yet, if only partially realized, they would far

---

[195] Pointing to the period of the Homestead Acts, championed by President Lincoln, as the closest correlative to the open private property system, the Kelsos identified a sustained period of non-inflationary growth and broader income distribution which lasted until the operative provisions of the Acts expired and the U.S.A. returned to the closed private property system. Kelso and Kelso, *Democracy and Economic Power* (1986) at p. 16, 19, 159.
[196] *Id.* at 98-100.

surpass the most optimistic forecasts of traditional economists expected to be achieved by implementing proposals based on their various theoretical approaches.[197]   Indeed, by widely-shared, experience-conditioned expectations (based on the existing closed private property system), the Kelsonian predictions so far outstrip the promise of traditional economics that they may seem unrealistic, fanciful, beyond the realm of the possible.

So how can ordinary people, who are not economic experts, when faced with two economic paradigms for understanding growth, decide for themselves how big binary growth might be? One way to derive a sense of its magnitude is to focus on the fact that the two different economic paradigms are also two different *private property paradigms*, and with that understanding, then consider some evidence readily at hand.

Thus, permit a thought experiment to test the relationship between different property systems and the way people conceive the realm of the possible. Suppose no large and relatively affluent unfree market economies existed anywhere on earth. Suppose also that some well-meaning reformers were to go to the republics of the former Soviet Union or to the countries of Eastern Europe or the Third World proclaiming that they could create a market economy (modelled on a vision of the U.S.A. economy) where mile after mile of shopping malls boast stores full of goods. Suppose they said there are mountains of food and rivers of milk with farmers being paid *not* to produce more. Suppose they said there are also vast discount sales continually everywhere available, lavishly supported by massive advertising pleading with people to buy........

Of course, the reformers would also warn that there would be some initial, temporary dislocation and a drop in Gross National Product resulting from the 'shock therapy' of the 'big plunge' into market principles. They would admit that there would be considerable (but politically 'manageable') residual poverty. However, they would add, the economy will nevertheless begin to

---

[197]   See, for example, M. Weitzman, *The Share Economy* (1985).

experience substantial, unprecedented growth which would produce (within a generation or so) a large, relatively affluent, (though still worried) middle class.   In aid of their case, the reformers might then present an illustrative drawing such as this:–

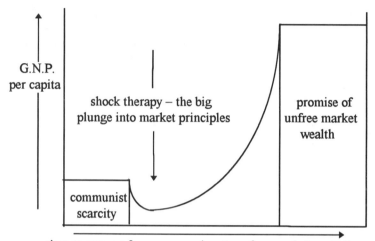

Fig. 10 – 3. The promise of unfree market wealth.

Nevertheless, even with their chart, the reformers would not be believed.   The promised growth would simply be incredible.   In truth, to most people, the growth predictions would become credible only if the reformers could point to the *actual experience* of, say, the U.S.A.   Without that experience, the reformers would be labelled as dreamers and perhaps be ignored for decades, generations or even centuries.[198]

Yet large capitalist economies, such as the U.S.A. today, are economies with *less than 10%* of the population enjoying

---

[198]   Aristarchus of Samos, in a remarkable insight, first proposed the sun-centered solar system in the third century A.D.   It is to be hoped that binary growth will not have to wait as long as Aristarchus' insight did to be recognized.   For Aristarchus' work, see T.L. Heath, *Aristarchus of Samos, the Ancient Copernicus* (1913).

effective capital acquisition rights. Binary analysis therefore
invites us to ask how much larger might those economies be –
how far beyond our experience-conditioned expectations – if they
were founded on a private property system in which *all* people
enjoyed effective acquisition rights. If the socialist economies
with only black market private capital are small, and the existing
capitalist economies are significantly larger even though only
10% of their populations own viable capital estates, how much
larger might those economies grow as increasing numbers of
people acquire a binary competence to become binary capitalists
on true free market principles? The reformers might well present
another drawing:–

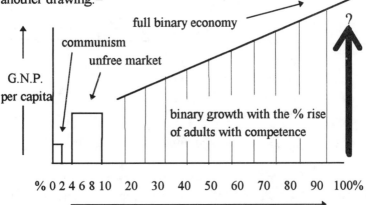

*Fig. 10 – 4. The road from communism and the unfree
market to the binary economy.*

This drawing shows the considerable growth in output as the
transition is made from communism (with 0 - 2% private capital
ownership) to unfree market capitalism (with about 5 - 10%
private ownership). It then shows the almost unimaginable
growth which could come with the transition from unfree market
capitalism, (with capital effectively benefiting only 5 - 10% of the
population) to the full binary economy in which capital

acquisition rights are effectively enjoyed by 100% of the population.

Lastly, readers might like to ask themselves another question. Even if binary growth were to be only a half or a quarter of the magnitude predicted by the Kelsos, then might not the presently endless debates (among those of left, right and center) regarding jobs, welfare and trickle-down amount to mere squabbling over spare change in the gutter? Can not the debaters see that, all the while, the real action – the all-important access to long-term economic well-being – is being negotiated for the few up in some high-rise building behind closed doors? And even if the binary growth is just 10% of what Louis Kelso predicted, is it not yet better for the people to have the binary property right than to continue without it? And just what is there to lose from trying the binary approach? Asking such questions is not to answer them, but it underscores the importance of remaining open to the implications of new ideas, and of resisting the self-imposed restraints of unexamined, limiting assumptions.[199]

---

[199] "When you adopt a new systematic model of economic principles, you comprehend reality in a new and different way." Paul A Samuelson, *Economics and Introductory Analysis,* 7th Ed. (1967) p. 10.

Book IV

Chapter Eleven

The choice in private property systems

1. New paradigms offer new choices

New paradigms offer new choices. With the advent of the binary paradigm, all the old economic and political choices made over the last century or so (which are implicit or explicit in all the economies of the world, from far left to far right), are called into question.[200] So, in considering how society should reform itself to adapt effectively to the future, one thing becomes clear – the present patchwork of public and private institutions and solutions based on a mix of conventional capitalist and socialist principles is *not* all there is to choose from.

In addition to the old choices, there are the new binary choices which will arise in many contexts. The new choices will involve

---

[200] Indeed the entire history of economic and political choices since the advent of industrial revolution should be re-evaluated in the light of the binary paradigm.

the reconsideration of many kinds of far-reaching decisions. Furthermore, inevitably, the new insights provided by the binary paradigm will point to new, more just and more efficient choices than can be seen from a conventional left-wing, right-wing or mixed-centrist economic perspective.

Of the new choices offered by the binary paradigm, perhaps the most fundamental is the choice in private property systems. It is a particularly timely choice because the apparent triumph of unfree market capitalism over state sponsored communism reflects, in and of itself, a choice in property systems. That choice was between economies in which the capital is
  either
- primarily *state-owned* (i.e., state sponsored communism or socialism);
  or
- primarily *privately owned*, although also largely concentrated *in the hands of less than 10% of the population* so as to require massive earnings redistribution (i.e., unfree market capitalism).

But, with the development of the new binary paradigm, it becomes obvious that the above choices are not the only possibilities. Just as the primarily privately owned unfree market economies (with capital concentrated in the hands of less than 10% of the population) have performed with greater efficiency than the primarily state-owned ones, so the binary economy (which over time will become almost entirely individually owned by 100% of the people) offers an efficiency even greater than that of the unfree market. This is because the broader acquisition of capital in the binary economy fuels a greater growth in proportion to its distribution.

So the triumph of unfree market capitalism over state-sponsored communism/socialism represents not only a choice between economic theories, but more fundamentally, as reflected in the national laws governing the economy, a choice between property systems. That there is an inextricable connection between economics and property should come as no surprise.

When considering economic issues, both the left and right (and everybody in between) focus on the property system. For example, when Marx set out to improve the economic plight of poor and working people by reforming the economic system, he inevitably had to propose a change in the system of property. And, by reason of the same inextricable connection between economics and property, people on the right-wing of the economic spectrum staunchly defend private property rights. They do so because they see not only a moral foundation for private property reflected in two basic principles:–

- You deserve to keep what you produce; and
- Thou shalt not steal

but also an economic efficiency connection which is inherent in their view of the relationship of private property to markets.

Thus the victory of unfree market capitalism over communism or socialism is only the victory of *one kind* of property system (a closed private property one) over another (a state-controlled one). But, the closed private property system of the unfree market economies is *not* the only private property alternative. The open binary private property system described in Chapter Eight can easily be gently and democratically adopted while honoring all existing property rights.

Therefore to understand the true range of private property choices realistically available after the collapse of state sponsored communism, people on all levels of society should develop a deeper understanding of private property and its potential for enhancing efficiency and distributive justice. This chapter explores the subject of private property more fully.

2.   The meaning of 'private property'

There is considerable confusion in much twentieth century speech and writing regarding the meaning of 'private property' and its relationship to things. For example, people often speak of a parcel of land, a structure, a vehicle, a machine, a tool, or a patent as their 'property'. Students of the law, however, soon learn that property is not one or more physical or intangible things, but *human rights in respect of those things*. Because the rights can be separated and apportioned in many ways convenient to serve different purposes, property is often referred to as a 'bundle' of rights with respect to things. For example, there can be permanent or temporary rights of exclusive and non-exclusive use, income rights, residual rights, rights to buy and sell (often called 'options'), and collateralization rights (i.e. rights to use capital assets as security for credit to acquire additional capital assets).

In referring to a 'private property system', therefore, a social system that recognizes individual human rights over things is meant. Accordingly, if the law courts uphold a man's right to the profits from a particular piece of land, or uphold his right to grant a tenancy of that land, then he has a private property in it. Similarly, if the law courts uphold a woman's right to receive the income from shares of a company, they are recognizing her private property in those shares. Indeed, the shares (which are evidenced by share certificates indicating the number of shares owned) themselves reflect a property interest in the underlying capital owned by the company. The woman's property interest is further reflected in the equity accounts of the company's financial statements and is respected in every lawful transaction undertaken by the company.

a)   *Private property in capital*

Conventional left-wing and right-wing economists and binary economists all give special consideration to the importance of private property in capital, but they approach the issue in very different ways.

In critiquing the raw capitalist economies of the nineteenth century, Marx distinguished between private property in personal possessions and private property in capital. Interestingly, most socialists did not, and do not, reject private property in personal possessions.   However, because they were concerned with real economic power, Marx and his followers focused on the question of private property in capital.   They recognized property in capital as vitally powerful because of the increasing power of capital to produce more and more of the wealth.   Yet admitting the increasing productive power of capital *as an independent productive* power would have exposed a fundamental contradiction in socialist analysis because, at the same time, the socialists upheld the labor theory of value – the idea that labor and not capital was creating the surplus value.   So, on the one hand, they protested the concentration of capital ownership because they knew that machines were doing an increasing percentage of total production while, on the other, they were alleging that an increasing percentage was being done by the humans.   They could not admit the work of the machines without debunking the labor theory of value.

There is also a contradiction in the position of proponents of today's unfree market capitalism who see private property in capital as being the vital key to economic growth and greater affluence.   Yet, holding to the idea that increasing human productivity is the cause of growth, those same proponents deny that capital is doing most of the work and has a distributive relationship to growth that is independent of human productivity. They repeatedly stress the need for more capital investment to increase productivity, but maintain that it does not matter whether the new capital is narrowly rather than broadly acquired.   They also stress the need for laws, institutions, and practices that facilitate capital formation for existing owners, but oppose or ignore binary ways that offer to facilitate much more capital formation much more efficiently for everyone.

The contradictions of both left and right stem from the same erroneous thinking.   This thinking wrongly denies the independent productiveness of capital and therefore wrongly concludes that all growth is some function of productivity.   Binary economists, however, fully understand the independent productive and distributive role of capital in creating wealth. Thus the private property issues with which they are primarily concerned are the question of private property *in capital* and the further question – *Who has rights to acquire it?*

b)   *Private property in self and labor*

Of course, a private property right that humans have individually in themselves is the other vital property right necessary to individual freedom and fulfilment. To have an inalienable private property right in one's own body and labor is an essential element of what it means to be a free person in a society governed by laws. In slave societies, regrettably, people can be owned by other people or institutions just as donkeys and trucks can be owned. In such societies, human beings are truly 'human capital'.

But in free societies, no person can own another person's body or labor. With a property right in their own labor, people are free to produce consumer or capital goods for use or sale and also to sell their labor in the labor markets. Also with this right, people cannot be compelled to work for nothing; nor can they be compelled to work against their will even though they might be handsomely paid for that work. In 'free' societies, military conscription is a notable (and, for some people, irreconcilable) exception to a free person's private property right in his labor.[201]

However, a free person's private property right in labor has economic limitations. For example, such a right cannot on market

---

[201] It seems to be the case that, at common law, there is some sort of limitation on all rights. The justification offered for the limitation on individual liberty manifested by military conscription is the need to protect the society as a whole. Thus an individual's rights in body and labor are subordinated to the requirements of the society. Of course difficult moral and political issues arise when an individual's view of what is a requirement of the society differs from that of the government of the day.

principles compel labor compensation from another who has not agreed to pay for the labor (even though the services are highly valuable). Nor can such right make human labor more valuable than it is. Thus many people (such as women caring for children) perform valuable services, but receive little or no monetary compensation. And many people are free and willing to work, yet they cannot produce enough (in competition with other people or with capital) to earn a living.

c)   *Private property in capital is necessary for individual survival, economic well-being, distributive justice and sustainable growth*

From a binary perspective, in the light of the industrial revolution, having private property in one's own labor while essential to individual liberty, is *not* enough for individual economic survival, much less robust economic autonomy and prosperity. In other words, *a private property right in labor has little or no economic meaning if people cannot get jobs* or if jobs, in reality, are no longer doing a substantial part of the wealth creation. Increasingly, for survival, economic autonomy, and material prosperity, people need not only private property rights in their own labor, but also private property rights in the capital that is doing ever more of the work. And the same requirements are necessary for distributive justice and sustainable growth.

Thus, from a binary perspective, a just and efficient property system cannot be one that limits people to personal rights and restricts capital rights to the state (as in communist economies). Nor can a just and efficient private property system be one that rhetorically elevates personal rights above property rights, while restricting effective capital acquisition rights to those already well-capitalized (as in unfree market economies). A just and efficient private property system requires that *all* individuals have effective property rights not only in their labor and personal possessions but also increasingly in productive capital.

The reasons for preferring the binary private property choice will become yet more apparent in the light of the purposes, principles, and limitations underlying private property, which are discussed in the next three sections.

3.   Purposes of a private property system

A private property system has several purposes.   The main ones are:–

a)   Social purpose

A private property system is *socially* valuable because, when properly structured, it enables people in society to exercise dominion over things in a free, peaceful, orderly, efficient and mutually respectful manner.   However, the value cannot be maximized unless all individuals have effective private property rights to acquire a viable share of what produces the wealth.   If, therefore, what produces most of the wealth as a practical matter can be privately acquired *by only a few people*, then freedom for the few suppresses the freedom of many others; peace becomes a cosmetic illusion built on strife; order unravels into disorder; efficiency and distributive justice are compromised; and mutual respect for law and order is replaced with contempt.

b)   Motivational purpose

A private property system is also *motivationally* valuable because it protects individuals in the receipt and enjoyment of what they produce through their labor *and* their capital, or both.[202]   In this way, individual incentives for efficiency are maximized. Again, the value cannot be maximized unless all individuals have effective property rights to participate efficiently in the capital and labor markets. However, when *only a few* can acquire the capital that increasingly produces more of the wealth, demand for production is strangled; the motivation of the many is suppressed; and negative, destructive attitudes prevail.

c)   Democratic purpose

Besides being socially and motivationally valuable, a private property system is *democratically* valuable because the considerable power which comes from individual economic autonomy enhances and supplements the small power of the vote. However, when *only a few* have the considerable power which comes from individual economic autonomy (as in the present unfree market), the many, individually, have relatively little or no power at all. Thus, when there is a great imbalance of power, there can be no true democracy because political power cannot be effectively diffused throughout a population as long as economic power remains concentrated.   Indeed, when only a few have individual economic autonomy, *democracy turns into plutocracy*.[203]

d)   Binary purpose

A   private   property   system,   therefore,   is   socially, motivationally and democratically valuable. However, its value is severely compromised when only a few can acquire effective property rights in what really creates the wealth (that is to say, the capital assets). So it can be easily understood that, just as binary

---

[202] Louis & Patricia Kelso, *Two-Factor Theory*, p. 60.

[203] Significantly, frequently no more than 50% of the eligible voters in U.S.A. actually vote in elections. And, of course, many U.S. citizens do not register to vote.

economics offers a new economics (founded on productiveness), so it also offers a new private property system significantly different from the present one.   A major difference is that *all* people (not just some) are enabled to participate in the increasing productiveness of capital on market principles.   As a result, capital ownership will tend to diffuse rather than concentrate. The new binary property system provides a much fuller democracy.   Combined with the new economics it offers to help put people at peace with each other, with the advance of technology and with the environment, in a way that produces sustainable growth, distributive justice, and widespread material prosperity.   These are high purposes for a private property system, and binary economics offers to fulfil them.

4.   The three private property principles

In a very important sense (unlike the binary economic analysis built on productiveness which is entirely original in the history of human thought), the binary private property system is *not* fundamentally new.   Although the binary infrastructure, and the precise definition of the binary property right in a modern industrial economy, are new in their particularity, the basic binary property right itself is founded on ancient principles of private property with deep roots in the English common law.

The basic binary private property principles are principles of *participation, distribution, and limitation.*   These principles closely follow the principles of truly free and competitive markets and are discussed below.

a)   Participation

The participation principle holds that *all* people should be able to participate in the private property system on private property principles.   No one who is willing to play by the private property rules should be excluded.   Thus the participation principle is one of inclusion and universality. It reminds that if I would be a capitalist, then I cannot deny that goal to any other. It demands that, as with the conditions for efficient markets, to maintain its efficiency and universal legitimacy, the private property system should not be subject to entry barriers.

b)   Distribution

The principle of distribution (or distributive principle) in a private property system holds that each participant in production is rightfully entitled to receive the wealth that participant produces.   By the distributive principle, the producer (or the owner in the case of a non-human producer such as a machine or donkey) deserves what she or he produces, and need surrender production to others only voluntarily.   Thus the distributive principle reflects both the property right of producers in their production and the principle of free exchange.   (The producers can either consume their production, or exchange it voluntarily for the production of others.)

In other words, the producer gets the income. As a corollary, people should not steal.

c)   Limitation

The limitation principle is a recognition of the fact that property rights can equip individuals with such power as to enable them to injure the rights of other individuals or of society in general. When John Locke, for example, justified one person's taking from nature, he limited the taking so as to require that person to leave enough for a taking by others.   Thus the participation of all is limited, if necessary, to ensure the participation by all.

So the binary private property system upholds a general right of private property but inherently subjects the right to limitations necessary to ensure that universal participation and just distribution are honored. These principles are further developed in section 5 below.

The idea that limitations on property are necessary is all but universally recognized among peoples of the world. Such limitations are necessary because property gives power. Property in the hands of the few can concentrate so much power that others cannot have effective participation rights and are thereby denied the participatory basis for distribution rights. Property in the hands of the few can also concentrate so much power that the functions of government are bent to serve special interests. Consequently, the civil rights and liberties of the many are infringed and there is an erosion, and ultimately a destruction, of democracy.

5. Two inherent limitations on property

The limitation principle underlying private property rights, with its deep roots in the Anglo/American common law, can be restated as follows:–

- the ownership of private property does *not* include the right of an owner to use his property in a way that injures the property or person of another; and

- the ownership of private property does *not* include the right to use that property in ways which injure the public interest or the public welfare.[204]

In other words, property rights are inherently limited to the extent that they interfere with the rights of others or the rights of society. Thus the ostensibly unrestricted property rights associated with a less congested, less inter-related, pre-industrial world, have always carried with them the two inherent limitations

---

[204] Louis & Patricia Kelso, *The Right To Be Productive:* (2, *The Financial Planner*, 1982 at p. 51 and 54). See also Louis & Patricia Kelso, *Democracy and Economic Power*, p. 36.

set forth above.[205]   Accordingly, as society has industrialized, legislatures and courts have subjected those rights to more specified limitations for the protection of individuals and society.

Yet, in attempting to give protection to individuals and society, the legislatures and courts have been trying to correct for market failure resulting from the unfettered operation of the private property system, frequently *without understanding the underlying cause of that failure*.   Therefore an important question addressed by binary analysis is how the limiting principles (inherent in a balanced system of private property) apply to a post-industrial world in which capital produces an ever-increasing proportion of the wealth and so has the increasing ability to buy itself either for existing owners or, initially as easily (*and eventually more easily*), for all people individually.

The binary analysis of production based on increasing capital productiveness indicates that unrestrained capital acquisition rights in the hands of a few can become so substantial and concentrated that they begin to monopolize and effectively extinguish the capital acquisition rights of others.   With no effective market participation for the many, there develops growing distributional imbalance that forces a political distortion of the distribution principle to meet the needs of those who have been excluded from participation in capital acquisition.   So the binary infrastructure uniquely corrects the unfree market's productive and distributive failure.   It does so by providing a bigger, more robust and competitive market solution that honors everyone's private property rights.   Unlike other proposals for reform, the binary proposals respect all existing property rights

---

[205] The principles of limitation have been recently articulated by the U.S. Supreme Court in *Lucas v. South Carolina Coastal Council* (1992) holding that a state's right to regulate without rising to a 'taking' of property in a Constitutional sense (so that the owner of the property subject to regulation must receive just compensation) is bounded by the common-law of nuisance.

with respect to things, and leave existing owners entirely free to compete for additional acquisitions.

However, in a binary economy, *others are also able to compete* for capital acquisition as well. This increased competition resulting from the effective extension of participation rights in capital acquisition to all people, is *not* a taking of the acquisition rights of existing owners. Their acquisition rights *are, and always were, inherently subject to limitation* as necessary to insure universal participation and to protect society.[206] More particularly, at common law, the capital acquisition of rights of existing owners were never so extensive as to enable them to monopolize the acquisition rights of others. The binary infrastructure merely provides the institutional arrangements whereby the private acquisition rights of existing owners are not allowed to monopolize and extinguish the capital acquisition rights of others. Only in this sense are the rights of existing owners limited. And this limitation is inherent in all private property rights at their foundation. It is a limitation only in the sense that it prevents people from monopolizing the participatory rights of others.

Thus, from the binary perspective, the binary infrastructure based on the binary property right (as described in Chapter Eight) achieves the optimal harmony of participation, distribution and limitation for a democratic, industrial economy. Furthermore, the binary paradigm reveals that if everyone is vested with the binary property right within a binary economy, there will be sufficient binary growth so that the private property rights of existing owners will *not* be restricted in any material way.

---

[206] John Locke, *Second Treatise on Civil Government*.

6. The basic binary property right

The binary property right has been discussed in some detail in Chapters Seven and Eight. For present purposes, however, it is helpful to restate its salient features.

The basic binary property right is the right to acquire capital at competitive rates; to pay for the capital out of its future pre-tax earnings; and to receive indefinitely the full net income earned by the capital in producing goods and services. The economic market power underlying this right (which is entirely consistent with free-market and private property principles) springs from two fundamental binary tenets:–

- capital productiveness increasingly replaces labor productiveness in the wealth-creating process while increasing total productiveness; and
- capital has a distributive relationship to growth so that the more broadly capital is acquired on market principles, the more growth an economy will experience.

Thus, underlying the binary property right is the promise that, over a binary time frame, much of the capital that buys itself for existing owners can even more profitably buy itself for all people if they are individually able to participate in capital acquisition on market principles.

Furthermore, for the purpose of understanding the new private property choice presented by the binary paradigm, it is important to remember that the binary property right has two components, which can be thought of as separate, though related, rights – a capital acquisition right and a capital income right. In view of their importance, they are dealt with in a little more detail below.

a) The capital acquisition right

The acquisition right to capital is critical. Individual acquisition rights are the gateway to all other private property rights. Although the unfree market alleges that the acquisition right to capital is open to all people, the facts are to the contrary. In the vernacular, everyone knows it takes money to make money. To be sure, millions scrimp and save and retire with a small nest egg, and perhaps tens or hundreds of thousands start with nothing and become wealthy. However, many more in the U.S.A. and the U.K. (and billions more around the world) end up with little or no capital. The general rule is that *the right to acquire capital is effectively open only to those people who are already well-capitalized* Without a competitive acquisition right most people are effectively excluded from capital acquisition.

b)   *The capital income right*

The capital income right is just as critical as the capital acquisition right.   Indeed, without the income right, the acquisition right would have no coherent purpose and would be denied its full efficient power.

The income right is the right to receive indefinitely the full income earned by the capital in producing goods and services. *After* the capital has paid for itself (and after sufficient reserves have been set aside for depreciation, research and development to restore the capital to technological currency), *all* income is paid to the employee or other individual owners.

This market-based income right completes the long-term linkage between supply and demand that is required for sustained binary growth. Indeed, in the long run, it is the income right which, providing the basis for growth, makes the extension of credit to the binary beneficiaries not only profitable to the participants (companies, lenders, capital credit insurers, investors, and binary beneficiaries), and non-confiscatory as to any investment opportunity for existing owners, *but also a boon to existing owners in the form of increased investment opportunities.*

c) *The right to an open market infrastructure*

Nevertheless, as we developed in Chapter Eight, to be competitive with the capital acquisition rights of existing owners on market principles, the binary capital acquisition right (which entails payment for the capital out of *future* earnings of the capital acquired) must be backed by credit; and that credit must supported by appropriate collateral or credit insurance on market principles. Whether that credit and insurance will be forthcoming for particular transactions will depend almost entirely on private market decisions.   However, it should be said that the actual availability of credit or insurance in particular transactions is a matter *quite distinct* from a nation's decision to establish the market infra-structure to facilitate:–

- the voluntary provision of that credit; and
- the voluntary private consummation of binary financing transactions as competitive alternatives to conventional financing transactions.

Thus, just as governments of the unfree market economies

- do much to facilitate conventional financing by ways of their fiscal, monetary, insurance, tax, international trade, and labor law and policies, and yet
- leave the specific decisions as to individual private, conventional capital financing to private parties;

so also the governments could

- extend that facilitation, by opening the infrastructure, so as to honor everyone's capital acquisition rights on market principles, and yet
- leave the specific decisions as to individual, conventional *and binary* private capital financing to private parties.

There is no reason why the sauce which enriches the goose cannot also enrich the gander.

d)   Binary rights are market rights limited by market principles

It is important not to confuse the binary capital acquisition and capital income rights (which are entirely dependent on market principles) with a socialist redistribution right. *A socialist redistribution right exists specifically to disconnect monetary outtake from work input.* Indeed, the socialist redistribution right is intended to transfer income from those who have produced to those whom the state views as being in need. Thus on socialist principles, capital ownership or income can be redistributed from one person to another without the owner's consent and without worrying about ever paying for it.

In contrast, binary transactions occur only between willing parties, willing buyers and sellers of goods and services. In binary transactions, private companies acquire capital from willing sellers for cash received from the constituency trustees in exchange for share of company stock held for the benefit of employees and other beneficiaries. The cash is available as a loan to the trust to purchase the binary shares only if willing lenders and capital credit insurers see a profit in the transaction. Thus, even though everyone will have the binary property right, that right does not enable them to demand participation in, or credit and credit insurance for, any particular capital acquisition. Participation in any specific transaction requires voluntary assent by the company, lender, and capital credit insurer within a binary economy.

But critically, in a binary economy, the financial infrastructure that facilitates capital acquisition on private-property market principles is opened to all people. As we have previously explained, this opening has profound implications for the market distribution of income and growth. This is because, over a binary time frame, the new binary owners have consumer needs and wants which, when fortified by the productive capacity of their fully-paid-for capital, will provide the market basis for increasing growth and distribute justice.

In contrast to the socialist redistribution right which typically transfers wealth or income from those who have produced it to those the state views as being in need, the binary income right pays income *only* for profitable production. Specifically, it pays income to people *as owners* and *only* if their capital produces goods and services which earn that income on market principles. In other words, the binary income right honors the basic distributive principle of a true free market, viz.:–

*Monetary outtake **must equal** work input.*

Stated in other words, it expresses the private property principle that *if you produce it (either as a worker or an owner) you should get to keep it.* Likewise, the realization of binary property rights is not redistributionary. *All* capital acquisition is paid for at competitive rates; *all* income paid to binary beneficiaries is earned in the markets by *their* capital. Thus the operation of a binary economy works to satisfy the consumer needs and desires of poor and working people without redistribution – without taking from existing owners. In this respect it is fundamentally different from all left wing alternatives.

At the same time, the binary market right is built on honesty and internal consistency. It does not (like the unfree market) offer a market solution that is theoretically open to everyone, but which in practice gives only some people competitive acquisition rights. Rather, it offers a market infrastructure in which *everyone* has competitive acquisition rights. In this respect it is fundamentally different from all right-wing alternatives.

In summary, the binary property right (the effective right to acquire capital and receive its earnings on private property free market principles) is a market right that requires no redistribution of physical assets or earnings. It does require an opening of the financial infrastructure which presently facilitates capital acquisition effectively for people who are already well capitalized. Thus to pursue further the new choice in property systems it would be well to consider how the rights of existing owners might be affected by an opening of the financial infrastructure, and to consider also the effect that opening (and not opening) the financial infrastructure may have on the great majority of people who presently own little or no capital.

7.   The property rights of existing owners

It is the claim of binary economists that the institution of a binary economy, with its open financial infrastructure and the subsequent voluntary consummation of capital acquisition transactions (based on binary property rights and using insured capital credit), involves no confiscation of existing assets. However, existing owners, from their point of view, may object to the establishment of a binary economy by saying that, although it does not change title to existing assets, it will change the ownership distribution of subsequent capital acquisitions because the new binary competitors will be acquiring from the pool of capital previously open primarily to existing owners.   The existing owners' objection is that but for the 'interference' of the binary program, *they* would have acquired the new assets by exercising their hitherto essentially unlimited collateralization rights. Thus, the objection goes, the government's promotion and provision of binary insured capital credit will crowd out existing investors and deprive them of their rightful investment opportunities. In other words, existing owners may say that the opening of the infrastructure to enable people without capital to become more competitive in the capital markets is an interference with existing property rights.

Therefore the choice in private property systems presented may be viewed as a straight choice:–

either

A – the present closed system of private property rights which restricts the acquisition capital assets primarily to existing owners, but which leaves collateralization rights of existing owners unlimited (in the sense of being protected from competitors)

or

B – the binary open system which extends capital acquisition rights to all on market principles, which may thereby limit or enhance the economic value of pre-existing collateralization rights.

Some existing owners, of course, have no doubt as to what choice should be made. They bluntly say that *A* is the most just and efficient alternative. But others are not so narrow in their attitudes. And many have been persuaded by the arguments that follow.

First, on the question of government 'interference' or 'intervention' in the markets for capital acquisition, there is in fact a long beneficial and welcome government involvement by way of protective laws, regulations, and institutions, which has provided the protective foundation for the great global capital expansion of the last several centuries. Along with the question of financial feasibility, one of the first questions raised by investors is whether there is law and order in the land where the capital is supposed to do its work and earn its income. Law and order, including the rights of private property, are as a practical matter anything but *laissez faire*. So the unfree market governments are already up to their eyeballs in maintaining the vital financial infrastructure by which prospering firms and existing owners acquire additional capital on the earnings of capital. Therefore the only issue of additional involvement is whether those governments are now prepared to take the additional steps to let everyone in on the capital acquisition game so as to provide the basis for sustainable growth and distributive justice.

Further, even assuming that extending to all people the binary property right (i.e. the competitive right to acquire capital on the earnings of capital acquired) can be fairly characterized as an opportunity cost to existing owners (and therefore a 'taking' of their property), any cries from existing owners as to lost opportunity costs rest on a fatal circularity. The opportunity costs of existing owners are also the opportunity costs of those who are now effectively excluded from *all* market opportunities for capital acquisition. *So the choice between two property systems is inescapably the choice between two different allocations of opportunities and their costs.* But the notion of opportunity costs supposedly suffered by existing owners (as a result of enabling all people to compete on market principles) cannot be fairly used to extend the property rights of existing owners beyond the limitations inherent in private property. Recognizing unlimited opportunity costs in this context for existing owners, would effectively deny all practical opportunity to everyone else.

In other words, the objection from existing owners that their rightful investment opportunities will be given to others (or that their capital acquisition rights will be 'redistributed' to others) amounts to a demand for a monopoly on capital acquisition. The demand contradicts the ostensible rules of the unfree market which insist that all markets be as barrier-free as possible.[207] It also contradicts the participation principle of private property, and runs afoul of the limitation principle. How can existing owners convincingly complain about being crowded out of investment opportunities by the opening of the market infrastructure when, otherwise, most other people will remain entirely excluded?

As a general rule, *any* claim by one group that it has unlimited rights over anything is automatically suspect because, at some stage, the unfettered exercise of individual right will usually come into conflict with the right of another. The claim of unfettered

---

[207] The objection becomes even more revealing when the existing owners are asked what they would do with the income which, if in the hands of the new binary owners would be spent on food, clothing, shelter, education and health-care; and back comes the answer, "We will reinvest the income to acquire even more excess earning capacity."

collateralization rights in the post-industrial world is no exception to this rule. Binary economics says that unlimited collateralization rights, which have remained narrowly owned despite massive industrialization, must not be allowed to monopolize the vital acquisition rights of others. In this sense only must the acquisition rights of existing owners be limited, as necessary, in order to extend effective universal capital acquisition rights to all people.

Thus, binary economists respect the rules of private property, *beginning with their foundation*, and therefore do not countenance an abandonment of the limitation principle. Without the limitation principle, and with the help of the independent productive power of capital, a few people are able to monopolize all capital acquisition and therefore effectively to squash the acquisition rights of everyone else. But happily the only so-called limitation on the rights of existing owners that a binary economy would create is the condition that everyone be vested with effective capital acquisition rights (and this condition is inherent in the requirements of open markets and respect for the participation rights of all people).

Thus, to claim that an opening of the private property economy to enable all people to participate in capital on market principles is a limitation on investment opportunities, and therefore a taking of property, is to lose sight of the fact that all property carries the two inherent, historical limitations set forth in Section 5 above. Although the ostensibly unlimited collateralization right has itself a long history of wide acceptance in the unfree market legal system, it has likewise always been inherently circumscribed by the two historic limitations. In the binary view, since the industrial revolution, the maintenance of unlimited collateralization rights of existing owners has created a concentration of economic power that increasingly intrudes on the acquisition rights of others. Because they effectively deny all other people the right to be productive, the concentrated collateralization rights of existing owners are the proper subject of governmental limitation (if necessary) to realize the right of all citizens to be productive as capital-workers as well as labor-workers.

Moreover, binary economists insist that, as a practical matter, the limitation of existing owners' collateralization rights is no more than an opening of the financial infrastructure to all people on market principles. Existing owners may complain that they are being crowded out of their rightful investment opportunities, but in reality they are merely being asked to compete fairly with others for those opportunities. As a result of this competition, they may have to move some of their investments from present blue-chip capital acquisition on debt to more venturesome investments. Even by conventional analysis, this move in response to more competitive capital acquisition may have beneficial growth potential.[208] It will provide a greater source of credit and capital for entrepreneurial individuals and firms. Among the new investments that will be available in a binary economy, existing owners will be able to invest in the private firms which will provide binary capital credit insurance and so receive a share of the market return for any investment risk the firm profitably underwrites.

8. *Binary growth offers opportunity for all*

The binary analysis reveals, however, that *binary growth*, because of its size, will provide plenty of investment opportunity for existing owners. The material concerns of existing owners are ultimately predicated on the dismal productivity-orientated conventional economic analysis. That analysis is confused as to who or what is producing the wealth and distributing the income on market principles. The conventional analysis says that it makes no difference who owns the capital, ignores the potent

---

[208] Louis Kelso & Mortimer Adler, *The New Capitalists* (1961).

distributive relationship between capital and growth, and denies the powerful long-term property connection between the incremental productiveness of capital and the incremental consumer income necessary to support sustainable growth. This production-based (and therefore non-inflationary) widespread earning power materializes after the binary capital has paid for itself and (if properly managed) grows in perpetuity. It will provide sufficient growth to open ever greater opportunities to existing owners as well.

Therefore, as a matter of property law, the binary system will institute no material limitation on the collateralization right of anyone. As a practical matter, existing investors will be crowded out of nothing because of the opportunities provided by binary growth. In a binary economy, no one is effectively excluded from the capital markets as they are now. Rather everyone is invited into a much larger economy which grows by increasingly linking the ability to produce with the ability to consume.

9. A new choice in private property systems – the closed conventional system or the open binary one

Based on what we have written so far in this and preceding chapters, we can now offer a summary of the attractive new private property choice provided by the binary paradigm. Louis Kelso's conception of an alternative private property system provides all people of good will with a fundamental new choice:−

either

- they can choose to stay with the present closed unfree system which mixes an undesirable capitalism with an undesirable socialism thereby making for vast inequalities in productive and consuming power while also concentrating economic and political power and

suppressing efficiency growth, distributive justice, and
widespread prosperity;

or

- they can move on to the open binary system which, by
opening the financial infrastructure, extends to all people
efficient capital acquisition rights on market principles,
makes everyone more productive, and provides the basis
for sustainable growth, distributive justice, widespread
prosperity, and a strengthened democracy.

Because capital is independently productive and doing ever
more of the work, if there is to be distributive justice, sustainable
growth, and widespread prosperity, an economy must be built on
an open private property system that vests all people with
competitive capital acquisition rights.   Conversely, distributive
justice, sustainable growth and widespread prosperity cannot be
achieved in a property system that is closed in the sense that it
generally takes capital to acquire more capital.

For these reasons, despite its obvious superiority in producing
and distributing wealth as compared with the communist system,
the existing private property system of the unfree market
economies is fundamentally flawed.   It is a closed system of
private property with a system of corporate finance which limits
efficient capital acquisition primarily to existing owners and so
excludes the vast majority of other people from participation in
the capital acquisition.   With only statistically insignificant
exceptions, only those with capital have the access to credit and
collateral which enables the acquisition of additional capital on
market principles. Of the billions of dollars worth of new capital
acquired each year by way of the present unfree markets for
capital and labor, the vast preponderance is paid for with the
earnings of capital and much of it is acquired with borrowed
money. That is to say, it is acquired by existing owners, *not* new
ones. The traditional means (work hard, save and invest wisely)
recommended by conventional economists for becoming an owner
of a viable capital estate are an unreal alternative for the vast
majority of American and British citizens. As for those in the

poorer parts of the world, the traditional means are a fantasy. Although nothing in the traditional productivity approach says that laborers cannot also be capital owners, the plain fact is that the existing productivity-based closed private property system has *not* produced many substantial capital owners and will *never* do so.

Inasmuch as the existing private property system is demonstrably closed in a way that is:–

• inconsistent with private property roots (which require open participation, just distribution, and limitations to protect society and others);

• inconsistent with free market principles (which require as a condition of market efficiency that there be no unnecessary barriers to entry to anyone willing to play by the free market rules); and also

• at odds with egalitarian values in individual participation, equal opportunity, fair competition, and a level playing field,

then how can the closed private property system of the unfree market still be preferred to the new binary alternative?

In their arguments against the communists and socialists, despite disturbing, unexplained, and unremedied symptoms of unfree market failure, including:–

• great disparities in wealth, opportunities and distribution;

• chronic unemployment and underemployment; and

• a spotty record of booms followed by busts,

the proponents of the unfree market system could always play the 'optimal efficiency' trump card. Thus proponents of the unfree market system would argue as follows:–   "The present private property system may create a rich class, but the rich are the ones who can afford to acquire the capital, provide the jobs, increase worker productivity, and thereby enable more people to live well. Compared to communist/socialist alternatives, policies that favor and respect open markets and private property manifestly increase the pie for all people to share in optimally efficient portions as workers and owners, and to provide an additional amount available for redistribution."

But the optimal efficiency trump card used by unfree market proponents against communism, socialism, and Keynesian redistribution, carries no weight against the binary private property choice which is more faithful to private property principles than unfree market capitalism and in no way relies on redistribution. To the contrary, binary economics relies on markets that are much more competitive and open than the existing markets because they do not require participants to own substantial assets before they can have competitive acquisition rights.

So the choice for people of good will really boils down to this:–

If, as conventional economists claim (but never offer in writing to show), the binary offer to extend capital acquisition rights to all people (so as to create greater efficiency, distributive justice, and individual prosperity for growing numbers of people) cannot be achieved without self-defeating inflation and *de facto* confiscation of the property of the rich (thereby undermining incentives for investment and efficiency), then perhaps the present unfree market system, by its relatively efficient operation (as evidenced by its materialistic triumph over communism and socialism) may produce the optimal standard of living based on a strategy of capital acquisition for the rich and jobs and welfare for everyone else. As a consequence, the binary alternative may be disregarded as an superficially plausible idea, but one lacking in practicality.

But if, as binary economists claim, effective capital acquisition rights *can* be extended to everybody (without inflation, confiscation of existing assets or abridgement of property rights) and *if* that extension produces distributive justice and sustainable growth beyond left-wing, right-wing, and mixed centrist strategies, then the unfree market alternative is *not* optimal, and the new binary paradigm offers humanity a great new alternative choice in private property that was not apparent from the conventional view of economics.

Readers are invited to decide.

Book IV

Chapter Twelve

The broad beneficial promise of binary economics

1. The economic promise

Thus, having denied the prowess of an unfree market built on a closed private property system, binary economics offers a true free market based on an open private property system in which everyone can participate in the economy on market principles not only as a labor worker but, increasingly, as a capital worker. With this expanded, democratic, market system of private capital acquisition, the incremental income from the incremental productiveness of capital will be increasingly earned by the very people expected to buy what it produces. So there will be diminishing need for earnings redistribution or inflated wages.

On private property principles, the binary economy offers increasingly to match the incremental supply produced by capital with the incremental consumer income it is capable of generating and distributing, and to do so without confiscation, taxation, or other redistribution. Year by year, the consuming population of every binary nation will become more capital-rich and less dependent on their labor and redistribution for survival. The binary economy therefore promises a basis for sustainable economic growth, distributive justice and widespread prosperity without inflation or recession.

By enabling full, universal, individual economic participation, not only as laborers but also as owners of productive capital, the binary economy offers:–

- to release the full potential of technology to the immense advantage of humankind and the environment;
- to lower and eventually remove the need for redistribution, consumer debt, and deficit spending;
- to tame, if not eliminate, the destructive economic cycles that have blighted economic history certainly since the start of the industrial revolution;
- to establish economic justice; and, eventually,
- to eliminate material poverty.

2.   *Other promise*

However, binary economics offers more than a good system of market economics and private property that simultaneously promotes sustainable growth and distributive justice. It also has within it benign, creative and very powerful forces which seem likely to permeate and transmute many other aspects of life on this planet. As capital acquisition and income on market principles become increasingly more widespread, a binary economy offers other beneficial changes, political, environmental, psychological, social and spiritual.

3.   A strengthened democracy

As indicated in Chapter Eleven and elsewhere, the binary system offers to strengthen democracy by fortifying universal political suffrage with universal economic participation as individual owners of productive capital. Thus, to the extent that universal individual political power is distorted by concentrated economic power (whether in private or government hands), the distortion will be gradually reduced as more people come to acquire substantial capital estates.

Not only will the broader distribution of capital acquisition on market principles fortify democracy by broadening the population of economically autonomous citizens, it will also create in people a deeper understanding, a binary understanding, of the meaning of democracy. That understanding has been succinctly expressed by Louis and Patricia Kelso. After defining an economic democracy as one in which every citizen individually owns and possesses the power to produce the income needed to enjoy a reasonably chosen lifestyle, the Kelsos wrote:–

> The importance of democracy is that *it is designed to the scale of human beings*: not to dynasties, nor to giant corporations that are narrowly rather than broadly owned, nor to other vast ownerless institutions. Democracy was conceived on the idea that power should reside in the individuals who make up a democratic society. But there are two forms of non-violent power. Political power, consisting of the power to make, interpret, and administer laws, and economic power, the power to produce goods and services. Political power and economic power are equally potent. *Neither gives a citizen democratic power without the other.*[209]

---

[209]   Louis & Patricia Kelso, *The Right To Be Productive, Part 2* (*Financial Planner*, September, 1982).

Several aspects of this passage are noteworthy. First, the emphasis is on *individual power*, not on majority rule as an end in itself (although there is prominent place for majority rule in making and administering the laws and regulations). The emphasis on individual power is fully consistent with the binary value implicitly placed on every individual's life, liberty, equal opportunity, and right to private property. The passage warrants political action to facilitate universal individual power, and sometimes to limit some individual power when necessary to protect the interests of society as a whole. Those interests include society's interest that *everyone should have the practical opportunity for competitive economic power* (i.e., for competitive participation in the production of goods and services).

A second noteworthy aspect of the passage is that it states that democracy has *two* discrete components – the political and the economic – and universal individual and discrete participation in *each* is necessary for true democracy. Thus, the passage expresses the important distinction between:–

- *political power* – the power to make and administer laws and regulations (which in a democracy is a majoritarian power, subject to safeguards to protect the fundamental rights of individuals and minorities);
  and

- *economic power* – the power to produce goods and services.

To optimize individual (i.e., fully democratic) economic and political participation, binary economists wish to establish open market institutions (such as those described in Chapter Eight) which facilitate the distinction between, and practical separation of, political and economic participation in society.

This distinction between, and separation of, economic power and political power, by way of open market, private property mechanisms, may seem to run contrary to much twentieth century thought. For example, if asked to define 'economic power' and if allowed to go on talking long enough, many if not most people will begin to discuss *political* power. Political power, however, is not a power to produce goods and services, but rather is a power to command (by way of laws, regulations, or other authority).

Furthermore, the binary distinction between, and separation of, political and economic power may appear naive and inconsistent to those who say that economic and political power are inseparable. Similarly, it may appear inconsistent with much socialist strategy that expressly seeks to burden economic power with the commands of political power.

Nevertheless, to confuse economic power with political power is to confuse:–

* who or what is doing the work
  with
* who or what can command (for example, that earnings be redistributed).

Theoretically, in a true free market system, it is the producers who can command production by reason of their property interest in their productive capacity and in what they have produced. Yet, in the unfree market, through the exercise of political power, the command on resources that results from productive power and private property is diluted or replaced with the command that comes from political power. Yet the political command produces nothing by itself. After all, *someone or something must do the actual work*. The political command merely redistributes what others have produced either by their labor or their capital or both.

To fail to comprehend the difference between economic power and political power is to also fail to comprehend who or what causes growth. More particularly it is to fail to comprehend that capital:–

* is productive independently of labor;
* can efficiently replace labor in production *and* vastly add to total ouput;
* can purchase itself on its future earnings; and
* can distribute to increasing numbers of individuals the income necessary to purchase its output.

To deny the distinction between economic power and political power is, as a matter of politics, to deny people universal individual participation in capital acquisition, and thereby to deny people economic autonomy independent of political will. This denial has momentous consequences because, contrary to Marxist ideology, *private property is **not** theft*. Rather, private property in capital is vital to the economic survival of all individuals. It is only by way of private property that people can earn without laboring and all people need to be able to acquire private property in capital if they are to be competitively productive in a modern industrial economy.

Nevertheless, in making the distinction between economic and political power, binary economists do not deny that economic power can be used to purchase and distort political power. Indeed, the recognition of the use and abuse of economic power to purchase and distort political power is one reason (but not the only one) why binary economists seek to redress the present concentration of wealth by opening the capital markets to all people.

Likewise, binary economics does not deny that when people are precluded from sufficient legitimate economic power via market participation in capital acquisition, many will look for ways to appropriate the earning power of others. Thus many people vote, contrive, and otherwise act to redistribute the economic product of others by way of subsidies, inflated wages, social convention, and even outright theft. Yet these all-too-human exploitations of economic power by the exercise of political power, and *vice versa*, should not obscure the intrinsic distinction between:–

- the power to produce goods and services;
  and
- the power to command the redistribution of the goods and services produced by others.

From a binary perspective, in order to minimize the use of political power to distort economic power and *vice versa*, a true democracy requires the full participation of individuals in both the political and economic spheres. Only in this way can all members of society obtain proper opportunity for voluntary fulfilment of their potential. In summary, without effective individual participation in capital acquisition in an industrial economy, people are denied the full power of democratic citizenship.

4. *Beneficial political realignment*

The new binary paradigm offers the possibility of a major political realignment having ramifications around the world. The possibility arises because, although a society may have issues of religion, secular morality or ethnicity which cause division, *most political differences are rooted in some aspect or conception of economics*. Furthermore, an issue which is apparently non-economic can often be made even more divisive by reason of economic forces and views acting on and influencing it. So, while it would not be quite true to say that economics is behind everything in society, it certainly has a massive impact on politics. And politics then becomes left-wing, right-wing or mixed centrist in its analysis of problems and its preferred solutions *because of its underlying economics*. But the binary paradigm offers a systemic new alternative that is neither left-wing, right wing nor mixed centrist.

Firstly, binary economics is not a left-wing economics. It readily acknowledges the obvious superiority of open market and private property principles in producing and distributing wealth and in providing the necessary efficient and moral foundation for a widely prosperous, just and free society.

Secondly, binary economics is not a right-wing economics. Unlike right-wing thinking, it recognizes that markets cannot operate in a way anywhere near optimal efficiency or distributive justice unless *all* people are equipped with private property rights that provide efficient individual participation in capital acquisition. It rejects trickle-down theory on the same basis that it rejects redistribution.

Thirdly, binary economics is not a mixed centrist economics. Unlike the mixed centrists, it recognizes that widespread prosperity, distributive justice, and freedom cannot be maintained on a foundation attempting to combine the defective strategies of the right- and left-wing. The mixed centrists combine a private property system that is inherently closed to most people (and therefore unjust and inefficient) with a redistribution system that is inherently still more inefficient.

So, because it is neither left-wing, nor right-wing, nor mixed centrist in its economics, the binary paradigm offers the possibility of a systemic, distinct, new *political* alternative. Indeed, in increasing numbers, the most thoughtful people from the left, right and center are coming to doubt the value of conventional politics, are calling for new ideas and, in some cases, are already recognizing the possibility of that new alternative. The appeal of binary economics to the most thoughtful people of the left, right and center is explored further below.

a)   The right-wing Generous and Not-So-Generous defenders of private property

As regards the right-wing, it is noteworthy that, in addressing people who consider themselves right-wing or conservative, Louis Kelso encountered two distinctly different groups reacting to his offer of universal capitalism – the *Generous* and the *Not-So-Generous*.

i)   The Generous

The first group we call the *Generous*. In essence, it enthusiastically said, "Louis, if you have truly figured out a way to extend the marvelous benefits of capitalism to everyone on market principles, then God bless you, and on with your important work!" This group extended helping hands, invested in his ownership-broadening work, and opened many doors, some even to the closest advisors of presidents and prime ministers.

ii)   *The Not-So-Generous*

But there was a second right-wing group – the *Not-So-Generous*. Never speaking directly, but rather by way of their reactions and their silence, this group in essence said, "Louis, you don't understand...... – the most marvelous thing about capitalism is that there are so few of us at the top. Opening the capital markets to all people, even purely on market principles and even if necessary for sustainable growth and distributive justice, will crowd our playgrounds and take away our exclusive place in society. We can't have *that*, can we?"

Thus, the two groups on the right (which exist to this very day) have very different reactions regarding private property in capital and the effect of broadening market access to it. The *Generous* find plausibility in the idea of binary growth. They are willing to entertain the idea that, by opening the capital markets to all people, greater efficiency and distributive justice will result. They are receptive to the notion that a private property system which gives everyone competitive opportunity to acquire capital is a better capitalism even for the wealthiest people.

In complete contrast, the *Not-So-Generous* claim to be highly skeptical about binary growth. In order to reinforce their skepticism, they assert that the whole burden of proof is on the binary reformers. In so doing, they conveniently ignore their own responsibility to discover the truth and forget the possibility that they may suffer consequences from failing to do so. The *Not-So-Generous* are firmly entrenched in the unexamined notion that productivity accounts for all growth. They think that the rights of existing capital owners entitle them naturally and morally, without limitation, to all new capital acquisition. They see whatever binary gains that might be provided to poor and working people as something taken from existing owners, a taking, they further allege, which also compromises efficiency. They see the world as a 'zero sum game,' and are unwilling to recognize that it is only the present zero sum closed private property system, which they are selfishly defending, which most certainly stands in the way of greater growth and broader, more just and efficient distribution.

b)   The left-wing Eager and Reluctant Redistributionists

As regards the left wing, there are also two distinctly different groups reacting to Louis Kelso's offer of universal capitalism. We call them the *Eager* and the *Reluctant Redistributionists*. In both cases, it is helpful to consider the reactions in their historical context.

Beginning with the earliest socialist thinkers, and continuing through Marx and others, there is in the work and activism of the left wing an abiding, central concern for the economic plight suffered by poor and working people. Over the years, concern for the plight (marked with hunger, disease, premature death, insecurity, depression, and despair) has grown all the greater as these hardships persist despite ongoing efforts of enlightened and public spirited people to remedy the situation. The *Eager* and *Reluctant Redistributionists* are united on their expressed ends (addressing poverty and economic injustice) but divided as to means. The various means include complete state ownership of capital and partial state ownership of capital with private property rights, restricted, regulated and redistributed on the basis of need as politically determined.

Thus, given that means are subordinate to ends, it would seem that Kelso's attempt to address the very ends that unite the left, and to help the very people that the left wing seeks to help (and to do so in a way that would defeat plutocratic capitalism on its own terms with yet greater efficiency), would be an attempt that would be roundly welcomed in left wing circles. Sadly this has not been the case; and the reason is that, like the right wing, the left wing is not of one mind on some basic, but generally unarticulated, principles related to private property. As in the case of the right wing, the left-wing has a negative reaction and a positive reaction to binary economics.

i)   *The Eager Redistributionists*

The left wing negative reaction comes from the *Eager Redistributionists*. They are people who simply *prefer* state capital ownership to private capital ownership. They prefer state capital ownership because they see political power as essential to constrain private economic power. They offer the state as a better proxy for all the people than a private property plutocracy (although in making their offer of state ownership, they do not always volunteer the fact that communism, socialism, and social democracy create plutocracies of their own).

The *Eager Redistributionists* recognize the monopoly on capital acquisition caused by the closed private property system of unfree market capitalism, yet their only solution is a state-owned monopoly on capital acquisition. Some of these left-wingers are uncomfortable when pressed to admit that the privately owned capital monopolies create and distribute more wealth than their state-owned monopolies. Some are uncomfortable when pressed to admit that there might be an open private property system (such as the binary system) capable of creating yet greater wealth and distributing greater wealth even more broadly, on free market, private property principles than the present unfree one. And some of these left-wingers are uncomfortable when pressed to consider that this open private property system may offer so much greater wealth-creating and distributing power, that the use of political power to monopolize and burden economic power may become increasingly unnecessary and unattractive as an alternative.

But, despite their discomfort and like the right-wingers who prefer to keep their private monopoly on capital ownership, these left-wingers prefer to keep their monopoly of state-owned capital. Consequently, they take little or no hope or joy in the promise of binary growth which will result from a truly open binary property system. Clinging to the labor theory of value (which is itself an expression of the human productivity theory of growth), these left-wingers are highly skeptical of the idea that capital has an independent productive and distributive relationship to more effective wealth creation. They allege, moreover, that without effective left-wing political action, any potential benefit of binary economics (by way of binary growth or otherwise) will be grabbed by those in power, as class interest and greed dominates the decision-making process. In this way, these left-wingers (all in the name of 'the people') justify the continued use of political power to monopolize and dominate economic power.

Some of these left-wingers also take offense at the binary claim that growth can be achieved without taking anything from existing property owners. Still holding to the notion that private property is theft, they say they have no obligation to respect thieves. Unlike binary economists (who consider a binary economy's ability to encapitalize poor and working people without taking from those who already have capital as one of its most appealing, potent and unifying qualities), they show no serious misgivings about the present-day massive redistribution of income from earners (including not only capital owners *but also many ordinary workers*) to poorer workers and non-earners.

ii)   *The Reluctant Redistributionists*

Fortunately, there is a second group on the left. It includes many people who are not comfortable with the massive abrogation of private property rights that majoritarian redistribution inevitably requires. People within this group might be called *Reluctant Redistributionists* or redistributionists of last resort. They accept redistributionist strategies not because they believe it is inherently good to abridge private property rights, but rather because they see that abridgement as the only practical means to the end of ameliorating horrific poverty. In particular, they accept redistribution because nobody has ever shown them that there could be better (binary) means of achieving the aim of economic justice, one that does not require redistribution.

c)   The Well-Meaning Center

Also, over the years, various centrist and non-aligned political forces have emerged and attempted to combine the best of the left and right into a so-called 'third way' that works better for everyone. We call these forces the *Well-Meaning Center*. Their attempts at reform have been frustrated, however, not for lack of good intentions, but for lack of an open market system capable of producing sustainable growth, distributive justice, and widespread prosperity. Unfortunately, the *Well-Meaning Center* fails to understand that such a system can never be built on an old paradigm that falsely comprehends who or what produces the wealth and what causes economic growth.

To the *Well-Meaning Center* can be added two properly-motivated groups as follows:–

- people *on the right wing* who are willing to open capital ownership on market principles to all people, and
- people *on the left wing* who are willing to cut back on, and eventually replace, redistribution policies with binary open-market policies *if* binary economics is truly an efficient, democratic, capitalism that works better for everyone on market principles.

d)   Beneficial political realignment

The existence of the *Well-Meaning Center*, the *Generous* defenders of private property, and the *Reluctant Redistributionists* shows that the present political spectrum is not occupied only by right-wingers who mouth private property principles but have only *their own* private property in mind. Nor is it occupied only by left-wingers who like state-owned monopolies and are happy to redistribute *other people's* private property.[210] Indeed, the splendid news is that there are now plenty of people capable of seeing binary economics as offering a sound, economically powerful foundation for unifying what some might consider to be the best of left, right, and center in constructive new political ways. In other words, there are today plenty of people capable of seeing that a major beneficial political realignment is now very much on the cards.

Thus, binary economics offers to unite the best of right, left and center because it resonates with generosity, inclusiveness, and a concern for everyone's well being. At the same time, it squarely and practically addresses questions of efficiency, production and distribution in terms that respect individual autonomy and the power of private property and free markets. It offers to replace state and privately owned monopolies of capital acquisition with more efficient systems of universal individual ownership, and to do so without any confiscation. Thus, binary economics avoids the failure of both left and right to recognize that a fundamental reality – *a just and efficient social system – cannot be maintained without a private property, free market system effectively open to all people.*

Accordingly, binary economics has the potential of uniting people who share the values of individual freedom, equal opportunity, and private property for all people, and who also value truth and honesty as to who or what is really creating the wealth. Those people can combine their values with a practical concern for efficiency and a generous concern for the participation and welfare of everyone.

---

[210] Louis Kelso has wryly defined a conservative as a person very interested in defending private property – *his own*: and a liberal as a person very interested in redistributing private property – *someone else's.*

5.   *Reversing the increasing sense of alienation*

The change from labor-intensive to capital-intensive production, occasioned by the industrial revolution, while providing great economic growth, has also produced much unnecessary psychological alienation. The alienation can best be understood in the light of the increasing productiveness of capital (as a percentage of total output) when compared with the declining productiveness of labor. The change in production almost invariably results in the creation of more goods and services, more efficiently, with more capital and less labor. The capital contribution to production replaces the labor contribution and then adds a vast further contribution to total output.

So, although total production increases, *the human contribution to total production grows proportionately less*. The good news is that more human life can be supported with less human effort and with more comfort, leisure, and opportunity for personal development. The bad, indeed frightening, news is that there is much surplus labor which will never be able to compete with the capital that has replaced it. As a result, people are not able, on their own labor earning power alone, to buy what capital increasingly produces. *That inability is the economic foundation of alienation* which some think transcends all the other physical and psychological effects of the industrial revolution.

Other physical and psychological effects are also noteworthy. For example, the industrial revolution has changed many aspects of the relationship of people to one another and to their environment. It removed people from the land because great machines and few hands can work with the land to produce much more than can many hands with simple tools. It also reduced individual and family autonomy by requiring increasing specialization of human labor to remain economically competitive, so that a decreasing percentage of the population is personally capable of producing all the basic necessities of survival.[211]   Today, as tools, machines, structures and manufacturing processes grow ever larger and more complicated, people become ever more dependent on capital to earn their livelihood. People have become dwarfed by productive capital in almost all economic activity.

The industrial revolution, moreover, changed the dominant work relationship from small and personal to large and impersonal. It created massive, bureaucratic employers, with factories where workers were assembled for the greater efficiency of capital. It scattered families widely apart in pursuit of work. Often the new work became more mindless, dangerous, and otherwise de-humanizing, increasingly performed without experiencing the satisfaction of creating a whole product or facing the pleasure (or displeasure) of the customer. Quite apart from their economic and social consequences, these and other changes would have certainly contributed to feelings of alienation.

However, well-capitalized individuals with full participation (not only in the labor markets but also in the increasingly more potent capital markets) can better adjust to the move to the cities and the other changes in production in ways that most people (whose economic participation is only via labor) cannot adjust. This is because in virtually all production, per unit of output and in the aggregate, the encapitalization process almost invariably reduces the participation of labor while increasing capital participation. In other words, the most serious alienating effect of the process of technological advance is an *economic alienation* that eliminates labor from the production process by requiring ever less labor per unit of output. And individuals cannot escape the personal consequences of this economic alienation of labor from production unless their diminishing labor productiveness is replaced and supplemented by the acquisition of sufficient capital productiveness. In a closed property system, this vital replacement and supplementation occurs for existing capital

---

[211] In the U.S.A. one hundred years ago, it took 60% of the people to feed the rest of the population. In 1990, it took only 3%.

owners but not for those who have only their labor to rely on. In the communist societies, this process of alienation of labor from production has the effect of further concentrating productive and political power in the state, which owns all capital except the capital of the black market.

In truth, most people know intuitively when they are being excluded from something even though they cannot always express it in words. And when they are being excluded from something truly marvelous (like the ownership benefits of wondrous machines that dramatically increase production with less human effort) they manifest a restlessness, an unease, a resentment, all of which contribute to the sense of alienation. Of course, *as long as they are well employed at good and stable salaries*, that sense can be evaded, denied and suppressed by those who have swallowed the conventional human productivity explanation for growth, and who see their self-esteem all tied up in human labor. But for those on the short end of the (ever-shortening) productivity stick (who increasingly find themselves working double shifts, or scrambling for low paying jobs or, simply, unemployed), the alienation cannot be as easily evaded, denied or suppressed as it daily hits them in the face.

Given an economy in which most people are expected to be productive and survive entirely by their labor, and given the increasing impossibility of being sufficiently productive without participation in capital ownership, *most people live with the frightening sense of not being able to support themselves either immediately or in the not-too-distant future*. The result is that they either blame themselves for not being competent, or they blame the system for not providing them with the opportunity to become competent. They then further blame the system for conferring additional earnings on others (whom they may also blame for owning, for earning well beyond their personal consumption needs and desires, for not personally working for what they earn, and – even if they do work – for not having to work). Whether the blame is placed on self, 'the system', or others, the alienation grows and feeds on itself, as the concentration of capital continues and most people remain unnecessarily excluded from the closed capital markets.

The manifestation of this alienation has many facets – vandalized private and public property; theft by employees and consumers that seriously compromises company profits and revenues available to pay honest workers and shareholders; tax evasion; welfare fraud; and radical anti-private property and anti-government political activity.[212]   And all that alienation happens because conventional capitalist and socialist systems do not provide a way in an industrial economy for most people to survive, much less flourish, while playing by the free market private property rules. It happens because the markets are *closed* thereby excluding most people from capital acquisition. It is not therefore surprising that alienation becomes not only an alienation from self, the system, or others, but also from a sense that honesty and integrity have practical meaning.   Survival for too many people seemingly requires compromise and corruption to be competitive with others who may be doing the same or worse.

However, binary economics offers a way out of this dismal situation – a way that respects all people and their participation in private property. Thus:–

- by opening the capital markets to all people individually, the binary system offers to end economic alienation and therefore the resultant psychological alienation caused by the industrial revolution;

- by accurately perceiving the increasing growth in production and productive capacity as resulting from increasing capital productiveness rather than increasing labor productivity, the binary paradigm reveals that the economic alienation of labor from most production by the substitution of capital can come to be a naturally enriching

[212]   Louis & Patricia Kelso, *The Invisible Violence of Corporate Finance* (*The Washington Post*, Business and Finance Section, June 18, 1982).

process, indeed, a blessing of high esteem because it gives
people more time for their highest callings;

- by involving everyone in production not only as laborers
but increasingly as owners of productive capital, binary
economics enables people to come to a new, much more
realistic, sense of self worth;

- by becoming more accurate and honest on the question of
who or what is doing the extra work, people will also come
to understand the meaning of private property and why
being able to acquire it on market principle is essential to
everyone's individual dignity;

- by enabling everyone to participate in the potent productive
and distributive power of capital, binary economics
squarely addresses how people can earn to buy what is
increasingly produced by capital so that abundance,
leisure, and the opportunity for self development can
become increasingly widespread.

Thus the binary system provides a coherent way in which an
increasing portion of people can survive and flourish while
playing by private property, free market rules. It eliminates the
economic alienation resulting from the substitution of capital for
labor by accepting the separation of labor from the productive
process as being good and natural. It then provides an enriching
substitute for labor participation, namely individual participation
in capital acquisition on private property, free market principles,
which offers increasing abundance, leisure and opportunity for
self development.

6.   A new honesty

The importance to human psychology and to social psychology
of the discovery of a new system (based on reasonable
assumptions and internal consistency) that just *might* provide a
way in which an increasing portion of the people (not just
increasing numbers) can survive and flourish on private property,

free market principles, should not be underestimated. To be sure, many people are steadfastly seized with greed and will continue to use property or social advantage to appropriate the work and rights of others in a binary system just as they do in the unfree market and communist systems. Nevertheless, many other people prefer the comfort, serenity, healthier attitudes and good feelings that come from playing by the rules even if they might sacrifice greater material prosperity out of respect for their values.

However, in order to materialize, the principle of binary growth does not require people to behave any better or more kindly, just as it does not require them to work more productively. One of the marvelous aspects of the productive relationship between capital and growth is that it does not require a change in human nature. Nevertheless, once it is understood, the principle of binary growth *does* have the potential for changing people for the better precisely because it offers to change the economic environment in which they live. The principle of binary growth builds on the good inclinations of many people to play by the rules and to have a compassionate and practical concern for the welfare of all people. It further fortifies these inclinations with a newly available economic power that naturally develops in a binary economy because of the independent productive and distributive power of capital.

Resonant with both a generous and truthful spirit, the principle of binary growth is both inclusive and honest. It includes everyone in its promise of material well-being based on open market principles. However, it offers beneficial material results only to the extent that free market and private property principles are truly respected every step of the way.

Honest, efficient, private property, free market principles require:–

- an honesty as to who or what is doing the work;
- respect for the principle that people are entitled to keep what they produce; and

- respect for the principle that the markets should be truly open to everyone.

Thus, by way of the abundance and distributive justice promised with binary growth, the new binary paradigm provides people with a new basis for personal and social optimism that builds on their honest inclinations, generous spirit, and their practical concern for the well-being of all people. Furthermore, the optimism is a rational optimism, based on reasonable premises, internal consistency and a concrete program of reform. The program offers a practical means (using efficient market-proven principles of finance, banking and insurance) to enable everyone to prosper by participating in production in a technologically competitive way (i.e., as both a labor worker and increasingly as an owner of productive capital).

The new honesty will appeal not only to those who have morally compromised little or nothing to survive and flourish, but also to those who have compromised greatly yet who would wish to compromise less. The depth of this appeal can be understood by first recalling that productivity theory is based on a fundamental misapprehension as to who or what is creating the wealth. This misapprehension might be thought a mere intellectual confusion traceable to Adam Smith. Its effect, however, is deep because it compromises and corrupts all economic and social interactions.

For example, on the one hand, people have a natural desire to live comfortably and securely and to provide generously for self and family. The sense of being able to produce enough to meet this desire is an important element of self esteem. Furthermore, people desire not only recognition for good work done but also wish to reap the rewards of that recognition *honestly*. Yet, on the other hand, with unfree market scarcity and insecurity, and with the shortcomings of human nature, there is the temptation to steal the product of others and falsely to claim credit for others' work. The stealing and false claiming are given wrongful license by the productivity paradigm which is foundationally wrong as to who or what is doing the work and therefore truly earning the income.

Louis Kelso once said that if a person will lie about the way he earns his living, he will lie about anything. If people are confused, or in denial, or even lying about who (as among the man, the donkey, and the truck) is, and is not, doing most of the work, then they may be prone to being similarly confused, or in denial, or lying about which humans, including themselves, are doing the work and which are not.

Thus, despite the incessant emphasis on human productivity, many people find themselves working in companies, government agencies, universities and foundations where some people do all the work while others get all the credit. Furthermore, when it comes to promotions and other opportunities, why, if productivity drives growth, is it so often not what you know, but whom you know that counts? Indeed, how often is the productiveness of industry, government and education compromised at the expense of customers, employees, investors, taxpayers and students?

The reality is that the productivity paradigm shackles and compromises industry, government, and education in many different ways, resulting in injustices and inefficiencies adversely affecting millions of people. The wrongful denial of the productive work of other people and things is demoralizing to honest, hardworking people who believe in fair rewards for production. A growing binary consciousness, however, premised on an accurate perception of who or what is doing the work, and nourished by a growing capital participation in production, will provide incentives to expose such injustices and inefficiencies while fortifying instincts and preferences for honesty.

7.   *Mitigation of social distinctions and material preoccupations*

By enabling everyone to acquire a binary competence over time, binary economics offers to reduce the barriers to upward social mobility, increase respect for private property, and diminish the importance that people now attach to excessive consumption and disparities in wealth. Much class division is caused by differences in (and judgements about) the way people earn (or do not earn, or do not legitimately earn) their income. When there are great disparities in wealth and opportunity, the richer often look down at the poorer while the poorer resent the better off. In the binary economy, however, *everyone* will have effective capital acquisition rights, without regard to race, color, creed or sex. Thus participation in capital acquisition will be no longer entirely a matter of elite status, lineage, or supposedly superior endowments, talents, or performance (although such advantages will still exist), but more broadly a matter of simple, universal, individual dignity.

When *everybody* is a capital owner, moreover, people will attach less importance to ostentatious display, excessive consumption and disparities in wealth. The flaunting of wealth to show social superiority (see Thorstein Veblen's *The Theory of the Leisure Class*) may well diminish. To demonstrate social superiority, therefore, people will have to succeed in the things which really command the respect of good minds and hearts – self development, endeavor, serving others and creativity.

8.   Conservation of the environment

Binary growth has remarkable implications for improving the environment because it offers a new way out of the quandary which seems to pit concern for the environment against immediate needs, desires, and convenience. Indeed, the promise of binary growth is a promise of *green growth*. It includes the promise not only of a population better able to afford more food, clothing, shelter, health care, transportation and communication around the world but also the promise of greener products, greener processes, greener activities and tastes as well as a consumer population with stronger property interests in the environment and better able to afford the greener choice.

Many difficult environmental issues (that are frequently the source of much conflict) are evidenced in the U.S.A., the U.K. and other industrial nations, where people face choices that oppose social concerns for the environment against certain needs, conveniences and preferences and where some people must choose between policies that threaten the environment or their very livelihood. Such choices (which are hard enough for members of the middle class and working poor in the industrialized economies of the world) are yet more difficult in poorer nations where people, in far greater numbers and proportions, suffer and perish for lack of necessities.

The fact has to be faced that it is difficult, and frequently impossible, to raise the 'green' consciousness of people when they exist with pain, disease and poverty. Many will have trouble accepting 'deep green' proposals that seemingly demand a *cut* in the standards of living for the millions of people who have no proper standard of living to cut in the first place. At the moment, existence for most of the world's population is a painful one in which, too often, children, partners and friends suffer and, as a result of poverty, die prematurely. Any demand, therefore, for that population to sacrifice what little wealth it has and to take a long-term view rather than a short-term one will, at best, be heard by many with incredulity or, if acknowledged, honored in the breach and not the reality.

Binary economics, however, provides a way out from the deep green dilemma, for it understands that 'green' matters generally require one or more of the following:–

- a change in tastes and lifestyles;
- a change to more costly processes, products, or activities;
- a discovery of greener substitute processes, products or activities;
- a tax on or a straightforward prohibition of activities;

and none of these changes, discoveries, taxes or prohibitions is practicable unless enough people and their society can afford them. Crucially, binary economics enables increasing numbers of people within any society to become better able to afford these alternatives. Any society has a theoretical power to stop people destroying something but binary economics offers people a *practical* power to stop environmental degradation by better enabling people to chose, discover, and accept greener ways.

For example, many of the products widely sold in the unfree market economies are manufactured in environmentally harmful ways. Greener ways are possible, but they are more expensive, and many customers cannot afford them, which means many producers cannot afford to make them. In the unfree market, all producers might be required by law to use the more expensive, greener ways, so there will be fewer producers, fewer products, and fewer people will be able to afford the products (or so that the products will be removed from the market) and other people employed in making the products will be laid off. The results in terms of i) overall wealth creation; ii) the distribution of costs and benefits among the population; and iii) the environment itself, are problematic and debatable. Moreover, the problems and debates have been divisive, often splitting families, friends and communities. Binary growth, however, offers a new possibility – as customers become better capitalized in a binary economy, they will become wealthier customers, better able to afford greener products and processes.

To take another example of the green potential of binary economics, as developing nations with binary economies become better and more broadly capitalized, their people will be better able to resist the economic pressures to destroy their environments. A well-capitalized binary nation comprised of well-capitalized citizens does not need to sell its rain forests, or its wild game, or its other precious resources in ways that threaten their renewability and viability in the long run.

The binary economy also vests more people with a property interest in the economy. It is noteworthy that in the U.S.A. and Western Europe, much activity to restrain environmental degradation came from activists eager to restrain private economic power by the use of effective political power. This involved the simultaneous effort of convincing members of the consuming public that they did not really want the products they believed they wanted, and persuading the owners and workers that they did not really need their profits, wage increases, or jobs. In the unfree market economies, the protective actions required to preserve the environment against market forces required a political effort that faced opposition from well-capitalized interests.

Yet, in communist Russia, when political will could be achieved without private capital opposition, when consumers had little say regarding products, when there was less private property interest in manufacturing profits to resist regulation, and when jobs could be eliminated or created by government fiat, there was far greater environmental degradation to the soil and air, and far greater safety risks imposed on the people, than what generally occurred during the same period in the unfree market economies of the West.   In comparing environmental degradation in communist and unfree market capitalist countries, the binary paradigm reveals that:–

- environmental problems are, to a significant degree, economic problems;

- with the best in green consciousness, we can have only as green an environment as we can afford; and

- a widespread, individually owned private interest in productive capital can enhance, rather than detract from, the prospects for a rich, green coexistence with other life on earth.

As another example, consider the problem of 'planned obsolescence' which was once a scandal, but which now is so commonplace it receives scant mention in the media.   In many instances, companies could as cheaply manufacture products that last longer, but they would fast run out of customers if they did so.   In other words, the economies of more enduring (less wasteful) production cannot be supported by sufficiently widespread consumption.   But with a growing portion of poor and working people steadily becoming more able to afford the basics (food, clothing, housing, health care, transportation and communication) producers will no longer be faced with as great a need to produce according to a planned obsolescence. For example, rather than produce shoes and clothes that wear out in two years for a consuming population of a certain size, and then producing an equal amount for the same people to last another two years, competitive pressures to maintain global market share and profits in a growing binary economy may induce companies to chose to produce shoes and clothes that last five years for a consuming population of twice the size. Thus more people may be better served with better, more durable shoes and clothes, but with relatively fewer resources consumed.

A binary economy, therefore, taking the fullest possible advantage of technology, offers to provide greater wealth and a more broadly based viable standard of living for a growing portion of the population to support both a greater voluntary market-oriented approach to improving the environment, and also, to the extent necessary, greater and more effective public investment and regulation. And with a deeper understanding of the economics of environmental issues, with a stronger market for green products, and with a stronger private property interest in the environment, there will be greater incentives for the discovery and promotion of greener ways of life.

Nevertheless, material progress and a growing population having viable standards of living may not be enough to address all pressing environmental concerns. As long as people behave as though they have almost limitless material wants (as many economists seem to assume), the prospects for the conservation of natural resources might seem dim. Indeed, to many people, the prospects appear yet dimmer if no way is found to restrain the growth in population beyond the capacity to sustainably support it. Yet binary growth holds out helpful possibilities on these matters as well.

First, in regard to population questions, as developed more fully in Section 10 of this Chapter, there is considerable evidence that stable, affordable populations are most readily achievable on a voluntary basis in stable economic circumstances characterized by a robust base of general middle-class affluence – precisely the circumstances increasingly promised with binary growth.

Second, on the question of the limitless wants of people, there is a noteworthy possibility – because poverty (with its associated suffering, fear and insecurity) promotes the desire to be as far away from poverty as possible (i.e. to have great material wealth), the increasing elimination of poverty and provision of greater material security by the binary economy will result in the diminution of perceived need with extensively benign consequences for the planet. That noteworthy possibility could turn out to be one of binary economics' greatest achievements.

In summary, the prospect of binary growth, manifested by a more efficient creation and distribution of wealth, and by a growing population with viable standards of living, offers the practical basis for:–

- a deeper, understanding of environmental issues;
- a voluntary turning to greener ways through market and life-style choices; and
- an economy in which it will be more practical for government to insist on solutions for protecting the environment when market choices fail to do so.

Thus, binary economics offers a just and practical way for people to make peace with technology, with one another and with the environment while enhancing rather than compromising efficiency.

9.   *The developing economies*

a)   *Introduction*

Although it is well for any developing economy to take profitable advantage of foreign demand for its output and potential output, a binary understanding recognizes the more fundamental need for every developing nation to distribute incremental earning power, by way of competitive capital acquisition, to its own citizens in connection with *any* planned financing.   To become steadily more prosperous, developing economies need to develop a growing competitive capacity to produce quality, marketable goods and services, together with a growing indigenous population able to afford to purchase such goods and services.

These things cannot be done by the unfree market approach. Conventional financing, whether domestic or foreign, whether in the form of equity investments or conventional loans, and whether by private entrepreneurs or governments cannot provide the foundation for sustainable growth, distributive justice, and widespread affluence because conventional financing fails to take full advantage of the independent productive and distributive power of capital to create and distribute wealth. The conventional strategies offer capital acquisition primarily for existing owners (whether foreign or domestic, private or state) and jobs and welfare for everyone else. Jobs and welfare generally provide no more than a marginal existence; whereas individual affluence requires at least some substantial measure of private, individual capital ownership.

It is true that conventional financing provides some jobs in developing countries, but never enough work opportunities to employ more than a small portion of the unemployed and underemployed work force. Indeed, whatever promise of jobs may be offered with a proposed investment, it is certain that the long-term profitability of that investment will be maximized to the extent that labor costs are kept to a bare minimum.[213]

---

[213]   In understanding the need for universal, individual economic participation in capital acquisition by way of capital productiveness (and not merely by way of labor productivity) as an essential and simultaneous part of a capital development program, it is well to note that the industrialization of a primitive economy in the twentieth century is not analogous to the Western industrial revolution of the eighteenth and nineteenth centuries. The creation and maintenance of

Happily, however, from a binary perspective, much of the productive capital investment opportunity that exists in a developing country which can be profitably financed with foreign or domestic equity or loans so as to encapitalize existing owners, can also profitably be financed in a binary economy through binary techniques so as to broaden the private ownership base by encapitalizing people who presently own little or no capital. Likewise, much of the investment in infrastructure that truly raises the productive capacity of the nation in the form of state-owned property can be achieved even more efficiently on market principles through binary financing so as to broaden the private ownership base. Therefore, people pursuing any economic or social strategy in any country of the world would be wise to study binary economics; wise to include the binary property right as a fundamental human right; and wise to implement a voluntary binary market financial infrastructure such as described in Chapter Eight.

b)   The failure of conventional solutions

Without the sound foundation of a binary economy, the traditional attempts to promote sustainable development and distributive justice will simply further increase the concentration of capital in the hands of existing owners, continue the exportation of capital to other countries, and continue the

---

a steel mill, power plant, or factory introduced into an developing country today does not require the labor work it once did. The first transcontinental telephone lines required armies of workers over many years yet a comparable infrastructure can be achieved today by installing a string of relay stations with a handful of workers using highly productive equipment. Thus the promise of labor participation in the creation of the public and private capital base does not carry with it the same distributive economic potency it did a century ago. L.O. Kelso & P.H. Kelso *Uprooting World Poverty: a Job for Business* (*Business Horizons*, Fall, 1964).

dependence of most people solely on their labor, which is to condemn them to a marginal economic existence if they play by the rules. This is true of all conventional debt financing (whether foreign, domestic, private or public) because, after any financed capital has paid for itself, the added equity on the company balance sheet representing that capital is wholly owned by existing owners. In the case of foreign equity investment, the capital and capital earnings end up in the hands of foreign owners. In the case of domestic equity investment, the incremental productive capacity is acquired by a tiny percentage of the domestic population.

This tiny privileged elite is so rich that, in practice, it can never increase its consumption sufficiently to promote indigenous economic growth. Its consumer appetite, if not already satiated, will be for consumer products made abroad; and mindful of the need to diversify investments and hedge against domestic instability and monetary restrictions, its investment strategy will also point to foreign opportunities. The weak indigenous, labor-dependent market for consumer goods simply does not offer the most attractive investment opportunities for a competitive return.

Thus, the net domestic effect of conventional financing in a developing nation is to enrich a small elite; to create a small, insecure, malleable middle class to support a frail democracy; and to leave the vast majority of the population less able to buy what the economy is increasingly capable of producing by reason of capital investment. Driven by closed market forces, the developing economies increasingly allocate resources and production to cater to the demands of foreign consumers while distributing grossly insufficient earning capacity to their own people to purchase necessities that might otherwise be profitably produced locally. As more resources, production and earnings are exported, the vast majority of the people (those who do not own a viable capital estate) are increasingly alienated from vital economic participation in the process. Pressures to tax, redistribute, and restrict the earnings of the producers grow – pressures made worse by increasing population among the poor.

As in the case of the developed countries, the concentration of economic power in the developing economies carries with it a concentration of political power, so that the government's ability to help the most disadvantaged is compromised. Foreign loans and grants to help governments promote the economic development and welfare of all their people, and particularly the most needy, are not always used in that way. Special financing and grants designed to help the poor and working people, or designed to aid the government in helping those people, may (with the distortion of political power by concentrated economic power) be instead used to help those in power who, if they are not already rich, have plans to become rich. Although *competitive* financing opportunities in the developing nations to minister to the consumer needs of the indigenous population may not be attractive to the local rich in comparison to competitive investment opportunities abroad (because the would-be local consumers cannot earn enough to purchase what might be produced), *non-competitive* investments (i.e., those that are attractive because they are supported by subsidies and monopoly profits, such as some regulated utility companies) can be quite attractive.

Therefore, with subsidies and monopoly power, and with the promise of a few thousand jobs and some lucrative construction contracts, such opportunities become highly attractive to the people favored with effective political and market participation. The favored participants rarely face the fact that, in the long run, the private capital acquired must distribute a good portion of its income to those people expected to purchase its output if investment is to *remain* profitable on market principles and if a growing portion of the nation's resources is to be allocated to those people efficiently on market principles. Nor do they face the fact that public infrastructure must likewise truly raise the productive capacity of the people who use it if they are ever to be able to afford to keep the infrastructure in working repair.

Thus, too often, credit to developing countries is offered for economically unprofitable projects that enrich certain participants along the way, but leave the government directly or indirectly in hock with the financing bank or the international monetary authorities when the credit *plus interest* has to be repaid. As a price for refinancing the debts, or shoring up the economy or the government, creditors or monetary authorities then demand 'austerity measures' which leave the governments that much less able to minister to the immediate needs of their growing poor.

A vicious cycle sets in whereby the rich get richer and the poor generally remain poor while some become even poorer. The ensuing politics is easily predictable. Some people conclude that most people cannot survive playing by the rules. They point to those who profit from corruption, redistribution, and earning without personally laboring. Respect for private property and free markets erodes. Other people, seeing the deterioration of morality and social order that results from the erosion of private property rights, call for law and order. An alliance between the rich and many of those workers with better paying jobs (who may prefer to think that maybe they *can* survive playing by the rules, even though they will not get rich themselves) begins to tear families, friends, communities, states and nations apart. Societies become more polarized. Extreme left-wing politics, or extreme right-wing politics, or both at the same time, take root and spread with much injustice, tyranny, torture and death. Again, the situation is made worse by a growing population among the poor.

c) *The binary solution*

So how, in simple terms, does binary economics remove the poverty of a developing country? Firstly, the country must have considered the binary approach and enacted the laws necessary to establish the binary infrastructure so that, potentially, a binary economy can operate.

The binary economist then takes an inventory of the country's assets. Most countries have land, sea, lakes, rivers, sun, rain, wind, a trainable work force, and at least some other natural resources. The industrial nations have technology, manufacturing capacity, machines and equipment, and companies and individuals experienced in creating and operating virtually every aspect of every industry that might be profitably established in the developing nation. The developing nation needs an comprehensive plan to induce the owners of these factors of production to contribute them, in such amounts and at such times, as needed to create efficient, productive enterprizes in the developing country, and the contributors must each be compensated for their contributions at competitive rates.

By facilitating the creation of joint ventures of indigenously-owned operating companies and foreign assistance companies, a developing nation could provide a legal means to facilitate the inputs of the potential participants and to structure the timing of their compensation so as to create competitive, profitable, lasting economic activities. Based on private property, free market principles, in the light of the nation's available resources and location as well as market conditions at home and around the world, the joint ventures would identify, plan, and build 'project businesses' likely to provide competitive sustainable, broadly owned, capital investment. Some of the project business enterprizes would serve anticipated domestic consumption needs; other ventures would offer products for foreign markets; some would do both.

The indigenous operating companies would be privately owned by their employees and other citizens who are otherwise without effective access to capital acquisition. Generally, all people, except those already well-capitalized, would be eligible. As described in Chapter Eight, their binary stock in the indigenous operating companies would be acquired and held in trust with borrowed money supported by capital credit insurance. All net income earned by the stock would be used first to repay the acquisition loans and then to pay a growing non-inflationary production-based income to the owner-citizens of the developing country, thereby providing the market-based consumer demand for additional capital investment.

The foreign assistance companies would be owned by those foreign contributors of technology, capital goods, supplies, and expertise necessary to build and operate the planned enterprize who accept a security interest in one or more foreign assistance companies in full or partial payment for their contributions. (Those foreign contributors that require immediate payment for part or all of their contributions would be paid by the operating company with some of funds it received by selling binary stock to the constituency trust).

Foreign participation in the joint ventures by way of the foreign assistance companies would be of limited duration. The foreign assistance company would be required to commit itself by private or governmental contract (or both) to maintain its participation in the joint venture not perpetually but for a specified time period to achieve specific objectives in return for a reasonable profit. After start-up and initial operations of the project businesses, the foreign assistance company would sell its interest in the project business through secondary re-offering of shares to eligible local households who own little or no capital, again using insured capital credit to finance the acquisition.

The cumulative net effect of such a development program will be to create the indigenous productive capacity and widespread earning capacity to provide the basis for sustainable growth, distributive justice, and growing affluence, while creating a credit-worthy history of profitable international economic relations which will make future international commerce all the more auspicious. These benefits will be achieved without abridging the private property rights of existing owners within the developing economy or beyond its borders. Within the developing economy, existing owners will be free to compete for capital acquisition as before. Increasingly, they will be able to invest in an economy having:–

- a more prosperous, broadly based consumer population;
- a reduction in the need for redistributionary taxes and in restrictions on capital exportation; and

- an improvement in the conditions that otherwise spawn
  sentiments and threats against both private property rights
  and the government.

10. Population issues

Many people believe that the most intransigent problem we
face is the world's burgeoning population. That population (at
present nearly 6 billion) has been estimated to be around 10
billion by the year 2030 with standards of living just above the
starvation level producing a vicious circle of poverty, lack of
education, unrest and violence – for signs of what is to come, see
the megalopolises of the modern world. Without a systemic
solution, such as that offered by binary economics, the prospect is
one of massive, growing and needless suffering.

Now nothing in binary economics will eliminate natural
scarcity.[214] Nor do binary principles suggest that capital
productiveness will inevitably rise to satisfy the material needs
and desires of an unlimited population. Nevertheless, it is
noteworthy that Louis Kelso's earliest exploration of the paradox
of surplus alongside poverty lead him to study the seemingly
hopeless population problems forewarned by Malthus; and it is
significant that the beneficial impact of binary economics offers to
aid efforts to limit population growth around the world, and to do
so in a wholly voluntary manner.

Present programs to limit population growth are hampered in
situations where:–

---

[214] It can however, eliminate much of the scarcity now faced around
the world which is an unnatural scarcity resulting from the monopoly
on capital acquisition. As the full independent productive and
distributive power of capital is released according to true free market
and private property principles, the unnatural scarcity of monopolized
capital formation will be replaced by the greater bounty resulting from
the accelerated and broadened capital ownership pattern of capital
acquisition in a binary economy.

- families have large numbers of children to ensure that some survive;
- children are the only hope for an adult to have sustenance in old age;
- the uneducated have little understanding of a better life, or how to achieve it; and, in particular,
- women have a lack of choice as to whether or not they have children.   Concerning that lack of choice, generally, the main deciding factor is the low *economic* status of most of the world's women.

But there is considerable evidence that societies which have a reasonable standard of living; which can afford education; and which empower women, even if only minimally, have the best hope for achieving a stable level of population. In the U.S.A., the U.K. and much of Europe today, the middle classes (with a degree of prosperity, education and status for women) are demographically stable. For similar reasons, binary societies promise to be demographically stable. With growing, universal individual capital ownership to provide the foundation for material security, universal education, freedom from poverty-related death, and improved economic status for women as well as men, the binary societies will have voluntary control over their populations levels in a way which is just not possible for large areas of the world at present.

Further, with the introduction of binary economies throughout the world, pressures of immigration and talent drain will subside, as more and more nations create in their own people a robust, productive, widespread, market-based earning capacity, represented by their growing viable capital estates. In time, when vested with that market-based individual ownership, growing numbers of people will have no unending poverty from which to escape, no pressing economic need to uproot themselves from an impoverished home to move to a richer land and, because binary economics empowers individuals and deepens democracy, no torturing murderous autocracies from which to flee.

11.   *The empowerment of women, minorities and others*

The binary analysis we have applied to both advantaged and disadvantaged nations applies to individuals and groups within nations. Participation in capital acquisition on market principles enhances growth and distributive justice no less if it is extended to people who have been heretofore the subject of economic discrimination (such as women, racial and ethnic minorities and other historically disfavored groups and individuals) than if it extended to already-favored groups and individuals.

Indeed, the generous, productive and distributive power of capital is not limited by the sexual, racial, ethnic, or other barriers that are created by people to exclude other people. This is because the beneficent productive and distributive power of capital derives its strength from a natural law (the law of supply and demand) having natural consequences. The ugly consequences of exclusion from its benefits are felt by the excluded and the excluders alike; the benefits of inclusion shine on the good and bad alike. In truth, the bounty from inclusion has the potential of enriching all people, individually, without regard to race, creed, sex or other classification *provided only that there be a political will to include them.*

Many women, racial, ethnic and religious minorities and other socially and politically disadvantaged people have experienced first hand the great economic denial at the foundation of productivity theory even though they may not yet understand it in binary terms. If those in power can deny or minimize the work of donkeys and trucks, they can also deny or minimize the work of women, hired hands, peasants, serfs, slaves, and other disfavored and therefore 'inferior' people. When productivity (a ratio) is confused for productiveness (i.e., actual work done), then the distributive justice owing to each individual (a justice fairly recognizing the actual and potential contribution of each individual) can be flagrantly compromised thereby denying to that individual and to society both i) the individual's right to keep what that individual has produced and ii) the individual's opportunity to produce and keep even more without taking anything from anyone else.

Once it is understood that women and other disfavored individuals and groups can thrive and prosper without taking anything material away from those in power, an element of prejudice driven by a fearful view of economics may subside. Thus, the voluntary operation of a binary economy in which all people have competitive capital acquisition rights offers to empower women and other disadvantaged people substantially by vesting in them increasing economic power to produce goods and services, and to do so in a way that takes nothing away from anyone else. If binary economics is valid, women and other economically disadvantaged individuals stand to gain far more in the long term by competitive entry into open capital markets than by equal participation in rigged labor markets. Indeed, some binary economists have observed that capital in the form of washing machines and other domestic labor-saving devices, along with the growing need for two-family incomes, has done much to liberate women from domestic servitude, and that a binary perspective will do much to support the development of widely shared enlightened attitudes on the subject of equal opportunity.

Growing numbers of women and economically disadvantaged minorities and individuals have correctly identified major inaccuracies in the unfree market's pricing of labor which indicate that they are grossly underpaid compared to some men. They recognize that their experience in the labor markets calls into serious question the unproved claims of efficiency and justice made by the proponents of the neo-classical productivity theory of growth and efficiency.

The binary paradigm reveals, however, that the inefficiency and injustice experienced in the labor markets are but symptoms of a more serious market failure, namely the fact that most people are effectively denied competitive participation in the capital markets. Thus we urge people to consider whether they might have much more to gain in the long term by their having competitive universal individual capital acquisition rights rather than by receiving higher compensation for their labor in rigged labor markets. Furthermore, the binary logic that supports the pre-eminent importance of universal individual acquisition rights as compared with more equal labor rights will add force to the rightful claims of women, minorities, and others for competitive pay in competitive labor markets, while simultaneously reducing white male resistance to those claims.

Discrimination is experienced differently by every woman and every man; but certain economic principles transcend the individual experience. The small percentage representing the wealthiest of a disfavored group can generally fend for themselves, and sometimes flourish indefinitely within a broader discriminatory society. The vast majority of women and members of other economically disadvantaged groups (i.e., those who are from the poor and middle classes) suffer the worse consequences of discrimination. And their progress is most likely to be resisted not primarily by the rich who (with their capital autonomy) can always make room for a few more talented hired hands, but rather by the poor and middle classes of the dominant group whose prejudices are fuelled by financial insecurity and fear of the competition in the labor markets. In a binary economy, as all people become more capital-rich, the victims of discrimination will be better able to afford to protect their interests and compensate for the consequences of discrimination while members of the group in power will be less threatened by the progress of those historically the victims of discrimination.

Binary economics will not immediately end prejudice or change destructive social attitudes of groups in power toward those not in power. Nor will it immediately stop some people believing themselves 'higher' on the social hierarchy than those people they regard as beneath them. Yet it does offer the promise of providing an enriching economic environment, effectively open to all people, in which prejudice and destructive attitudes are less likely to emerge or be reflected in public or private economic activity, and in which the victims of prejudice and destructive attitudes can better afford to protect themselves from discrimination and its consequences.

12.   Summary of the broad binary promise

In summary, binary economics offers a broad beneficial promise that extends far beyond its promise of sustainable growth, distributive justice, and general material affluence.

By enabling all people to acquire independent economic power, as well as voting power, binary economics offers to strengthen democracy.

By offering a private property and market system open to all people in ways that promote efficiency and distributive justice, binary economics has the potential to unite people from throughout the political spectrum into a powerful new constituency for practical economic reform that respects the dignity and rights of all people.

By enabling all individuals to acquire a competitive, viable, long-term, individual, private property stake in the economy, binary economics offers more hope for honesty and fair play by providing a system in which people in growing numbers can prosper while playing by the rules.

By replacing the relatively decreasing labor contribution to production with the vastly increasing capital contribution, binary economics offers a new self-esteem and a substantial decline in destructive attitudes, negative behavior and in social divisions.

By enabling people to afford greener products and services, and by allowing an alternative means for people to earn their living, a greener consciousness can be developed. As a result, environmental depredations can be minimized, and the environment preserved and enhanced.

By providing a sound economic foundation, binary economics provides the social environment in which individual families, and therefore entire populations, are more likely to grow voluntarily within their practical means to support a comfortable standard of living suitable for individual fulfilment.

By providing a means of encapitalizing the individual households of developing nations, binary economics offers to establish the indigenous productive capacity and purchasing power in every nation to provide for sustainable growth, distributive justice and general affluence.

By enabling all individuals to acquire an independent productive capacity, it offers to empower and give more equal status to women, racial minorities, disadvantaged individuals and groups throughout the world.

By profoundly involving all individuals in the operation of the economy binary economics enables them individually to acquire a substantial, growing, capital stake in its success. Binary economics can therefore be immensely helpful in evolving political unity across non-economic issues that frequently divide people of good will in their politics. Moreover, countries with different ethnic, religious or other groupings will be able to give all their people a strong sense of common cause and purpose.

13.   Is there a catch?

Does the binary offer seem too generous? Too naive? Too good to be true? Where, the reader could still be wondering, is the catch?

If by 'catch' is meant the fatal flaw that makes a seemingly good idea impossible or impractical, then your authors have discovered no catch.   They say that after having studied the subject for over forty years between them.

Admittedly, there are some important questions to be considered more fully before implementing a binary economy in any particular nation, and there are some important conditions to be met for the successful operation of a binary economy. Nevertheless, these questions and conditions should in no way deter readers from exploring binary theory, or from using its powerful logic to assist them in understanding how best to improve the economy.   The questions and conditions are not serious concerns when compared with the continued futility of pursuing the present mixed approach of conventional capitalism and socialism.   Moreover, the questions and conditions to be met appear readily capable of resolution in practice as people explore, debate and proceed democratically to implement a binary economy.   In short, they in no way render the binary promise impractical or impossible and are set out briefly below.

14.   Conditions for a binary economy

a)   No immediate 'fix'

As a first condition, the binary approach is *not* an immediate fix.   The harmful effects of the closed private property system – massive welfare dependence; personal, town, state and national government debt; distortion of the capital and labor markets; economic cycles; and widespread economic alienation – did not develop overnight and will not be eliminated overnight.   It will *take time* for the binary broadening of capital ownership to reverse these effects because binary distributive and growth effects are gradual.

b)   *True free market principles to be strictly respected*

As a second condition, the economic success of the binary program is promised *only to the extent* that true free market principles are strictly respected.   The binary benefit is not something for nothing (except insofar as the effective right to acquire capital on market principles is an inalienable binary private property and market right).   Beyond the maintenance of the infrastructure necessary for effective, universal, individual acquisition rights, the binary economy does not operate by government fiat, but by market principles.

Accordingly, people have no right to participate in any specific binary financing.   All proposed binary financing transactions must satisfy competitive market standards indicating that the capital will acquire itself at a competitive rate.   Before the employees and other beneficiaries of binary financing can begin to enjoy their capital income, the capital must first have earned sufficient income to repay its acquisition costs (just as it must pay for itself under conventional financing techniques for existing owners).   Even after the capital has paid for itself, no income is paid to the binary beneficiaries in any year until the capital has earned that income by producing goods and services.   Only income paid on this basis will support sustainable binary growth.

Therefore, let those who would favor a binary economy because it appears to be a way of achieving socialist redistribution by way of capitalist rhetoric be warned – if the political pressures to satisfy immediate distributive needs are allowed to compromise efficient capital investment and maintenance, then the growth that springs from the independent productive and distributive power of capital will also be compromised.

c) Commercial insurance as a substitute for collateral

The third condition concerns collateral (i.e. the provision of sufficient security to support a loan for capital acquisition). Because the employees and other binary beneficiaries are enabled to undertake binary financing on the strength of non-recourse capital credit loans from banks and other lenders, the question of collateral or other satisfactory security to support the loans is critical. On market principles, to maintain a stable monetary system, banks cannot extend capital credit without security to cover the risk of the borrower's inability to repay the loan. Further, on free market principles, existing owners cannot be involuntarily saddled with the risk of business failure. Rather, anybody who voluntarily assumes investment risk will request financial compensation.

Thus the practical success of the binary program requires that the risk of capital investment failure (a risk that is now borne primarily by existing owners, but with considerable governmental back-up mediation through economic intervention by way of taxing, borrowing, monetary, regulatory and other powers) can instead be commercially insured. More specifically, binary economics holds that this risk of failure can be priced on market principles by commercial insurers and government reinsurers, and included as an element in the cost of borrowing in the case of each binary financing.

If the binary concept of insured capital credit, based on the profitable experience of the U.S. Federal Housing Administration (FHA), is viable (and there is good reason to believe it is, provided that it is founded on a binary private property system), then the most formidable financial barrier that prevents most people from effective capital acquisition (i.e. the requirement of collateral) can be overcome. Thus people's long-term income requirements can be met more efficiently on market principles than on principles of redistribution.

Once the people determine to open the existing infrastructure to establish a binary economy, it is an open question whether government involvement (and how much and in what form) is necessary to promote the market provision of capital credit insurance.   It is possible that the market provision of such insurance might spontaneously develop as the market participants come to understand the principle of binary growth and its potent relationship to market efficiency.

Nevertheless, in his writings Louis Kelso consistently proposed the creation of an agency to operate on the broad principles of the U.S. Federal Housing Administration in providing loan insurance to homebuyers.   Moreover, in view of the urgent need that most people have for sound market-based credit for capital acquisition, it would appear appropriate for any nation adopting a binary economy to build on the principles underlying the FHA's years of profitable success for more than half a century in facilitating the financing of broader home ownership throughout the U.S.A.

It should be noted that the provision of capital credit insurance is not a back-door way out of the requirement that the binary program proceed on market principles. Capital credit insurance is *not* a government guarantee. To the contrary, capital credit insurance is provided on binary principles *only* if the premium is competitively attractive in view of the risk insured.   Any investment risk that is not insurable on market principles should not be undertaken.   The government's reinsurance corporation would be expected to meet the profitable performance standards of programs like the FHA's home loan insurance program.

d)   *Understanding binary economics in its own terms*

The fourth condition is that, before a binary system can be properly implemented, binary economics must be understood in its own terms, *not* merely in terms of traditional left, right or mixed centrist economic theory. This requires a fresh look at economics and private property – a look that suspends belief in foundational assumptions explicit or implicit in almost all of twentieth century economic and political thought. Those involved in important questions of political economy should abandon their foundational, homocentric reliance on human productivity in analyzing growth and distributional issues and instead focus on the concept of productiveness. Further, they should take more seriously the long-term economic characteristics of the alternative binary private property system.

Thus, in considering, for example, the question of capital credit insurance in an open private property system, they should suspend preconceptions based on the conventional analysis of other forms of insurance in a closed private property system and, with an open mind, try to understand how capital credit insurance would work in a binary economy. This sort of fresh look is not easy to do. It sometimes takes decades, even centuries, for foundation-altering ideas to permeate the social hierarchies that prescribe and reward acceptable mainstream thought while ignoring and marginalizing the rest.

Nevertheless, with the collapse of much state communism; with the growing recognition that the surviving capitalist economies are facing worsening problems in achieving a just and efficient distribution; and with increasing calls for new alternatives beyond right, left and center, there is some reason to hope that people are sincerely ready to take a fresh look at economic assumptions. That look will come not a moment too soon.

Book IV

Chapter Thirteen

A brief history of binary economics

1. Binary economics grew out of a struggle to understand the Great Depression

The thinking that led to the formulation of the new binary paradigm began in the 1930s when a young man in a Colorado (U.S.A.) mountain town struggled to understand the reasons for the Great Depression. Night and day, long trains rumbled past his home; and he noticed that, as in some mysterious dream, the passenger trains had no passengers while the freight trains carried no commercial freight but were full of unemployed people roaming the country in search of work. Here, indeed, was a paradox and Louis Orth Kelso, an honors student of finance and law, was determined to solve it.

Kelso's determination was the stronger because he realized that the trains encapsulated the great paradox of unfree market capitalism, then as now – on the one hand, a great, and growing, capacity to produce while, on the other, millions of people incapable of earning enough to purchase what can be produced. The classical economic theory of Adam Smith alleged that such a paradox should not prevail for long. Price adjustments in supposedly efficient markets would mediate supply and demand to clear markets (i.e. falling prices would lead to unutilized resources, goods and services being acquired and unemployed workers hired) and thereby compensate those providing productive inputs with the income to purchase what is produced. Yet recurring business slumps and the prevalence of poverty, manifested only too painfully in the Great Depression, showed that classical theory was fundamentally at odds with reality.

So, thinking that somebody, somewhere, must have already identified and resolved so fundamental a paradox, Kelso began to read widely. He dug into many authors – all the great economists, philosophers and political scientists. To his disappointment, however, he could find no satisfactory explanation for those mysterious trains. Still worse, the more he learned about business and finance, the more certain he became that none of the authors had come to grips with the changes brought about by the industrial revolution. Those changes meant that capital assets such as machinery (owned by a few) were doing more and more of the production while, in percentage terms (per unit of output and in the aggregate) labor was *doing less* and consequently would be receiving less (if it were not for the redistribution of capital earnings).

So a disappointed Kelso was forced back onto his own intellectual resources and he began to realize that conventional capitalism is a mass of contradictions with no coherent theory to explain how most people can be expected to earn to buy what is increasingly produced by capital. More specifically, he came to understand that:–

- the over-riding, long-term effect of the industrial revolution is to squeeze the labor content out of production and increasingly to put people out of work by substituting ever more bountiful capital productiveness for relatively less bountiful labor productiveness;

- without an open private property system in which all people have the effective right to acquire capital on market principles, a market economy *cannot* efficiently distribute the income necessary to enable people to purchase what is increasingly produced by capital and thus to achieve sustainable growth.

Kelso's thinking began to coalesce. His analysis sharpened. He was coming to understand the causes of the train paradox and, at the same time, the possibility of its happy resolution. During the Second World War (1939-45), while serving as a naval intelligence officer in Panama, he completed a manuscript, yet unpublished, entitled *The Fallacy of Full Employment* which offered the first statement of the binary approach.

2.   The published writings

It was not until 1958, however, that a comprehensive presentation was published in *The Capitalist Manifesto*. This remarkable book, (written with the renowned philosopher and educator Mortimer Adler) was translated into several languages. It was to be widely praised in intellectual circles around the world, especially in the U.S.A. and U.K.[215]

Then came *The New Capitalists* (1961), also written with Alder. This book builds on the analysis of *The Capitalist Manifesto* and is especially important for its succinct explanation

---

[215]   In the U.K., where some circles have long held Kelso in high regard, David Howell, M.P. has described Kelso's work as being of "dazzling prescience" and concluded that, in attempting to solve the problems of distribution through capital ownership rather than labor, Kelso was clearly correct where Keynes was wrong.   See David Howell, *Freedom and Capital* (1981, pp. 77-90) and *Blind Victory* (1986, p. 117).

of the economic function of collateral, the concept of capital credit insurance, and the formation of capital without the use of financial savings.[216]

For a time, Kelso's new 'theory of capitalism' as it was then called, showed promise of catching on intellectually in a big way. The excitement, however, was to be dampened by economists who never addressed the binary challenge to conventional thinking. Moreover, of the many who praised the theory, most did not fully recognize the distinctly new paradigm being presented.

Then Kelso and political scientist Patricia Hetter Kelso, forming a life-long partnership, published over the years two ground-breaking books and many important articles which, together, comprise the definitive expression of binary theory as it developed during Kelso's lifetime. Their first book, *Two-Factor Theory* (1967), is a timeless critique of conventional capitalism and socialism. It documents Kelso's early efforts to make universal, individual capital ownership an important part of U.S.

---

[216] In passing, it should be noted that Mortimer Adler, as a chief editor of *The Encyclopaedia Britannica*, is a man who has widely read the vast spectrum of human thought. An excerpt from his Preface to *The Capitalist Manifesto* is instructional at this point:–

"While signing my name to *The Capitalist Manifesto* as co-author with Louis Kelso, I wish to disclaim any credit for the original and basic theory of (binary) capitalism on which this Manifesto is based. That theory is entirely Mr. Kelso's. It is the product of many years of inquiry on his part.....I came to appreciate the critical importance of the theory of (binary) capitalism; and ....I felt that its revolutionary insights and program should be briefly summarized in the form of a manifesto addressed to all Americans who are concerned with the future of a democratic society....and with a twentieth century interpretation of everyone's right to life, liberty and the pursuit of happiness....It was with these discoveries in mind that I persuaded Louis Kelso to engage with me in writing *The Capitalist Manifesto*." (*The Capitalist Manifesto*, Mortimer Adler's Preface at ix, xvii).

economic strategy, and provides a comprehensive proposal to achieve that result.

The year 1986 then saw the publication of the Kelsos' second book together – the important *Democracy and Economic Power: Extending the ESOP Revolution Through Binary Economics*. Republished in 1991, and translated into Russian in 1993 and into Chinese in 1996, this book represents the last major writing of Louis Kelso before his death in February, 1991. Inspirational for its brilliant insights as to the essential economic condition for a true democracy (universal, individual participation in capital acquisition on market principles), it has a special message for leaders and members of labor unions regarding their most effective role in the years ahead. Patricia Kelso carries on their common mission through writing and lecturing to this day.

All in all, Louis Kelso authored or co-authored four books and scores of articles, papers and speeches.[217] He gave hundreds of pages of Congressional testimony. He sent hundreds of letters to U.S. Presidents, cabinet members, Senators, Representatives, agency officials, corporate officers, foundation representatives, labor union leaders, economists and educators. Always, his intent was to alert political and social leaders to the importance of opening the private property system to all individuals on market principles. His writings are carefully structured – drafted with the precision of a financial contract – to secure for people, beyond their personal freedom, the most important private property right

---

[217] Among the most important articles are:– L. Kelso & P. Hetter, *The Great Savings SNAFU* (*Business and Society Review*, Winter, 1988, p. 42); *The Right to be Productive, Parts 1 & 2* (*The Financial Planner*, August and September, 1982); *The Invisible Violence of Corporate Finance* (*The Washington Post*, Business and Finance Section, June 18, 1972); L. Kelso, *Labor's Great Mistake: The Struggle for the Toil State*, (American Bar Association *Journal*, Feb., 1960); L. Kelso & P. Hetter, *Poverty's Other Exit*, (*41 N.D.L. Rev.*, p. 147, 1965); L. Kelso & P. Hetter, *Uprooting World Poverty: A Job for Business*, (*Business Horizons*, Fall, 1964); and L. Kelso, *Karl Marx the Almost Capitalist* (43 American Bar Association *Journal*, March, 1957).

in the post-industrial world; the right to acquire capital on market principles.

Others began to write about Kelsonian (binary) theory. Two works are noteworthy for having Kelso's endorsement as offering an accurate presentation of his new paradigm. First, in 1977, Rodney Shakespeare and G.W. (Wilf) Proudfoot, then a Conservative Member of Parliament, proposed *The Two Factor Nation*. This book took the principles advanced in *Two-Factor Theory* and presented them with an eye to reforming the institutions of the United Kingdom.[218] Second, in 1990, Robert Ashford published the first comprehensive, scholarly examination of binary economics as a distinct paradigm.[219] This work is particularly notable for its explication of productiveness, its comparison of conventional and binary analysis, its focus on binary growth, and its insights into new areas of academic inquiry.

3. *The media coverage*

Over the years, Kelso also succeeded in generating a steady stream of publicity for his new economic theory and the ESOP (Employment Stock Ownership Plan) or 'Kelso Plan' as it was sometimes called. Newspaper and magazine articles were

---

[218] For years in the U.K., Rodney Shakespeare struggled to identify precisely the reason for the failure of all conventional economics and, in 1976, independently concluded the failure was due to a misunderstanding of who or what really creates the wealth. Knowing nothing of two-factor (binary) developments in the U.S.A., he happened to discuss the matter with Wilf Proudfoot who saw the connection with the work of the Kelsos and Adler in the U.S.A. Shakespeare and Proudfoot then co-authored *The Two Factor Nation*.

[219] *The Binary Economics of Louis Kelso: The Promise of Universal Capitalism* (22 *Rutgers Law Journal* 3, pp. 3-121, 1990).

generally sympathetic.[220] Several noted columnists and television correspondents took a special interest in Kelso. They understood that his approach offered a fundamentally new paradigm that promised prosperity and reconciliation beyond the dreams of the left, right or mixed approaches of conventional economics.[221]

4. The economic stone wall

However, in the mainstream, the books and writings generally evoked a peculiar reaction – right-wingers condemned and dismissed them as being 'on the left', while left-wingers condemned and dismissed them as being 'on the right'. In respect of both left and right, the condemnations and dismissals were almost never in print.[222] Sensing, correctly, that the powerful and efficacious logic of binary economics would reveal foundational errors in their ideology, plutocratic capitalists and power-loving socialists each perceived the threat of binary theory to their institutional interests but mistakenly took Kelso's approach as a Trojan horse put up by the other.

During the Cold War, the communist and unfree market capitalist systems were engaged in ideological, material and spiritual battle. The new binary paradigm (which identifies the obsolete paradigm underlying both communism and unfree market capitalism) offended the foundational ideology of both sides. Communists and socialists, therefore, saw the binary criticism

---

[220] See, for example, articles in *New York Times*, *Wall Street Journal*, *Newsweek*, *Barons* and *Village Voice*.

[221] See, for example, columnists Nicholas Von Hoffman and Milton Moscowitz: and broadcasters Michael Wallace (*60 Minutes*) in 1975 and Bill Moyers (PBS's *A World of Ideas*) in 1990.

[222] The condemnors and dismissers seemed unprepared to explain their opposition to a capitalism that works for everyone. Preferring to support plutocratic capitalism, or some form of socialism, they ridiculed Kelso privately and ignored him publicly.

and new paradigm as a conspiracy put up by the capitalists. Similarly, capitalists saw binary economics as a conspiracy put up the communists. Any person asking for a fair examination of something as far-reaching as binary economics, therefore, was isolating himself and creating hostility on all sides. Rare indeed is the person who can withstand a combination of isolation and hostility particularly when status, friendships, promotion within a department and jobs are at stake.

So, with a few honorable exceptions, nobody seemed to understand that something very unusual *had* to be happening. If the right condemned as left precisely what the left condemned as right then *either* the right had got things wrong; *or* the left had got things wrong;[223] *or both had got things wrong*.

Rather than respond to the profound binary challenge, however, the conventional economists determined to stone-wall 'Kelsoism' as it was called by its foes. Their particular and insidious method was to exclude binary economics by denying it recognition in the make-or-break journals that legitimize thought within the economics profession. Indeed, Nobel Laureate Paul Samuelson boasted of this exclusion.[224]

Though they were outwardly opposed to each other ideologically, proponents of the left and right were united in keeping binary economics out of the national debate over economic policy, out of the universities and off the intellectual map. Kelso himself was blackballed from governmental exploration of his ideas because leading economists refused to debate with him face to face.

---

[223] It is an interesting by-note that when *The Capitalist Manifesto* had been translated into Hungarian it was circulated to the very highest circles in the Hungarian Communist party under the category of "Works of the Enemy." *Pravda* reviewed it as 'ramblings based on thinking along a dead end of history.'

[224] *118 Congressional Record*, p. 20, 207 (1972). Statement of Paul Samuelson read into the record by Senator Harris.

As for the private economics and public policy think-tanks and foundations (living on tax-deductible donations and professing to be dedicated to the exploration of new ideas in the public interest), the response of the prestigious Stanford Research Institute (SRI) is atypical only in that it is documented in writing. Although concluding that Kelso's theory raised important questions for which research could make a difference, the SRI reported that it could find no one who felt qualified and stimulated to do the research.[225]

Of the most notable economists, only Milton Friedman agreed to debate publicly with Kelso. Although he won over many of the students attending the debate, Kelso apparently did not get through to Friedman, who later referred to Kelso's approach as a "crackpot theory" and said that "Kelso .... is Marx stood on its head."[226]

To be sure, soon after the publication of *The Capitalist Manifesto*, there was a flurry of interest in the questions of capital-labor substitution,[227] and labor and capital factor shares of income.[228] Yet nobody attributed the flurry to Kelso's theory. For example, Kenneth Meade published *Efficiency, Equality and the Ownership of Property* (1964), just six years after the publication of *The Capitalist Manifesto*, without reference to Kelso.

---

[225] Letter to Louis Kelso dated April 12, 1963, from its General Manager, Economics and Management Research, P. J. Lovewell.
[226] *Time* Magazine, June 29, 1970.
[227] J. R. Hicks, *The Theory of Wages* (London: Macmillan and Co., Ltd., 1964) especially Chapter VI, "Distribution and Economic Progress."
[228] See, for example, Nicholas Kaldor, *Essays on Value and Distribution*, 209-236; Irving B. Kravis, *Relative Income Shares in Fact and Theory* (*American Economic Review*, 49, December, 1959, at pp. 917-949); Piero Sraffa, *Production of Commodities by Means of Commodities* (Cambridge, Middlesex, England: Penguin Books Ltd., 1971).

414   Binary Economics – *the new paradigm*

5.   *The honorable exceptions*

But not all economists agreed that Kelso's theory should be black-balled and ignored. There were honorable exceptions, and the honor is high because open-minded intellect and unselfish courage were involved.

Top honor goes to Professor James Green (University of Georgia), who was the first economist in print to lament the failure of conventional economics to explore binary analysis openly. Addressing the Joint Economic Committee of Congress in 1973, Green declared that Kelso's binary analysis took modern economics a major step beyond Keynes by supplying the self-sustaining missing link in the private property system that prior economists had failed to identify.[229]

Green also said that by harnessing capital credit for all people, individually, through the private property system, a binary economy could achieve sustained growth beyond any traditionally conceived strategy.[230]   Repeatedly Professor Green tried to publish articles on Kelso's theory but was turned down by the major economics journals.

Second honor goes to Economics Professor Timothy P. Roth[231] who in 1980 examined binary economics. He concluded that there was no principled reason for rejecting the Kelsos' growth predictions. Roth decried the general failure of economists to focus on property rights and praised the Kelsos' writings as an important catalyst for making them do so.[232]

---

[229] See Steven V. Kane, *Kelso and Keynes: A Comparative Analysis* presented to the Conference on Binary Economics, Syracuse University, March, 1992.

[230] *Employee Stock Ownership Plans (ESOPs): Hearings before the Joint Economic Committee*, (Part 1), 94th Cong., 1st Sess., 831-845.

[231] Chair of the Economics Department, University of Texas at El Paso.

[232] *The Economics of Property Rights Transferral: The Case of ESOPs, GSOPs, and CSOPs* in *Privatisation Theory and Practice:*

However, despite these few courageous written acknowledgements and repeated calls for open inquiry, the economics profession has long stood closed to the benign concepts of binary economics that offer to replace the unnatural scarcity of conventional economics with the natural bounty of a market economics open to all. It is only recently that conventional economists have begun to recognize the importance of understanding binary economics.[233]

6.   Implementing the binary paradigm in the real world

Yet Kelso was more than an ingenious, self-taught economist and political philosopher (in the tradition of Adam Smith, J.S. Mill and Keynes) for he was that rarest of beings – the intellectual who is also a man of practical action, a financial wizard, and a person dedicated to individual economic opportunity for all people.

Confident that he had discovered a new, acute insight into reality which offers a totally original understanding of the cause

---

Distributing Shares in Private and Public Enterprize, (The Fraser Institute, 111, T. Ohashi and T. Roth, eds).

[233] At the 6th International Conference on Socio-Economics in Paris, 1994, two ground-breaking sessions featured binary economics. Five Ph.D. economists from three countries presented papers or commentary. All agreed that binary theory raised important new questions worthy of exploration. The *Journal of Socio-Economics* has published three articles on binary economics: i) R. Ashford, *Louis Kelso's Binary Economy*, (vol. 25, pp. 1-53, 1996); ii) T. Roth, *Binary Economics: A Supply-Sider's View* (Id., pp. 55-88); iii) Jerry Gauche, *Binary Economic Modes for the Privatization of Public Assets,* (vol. 27, pp. 445-459, 1998). At the 10th International Conference in Vienna, 1998, Dr. Richard E. Hattwick (Dpt. of Economics, Western Illinois University, and Editor, *Journal of Socio-Economics*) presented a paper *Binary Economics in the Evolving Global Economy.*

of post-industrial poverty and depression, Kelso concluded that the elimination of the poverty and the basis for sustainable growth all boil down to one thing – a private property right to acquire capital on market principles. He further concluded that the right can be realized for all people individually, just as easily, indeed in the long run more easily, than it has been realized for the well-capitalized.

Fortunately, Kelso was also a man with the courage needed to implement his intellectual and moral convictions in the real world. Having conceived of productiveness with its market relationship to distribution, poverty, affluence and growth, and having conceived of the private property right necessary to link all people to capital productiveness on market principles, he set out to realize that right in everyday life. He knew that, while it is one thing to claim that capital can buy itself for poor and middle class people just as easily as it can for existing owners, it is quite another to prove the claim time and time again in a hostile economic environment, frequently dominated by people more committed to greed than market integrity. Yet, Kelso did just that.

With pioneering bravery, beginning in 1956, he set about implementing his economic strategy by establishing Employee Stock Ownership Plans (ESOPs) to enable workers to acquire stock in the firms that employed them. Then as now, almost none of the employees had the income, cash, savings, or credit necessary for acquiring stock of the companies outright. But in company after company, Kelso structured the financing to enable the employees to buy shares of their companies with borrowed money and then to repay the loan with a share of the pre-tax company profits.

Initially, the 'Kelso Plan' as it was then called, was used by small family-owned firms seeking the orderly liquidation of family holdings while passing on a successful business to the employees who helped make the success. Kelso started with small companies, but it did not take him long to convince larger, public companies of the value of ESOPs as well.   Today, ESOPs are maintained by some of America's largest companies.[234]

Interestingly, not only did Kelso succeed in institutionalising the ESOP, but he prospered in the process.   In fact he did the one thing intellectuals are not supposed to do – he made a fortune – and so shares with Keynes the distinction of being an economist who became rich.

7.   *Congressional recognition*

All the while, on the educational front, the Kelsos took the fight to the opponent by lecturing,[235] debating and lobbying. Gradually, the message began to sink in, particularly in political circles. After reading *Two-Factor Theory*; after a steady stream of correspondence; and after personal meetings with Kelso, members of the U.S. Congress (particularly the then Senators Russell Long of Louisiana and Mike Gravel of Alaska) began showing strong interest.[236]   Whereupon the first (of what were to be many) legislative steps were taken to implement but a small part of a binary economy.[237]

---

[234] These include Proctor & Gamble, Hallmark, E-Systems, Anheiser Busch and United Airlines.

[235] One particularly notable lecture was given by Louis Kelso at the Bicentennial Forum sponsored by the New England Mutual Life Insurance Company (among others) in 1976. Entitled *The Economic Foundation of Freedom* and contained in the volume *The American Prospect* (ed. H.F. Thoma, 1977), the lecture was a masterful address to a distinguished audience and was greatly to influence thinking.

[236] This happened despite the continued cold shoulder, and sometimes oppositional meddling, from conventional economists (right, left and mixed-centrist).

[237] For example, when Chrysler Corporation received its Government bail-out, it was required to establish an ESOP so that not only its shareholders and top management, but also its rank and file employees, could participate in its capital acquisition and maintenance.

In 1974, in enacting the first ESOP legislation, the U.S. Congress finally officially recognized what Kelso had for twenty years been doing for companies and their employees. At that time, there were already some three hundred ESOP companies, almost all of them personally established by Kelso. By 1991, when Kelso died, the number of ESOPs in America numbered around ten thousand, covering roughly ten million employees.

8.   The American ESOP is a capital credit device and a technique of corporate finance

We have discussed the ESOP in Chapter 8. Here we repeat and develop some of the salient ESOP features in their historical context. Essentially, the ESOP is a capital credit device which institutionalizes the basic binary property right – the right to acquire capital, to pay for it out of its pre-tax earnings, and then to receive its income.[238] The legal entity that acts for the employees, and that oversees the capital acquisition and distribution of profits, is the ESOP trust. The ESOP trust is authorized to borrow money for the benefit of employees to acquire common stock of their employer. The employer-company is authorized to commit to make payments to the ESOP to enable it to repay the loan.

As a capital credit device, the ESOP is very flexible with many applications in the world of corporate finance. Given any contemplated corporate capital acquisition or transfer that might otherwise be acquired in corporate form by existing owners, the capital may instead be acquired in competitive bidding by an ESOP for the benefit of the employees. Likewise, any secondary offering of shares owned by existing owners can be acquired by

---

[238] The American ESOP is thus dissimilar to the ESOP of the U.K. which, originally, was not empowered to acquire stock on credit, and which was not legislated to realize the binary property right.

an ESOP.   Thus, ESOPs have provided employees with their most practical and enriching entry into the world of corporate finance on market principles.[239]

One application of the ESOP enables companies to satisfy their capital requirements at the cost of pre-tax corporate debt, while simultaneously enabling employees (who are the natural shareholders of their corporations) to acquire the capital on the pre-tax earnings of that capital.   Another use is to enable employees of a subsidiary to buy it from a parent corporation over time and pay for it with the subsidiary's earnings. This sort of divestiture was accomplished in the case of *Avis America*, which bought itself for its employees on its own corporate earnings.

Another application involves the sale of all, or a portion, of the outstanding shares of a family business to the employees, in cases where the founding owners intend to retire or diversify their holdings. In all of these cases, the major binary consequence is to increase the number of capital-owning consumers who are more able to buy the products of those wealth-creating assets.

As the continued operations of thousands of companies covering millions of workers might suggest, the ESOP program in America has been an impressive success.[240] When ESOPs are set

---

[239]   For a book with much information, see Jeff Gates, *The Ownership Solution* (Penguin, 1998).   See also J. Blasi and D. Kruse, *The New Owners* (New York, NY: Harper Collins, 1991); J. Blasi, *Employee Ownership: Revolution or Ripoff*, (Cambridge, MA: Ballinger Pub. Co., 1988); M. Quarrey, J. Blasi & C. Rosen, *Taking Stock: Employee Ownership at Work*, (Cambridge, MA: Ballinger Pub. Co., 1986); C. Rosen, K. Klein & K. Young, eds., *Understanding Employee Ownership* (Ithaca, NY: ILR Press, 1991); C. Rosen, K. Klein, & K. Young, *Employee Ownership in America: The Equity Solution* (Lexington MA: Lexington Books 1986).

[240] Jeff Gates, *The Ownership Solution* (Penguin, 1998).   General Accounting Office Report, *Employee Stock Ownership Plans: Benefits and Costs of ESOP Tax Incentives for Broadening Stock Ownership* (1986).

up for the right reasons and administered well, company profits and value increase while employees grow wealthier.   Success stories clearly outnumber the failures;[241] and employees are generally pleased with their ESOPs.[242]

The success of the American ESOP program shows a number of things.   First, it is testimony to the power of capital simultaneously to produce wealth while enriching and motivating workers when they are allowed capital participation in production.   Second, the success shows that, properly implemented, the ESOP does *not* dilute the investment of existing shareholders.   Third, it shows the appeal of the binary concept to investors,   company   managers,   bankers,   employees,   and politicians.   And, of course, it is testimony to its advocates, most especially Louis and Patricia Kelso.

But judging the success of American ESOPs in the present closed private property system is a little like gauging the practical potential of the first horse-less carriages before the roads, service stations, and other infrastructure were established.   As presently

---

[241] Over the period from 1983 (when it introduced an ESOP) to 1991, Oregon Steel Mills halved its accident rate, halved its labor costs per ton, trebled its output per hour and quintupled its total output.   The implications of such possible achievements for the economy as a whole are almost beyond belief.   Rather similarly, over the period 1986-1991, Reflexite (another ESOP corporation) tripled its workforce (because of expansion), quadrupled its sales, sextupled its profits and opened up new markets in other countries.

[242] Jeff Gates, *The Ownership Solution* (Penguin, 1998).   J. Blasi and D. Kruse, *The New Owners* (New York, NY: Harper Collins, 1991); Warren L. Braun, *On the Way to Successful Employee Ownership*, 1992; M. Quarrey, J. Blasi and C. Rosen, *Taking Stock: Employee Ownership at Work*, (Ballinger Pub. Co., 1986); C. Rosen, K. Klein and K. Young, eds., *Understanding Employee Ownership* (Ithaca, NY: ILR Press, 1991); C. Rosen and M. Quarrey, *How Well Is Employee Ownership Working?* (*Harvard Business Review* 65, Sept.-Oct. 1987; C. Rosen, K. Klein, and K. Young, *Employee Ownership in America: The Equity Solution* (Lexington Books 1986).

legislated and regulated, the American ESOP is burdened by self-defeating, conventional economic institutions and practices that shackle its optimal performance. But the analogy of the promise of early automobiles (in circumstances when the transportation infrastructure was largely non-existent) is not perfect. In the case of ESOPs, the financial infrastructure is already largely in place: it need only be opened so that the market-proven means that have served existing owners can be used to enrich all people individually. In this way, the acquisition rights of ESOPs will become much more competitive with the acquisition rights of existing owners.[243]

At present, without the binary infrastructure, people without capital may theoretically have capital acquisition rights, but those rights are not competitive on market principles with the acquisition rights of existing owners. As a result, all of the best capital is generally acquired by those with ready cash. The second-choice capital is generally acquired by existing owners with collateral to secure borrowed money. The third-class capital is acquired by managers in leveraged buy-outs who can capitalize on their experience, knowledge, and position. And, finally, the fourth-choice capital remains for acquisition by employees through ESOPs. Sometimes, one or more of the first three preferred acquirers will include employees in the deal for idealistic reasons or, more often, in return for labor concessions (which Kelso did not believe are necessary for binary growth).

Thus, as potential purchasers of capital for employees, ESOPs do not have acquisition rights fully competitive with those of existing capital owners; and as a result the capital acquired by ESOPs is likely to be not inherently the most productive capital. For fully competitive acquisition rights (so that ESOPs can

---

[243] In passing, it is interesting to note the early awareness of the self-productive quality of capital in the word 'automobile' which conveys the meaning of a vehicle capable of moving itself without human help. Unfortunately, the original meaning has been lost in the increasing twentieth century preoccupation with productivity.

compete more effectively for the most productive capital acquisition), ESOPs need to be operating within the entire binary infrastructure described in Chapter Eight.   Therefore, as impressive as the American ESOP program is (and there are some ESOP gems, and some ESOP duds), it does *not* fairly reflect the ESOP's true potential as it would exist in a binary economy that fairly respects the capital acquisition rights of all people on market principles.

Among researchers, there is some dispute on the effect of ESOPs on productivity, company performance, and employee compensation. Some studies of ESOP companies compared with non-ESOP companies have concluded that, generally, ESOP companies cannot be shown to outperform non-ESOP ones in these areas in statistically significant terms.

In contrast, other studies show that companies combining employee ownership with employee participation (involvement in company decisions) programs seem to do better than non-ESOP companies, even non-ESOP companies with affirmative employee participation programs.[244] Pro-ESOP advocates argue that the data shows that 'good' ESOPs established for the 'right' reasons are both wealth-creating and wealth-spreading and therefore should be encouraged.

ESOP detractors argue that the beneficial effects to achieved by ownership compensation and employee participation should be achievable without tax subsidies and special incentives. How easily those detractors forget the tax and other advantages available to (and therefore deemed by lawmakers to be essential for) existing investors!

But binary economics reveals that this debate is hopelessly limited by the conventional productivity paradigm, and therefore it fails to focus on the crucial question of competitive acquisition rights which stands at the foundation of all sound financial and

---

[244] See generally *Employee Ownership and Corporate Performance Review* (National Center for Employee Ownership, Oakland, California, 1996).

economic analysis. The fact that ESOP companies (whether participatory or not) are able hold their own financially compared to non-ESOP companies (despite the fact that ESOP acquisition rights are presently not competitive with the acquisition rights of existing owners), by itself provides strong support for the wealth-generating and wealth-distributing power of ESOPs. In other words, even in a market structure that excludes them from the most profitable capital acquisition, it is remarkable that ESOPs continue to hold their own against non-ESOP companies.

Furthermore, when understood as integral part of the binary infrastructure, what appear (under the assumptions of the conventional productivity paradigm) to be 'tax subsidies' for ESOPs (to be either attacked or defended on grounds of 'productivity' or 'fairness') are (in light of the binary paradigm) not tax subsidies at all. Rather they exist to help open the capital markets to all people on market principles. Indeed, they operate only to level the playing field by extending to ESOPs, for the benefit of employees, a portion of the existing and unquestioned present tax advantages (including tax credits, deductions for interest, depreciation, and research and development, and capital gains treatment, and various forms of government assistance in maintaining the market infrastructure) that presently facilitate capital acquisition for existing owners but not for new owners.

Thus, the ESOP's growth and distributive potential will not be fully realized without the complete legal and institutional infrastructure of a binary economy described in Chapter Eight. This infrastructure is necessary to end the present effective monopoly of capital acquisition enjoyed by existing capital owners.

It is likewise necessary to unleash the growing power of capital to produce and distribute wealth in markets competitively open to everyone. It levels the economic playing field. It enables poor and middle class people – all people without substantial capital estates – to compete effectively alongside the well-capitalized for capital acquisition on market principles. Rather than offer a new deal from same stacked deck, the binary approach unstacks the economic deck.

9.   *The unfinished history*

Louis Kelso died before he was able to complete his legislative program to open the capital markets according to the principles underlying the ESOP. Therefore, as a matter of history, much of the institutional development of binary economics still remains on the drawing board. A brief summary of the unfinished binary work ahead will therefore aid the understanding of both the success and limitations of the present ESOP program in the U.S.A., and will also shed considerable light on its great potential for much greater wealth creation and distribution in a binary economy.

a)   *Other capital credit devices*

Kelso understood that to meet the requirements of sustained growth and justice, the market-property linkage for broadening capital ownership cannot be limited just to a relationship between employees of those companies which are sufficiently credit-worthy to enjoy prime credit rates. Rather, the capital credit logic of the ESOP may be extended beyond a company's own employees so as to benefit consumers of the company's products, residents proximately related to the company's facilities, employees of other companies (including major suppliers and customers) *and others*.

Moreover,

> the task of making capital workers out of the undercapitalized population as a whole....cannot end with employees of private sector companies. That would exclude the many millions of people who have the same rights and aspirations as corporate

employees: people who work for various functions of government and non-profit enterprizes and, finally, the elderly and infirm. Today the latter have little choice but to burden consumers and taxpayers with their support, but they could and should be supported by their own capital.[245]

Thus to serve people within these broader constituencies, in addition to the ESOP, a binary economy offers other binary capital credit devices. These include the Mutual Stock Ownership Plan (MUSOP); the Consumer Stock Ownership Plan (CSOP); the Individual Capital Ownership Plan (ICOP); the General Stock Ownership Plan (GSOP);[246] the Commercial Capital Ownership Plan (COMCOP); the Public Capital Ownership Plan (PUBCOP); and the Residential Capital Ownership Plan (RECOP).

Each of these eight methods is a capital financing tool...for financing new capital formation or....the acquisition of existing assets or both, while it simultaneously raises the capital-oriented earning power of otherwise economically underpowered consumers.[247]

---

[245] Louis Kelso & Patricia Kelso, *Democracy and Economic Power* at p. 52.

[246] See J. Gauche, *General Stock Ownership Corporations: Another Step in Broadening Capital Ownership*, (vol. 30 American University Law Review, pp. 730-764, 1981), which documents the early binary work of Senator Mike Gravel which continues to this day, and R. Ashford, *Evaluating the Potential Use of a Consumer Stock Ownership Plan (CSOP) Financing for Meeting the Capital Requirements of Public Utilities*, (Proceedings of the Fourth NARUC Biennial Conference, Columbus, Ohio 1984 (The National Regulatory Research Institute)).

[247] See Louis & Patricia Kelso, *Democracy and Economic Power* at p. 57. This book contains fuller details of the eight methods.

b)   The full binary infrastructure

But willing companies and their shareholders, employees and
other beneficiaries, and their fiduciaries cannot by themselves
effect competitive binary financing without the participation of
commercial lenders, who themselves will need the participation of
capital credit insurers.   At a minimum capital credit insurance
will require regulation like other forms of insurance. Moreover (if
the experience of opening home loan credit to ordinary people in
the U.S.A. is any indication of the barriers to efficient financial
innovation) substantial participation by private capital credit
insurers in binary financing will likely require sufficient
government support by way of the establishment of the Capital
Credit Reinsurance Corporation (CCRC) to reinsure a portion of
the risk of the primary capital credit insurers.   Furthermore,
consistent with sound monetary policy, central bank discounting
will likely need to be specifically undertaken to level the playing
field so that binary financing is competitive on market principles
with conventional financing. Thus, all of these developments are
necessary so that people without capital can have competitive
capital acquisition rights.

Once the binary infrastructure is established then, by using
one or more of the capital credit devices mentioned above, and by
operating competitively and yet co-operatively, any industrial
nation's largest prime credit-worthy companies can satisfy a
major portion of their capital requirements in a way which will
encapitalize millions of their shared consumers so as to provide
for them substantially increased market-based consumer income
after the capital has paid for itself. Accordingly, binary financing
can provide not only second incomes to working people but can
also provide a market mechanism whereby welfare recipients can
be progressively spun off from welfare – their endemic welfare
dependence being gradually replaced with capital autonomy as
their individual capital estates grow.

Thus, in the full binary economy, as managers of the largest
companies of the unfree market economies search for ways to

expand their profitable business and improve their corporate citizenship, the binary approach provides them with a new, vital, wealth-broadening way to do both. They can choose to meet their credit-worthy capital requirements while simultaneously encapitalizing not only their own employees but their customers and other citizens, whose consumption needs would otherwise be satisfied by non-market-based redistribution.

But, at present, the full binary infrastructure necessary to expand the ESOP concept so as to enable operating companies, banks, insurers, fiduciaries, and monetary authorities to facilitate capital acquisition for all people (not merely existing owners) is something still requiring further implementation. Thus, until the implementation of the full binary economy, market participants and other citizens can properly say they are not practically able to undertake binary financing. But nothing prevents them studying it, coming to understand it, and then going on to advocate it so that it becomes the reality.

Yet a close look at the actual situation today reveals that the seeds of the future already exist. For example, in one form or another, all of the potential participants of a binary economy are in being:–

- *employees and other citizens* in need of more productive power;
- *private companies* in need of productive capital, motivated employees, and consumers better able to afford to purchase their products;
- *lenders* seeking to expand their profitable loan volume;
- *insurance companies* looking for profitable new products;
- *large institutional fiduciaries* (including those controlling public and private employee pension, profit-sharing and other retirement plans) with obligations to maximize the financial interests of their beneficiaries, and interests in extending their service to more beneficiaries, and with funds that might be profitably used to underwrite capital credit insurance; and

- *insurance, banking, and monetary authorities* with legislative mandates to serve the public interest in their respective spheres.

So the potential participants are all on hand: but they have yet to put their heads together to study the binary potential and then take responsible action based on their study. In other words, since the enactment of the ESOP legislation, the history of binary economics as far as these participants are concerned has sadly been a history of inaction. But happily things may now be changing. At what point the essential features of the binary economy come to be reflected in the history of the future, first by way of a fair and open exploration of binary theory, and then by way of a careful implementation of its salient features, is explored in the final chapter.

Book IV

Chapter Fourteen

The binary future

1. New paradigms, new futures

By offering a fundamentally different way of understanding the past, a new paradigm generally also reveals a fundamentally new way of understanding possibilities in the future. Those possibilities are often beyond the imagination of those who hold to the old paradigm as they try to make sense of what has gone before.

But to those willing to question the old paradigm and suspend belief in its unproved assumptions, the new binary paradigm will reveal new, practical possibilities. Using the binary perspective, this chapter discusses the future in the light of the past and highlights some of the new possibilities. It then concludes by offering lessons from the common law to assist readers in approaching the future in the light of the new binary paradigm.

2.   A binary perspective on the past

From their earliest times, people have been concerned with the task of persuading nature to satisfy their needs and wants. The process of invention was periodically marked by certain crucial discoveries involving fire, agriculture; certain tools, weapons and processes; the wheel, the plough, and the sail. Over the millennia, the resultant increase in productive capacity and the shift from labor to capital in production were propelled by the cumulative effect of countless other discoveries. Since the start of the industrial revolution, the process has assumed gigantic proportions.

The process has allowed for a great increase in productive capacity and output with relatively less human work. Consequently, it has enabled a great increase in the absolute number of people living materially well throughout the world, as well as enabled a great increase in their life spans.

However, at the same time, the increase in productive capacity and output has allowed a marked increase in population levels, with the result that the absolute numbers living in or near poverty have also greatly increased. Thus, an apparent paradox – as greater numbers do materially better, so many more do poorly, being left behind, pushed aside and sucked under in the wake of developments seemingly beyond their control. Indeed, the over-all trend in the ratio of those doing well compared to those doing poorly is such that, far from being a cause for satisfaction and complacency, it is cause for alarm.

3.   A central thesis

The great growth in productive capacity and the shift from labor to capital in production are part of a process which began in pre-history and which will seemingly continue with increasing impact indefinitely into the future. There is no doubt that the process happened, is happening, and will continue to happen; but there is a conflict of paradigms over *how* it happened and what will happen. Moreover, it is a central thesis of this book that *it makes a great difference* whether the process is understood primarily as a function of increasing human productivity, or rather primarily as a function of increasing capital productiveness. The difference in paradigms affects not only our understanding of the past but also our strategies for the future. Indeed, the difference has the potential to influence all the most important economic, political, legal, and moral decisions that people and nations ever have to make. The difference can be summarized in a sentence:–

> Beyond the stale, 'zero-sum game' alternatives offered by the conventional left-center-right linear paradigm, *binary economics offers a new future of growth and distributive justice* in which everyone can flourish individually by playing according to the rules of a private property system truly open and dedicated to free market principles.

From the binary perspective, the conventional linear paradigm (consisting of left-wing, right wing and mixed-centrist approaches) is simply inadequate for understanding the past and meeting the challenges of the future. Significantly, although more has changed in the production of goods and services on Earth in the last two hundred years than in all the time gone before, conventional economics has yet to re-examine and revise the foundational assumptions made by Adam Smith in 1776 – assumptions which were formulated *before* all the great changes in the production process had become apparent.

So, once people comprehend that capital, and not labor, is producing ever more of the supply, and that in markets open to all people, capital income can increasingly satisfy more of the demand, then the past can be understood and the future met in a practical, just, and efficient new way. With a binary understanding that capital, and not labor, is increasingly producing ever more of the supply, the capital markets of any economy can be structured so that much of the capital that now buys itself for existing owners can also buy itself for all people individually and, in the long term, can do so (as fully-paid capital becomes more broadly acquired), even more profitably. In such an economy, as capital becomes more broadly acquired, it will thereby increasingly distribute the demand to purchase its output so as to provide the private property foundation for sustainable growth and distributive justice.

Significantly, as capital productiveness continues to replace labor productiveness and increase total productiveness, the distribution of capital acquisition and income will increasingly serve either to suppress or promote growth. In the closed markets of the present unfree market economies (which admittedly outperform communist economies), the continued concentration of capital acquisition for the benefit of the few existing owners will increasingly suppress the potential for total growth. Conversely, in the open capital markets of a binary economy, the broadening pattern of capital acquisition will increasingly provide the efficient market basis for sustainable growth and distributive justice.

4.   *The watershed moment in the future of nations*

The richer future offered to all people by the binary approach will not be accomplished by fiat, force, or confiscation, nor by the compromise of any free market private principles. The binary infrastructure will be established democratically, and recourse to the various forms of binary financing will remain entirely voluntary and consistent with existing private property rights. In a binary economy, everyone will be free to go about their ways as before with the difference that *new, more competitive ways will also be available.*

Therefore a time of crucial decision or a 'watershed' moment in the binary future of any nation will arrive when *enough* people come to understand the productive and distributive power of capital in open markets. We say 'enough' people, and not a majority, because the powerful and benign assumptions and logic of the binary paradigm have the ability to unite the very considerable numbers of opinion leaders of good will. These leaders are at present isolated from each other by political and intellectual barriers which create divisions along the conventional linear economic paradigm. Binary economics, however, will enable the leaders to overcome the barriers. Then, once binary economics is comprehended by a critical mass of leaders along the political spectrum, it is likely that the rest of the people will happily follow. Nevertheless, with an understanding of the binary paradigm, people in *every* walk of life and every station in society can also, in their own way, become effective leaders in aiding the comprehension process.

5.   *The critical questions*

At the close of Chapter One, we stated that the process of evaluating binary economics need not be surrendered by any man or woman to the experts. To that end, we offered a list of questions to aid in the exploration of binary theory. Readers might now wish to be reminded of them:–

i)   Is binary analysis new?

ii)   Does it rest on reasonable assumptions?

iii)   Is it internally consistent?

iv)   Does it explain an important range of experience in its own terms?

v)   Does it helpfully predict an important range of future events in its own terms?

vi)   Does it provide a specific proposal for helping people that is worthy of rigorous exploration by those professing a concern for questions of growth, distribution and democratic participation?

vii) What are the drawbacks if it is tried and fails?

viii) Is it worth trying?

6.   Our best answers

In this book, we have offered our best answers to each of the questions. By way of summary, we have shown that:–

i)   (*Is binary analysis new?*) The binary paradigm, based on productiveness, is distinct and new compared to all the antecedent approaches (left, center, and right) based on various theories of productivity.

ii)   (*Does it rest on reasonable assumptions?*) Binary economics rests on the assumptions that capital does work just as humans do work and that, in an industrial economy, capital is doing most of the work, is also doing ever more of the work, and is therefore is earning (and in competitive markets would be paid) ever more of the income. Binary economics also assumes that growth is better understood as a process whereby capital productiveness replaces labor productiveness and increases total productiveness, rather than understood as a process by which capital increases labor productivity. Based on the assumed validity of the law of supply and demand, binary economics further assumes that a) capital has a potent distributive relationship to growth and b) capital must be broadly acquired if it is to sustain the profitability of its increasing productive capacity. In other words, for any economy, the broader the distribution of capital assets on market principles, the greater the growth. (In contrast, conventional economics assumes that labor is doing most of the work and further assumes that in terms of promoting growth and broader affluence it makes no difference whether capital is broadly or narrowly owned unless the distribution somehow affects productivity.)

iii) (*Is it internally consistent?*) Based on productiveness and the distributive relationship between capital and growth, binary economics offers internal consistency by explaining how people will be able to afford to purchase what is increasingly produced by capital. It offers the internal consistency of recognizing that capital such as donkeys, shovels and elevators, does work just as humans do. It offers the internal consistency of capital markets actually open to everyone, rather than the inconsistency of capital markets that are supposedly open to everyone *but in practice are open to only a few*. In fulfilling the needs of the poor, it offers the internal consistency of answering a) the individual question of how shall people come to produce enough to meet their needs and desires; and b) the social question of how shall society pay for the good it would do and the harm it would prevent.

iv) (*Does it explain an important range of experience in its own terms?*) As a new approach, based on reasonable assumptions, and internal consistency, binary analysis explains the past in a way consistent with its premises, and also explains how past practices can be corrected to produce a better future. It explains how the great increase in productive capacity has produced much greater bounty in the closed unfree markets than in communist economies. With the same analysis, binary economics also explains how those unfree market economies can be opened to serve all people even more efficiently. Binary economics explains how the unfree market economies have consistently failed to distribute on market principles the income necessary to purchase what they can produce, and then prescribes how they can be opened to do so. It explains how those unfree market economies lurched from boom to bust, and then explains how they can be reformed to provide steady, sustainable growth. It explains how those unfree market economies have produced unnatural scarcity and suppressed growth by concentrating excess productive capacity so that it is acquired almost entirely by the few people without unsatisfied consumer needs and desires. It then goes on to prescribe how unfree market economies can be reformed to produce a growing binary economy in which capital ownership is increasingly more broadly acquired by people who will spend the earnings of capital on what it produces. Binary economics explains how increased productive capacity grows in unfree market economies for the few while welfare dependence (and the fear of it) grow for the many. Further, it explains how welfare dependence, and the fear of it, can be replaced with growing capital autonomy and greater respect for private property, without taking from existing owners.

v)   (*Does it helpfully predict an important range of future events in its own terms?*)   Binary economics has at its core a prediction eminently capable of being verified, or not, by events, viz.:–

The more broadly capital is acquired on true (binary) market principles, and its true net income fully paid to its owners, the larger the economy will grow independently of traditional productivity-based considerations.

This is called the principle of binary growth. To verify it unambiguously would require the enactment of the binary infrastructure so that the predicted broader distribution of capital acquisition and the greater growth might be either demonstrated or falsified on market principles. In this connection, it is interesting to note that neo-classical economists are quick to suggest that matters should generally be left to open markets. They are, moreover, quick to criticize those who would substitute their own arm-chair judgements for those of the market participants themselves. However, to our knowledge, no neo-classical economist has ever been willing to leave the question of binary growth to open markets, which is all that results from establishing the binary economy.

vi)   (*Does it provide a specific proposal for helping people that is worthy of rigorous exploration by those professing a concern for questions of growth, distribution and democratic participation?*)   Based on the foregoing i) – v), the new binary paradigm reveals a concrete proposal to open to all people the existing financial infrastructure that now facilitates capital ownership primarily for existing owners. Once the infrastructure is opened, binary analysis reveals that the voluntary operation of the economy will naturally enrich poor and working people everywhere without taking from existing owners. Because no taking of property is involved, but only an opening of the market infrastructure, any adverse consequences of adopting the binary approach are all but imaginary. No binary transaction occurs unless willing participants agree. All incremental risks of binary financing are either voluntarily assumed or not incurred at all. And in a binary economy, those risks can be more efficiently assessed and underwritten in capital markets open to all.

The only consequence of implementing the binary economy is to open the market opportunities presently available essentially only to existing owners and thereby to extend to all people competitive rights to acquire capital. As a result, much of the capital that presently buys itself for existing owners can also just as profitably buy itself for new owners; and in the long term (as fully-paid capital becomes more broadly acquired), it can do so even more profitably.

The binary system has great upside potential with virtually no downside risk (unless such risk is voluntarily assumed). Such a system is surely worthy of exploration by all people who publicly profess to be searching for new approaches to correct long-standing and seemingly insoluble problems of economic growth and distributive justice.

vii) (*What are the drawbacks if it is tried and fails?*) And if the exploration affirms the broad binary promise, as we are confident it will, the binary approach can seemingly be adopted without fear of systemic adverse consequence. Because binary financing operates entirely on a voluntary basis, any risks taken in the binary economy to participate in binary financing are assumed market risks. With binary financing, *no one* is forced to take risks. Binary financing that succeeds financially will enrich both the traditional investor-participants to the transaction and also the binary beneficiaries. And it will promote binary growth. Binary financing that fails will leave the traditional investor-participants and binary beneficiaries without valuable interest in the investments, but no worse off than if the same investment had been made by way of conventional investment and had failed. All investments are made voluntarily but in markets which will be more competitively priced and undertaken in the context of broadening consumer demand.

viii) (*Is binary economics worth trying?*) The matter is discussed in the next section.

7. *Proceeding with uncertainty*

Few things are certain. Important new choices raise doubts. Old paradigms that do not work raise doubts. And so do new paradigms that are not yet widely accepted. The resultant uncertainty can protect against unwise experimentation with the *status quo*; yet it can also needlessly prevent or retard understanding and reform.

In exploring your own answers to the critical questions set forth in Section 5 above, you may develop inclinations towards answers you find most convincing, yet fall short of certainty. If that is the case, it is helpful to consider several lessons from Anglo-American jurisprudence related to the 'burden of proof'. The lessons are designed to assist judges in making decisions in the context of uncertainty. They apply sometimes in general and sometimes in special circumstances. In the section below we consider the burdens of proof as they apply in the general case, and, in Section 8, as they apply in special circumstances.

In the general case, it is widely accepted that the burden of proof is on the reformers, the advocates of change, in this case, the binary economists. Indeed, binary economists have been saddled with this burden for years by complacent people comfortable with the *status quo*. Such people always demand much effort on the part of others before they themselves will admit to any obligation to re-think their intellectual positions.

a)   The shifting burden of proof in a civil case concerning ownership of assets

It is first important to note that frequently the burden of proof is not an all-or-nothing proposition. For example, as the process of providing convincing evidence continues, the burden of proof can shift back and forth between the parties.

For example, in respect of private property, Anglo/American law starts by *assuming* that, in civil matters involving individuals and/or companies, all private assets are in the rightful hands. That is to say, the civil law assumes the *status quo* to be correct.[249]

Take the case in which one person seemingly holds title to assets, but another person claims to be the rightful owner because, for example, the documents supporting title are allegedly forged. In such a case, the court will not order the transfer of the assets to the plaintiff unless there is sufficient proof that (contrary to the general assumption), the facts really do show that the assets are in the wrong hands. However, as explained below, even with the general assumption operating, the burden of proof is still not inevitably an all-or-nothing burden falling only on the plaintiff.

i)   Proof on pleadings

If by filing appropriate documents called 'pleadings', a plaintiff merely *alleges and offers to prove* requisite facts (called a '*prima facie* case') indicating that, 'more likely than not' (i.e., 'probably'), assets now in the name and possession of the defendant in fact belong to the plaintiff according to law, then the

---

[249] Otis Harrison Fisk, *Fundamentals of the Law of Proof in Judicial Proceedings*, 1928).

defendant (as defender of the *status quo*) must come forward with a responsive answer even though there has as yet been no actual avidence submitted and no final satisfaction of the burden of proof on the basic facts. Rather, on the strength of a *prima facie* case made by the plaintiff's pleadings, the defendant must answer with responsive pleadings or else lose the case by default without even a hearing.

ii)   *Proof at trial*

Furthermore, even if the defendant files responsive pleadings to avoid the default judgement and if the plaintiff presents enough evidence at the trial to make a *prima facie* case (e.g., indicating a probable forgery of title), then the burden of proof shifts to the defendant (as the defender of the *status quo*) to come forward with his own proof that the assets are lawfully in his hands. Moreover, if the defendant fails in this proof, then on strength of the plaintiff's *prima facie* case (i.e., on the strength of the conclusion that the assets are in all probability the property of the plaintiff and not the defendant), the court will order the property previously in the name and possession of the defendant be held as a matter of law to be property of the plaintiff, *even though some uncertainty as to the basic facts and proper course may yet remain.*

Thus, in aiding the judge to reach the proper decision on a matter of private property, American-Anglo law uses a pattern of shifting burdens of proof impacting alternately upon plaintiff and defendant. In this way, the law tries to develop a balanced understanding of the matter. The judge starts with a respect for the *status quo*. This respect is founded in the general assumption that all private wealth is in the proper hands.

Nevertheless, the law also assumes that the *status quo* may sometimes be contrary to law. Therefore the judge is willing to be persuaded to change the *status quo* as required by law. Accordingly, upon learning enough from the plaintiff to create a *prima facie* case that the *status quo* is probably wrong, the judge turns to the defendant for some explanation as to why the plaintiff's case should not be taken as proven. If there is no satisfactory proof coming from the defendant, the judge must decide for the plaintiff, because it is more likely than not that the asset belongs to the plaintiff than the defendant.

b) The shifting burden of proof in exploring binary economics

The trial judge *must* decide, *even in the case of uncertainty*. According to the applicable laws, the *status quo* is either correct *or* it is not. And on this issue, based on all the rules of evidence and procedure, the judge must decide what has been proven more likely than not.

Therefore the decision to be made by a civil trial judge is not exactly analogous to the choice to be made by a reader between binary and conventional economics. The reader is not forced to decide between the binary paradigm and the conventional paradigm and, in the face of uncertainty, can be indecisive and choose to endure the consequences of not deciding. Yet, in this context, the reader should remember that indecision is itself a decision. The basic decision is *whether or not to favor an economy that honors the binary property right of all people or one that ignores it*. People cannot have it both ways.

Thus to readers interested in moving forward on a decision as to whether or not it is better for all people to have binary property rights, a number of lessons can be learned by the American-Anglo approach to civil court litigation.

First, in deciding whether the binary economists or the conventional economists have the better view of reality, it is not necessary for people to do all the work themselves. Nor do they need to impose all the work on the binary reformers. This is especially true:–

• if there is independent reason to question the assumptions, logic, and alleged empirical evidence provided by conventional economics; and

- if the unfree market economies fail to perform as conventional economic theory predicts.

In such a context, people can rationally require from binary economists a *prima facie* case and, if that case is made, people can then require a convincing response from the defenders of conventional economics. Should they receive none, they can then open-mindedly decide the matter in favor of binary economics, at least tentatively, even though later they may change their minds. An open-minded approach is to be commended because, in the experience of the authors, the binary paradigm becomes more convincing the longer it is entertained.

We believe that years ago, a strong *prima facie* case (indeed, a convincing case) was made by Louis Kelso alone and with his co-authors in many writings. We believe that this book has done so once again in a timely new way and with added developments. Armed with the binary understanding provided by this book, people in all walks of life can now rightly go to the experts and ask for some clear, convincing explanation as to why the important binary ideas should not be expeditiously studied and acted upon.

8.   Fiduciary duties

The burden of proof as it applies in the general case was considered in section 7. This section now considers the burden as it applies in special circumstances;   and we open with the observation that some of the experts who might logically be asked about the merits of binary economics are not merely experts: they are people with *fiduciary duties*. When that is the case, it is noteworthy that, in special circumstances, the law uses other techniques involving *variations* of the burden of proof to assist in the discovery of truth and the promotion of justice in situations where there is uncertainty.   The variations have special application to people who (frequently for substantial compensation) have voluntarily assumed fiduciary duties to act for the benefit of others. Examples are given below.

a) Lawyers and trustees are fiduciaries

Consider the responsibility of an attorney in western Pennsylvania in 1850, who represented the children of two parent-farmers killed unexpectedly in an accident. He then found himself in a difficult situation. The children were incapable of fending for themselves and, under a court order and pursuant to the parents' will, he became the legal representative and the trustee for the benefit of the children. As trustee, he held title to a marginally productive farm, now thrown into insolvency by the death of the parents. The bank was owed money and was proposing to foreclose on the farm it held as collateral. Nor could the attorney see his way to turning the farm into a serious money-making operation – nasty, black, oily secretions oozed from large parts of the land. In town there had been some talk that, one day, the ooze could be valuable but such talk was dismissed as idle and the fanciful speculations of dreamers.

In such a situation, the lawyer's fiduciary duties are two-fold because he serves in two capacities:–

- as a lawyer for the children, he must identify and secure their essential rights and obligations; and

- as trustee, he must preserve and enhance the value of the assets held in trust (i.e., the farm) for the benefit of the children.

Now, in order to fulfil fiduciary duties according to the law, any lawyer who is a trustee sometimes has to decide questions of fact and law. One such question of fact, of course, was the value of that oily ooze – Was it valuable or not? One such question of law was the point at which the fiduciary becomes negligent in not discovering the true value of the ooze.

Although it is difficult to identify things precisely, it is clear that at some time between 1850 (when the ooze apparently had very little value) and 1870 (when it had become clear that the ooze had great value), it would have been a breach of professional responsibility for an attorney or a trustee to fail to discover and maximize the market value of the oil-rich land. The exact point when a fanciful speculation becomes fact (giving rise to obligations to act) may be uncertain, but the existence of an ever-present obligation of affirmative investigation to separate speculation from fact is clear.

b)   Fiduciary duty of affirmative investigation

Nor was the obligation of affirmative investigation automatically extinguished merely because the early advocates of a profitable oil industry had not sustained a burden proof necessary to satisfy a private investor or citizen. Any affirmative fiduciary investigation must be reasonably structured to:–
- reveal the underlying facts and circumstances under consideration; and
- identify the essential rights and obligations of the client, beneficiary, and other people relevant to the matters at hand.

At all points in conducting a reasonable investigation, the fiduciary should be skeptical of unproved assumptions that are prejudicial to the interests of the client and beneficiary. Conversely, when an idea like binary economics seemingly well serves client and beneficiary interests, the fiduciary should not easily decline to use the idea unless it is clearly shown to be wrong in some important way.

Based on the results of such an investigation, the lawyers and other fiduciiaries must then effectively advance the interests of client and beneficiary in a way consistent with applicable law.

c) *Broadly applicable duties*

These duties of which we speak fall not only on private attorneys and trustees, but also on other fiduciaries including financial advisors and underwriters. The duties exist with respect to all directors and officers of major corporations (including not only manufacturing companies, but also banks, insurance companies; public and private pension, retirement, and social security funds; and educational, religious, and other non-profit institutions). In light of the lofty aims of labor/trade union and government officials, to say nothing of the legal mandates underlying their authority and privileges, the obligations would seem to fall on them as well. Suffice it to say that the obligations enumerated above cannot be conscientiously discharged merely by saying that *someone else* has not met some generally applicable burden of proof.

9. *Critical questions of fact*

The new binary paradigm raises critical questions of fact which fiduciaries need to investigate and determine if they are to fulfil their duties of affirmative investigation. Some of these questions of fact can be expressed by the following propositions:–

* *either* capital is producing most of the wealth, *or* it is not;
* *either* the present capital markets are as open to people without capital as they can be, *or* they are not;
* *either* capital has a positive distributive relationship to growth that is independent of productivity, *or* it does not;
* *either* much of the capital that presently buys itself for existing owners can buy itself for all people individually, *or* it cannot;
* *either* the profitable principles of the American FHA can be extended to provide credit insurance to enable people

without capital to participate in the capital acquisition of prime credit worthy companies, *or* they cannot;

- *either* a nation's central bank can synchronize its monetary policies to accommodate low-cost binary financing while controlling inflation, *or* it cannot;

- either the binary propery right is essential to widespread individual economic well-being or it is not; and

- *either* a binary economy can facilitate voluntary transactions to promote growth and distributive justice, without redistribution, *or* it cannot.

For decades, individual and institutional fiduciaries and their legal counsel have voluntarily assumed the obligation of affirmative investigation necessary to maximize (within the bounds of prudent risk) the wealth of their clients and beneficiaries. If, however, they would now begin to address the above propositions, the long-overdue beneficial exploration of binary economics will proceed expeditiously and, we are confident, will eventually mature into a widely shared and powerful new way of understanding economic issues and achieving positive reform throughout the world.

10.   The buck stops here

Yet, in the deepest sense, the burden of investigation trumps the burden of proof and falls squarely not just on experts but *on each of us*. It can be fully understood only when balanced against the consequences of remaining ignorant. To meet it, therefore, people should study binary economics. If they then find that binary economics deserves an answer they can go to their pension and retirement plan fiduciaries, bankers, insurers, financial advisors, attorneys, union leaders, educators and government officials, and ask them to study binary economics and explain in writing what, if anything, is wrong with it. In this way, people can meet their burden of inquiry by prompting the inquiry of professionals who have the duty to learn and act in the best interests of the people they represent. Clients and beneficiaries have the right to responsive answers from their fiduciaries. They can initiate a process that will be enlightening and unifying.

11.   Everyone and everything is here

It is now time to return to key observations made previously. The first is that, in one form or another, *all* of the potential participants of a binary economy exist today, viz.:–

- *employees and other citizens* in need of more productive power, and the *unions and other organizations* that represent them;
- *private companies* in need of productive capital, motivated employees, and consumers able to afford to purchase their products;
- *lenders* seeking to expand their profitable loan volume;
- *insurance companies* looking for profitable new products;
- *large institutional fiduciaries* (including those controlling employee pension, profit-sharing, social security, and various other retirement plans) with obligations to maximize the interests of their beneficiaries, and interests in extending their service to more beneficiaries, and with funds that might be profitably used to underwrite capital credit insurance; and
- *insurance, banking, and monetary regulatory authorities* with legislative mandates to serve the public interest in their respective spheres.

These potential participants are all on hand, but they have yet to put their heads together to study the potential of binary economics and then take responsible action based on their study.

Likewise, the *market infrastructure* is essentially all in place. At present, ideas and plans for capital acquisition are developed and financed on the strength of anticipated future earnings and principles of corporate finance. The present market infrastructure has proven its effectiveness in enabling existing owners to grow richer on the earnings of capital. This is illustrated by the steady rise in value of the largest three thousand U.S. companies represented by the Russell Index, which pays for its replacement cost on an inflation-adjusted basis every five to seven years. However, the binary paradigm reveals that the potential of capital to produce and distribute wealth is *much greater* than the profitable results delivered by the Russell three thousand. That is because the present performance is depressed; and it is depressed because it has occurred in a capital market in which most people are denied effective participation.

12.   Let us begin......

It is true that until the existing corporate, banking, insurance and fiduciary institutions and the appropriate regulatory authorities are authorized to engage in binary financing based on the binary property right, present-day market participants and other citizens can properly say, "We are not practically able to undertake binary financing."

Yet *nothing* stops us from studying binary economics. *Nothing* stops us from coming to understand its potential. And *nothing* stops us from coming to advocate its adoption as the new paradigm.

So let us begin......

Binary bibliography

The Capitalist Manifesto, Louis Kelso & Mortimer Adler (1958)

The New Capitalists, Louis Kelso & Mortimer Adler (1961)

Two-Factor Theory, Louis Kelso & Patricia Hetter (1967)

The Two Factor Nation, Wilfred Proudfoot & Rodney Shakespeare (1977)

General Stock Ownership Corporations: Another Step in Broadening Capital Ownership, Jerry Gauche (30 *American University Law Review*, pp. 730-764, 1981)

Democracy and Economic Power – Extending the ESOP Revolution through Binary Economics, Louis Kelso & Patricia Hetter Kelso (1986 & 1991)

The Binary Economics of Louis Kelso, Robert Ashford (*Rutgers Law Journal*, vol. 22, pp. 3-121, 1990)

Curing World Poverty: The New Role of Property, J.H. Miller, editor (1994)

Louis Kelso's Binary Economy, Robert Ashford (*The Journal of Socio-Economics*, vol. 25, pp. 1-53, 1996)

Binary Economic Modes for the Privatisation of Public Assets, Jerry Gauche, (*The Journal of Socio-Economics*, vol. 27, pp. 445-459, 1998)

Binary Economics – the new paradigm, Robert Ashford & Rodney Shakespeare (1999)

Index

Author Biographical Sketches

Robert ASHFORD is Professor of Law at Syracuse University, College of Law, in Syracuse, New York, where his subjects include business corporations, securities regulation, professional responsibility and binary economics. He graduated with highest honors with majors in English Literature and Physics from the University of South Florida. As an undergraduate, he was elected the President of the Student Government and the Editor of the Literary Magazine. He studied creative writing at Stanford University as a Woodrow Wilson Fellow.

After graduating with honors from Harvard Law School, he practised law in San Francisco regarding, among other things, tax matters, securities regulation, and employee ownership. While practising law, he served as President of the Barristers Club of San Francisco, and as a Director of the Bar Association of San Francisco. Before beginning law teaching, he was Chief Operating Officer and General Counsel for Kelso and Company; and in that capacity, he worked with Louis Kelso for a number of years. He has authored or co-authored articles and chapters on binary economics, implied liability under federal laws, securities regulation, evidence, workers' compensation, banking law and tax law.

Rodney SHAKESPEARE studied history at Cambridge (Downing) where he obtained a MA and won a television writing competition. He then qualified both as a teacher and a barrister and has worked in education and business.

For about twelve years he tried to study conventional economics but found that *every* book on economics gave him a headache. He ruefully concluded that economics was beyond his mental capacity. Then, one day, he had a disturbing thought – perhaps it was not so much a matter of his mental capacity but rather that *all* the books on economics were wrong (although he could not, at that time, say why). So he started to examine the assumptions upon which conventional economics is based........

Rodney has an extensive range of interests. Among other things, he was many years in London local government politics and, recently, began to create musicals with a friend. Two have been completed and they are now working on a third.